MONETARY PROCESS AND POLICY: A Symposium

KRANNERT GRADUATE SCHOOL,
PURDUE UNIVERSITY
MONOGRAPH SERIES

HORWICH *Money, Capital, and Prices*

JENSEN *The Impact of Reparations on the Post-War Finnish Economy: An Input-Output Study*

HORWICH (Editor) *Monetary Process and Policy: A Symposium*

MONETARY PROCESS AND POLICY

A Symposium

Edited by

GEORGE HORWICH

Professor of Economics
Purdue University

1967

RICHARD D. IRWIN, INC.

Homewood, Illinois

First Printing, April, 1967

Library of Congress Catalog Card No. 66-28628.

Printed in the United States of America

FOREWORD

A new structure housing the Krannert Graduate School of Industrial Administration of Purdue University was dedicated May 6, 1965. During the following "dedicatory" year a number of conferences and symposia marking that event were held in the new building. Among these was the third annual Conference of University Professors of the American Bankers Association. Held previously at Arden House and Princeton University, the Conference of University Professors brings together representatives of academia, government, and banking to discuss problems of monetary theory and policy. The third annual conference was co-sponsored by the American Bankers Association and the Krannert School and was held at Lafayette August 29 to September 1, 1965.

This volume covers the proceedings of that conference. Included are 14 invited papers, seven discussants' comments, and eight comments contributed at the initiative of the participants. The program was drawn up by a committee consisting of Lester V. Chandler, Harold L. Cheadle, Gottfried Haberler, George Horwich, Harry G. Johnson, Paul W. McCracken, Roy L. Reierson, James Tobin, and Charls E. Walker. Professors Tobin and Horwich served as co-chairmen, while Mr. Cheadle acted as co-ordinator for the American Bankers Association.

The program committee made a special effort to broaden the range of topics usually discussed at monetary gatherings. Accordingly sessions were organized to treat structural unemployment and cost-push vs. demand-pull inflation in both the United States and Europe, the financial-institutional environment of monetary actions, and the interaction of domestic and international monetary policy.

Arranged into a sequence of three sessions under the title, "The Effects of Monetary Policy" were the more purely monetary topics: the impact of policy on financial variables, the link between financial and real variables, and the policy implications of recent research—as viewed by representatives of the Federal Reserve and academia. The paper by John Wood, "A Model of Federal Reserve Behavior," is in a sense an introduction to all three sessions, endeavoring to describe the process of policy formulation in a model of both financial and real variables.

West Lafayette, Indiana
April, 1967

George Horwich

LIST OF CONFERENCE PARTICIPANTS

THOMAS R. ATKINSON, The American Bankers Association
G. L. BACH, Stanford University
WILLIAM J. BREEN, Purdue University
DANIEL H. BRILL, Board of Governors of the Federal Reserve System
KARL BRUNNER, Ohio State University
PHILLIP CAGAN, Columbia University and National Bureau of Economic Research, Inc.
DEANE CARSON, Columbia University
SAMUEL B. CHASE, JR., The Brookings Institution
HAROLD L. CHEADLE, The American Bankers Association
JACOB COHEN, University of Pittsburgh
FRED DAHL, Board of Governors of the Federal Reserve System
FRANK DE LEEUW, Board of Governors of the Federal Reserve System
DAVID I. FAND, State University of New York at Buffalo
J. MARCUS FLEMING, International Monetary Fund
TILFORD C. GAINES, The First National Bank of Chicago
LOWELL E. GALLAWAY, University of Pennsylvania
CARTER H. GOLEMBE, The American Bankers Association
PATRIC H. HENDERSHOTT, Board of Governors of the Federal Reserve System
DONALD D. HESTER, Yale University
GEORGE H. HILDEBRAND, Cornell University
JAMES M. HOLMES, Purdue University
GEORGE HORWICH, Purdue University
HARRY G. JOHNSON, University of Chicago and London School of Economics
JOHN H. KAREKEN, University of Minnesota
BARON ALBERT KERVYN DE LETTENHOVE, Notre Dame University at Namur
THOMAS MAYER, University of California, Davis
DAVID MEISELMAN, Macalester College
ALLAN H. MELTZER, Carnegie Institute of Technology
HYMAN P. MINSKY, Washington University
WALTER A. MORTON, University of Wisconsin
DON PAARLBERG, Purdue University
S. POSTHUMA, Netherlands School of Economics
ROLAND I. ROBINSON, Michigan State University
ARTHUR M. ROSS, Bureau of Labor Statistics
PAUL A. SAMUELSON, Massachusetts Institute of Technology
FRANK SCHIFF, Council of Economic Advisers
HARVEY H. SEGAL, Washington Post
LEE SILBERMAN, Wall Street Journal
WARREN L. SMITH, University of Michigan

Beryl W. Sprinkel, Harris Trust and Savings Bank
Robert H. Strotz, Northwestern University
Frank M. Tamagna, The American University
Rollin G. Thomas, Purdue University
James Tobin, Yale University
Robert C. Turner, Indiana University
Charls E. Walker, The American Bankers Association
Henry C. Wallich, Yale University
Emanuel T. Weiler, Purdue University
William Wolman, Business Week
Paul Wonnacott, University of Maryland
John H. Wood, University of Birmingham

TABLE OF CONTENTS

KEYNOTE ADDRESS

Discussion

INTERNATIONAL CONSTRAINTS

EFFECTS OF MONETARY POLICY
II. The Impact of Financial Variables on Aggregate Demand

Discussion

EFFECTS OF MONETARY POLICY
III. Criteria for the Conduct of Monetary Policy— The Implications of Recent Research

CONTRIBUTED COMMENTS

INDEX

KEYNOTE ADDRESS

STABILIZATION POLICIES IN THE CONTEMPORARY U.S. ECONOMY

Paul A. Samuelson

I. CHASTENING REMEMBRANCES

In connection with stabilization policies for the contemporary American economy, we economists are at the moment riding very high. If there are malicious spirits running around [in] the universe, you might even say we are riding for a fall.

As we look up from our charts and computer print-outs, why is it that every prospect pleases? For one thing we are now in the fifth year of the post-1961 economic expansion. As the American annals go, that is a ripe old age. If you want to equate the age of a dog with the age of a man, I believe you multiply by seven. To bring phases of our business cycle up to a comparable basis, you have to multiply the number of years of expansion by a factor of more like 20. By this reckoning the Kennedy-Johnson expansion is just past 90, and, according to the only prediction I shall be unguarded enough to make tonight, I confidently expect it to go beyond the century mark. If the powerful magic of the modern generation of economic medicine men continues to operate, we may not soon see the euthanasia of poverty, but there might well ensue the euthanasia of the National Bureau of Economic Research—or at least an atrophying of its vital organs. To appreciate the euphoria of present day avant-garde economists that makes such joking possible, you must understand that I do not attribute the nation's recent good performance to anything as prosaic as sheer luck. Rather it is a case of the right thing being done for the right reason—and most miraculously being followed by the right results.

What really makes the cup of the econometrician overflow is the remarkable success of the 1964 massive tax cut. Economists flew in the face of all orthodoxy to recommend this measure. They used all their arts of persuasion to beat down ideological resistance. They predicted quantitatively the pattern of benefits to be obtained from the new tax measures. And, for once, all the universe conspired to bring the tale to a happy conclusion.

So perfect is the picture that it reminds me of another occasion of high spirits in our profession. Almost exactly 20 years ago this night, the best brains in our profession were gathered together in Washington. A great war had just come to an end. In the course of that war economists had conducted themselves with great distinction, worthy at least of the Victoria Cross.

For example, in 1941 President Roosevelt was told by practical men that gross national product was capable of but little expansion. Economists in the OPA and elsewhere took out their little slide rules—I will remind the younger men in this audience that electronic computers were not available to our gallant forefathers—and on the basis of economic calculation they reckoned that output still had a long way to grow. As events turned out, the economists were right.

I shall not go on to enumerate other triumphs of our profession in wartime, but—as I can say with good grace since I was then involved in other kinds of work—the triumphs were many and solid.

Little wonder, then, that the assembled experts of government felt considerable confidence in the rather gloomy forecast of heavy postwar unemployment that the cream of the various government agencies all arrived at. (I wish that my own guilt in this faulty diagnosis could be Freudianly forgotten.)

The rest is history. As a minority of economists *had* predicted, after an initial reconversion dip, there followed a period of strong aggregate demand. The honor roll of this minority included such diverse names as Sumner Slichter, Alvin Hansen, and William Fellner—who proved to be right for pretty much of the right reasons, namely [that] cumulative wartime backlogs of demand and need [existed], coupled with cumulative wartime accretions of purchasing power. (I shall omit reading the names of some of our distinguished brethren who were able to say "I told you so," but only on the basis of an ideological presumption that the good old American system can always be counted on to weather all storms.)

Very germane to the subject of my discussion, and indeed to the subject matter of this whole conference, is still another period of complacency within what Maynard Keynes called "our most agreeable branch of the moral sciences." I refer to what is said to have been a widespread feeling at the end of the 1920s—that Governor Strong in New York and the Federal Reserve Board in Washington—with only occasional help from cousin Montagu Norman on Threadneedle Street—had learned to utilize monetary policy to banish forever the instability of capitalistic enterprise. When you read in your modern textbooks about the "rediscovery of money," you can be sure that this rediscovery will include rediscovery of all the grandiose claims for control of the money supply as a panacea for eternal stability.

By now you may be thinking that the burden of my sermon tonight is that there is nothing new under the sun. It is true that I have been raking up the scandals of the past to warn the present generation, myself included, against overconfidence. But let the record also show that I do believe we have made genuine progress in learning how to reduce instability and promote real growth in the modern mixed economy. Furthermore, the development of economics as a science has, in my judgment, played an important role in this improved performance. And—what is, alas, not the same thing—an increased understanding of economic fundamentals on the part of the electorate and men of affairs has also helped. As far as the banishing of deep depression is concerned, the much talked-about contemporary "decline of moral fiber" has even had a constructive role to play. (I hasten to add, parenthetically, that the same complacency is not justified when it is a matter of long-term stability of the price index.)

II. FISCAL AND (RATHER THAN FISCAL OR) MONETARY POLICY

Let me now get down to business. Our chief instruments for macroeconomic control are obviously fiscal policy and monetary policy. In the days of Governor Strong, fiscal policy was given a very limited role in the stabilization drama. This is not because there is truth in the old wives' tale that the employment-creating effects of public works were unknown before the days of Richard Kahn and of J. M. Keynes. Actually, you will often find, going back into remote history, recourse by practical men to such devices in time of depression. (I was shocked to read Cecil B. Woodham-Smith's *Great Hunger,* which tells the unbelievable story of how laissez-faire England tried to cope with the terrible Irish potato famine of the last century. Then starving people were actually made to work on the roads in order to qualify for meager allotments of imported grain. This tragic misidentification of what was needed in the way of social policy is mentioned here only to emphasize the point that income maintenance by means of emergency public works was already so customary as to have become clothed in a spurious legitimacy.)

In 1929 American fiscal policy was of limited scope, not because the intricacies of the multiplier doctrine had yet to be developed, but rather because the federal government was still limited in its scope of operation and the state governments and localities had neither the will nor the financial leeway to do much in this respect.

Had people of that day the imagination to insist that extreme anticyclical federal fiscal policy be started late in 1929, I am convinced the debacle of the 1930s could have been much averted; and, in case anyone thinks this an unimportant consideration, we would probably have ended up by the late 1930s with a smaller federal debt than was actually the historical case.

The late Charles O. Hardy regarded fiscal deficits as at best an indirect and roundabout way of creating an expansionary money supply. Why burn houses to roast pig? And why list fiscal policy as a supplement to monetary policy, since—according to this extreme view of Hardy and of of some recent money enthusiasts—it is merely an unnecessary and roundabout way of getting the Federal Reserve to do what it ought to be doing anyway, namely, determining the supply of M (somehow defined) in the pattern best suited to overall stability and healthy growth.

I personally go along with the Irishman who said: "If whiskey is good and gin is good, how glorious must be whiskey and gin." I do not regard fiscal policy as the olive that wags the dry martini. I must confess that this was the view I held before I read the valuable *A Monetary History of the United States,* by Mrs. Schwartz and that other fellow. And I have to report that, while I ended up a better man for having read that work, I was left with no belief that the velocity of circulation of money remains unaffected by the level and financing of public budgets.

It is fortunate that fiscal policy does have a separate potency. For in this era of balance-of-payments deficits, militant use of credit expansion to restore full employment has not been politically feasible.

To be specific, consideration of domestic employment and growth would have called for the "Fed" to expand bank reserves enough after 1960 to bring the short-term bill rate down as much below 2 percent or 1½ percent as would be needed to promote an intensive deepening of capital in the United States. That would undoubtedly have sent dollars and gold abroad in great amounts under existing currency parities. Instead, unemployment was brought in the 1960s from a 7 percent level down to its recent 4½ percent level by determined recourse to expansionary fiscal policy.[1]

Since the money supply did rise substantially in the years 1961–65, I do not want to attribute the expansion to fiscal policy alone. It was a case of active fiscal policy which was coupled with or financed by a supporting monetary policy. I suppose a modern-day Hardy who believes "the change in money income—attributable to a change in federal spending or in taxing or in their budgetary difference—is negligible, provided the total of the money supply is held constant" might be tempted to dismiss the constructive role of fiscal policy in this period. I cannot agree. The macroeconomic models I consider realistic do not display a velocity

[1]The next two paragraphs have been added to the original manuscript to take account of the oral discussion that followed the paper.

of circulation of money that is invariant under substantial changes in fiscal policy. Instead, had we kept the Eisenhower spending and taxing programs while the Fed tried to make M (the money supply) grow as it actually did grow in 1961–65, I am confident short-term interest rates would have been strongly depressed. Cool money would have left our shores in considerable volume. At a much lower structure of interest rates, people could have been content to hold larger cash balances relative to their earning assets and income streams. So unemployment would not have fallen in the quantitative degree that it did; nor would production have shown its historical growth; and similarly for profits and other indicators of sustained growth.

In historical fact we used expansionary fiscal policy and expansionary monetary policy together. We wisely ignored the advice of those European and American financiers who said we should reduce taxes only if we [could] make sure that the resulting deficit be financed out of "genuine savings" rather than by money creation. As an academic question one might ask, "Suppose the latter-day Hardy view quoted above were correct? Couldn't the government still use budget deficits as the excuse to print new money, offsetting any tendencies for interest rates to fall by specific open-market sales in the money market?" I am inclined to answer in the affirmative to this leading question[2] as a possibility; but I think this would require a more complicated model than the limiting one in which the liquidity-preference demand for money is interest inelastic.

Let me say in what must be a brief aside, that abandonment of the "bills only" doctrine and embracement of "operation twist" did enable monetary policy to make a small deliberate contribution to economic expansion. Probably more important still was the raising of the ceilings on deposit interest set by Regulation Q. These adjustments were in any case long overdue but were precipitated by the desire to keep our large banks competitive with foreign branches here and to forestall direct investment in Treasury bills by large official and unofficial foreign agencies.

Here again was a case where economic law and knowledge of it triumphed over lay opinion. "If you let some banks pay higher interest rates on deposits," so it was said by easy money fanatics, "then all banks will have to pay the higher rate. The only way they'll be able to afford to do that will be by raising the interest rates they charge on mortgages and loans to borrowers." Trained economists like Undersecretary Robert Roosa and Economic Adviser James Tobin, drew the opposite conclusion. They agreed: "If interest on deposits is allowed to rise to the competitive equilibrium level, that will make *more* funds available for mortgage and commercial lending. More funds imply both cheaper interest rates and greater availability." It was a dramatic fact that the

[2]Of Paul Wonnacott.

long-term interest rate remained low unprecedentedly long in the current expansion. I think this indicates that the expert economists were thus proved right. But I don't honestly know whether any of them predicted what seems to have also occurred—namely, a willingness of all the banks together to reach out for riskier long-term investments in order to be able to offer high competitive interest rates on the new certificates of deposit. In a sense, one device we have used to stabilize domestic employment in the face of an international deficit has been a contrived deterioration of the quality of credit on a mild scale. It is a paradox that this may be sound social policy and one of its certain consequences is an implicit new responsibility thrust upon government—by which I mean the Federal Reserve and the federal government—to help bail out the banking system if widespread problems of insolvency should ever develop.

This reminds me of our shocking failure to avert the collapse of all the banks in the 1930s. Future historians will consider it fantastic that we did not print whatever money would have been necessary to have staved-off runs on the banks. You can be sure that present-day stabilization programs would include such super-duper Reconstruction Finance Corporation salvage operations where the nation's banking system is concerned.

In this sense I agree with Milton Friedman that economic policy from 1930 to 1933 constituted a tragedy of errors. With present attitudes and institutions of government I am convinced the worst of the Great Depression could have been averted. But I have to emphasize that the measures to protect a multiunit banking system from internal drains and disaster involve much more than mere conventional open market operations by the Fed. The errors of omission that must never again be repeated are not definable simply in terms of permitting the statistical total of the money supply to decline.

If important institutions that have nothing to do with money narrowly defined—life insurance companies, mutual funds, even the stock market itself—were to be plunged into a vicious downward spiral of liquidation and bankruptcy, economists and politicians would today take it for granted that government had an overriding obligation to stem the tide. And make no mistake about it—armed with the constitutional powers of money creation, taxation, and borrowing—a great country like the United States would have power to spare in avoiding such a disaster.

III. HOW TO SYNTHESIZE A STABILIZING SERVOMECHANISM

Suppose we agree that fiscal policy and monetary policy are complementary mechanisms to promote growth and stability. What rules, procedures, and policies ought we to choose to follow?

Notice my wording of the last sentence. What rules should we choose? This will seem almost self-contradictory to those who pose the debate in terms of polar opposites: government by rules and laws rather than government by the discretion and intelligence of men. I won't rehash the arguments and counterarguments here. Let me merely summarize by saying that it takes discretion to institute a system of rules; and it takes discretion to desist from interfering with those rules. There is no true philosophical difference between the competing approaches: discretionary policy by men in government can be venal or disinterested; can be intelligent or stupid; can be arbitrary and capricious; or consistent and equitable.

Purely on the level of tactics one can ask the question [of] whether a simple policy of using open market operations to keep some definition of the money supply growing at some-such rate as 3 percent per annum is the best servomechanism that present-day economics can devise for a mixed economy like that of the United States.

Even if we had the floating exchange rates that we do not have and the perfect flexibility of wages and prices that we do not have, wouldn't it be something of a miracle if this turned out to be the optimum rule of all rules? Indeed, until you have a specific notion of the statistical properties of the load that is to be put upon a servomechanism, you cannot know in advance what is the best combination of resistances, capacitances, and inductances needed to synthesize the optimal stabilizing circuit. If the American economy in the decades ahead is to be subject to Kuznetslike intermediate waves, attributable to such exogenous factors as construction, population, and cold wars, an intelligent jury would expect that destabilizing fluctuations in the velocity of circulation of money would be discernible in our statistical data. The Federal Reserve Board would not have to consist of saints and wizards to be able to make at least a modest contribution toward minimizing unemployment and accelerating maintainable growth. Why sacrifice this feasible improvement of the system to that almost paranoid distrust of government which some zealots inherited from the nineteenth century?

I go further. While admitting that there are hazards in anticipating turns of the business cycle, I think it lamentable that the footprints of the Federal Reserve were so often in the past to be found among the lagging indicators. Why always bring up the rear? Let us find such financial series as the money supply and interest rates more often among the current indicators or even among the leaders. Naturally this would involve some errors of the false alarm variety. But what is the vaunted flexibility of monetary policy for . . . its alleged ability to reverse its ground like a Big-Ten football quarterback?

Both fiscal policy and monetary policy are on an equal footing in this regard. Each [of them] involve time-lags of many months before they achieve their final effects. Such time-lags make it all the more important to use some measure of forecasting and anticipatory action. And what I am saying in this respect will become less controversial if, as many think, the important problem ahead is not that of a choppy 30-month National Bureau inventory cycle but rather that of longer undulations in the rate of growth of our economy. If it is the case that the servomechanism is to bear such a load, then many of the old clichés will go out of the window.

I refer to such bits of unconventional wisdom as the following: "Don't employ public works for stabilization purposes. By the time they get the money out you'll already be in the next boom." And yet, when President Kennedy came into office in January, 1961, his economic advisers could predict with some confidence that there would continue to be an unemployment gap for some considerable time.

I don't want to give away any secrets—and fortunately I don't happen to know any—but isn't it quite possible that some shrewd economic historian of the future will characterize the fiscal policy of the Kennedy and Johnson administration in the following provocative way:

> With much ingenuity and untiring zeal, the New Frontiersmen of the Great Society contrived to emasculate the automatic stabilization built-in on the upside by our progressive tax system. Brick by brick they hauled down the implicit budgetary surplus which would have prevailed at full employment if the Eisenhower levels of expenditure had been preserved with unchanged Eisenhower rates of taxation.

I don't say anybody planned it in quite that way, but perhaps I am underrating the perspicacity of our political economists. In any case the whole nation has been the beneficiary. And I can think of no better contrast to bring this out than a comparison of the anemic and short-lived business expansion from 1958 to 1960 with the current post-1961 cyclical expansion. I will remind you that unemployment stayed above the 5 percent level during the last years of the 1950s; yet the Federal Reserve—in its fanatical determination to root out any trace of inflation—engineered a tighter pattern of interest rates than can be found in the annals of the National Bureau for almost a century. At the same time the federal budget was permitted to go within a year from the largest peacetime deficit ever experienced to a whopping surplus. All this involved stabilization with a vengeance; but it was, if not stabilization of *rigor mortis,* something like the stabilization of hibernation.

I am a dutiful speaker—and when I am given the assignment to talk on stabilization I try to live up to it—but I am also a devious person with a Machiavellian cunning. If it is to be stabilization, it must be stabilization on my definition.

The pattern of stability that should interest people today cannot be one of sluggishness or stagnation. Nor does the problem pose itself as that of perpetuating an average level of unemployment midway between such extremes as 7 and 4 percent. Good economic performance means infrequent and only transient departures from high-employment production along a growth trend of some 4 percent per annum.

In part because of the new Viet Nam spending, I think we are beginning to approach our goal. I refuse to believe our public is so economically retarded as to have to rely on cold-war emergencies to back into full employment growth. I think that we have learned something since 1953 (when we lacked the imagination to offset the end of the Korean War with a massive cut in taxes). I even venture to think that the phobia against noninflationary deficits is beginning slowly to disappear.

So I stand before you tonight as something of a "cockeyed optimist." Most of us here are not bankers. But we have absorbed enough of the banker's neutrality to know that one ought to be wary in lending money or credence to optimistic idealists. In order then to restore my credit and standing as a man of prudence and sobriety, I must end my sermon with a warning of problems still unsolved.

Can a mixed economy like ours enjoy continued full employment without having wages and other costs push up the wholesale price index beyond a tolerable rate? Or, to use technical jargon, can we contrive stabilization devices to ensure a healthy Phillips curve for the American economy?

I don't know the answer. Few mixed economies have met with success in engineering an "incomes policy." Certainly our English brethren are no less intelligent than we in cooking up beautiful economic theorems and models and today London is swarming with civil servants recruited from the universities. Yet, even the most sympathetic observer must wonder whether the British are getting anywhere in the field of income-policy stabilization; and despite the many miracles we have been able to observe in Japan and the Common Market, conspicuously absent has been the miracle of full employment with free markets and reasonable price stability.

The first speaker at a conference ought to set a good example. Money, besides being the root of all evil, is the source of much bad temper among economists. If I have stepped on someone's doctrinal toes, I apologize and beg his pardon. Only the late hour can extenuate such gauche behavior. I hope you will agree that much can be forgiven a speaker who uses up only 45 minutes of his 50-minute hour.

HIGH EMPLOYMENT AND PRICE STABILITY

STRUCTURAL UNEMPLOYMENT AND COST-PUSH INFLATION IN THE UNITED STATES

George H. Hildebrand

For some years the ranks of the economists have been divided by two lively controversies, one concerning the causes of inflation, and the other the reasons for comparatively high and persistent rates of unemployment. I shall argue that with the postwar years the American economy has developed a relatively low inflationary threshold, one that is not well explained by the traditional competitive model of excess demand, although that model still has a role to play in any revised interpretation. I shall also contend that while deficiency of overall demand has been the primary reason for high rates of unemployment, the behavior of both the level and structure of wages must be incorporated in the analysis if the latter is to be made complete. In short, my thesis is that the failure of the labor market to work with full competitive efficiency has important consequential effects for the inflation problem, for demand expansion policy, and for unemployment.

I. THE POSTWAR INFLATIONARY PROCESS

The following summary observations about wage and price behavior since 1945 will prove useful for posing the basic problem and for providing a *raison d'être* for the model to follow.

(1) Through 1964, the wholesale price index passed through three major upswings: 1945–48, 1950–51, and 1955–57. The first two episodes were clear-cut cases of excess general demand, although the underlying nature of the inflationary process was obscured during the first one by undue attention to the great strike wave and the wage settlements that followed.[1] However, the upswing of 1955–57 was of a different order:

[1]It was at this time that the suggestion first appeared that the inflation originated from wage-push, although in fact it was a straightforward classical case of monetary disequilibrium, with origins in wartime finance and direct controls.

there was no general excess of demand, but a general rise of the wage and price levels did occur. This was the first occasion in which the wage-push hypothesis acquired plausibility. From 1958 through 1964, there was no price inflation. But during the first six months of 1965 wholesale prices have moved up 2.1 percent, although total demand had not yet touched the limits of productive capacity or of the labor reserve. However, the supply of experienced male labor is now about as tight as in 1953.

(2) Recessions occurred in 1949, 1954, 1958, and 1960. However, the price level fell only slightly in the first two declines, and not at all in the last two. Thus we can say that business slumps in the postwar years have not brought about downward adjustments of the price level, which contrasts with past experience.

(3) Measured by hourly earnings, money wages have risen without exception in every year since 1945, in manufacturing, construction, mining, transportation, wholesale trade, and retail trade. The evidence for salaries and for wages in other segments points in the same direction. In short, the trend of compensation per unit of labor service supplied has been consistently upward, maintaining a pattern that, with some prewar interruptions, goes back to 1896. However, in the postwar years wages ceased to fall in recessions. The main influence of unemployment has been exerted on the rate of wage advance, not the direction of change.

(4) Since 1948, unit labor costs in manufacturing (total wages and salaries plus fringe supplements, divided by an index of physical production) have followed an upward trend, registering a cumulative advance of over 20 percent by late 1964. However, at certain times this movement has been interrupted or reversed. Since 1959, when the unemployment rate was consistently above 5 percent, until this year, the index has fallen slightly and irregularly. Moreover, the Federal Reserve Board has estimated that unit labor cost of production workers in manufacturing rose 2.5 percent yearly during 1948–53; 2 percent yearly during 1953–57; and 0.5 percent yearly during 1957–60, although employment of these workers was falling after 1953.[2]

(5) Between 1953 and 1963, total employment in mining, construction, manufacturing, and transportation and public utilities fell by almost 800,000. In the first three segments, the number of production workers dropped 1.5 million. Altogether, these four sectors form the central core of union membership in the United States. Although the trend in this period was creating excess supplies of labor, nonetheless wages and salaries in these fields continued to rise without interruption.

(6) Between 1953 and 1963, employment in the four main white-collar

[2]*Federal Reserve Bulletin,* Vol. 50 (June, 1964), p. 677.

sectors—trade, finance, services, and government—soared by 7.2 million. Excluding government, the first three accounted for nearly three-quarters of the total increase in nonagricultural employment in the period. Wages and salaries rose consistently throughout the white-collar group, where excess demand for labor prevailed over these years. However, no permanent trend is evident for compensation spreads to widen in favor of these weakly unionized groups.[3] In other words, workers in the strongly unionized sectors maintained their general wage advantage despite a slow shrinkage of demand for their services.

Taken as a whole, it is difficult to explain this pattern of wage-price behavior following the Korean truce by appeal to straight competitive analysis. At no time in the ensuing 12 years has the economy experienced a general excess of demand for products or a general shortage of labor. Despite three recessions, neither the price nor the wage level fell. Indeed, the wage level has continued to advance during the years of comparatively high unemployment after 1957, and, until 1959–60, it did so faster than the rate of improvement in gross labor productivity in the important manufacturing sector. This pattern is inconsistent with what we might expect if wage determination were operative in a fully competitive regimen.[4]

At the same time, it is not easy to account for these developments as the simple consequence of a union-made wage-push. First, union members outside of government are concentrated in a few sectors, in organizations that vary in market power. In total they constitute (1962) only about a third of all private nonagricultural employees.[5] In public employment, the strike is usually forbidden, and formal collective bargaining is only beginning to spread. Second, postwar unionism in the goods sector has been unable to achieve a widening spread for wages relative to those segments where it is weak or entirely absent, which is sometimes taken to mean that unionism as a whole has no real power to raise wages. But this view is a mistaken one, because it overlooks the possibility of a one-way spillover from the union to the nonunion sectors.

---

[3] As of 1962, there were 2 million unionized government employees.

[4] Those who argue that unions are too weak to affect the money wage level or to produce significant distortion of the wage structure rely upon generally high partial elasticities of derived demand and upon the supposed inability of most unions to limit entry of new workers. This argument has three weaknesses: (1) union leaders do not usually associate employment losses with enforced wage increases, and in any case they concentrate upon the interests of the survivors; (2) unions commonly deal with all competing firms together, with the union acting as a syndicate or labor cartel. This makes the product demand schedule for the industry the relevant one, and it is less elastic than that of the firm. (3) In concentrated industries, entry of new firms is highly unlikely as a consequence of wage pressure and hence cannot act as a competitive check.

[5] *Monthly Labor Review*, Vol. 87 (May, 1964), pp. 501–7.

II. THE WAGE- AND PRICE-MAKING MECHANISM SINCE THE WAR: A SUGGESTED INTERPRETATION

Given a huge collection of observations involving actual wages and prices in historical time, we require a conceptual framework that can make this behavior meaningful, in the sense that one can say that "things seem to work according to the underlying mechanics established in the framework." If that framework is to perform its task, it has to join together both the union and nonunion spheres of the economy, showing how they are interconnected and accounting for wage and price behavior in both of them, and incorporating both the influence of market competition and of wage-setting institutions in the explanation of the behavior observed. Working independently, Duesenberry, Haberler, and Lerner worked out models of this kind in 1958 and 1959.[6] Extensive empirical research since then has done much to sustain the view of the postwar inflationary process therein presented.[7]

The analytical framework we shall use rests upon two main underlying premises. One is that employees throughout the economy now expect and can insist upon regular annual increases in total money compensation per unit of work performed, whether they are represented by unions or not, wherever they work and whatever their occupation, and regardless of any level of unemployment experienced since the war. In the nonunion sphere workers can enforce their demands by quitting, by refusing to hire out, and by slacking off on the job.[8] This bargaining power of the un-

[6]James S. Duesenberry, "Underlying Factors in the Postwar Inflation," in Charles A. Myers (ed.), *Wages, Prices, Profits and Productivity* (American Assembly, Columbia University, 1959), pp. 61–89; Abba P. Lerner, "Inflationary Depression and the Regulation of Administered Prices," in *The Relationship of Prices to Economic Stability and Growth* (Compendium of Papers, March 31, 1958, Joint Economic Committee, 85th Cong., 2d sess.) (Washington, D.C.: U.S. Government Printing Office, 1958), pp. 257–68; and Gottfried Haberler, "Wage Policy and Inflation," in Philip D. Bradley (ed.), *The Public Stake in Union Power* (Charlottesville: University of Virginia Press, 1959), pp. 63–85. See also Fritz Machlup, "Another View of Cost-Push and Demand-Pull Inflation," *Review of Economics and Statistics*, Vol. 42 (May, 1960), pp. 125–39.

[7]For examples, see John E. Maher, "The Wage Pattern in the United States, 1946–1957," *Industrial and Labor Relations Review*, Vol. 15, (October, 1961), pp. 3–20; Otto Eckstein and Thomas A. Wilson, "The Determination of Money Wages in American Industry," *Quarterly Journal of Economics*, Vol. 76 (August, 1962), pp. 379–414; Sara Behman, "Labor Mobility, Increasing Labor Demand, and Money Wage-Rate Increases in United States Manufacturing," *Review of Economic Studies*, Vol. 31 (October, 1964), pp. 253–66; and Lloyd Ulman, "Labor Mobility and the Industrial Wage Structure in the Postwar United States," *Quarterly Journal of Economics*, Vol. 79 (February, 1965), pp. 73–97.

[8]Dissatisfied employees know how to withhold efficiency, can raise the unorganized employer's turnover costs, and can also begin to take an interest in forming a union. The best account of all this is in Sumner H. Slichter, "Do the Wage-Fixing Arrangements in the American Labor Market Have an Inflationary Bias?" *American Economic Review* (Papers and Proceedings), Vol. 44 (May, 1954), pp. 323–24.

organized workers also enables them to resist wage cuts. In the union sector, the employee has the same expectations and the same personal weapons to enforce them, and in addition belongs to an organization that can both bargain for him and, if need be, conduct strikes to back up its demands.

The second premise is that by force of statute and of public opinion today government policy must be aimed at preventing depressions, or in this context at striving to keep the unemployment rate down within a range of, say, 4 to 3 percent of the labor force. This means simply that no recession will be allowed to deepen enough to permit wage cuts to take place; indeed, increases in wage and salary compensation will still regularly occur, although the rate of advance may slacken.[9] Since wage reductions are ruled out in recessions, the price level is shored up against decline. When good times return, it begins to rise again, as is now the case. Thus the overall trend in the price level is upward. More than this, the surrounding circumstances now make it impossible to break this trend by deflationary monetary and fiscal measures. In consequence, if excessive unemployment does develop, corrective action must take the form of further expansion of total money demand, which will underwrite the rise in the wage and price levels and, indeed, probably accelerate it. Thus, while it is clear that the we cannot have persistent inflation without an expansionary monetary policy, that policy will be enforced by certain constraints: an advance in the wage level that in the main is externally determined, and a commitment to fight recessions by methods that do not allow wage and price deflations.

The process we now have to examine concerns the way in which the wage and price behavior of the two spheres is interrelated. Consider the union sector first. Assume the artificial initial circumstance that total demand is stationary. A wave of wage increases is then negotiated, and in general the unionized employers will extend the advance to their nonunion employees as well, as a matter of good personnel policy. If the rise in wages and salaries is large enough to squeeze up unit labor cost, product prices will rise throughout the union sphere, and a demand shift to nonunion goods and services will be induced, creating some unemployment for the union group. But even if this were not the case, the union employers still must pay more per unit of work performed. In consequence, they will gain incentive to shift their production processes in favor of more capital and less labor per unit of output. In these circumstances, this process of substitution, now usually cited as "automation"—although it involves more than this—will also lead to some unemployment within the sector, particularly if the demand for output is only

[9]In some union industries, the rate need not even slacken, where, as in 1955–56, long-term contracts with large built-in increases are made in prosperous times and then extend into periods of slump, as in 1958.

slowly increasing. More than this, because these employers have become habituated to regularly recurring advances in labor cost, they will be following a continuing policy of reproportioning inputs to reduce the labor content of their products.

Now look at the nonunion sphere. There, too, employees are expecting regular annual increases. For these firms to stand out against comparable increases, they must accept higher turnover costs, withdrawal of efficiency by their workers, and perhaps invasions here and there by unions. Also, as in the union sector, some of these firms are believers in paying wages above the market, and as a matter of policy they will not allow themselves to fall behind. At the same time, if price movements in the union sector invoke a demand shift toward nonunion products, the nonunion employers will require more workers. All told, then, wages will also go up in the nonunion branches of the economy, the more so if demand is expanding. A cost-price squeeze may also follow here, along with a continuing process of displacing labor by capital.[10]

If, now, the government takes no action and total demand accordingly remains stationary, we get some unemployment in both sectors, made worse if a rise in the price level also occurs. But today's political circumstances dictate that the government must intervene against rising unemployment, and the only way it can do so is by enlarging total money demand. Two consequences then follow: the rise of unemployment will be checked and output will start upward. Any price increases enforced by higher unit labor costs cannot lead to falling sales and employment, because they are supported by fiscal and monetary measures leading to larger money incomes and higher money demands for products. And if the initial conditions were already those of low unemployment and higher utilization of capacity, demand-pull can now operate on the wage and price levels, masking out the underlying process of cost-push.[11] But even if this were not the case, if consumer demand is undergoing a long-term shift from goods to services, which was the case until quite recently, the nonunion sector will undergo still larger price increases invoked by a localized demand-pull on top of an underlying cost-push from wages.

Viewed as a whole, then, much depends upon the amount of initial

---

[10]As Sara Behman shows in her study of aggregate manufacturing, cited earlier, the pattern of wage advance is diffused among laggard employers by the actions of marginal groups of workers who can quit, refuse reemployment or initial employment, or reduce their efficiency on the job. Of these, the quit rate turned out to be the most powerful variable for explaining postwar wage increases in manufacturing. With unions, the morale factor can be given additional expression as a wage-raising force.

[11]Except for the inability of the price level to fall at any time and for the continuing advance in the wage level at all times, the cost-push will be concealed anyway, since wages and salaries will be moving upward in comparable fashion in both spheres. In other words, no permanently widening wage spread in favor of the unionists will be detected.

slack in the economy when a given round of negotiated wage increases occurs and upon the vigor with which the policy of demand expansion is pursued—matters to which we shall return later. At this point we need only point out that while the process calls for accommodating monetary and fiscal policies and depends largely upon market forces for its extension to the nonunion sphere, by no means is it a simple case of excess overall demand.

Moreover, expansion policy is not the only way in which government affects labor costs and prices, for it also serves as an institutional force of its own, in addition to collective bargaining as such. Through a variety of statutes, government contributes directly to the rise of employment costs. The most pervasive of these involve the social insurances, particularly the OASDI system. Labor costs under OASDI are raised both through increased rates of tax per wage dollar and through enlargement of the taxable maximum. Both are now mandated for further increase under the Medicare legislation. By the end of the decade, the employers' payroll tax rate for all social insurances may well rise from a current average 6.625 percent per taxable wage dollar to at least 8 percent, with a further increase in liability deriving from increase of the OASDI maximum from $4,800 to $6,600 per year.[12] Beyond these legislated general increases in employer costs, the federal minimum wage works to raise the wages of low-productivity labor. Between 1950 and 1963, the minimum in manufacturing rose from 75 cents to $1.25 per hour, or by two thirds.[13] Further extensions of coverage are now in prospect, along with an increase in the rate to perhaps $1.75 by 1968.

Clearly, direct government intervention has contributed an important thrust of its own to the rise of labor costs since the war, in good part as the consequence of the political power of unionism. However, let us consider somewhat more fully the economic power of unions as well.

If they can be said to have any market power, then they should be able to alter the behavior of the entire wage level and to bend the structure of relative wages in a different direction, both in comparison with what we might expect in an economy without labor organizations. Obviously it is an extremely difficult matter to detect either influence as against "what might have been." Nonetheless, a good deal of recent sophisticated investigation suggests that their influence is real and that it is of preponderate importance.

---

[12]OASDI now costs the employer 3.625 percent on all compensation up to $4,800 a year. By 1969, the rate is scheduled to go to 4.9 percent, of which 0.5 percent will be hospital insurance, applicable to a revised maximum of $6,600 (effective 1966).

[13]In 1961, the minimum was extended to certain parts of construction, trade and services, which will go up to the $1.25 hourly rate in September, 1965. The minimum for manufacturing was then raised to $1.15, going to $1.25 in September, 1963. As of now, 60 percent of all private sector employees are covered, with further extensions proposed for trade, hotels and restaurants, laundries, and farm workers.

Start with the overall wage level (strictly, the average level of wage and salary compensation, including supplements, per unit of work performed). Wage-setting through collective bargaining in the unionized industrial sector exerts what Maher calls a "demonstration effect" upon nonunion employees—resistance to wage cuts when workers are in excess supply, and establishment of norms for expected annual increases—norms that become enforced over the system through market forces exerted by potentially mobile employees and supported by aggregate demand policy. This consensus of expectations stabilizes the price level against decline at certain times and promotes its rise at others. By detailed study of postwar wage settlements in key industries within the union sector, Maher as well as Eckstein and Wilson have found that collective bargaining produces a strong tendency for conformity to a common pattern of wage advance in each bargaining round, instead of the diversity that competitive forces would bring about. As Maher says, this central tendency is so evident that one may speak of a strategic group of "central bargainers" who set the norm for wage advance, which then spreads outward to the nonunion parts of the system. On occasion, the wage-making activities of the central bargainers may well conflict with the efforts of our monetary authorities to stabilize the price level.

The more subtle question is whether this informal "central wage administration" has accelerated the trend rate of advance in the entire wage level. The issue is a complex one and is still under debate and investigation. Nonetheless, I think there is a persuasive case in favor of an affirmative verdict, provided that one also recognizes that aggregate demand policy in these years has been supportive rather than restrictive for the "central administration's" wage policy.[14] One cannot ignore the permissive role of total money demand, although in my view the real line of causation now runs from the wage level to adaptive fiscal-monetary policy, rather than the reverse.[15]

One element in the case for acceleration is that the wage level has continued to rise throughout the period, despite four recessions and generally slack labor markets after 1957. It seems impossible to reconcile this behavior, at least after 1953, with the traditional theory of general excess demand, and this suggests in turn that the central bargainers were able to force up wages despite excess supplies of available labor. The Eckstein-Wilson study points in the same direction, indicating that within industry wage advances were more sensitive to upshifts in the profit rate

---

[14] If demand policy had been deflationary enough to have produced a 10 percent unemployment rate for, say, two years, the wage-raising efforts of the central bargainers could have been broken. But in my judgment this was neither possible nor desirable.

[15] This is why most of the Western countries are now struggling with "income policies," which at bottom are nothing more than an effort to reconcile full employment with a stable price level in a context of strong unionism.

than to a fall in the unemployment rate. Although unemployment is important, it does not seem to be as strong a deterrent to wage advances as Phillips and others in England earlier had thought.[16] Let the profit rate rise, and even at 5 percent unemployment, the rate of wage advance will be faster. Along the same line, Ulman has found that within the industrial sector in the postwar period relative wage increases were not significantly associated with relative changes in labor demands (employment); however, except for 1948–53, they were significantly correlated with the level of the industry wage at the start of the period, although the initially high wage industries did not increase employment faster than the others and their quit rates were actually falling. In other words, the state of the labor market—as measured by particular shortages or surpluses of production labor—within quite broad limits was not a significant influence upon the patterns of wage advances being negotiated.[17]

Although the issues are not finally resolved by these bits of evidence, the view that they suggest is this: the institutional forces exerted by collective bargaining and government together have contributed to the trend line of advance in the overall wage level, and this trend has had much to do with the behavior of the postwar price level. Of course, market forces were also of some influence, but only in affecting the rate of advance—in other words, by affecting the business cycle monetary and fiscal policy can change the second derivative, but only within externally imposed limits. More than this, collective bargaining as such has produced a different kind of interindustry wage structure relative to what we could reasonably expect from the operation of market forces alone.

III. THE QUESTION OF STRUCTURAL UNEMPLOYMENT

Two primary facts have given rise to the notion that "structural" factors, rather than deficiency of total demand, have been responsible for recent excessive unemployment in the United States. One was the

[16] A. W. Phillips, "The Relation between Unemployment and the Rate of Change in Money Wage Rates in the United Kingdom, 1861–1957," *Economica*, Vol. 25 (November, 1958), pp. 283–99. For another study, which finds that union "pushfulness" contributed to the U.K. wage trend, see L. A. Dicks-Mireaux and J. C. R. Dow, "The Determinants of Wage Inflation in the United Kingdom, 1946–1956," *Journal of the Royal Statistical Society*, Series a, 122, Part 2, pp. 145–74 (1959).

[17] If shifts in particular labor demands and supplies become seismic, market forces then do begin to reshape the wage structure. "Seismic" is the right word here. Consider, for example, that between 1953 and 1963 Class I railroads lost 526,900 employees while wages rose 46.8 percent; transportation equipment lost 429,700 production workers, but gross hourly wages went up 46.8 percent; primary metals lost 230,500 production workers, and wages were up 47.6 percent; while foods and kindred products lost 174,700, and wages rose 51 percent. These are end-year comparisons and are at most only straws in the wind. But there is not much doubt about how the wind has been blowing.

emergence of price inflation during 1955–56, when the overall unemployment rate was still over 4 percent. The other was persistence of the unemployment rate at levels above 5 percent throughout 1958–64. Noting also that unemployment rates were particularly high for certain vulnerable groups—blue-collar workers, the unskilled, the poorly educated, and the Negroes—observers began suggesting that some basic changes had begun to assert themselves in the composition of labor demand, against which the composition of labor supply was unable to adapt either promptly or fully.[18] The changes usually cited were automation, the long-run shift in the proportion of consumer outlay assigned to services rather than goods, and the relative immobility of high-wage factory labor. Their supposed consequence was a growing structural mismatching between the demands for particular types of labor—which were moving upward in skill requirements—and the supplies available—which consisted increasingly of people without the desired skills and aptitudes and/or in the wrong occupational, industrial, and geographic locations.[19]

Probably the main implication of this loosely drawn theory is that, given some target rate for full employment, say 4 or 3 percent, it will be impossible to reach this goal at an acceptable rate of price inflation by policies limited to expanding total demand. The underlying reasoning is somewhat obscure, but seems to run as follows. (1) Any desired level of total output now requires an increased number of skilled workers, technicians, and professional employees, relative to earlier boom periods; (2) the short-run elasticities of supply for these groups are very low; (3) inputs of these types of labor are more or less technologically fixed relative to associated quantities of unskilled and operative labor, which is redundant on the market; (4) in consequence, the expansion of real output will soon be checked by bottlenecks in skilled labor supply. Demand expansion thus quickly leads to demand-pull inflation in compensation rates for these types of labor and for output as a whole. Thus the lower quality workers continue to suffer heavy unemployment, while the economy hovers on the edge of inflationary depression. Furthermore,

---

[18]See, for example, Charles C. Killingsworth, "Automation, Jobs, and Manpower," in *Nation's Manpower Revolution* (Hearings before a Subcommittee on Employment and Manpower, Committee on Labor and Public Welfare, U.S. Senate, 88th Cong., 1st sess., Part 5) (Washington, D.C.: U.S. Government Printing Office, 1963), pp. 1461–83; *ibid.*, "The Automation Story: Machines, Manpower, and Jobs," in Charles Markham (ed.), *Jobs, Men, and Machines: Problems of Automation* (New York, 1964), pp. 15–47; *ibid.*, "Unemployment and the Tax Cut," address before Conference on Employment Security, Michigan State University (October 26, 1963); and Gunnar Myrdal, *Challenge of Affluence* (New York, 1962), pp. 12–33.

[19]Since wages play no part in the argument, the implication is that for any particular group of unwanted workers, the demand and supply functions do not cross at any wage of zero or above. This virtually rules out the possibility of intrafactor or interfactor substitution.

this critical point in expansion may involve successively higher overall rates of unemployment as technical advance proceeds.[20]

In short, then, a supposedly novel shortage of skilled labor has lowered the inflationary threshold, making policies for operating upon aggregate demand inadequate as a cure for excessive unemployment. If so, effective solution requires the addition of measures for training, retraining, and relocating labor supplies to break these skilled labor bottlenecks, because we are not suffering simply from a demand-deficiency depression of Keynesian type.[21]

In my judgment, there is a problem of structural unemployment, although such unemployment is not the reason for high general rates of unemployment since 1957. The trouble with the theory is that it claims too much and, by leaving out wages, it explains too little. As a result, it reinstates the traditional excess demand theory of inflation in special form, to apply to a period in which it fails to fit at all well, and at the same time it unnecessarily downgrades the effectiveness of overall demand policy. Yet the latter approach has already cut unemployment by 1.6 million between February, 1961, and July, 1965, while boosting nonagricultural employment by over 7 million (all figures seasonally adjusted). Clearly, these statistics demonstrate the job-creating power of expanding demand, not the contrary.[22]

In a sense, this is really the acid test of the structural hypothesis, for its basic claim is that the volume of unemployment cannot be lowered significantly by increase of total effective demand. But other carefully formulated and more detailed statistical tests have also been made, chiefly by Knowles and Kalacheck, Gordon, and Gallaway.[23] They, too,

---

[20]R. G. Lipsey has developed the best exposition of models of structural unemployment, but even his account leaves out a wage-push by the central bargainers. Rather, the trouble is still said to lie in the scarcity of skilled labor and increased relative demand for such labor, for which the crucial test calls for expanding demand and then seeing what happens to the price level. Richard G. Lipsey, "Structural and Deficient-Demand Unemployment Reconsidered," in Arthur M. Ross (ed.), *Employment Policy and the Labor Market* (Berkeley, 1965), pp. 210–55.

[21]To my knowledge, Italy during 1947–60 is the first practical case of protracted mass unemployment for which a structural explanation was offered—only there it was capital shortage that was said to be the villain, along with fixed capital-to-labor coefficients. In other words, if Italy could not import the right kinds of machines and raw materials, and in the right amounts, nothing could be done about employing redundant labor. This, of course, was absurd as an explanation, but there was truth in the argument if fixed coefficients had been left out and the level and structure of wages brought in.

[22]For a sophisticated defense of demand theory and policy, see Robert M. Solow, *The Nature and Sources of Unemployment in the United States* (The Wicksell Lectures, 1964) (Stockholm: Almquist & Wiksell, 1964).

[23]James W. Knowles, assisted by Edward Kalacheck, *Higher Unemployment Rates, 1957–60; Structural Transformation or Inadequate Demand* (Subcommittee on Economic Statistics, Joint Economic Committee, 87th Cong., 1st sess.) (Washington, D.C.: U.S. Government Printing Office, 1961); L. E. Gallaway, "Labor Mobility and

Continued on page 26

fail to bear out the view that structural factors, rather than deficient demand, underlie the American unemployment problem. I lack space to review this important work here, other than to say that it shows that excessive total unemployment is not explained by increased mismatching of labor demands and supplies in specific markets.[24]

Let us now look at wages as a part of the unemployment problem. In Keynes's original formulation of the theory of effective demand and employment, the level of money wages was taken to be externally given and not to be affected by the expansion of demand for output and for workers.[25] We know today that this was an oversimplification, that for postwar conditions the wage level continuously rises, even in recessions. Now the softer version of the wage-push thesis suggests that when total demand expands, the central bargainers will be able to raise labor costs to employers more than otherwise, and, as the results of their efforts become diffused, unit labor cost begins rising over the system at a faster rate than gross labor productivity. More important, this point may well be reached *before* the 4 percent unemployment rate is achieved. By contrast, the harder version modifies this to say that the upward squeeze on unit labor costs and the price level starts at *successively higher* critical rates of unemployment with each successive expansion.[26]

I suggest that the hard version is difficult to verify and that the softer one is enough to sustain the view that central bargaining gives the nation a lower inflationary threshold than it otherwise would have. It means that we could still attain full employment at 4, or even 3, percent, but only if we accept some price inflation. But growing concern over the balance of payments has lowered our margin of tolerance for price inflation. And so official policy has taken the more cautious objective of seeking 4 percent as the "interim" goal for the unemployment rate, while striving to contain wage-price pressure by the guideposts policy. Accordingly, we have not gone all-out on demand expansion. Quite the contrary: unemployment rates have stayed above target for over four years. But the real trouble does not derive from some mysterious set of structural forces, but instead from the imminent threat of cost-push

---

Structural Unemployment," *American Economic Review,* Vol. 53 (September, 1963), pp. 694–716; and R. A. Gordon, "Has Structural Unemployment Worsened?" *Industrial Relations,* Vol. 3 (May, 1964), pp. 53–77. I do not find Professor Lipsey's adverse criticisms of some of these studies to be persuasive.

[24]For a contrary view, see Harold Demsetz, "Structural Unemployment: A Reconsideration of the Evidence and the Theory," *Journal of Law and Economics,* Vol. 4 (October, 1961), pp. 80–92.

[25]Unit labor cost would eventually rise with expansion, but only because marginal and average physical productivity would fall.

[26]In the soft version, the convex curve that relates the rate of general price change to the rate of unemployment is too far out from the origin to permit a stable price level at designated full employment. In the harder version, this function moves further out with the passage of time.

inflation as demand expansion proceeds and from our reluctance fully to accept that risk.

However, one may properly ask: does this mean that there is no structural problem at all? If so, why are the unemployment rates for the unskilled, for the Negro, for youngsters, and for the poorly educated so much higher than the overall rate, in good times and bad?

Again, I think the answer lies mainly in wages, or more accurately, in relative wages, where "wages" refers to total labor costs per unit of work performed. I have already cited Ulman's finding that within broad limits relative wages have not responded to changes in relative demands and supplies for particular types of labor. Since 1953, wages in the high-wage industries have kept up with the other groups until quite recently, despite declining demands. Indeed, this cost pressure has fostered labor displacement, and those displaced have inadequate incentive to move to lower wage jobs in other fields. Here it is of interest that average starting rates in eight high-wage industries rose 77.7 percent between 1950 and 1961, or at a simple average of 7 percent yearly before inclusion of supplements. This rapidly rising cost of employing new workers has been a deterrent to absorbing them in the high-wage industries, all the more so when the reduced corporate profits tax plus the investment credit plus more liberal depreciation guidelines—all good things on other grounds—have given employers every reason to substitute capital for labor. Here, then, we have one of the reasons for the high unemployment of youngsters and other vulnerable groups in the labor force.

A related type of evidence concerns the unskilled generally. Although this rather large and amorphous group has been in excess supply for at least a decade, the general tendency has been for their wages to move up relatively as fast as those of the more skilled or highly skilled groups of occupations.[27] In short, relative occupational spreads have failed to widen, and this makes it less profitable for employers to use unskilled workers than would have been the case otherwise.

The persistent rise in the federal minimum wage and the spread of its coverage, and the rise in the costs of social insurance, are additional factors adverse to the employment of unskilled workers. These forces can have no other effect, *ceteris paribus*, if one grants for the usual reasons that the demand for any type of labor has an absolute elasticity of greater than zero and less than infinity and that this elasticity is negative in sign. The sole question is: How much? Bear in mind also that the OASDI charges have applied to a $4,800 yearly maximum, which means that their incidence has been relatively greater upon the employment costs of low-wage workers. Fortunately, the recent amendments to the

---

[27]George H. Hildebrand and George E. Delehanty, "Wage Levels and Differentials" (forthcoming).

Social Security Act (Public Law 89–97) will raise the taxable maximum to $6,600 per year, which will temper this effect somewhat.

Nonetheless, it is probable that the unskilled group will continue to suffer disproportionately from unemployment, even if the overall rate is pushed still lower, as now seems likely. Collaterally, there is the continuing general problem of pushing the overall rate lower without incurring an unacceptable rate of inflation. Happily, we are not without weapons for mounting attacks on both problems.

For the unskilled and the vocationally unprepared in general, we are now spending about $1.8 billion in fiscal 1966 to upgrade their personal efficiency through literacy, training, and retraining programs. In time, these measures will improve employment opportunities for these workers. In my judgment, consideration ought also to be given to a return to the earlier policy of a multiple minimum wage, to allow for the differential effects of varying elasticities of labor demand in particular industries, now that coverage of the law seems likely to expand and the minimum rate itself to be increased. There is also merit to greater use of juvenile progression rates throughout industry, to take greater account of the relationship between length of initial job tenure and increase in personal efficiency, and in this way to make it more profitable for firms to employ youngsters.

Finally, there is the basic question: How can we shift the "Phillips curve" in toward the origin even more than these segmental measures would be likely to do, so that whatever may be our preferred full employment rate, it can be associated with tolerable behavior of the price level, in optimal combination? In my view, this will not be easy to achieve, and it is futile to expect anything constructive from direct efforts to break up trade unions or to regulate strikes. The best hope would seem to lie in avoiding too fast a rate of demand expansion and in pressing hard for continued and consistent adherence to the guideposts for price and wage behavior. Whether either is possible is beyond the predictive powers of the economist.

IV. CONCLUSIONS

The central argument of this paper is twofold. First, the American economy of today confronts a persistent problem of cost-push inflation, which begins to manifest itself as the profit rate starts up and the unemployment rate goes down, and before designated full employment can be reached. However, the process by which labor cost per unit of work performed is advanced does not rest upon institutional factors alone, although they are basic to its inception and to the formation of the general rate of advance. Rather, market forces promote its rapid diffusion over the system, while overall money demand is a necessary permissive factor.

Second, these institutional forces also work to produce a structure of relative labor costs that is unfavorable to the increased employment of blue-collar workers generally, and to those with little or no skill in particular. If that structure cannot be adapted by relative widening, then the whole burden of adjustment falls upon programs to upgrade the efficiency of low quality workers, and to promote their mobility. Expansion of aggregate demand alone will not solve this problem, because it would require excessive inflation of the price level. In this sense, then, we do have a structural problem, but its roots lie in relative wage costs and their strong tendency to rise against the market. Finally, if genuine full employment is to be reached with acceptable accompanying behavior of the price level, adherence to the general rules provided by the wage-price guideposts will be essential.

INFLATION AND STABILIZATION POLICIES IN WESTERN EUROPE

Albert Kervyn

INTRODUCTION

Attention will be focused in this paper on developments in the last three years, when inflation has been the main preoccupation of economic policy everywhere in Europe. It has, however, appeared useful to include some quantitative background material covering a longer span so as to put the recent period in its proper perspective. The paper will therefore be divided into three parts. The first will contain a brief presentation of the main relevant data for the last ten years, divided into five-year periods. The second will discuss the various types of policies which have been used since 1962. The third will present some of the main quantitative indicators for the recent period, so as to try to draw some conclusions about the effectiveness of the policies pursued.

A difficult choice had to be made about country coverage. One could take two or three and deal with them seriously, or broaden the field at the cost of superficiality. The latter choice has been made, since the great diversity of situations could not be exemplified from too limited a basis. Thus, an attempt will be made to cover developments in the seven major Europeans countries, and, where data are available, in the eighth, Switzerland.[1] A measure of selectivity has been used and not all aspects are discussed in all countries.

A final introductory caution before we get on with the story: this is not a theoretical paper and no attempt will be made to present a formal model of inflation, or even to define it too precisely. The usual definition,

[1]Their weights, as measured by 1958 GNP, are as follows:

U.K.	27.5	Belgium	3.3
Germany	27.1	Netherlands	3.2
France	13.7	Sweden	3.1
Italy	8.8	Switzerland	2.5

(OECD Europe = 100)

an excess of effective demand over capacity to supply at current prices, is good enough. But such an ex ante concept is extremely difficult to measure statistically. Even the national Economic Budgets, a forecast prepared annually for the guidance of policy makers, do not often attempt to measure this gap; and when they do, they are often too far out to be of much use. Successive revisions show that the inflationary gap is an elusive concept indeed.

One is thus thrown back on the classical indicators: rising prices and an external deficit. But here new troubles arise. If one is to trust to the price indicators, all countries have experienced inflationary pressures practically all the time. Following the 1958 recession, the GNP price deflator has remained stable or fallen by a fraction of a point in only three countries during one year. Otherwise, the price picture is one of uniform increases. The conclusion this suggests is obviously nonsense in terms of the definition of inflation given above. Of course, a 2 percent and a 5 percent price increase are not the same thing, but where is one to draw the line?

The foreign balance indicator appears on the other hand as overly optimistic. Germany, for instance, despite all the talk about "überhitzung" never had a deficit in the ten years covered. Yet, the balance on goods and services comes closest to the definition of inflation; it does represent ex post the difference between home resources and home uses.

The sharpness of the difference presented by the two indicators suggests that a distinction will have to be made between demand and cost (or price) inflation. In the following pages, the main indicators will be presented, both on the demand and on the cost side, without, however, attempting a more precise definition. This is not necessary for policy, and policy is what this paper is mostly about.

I. BACKGROUND MATERIAL

Prices

It is probably easiest to start by presenting the price movements. The GNP deflator is chosen as the best single indicator. Taking five-year periods in Table 1, it appears that in two cases only has the average rate of price increase been less than 2 percent per annum, and both occur in the first period. The general experience is one of acceleration from one period to the next—quite a dramatic one in Italy and Switzerland, and more moderate elsewhere. France and the U.K. are the exceptions; open inflation in France in 1956 and 1957 led to the 1958 currency devaluation and an important upward movement in the price level. The case of the U.K. will receive attention below.

These are just averages. Year-to-year changes reflect, usually with a one-year time lag, the cyclical fluctuations. Price increases usually accelerated following the boom years of 1956–57, while the 1958 recession produced either complete or relative stability in 1959 (except in France, where devaluation was followed by a 12 percent rise in the price level). In the second period, the phasing is not so uniform; the maximum rate of increase was reached in 1962 in Germany, Sweden, Switzerland, and the U.K.; in 1963 in France and Italy, while in Belgium and the Netherlands the acceleration continued until 1964.

TABLE 1

ANNUAL AVERAGE RATES OF PRICE INCREASES*

Countries	*1954–59*	*1959–64*
Belgium†	1.9	2.3
France	6.0	4.0
Germany	2.5	3.4
Italy	2.1	4.9
Netherlands	3.4	3.9
Sweden	3.4	4.0
Switzerland	1.9	4.2
U.K.	3.5	2.3

*Year-to-year changes are given in the appendix tables, along with sources. This will be the case wherever only averages are given in text tables.

†The figures for Belgium are not entirely comparable to those of other countries. The method of deflating value added in government treats as quantity increases what in other countries would be regarded as price increases. The difference probably amounts to approximately 0.2 percent a year for the first five-year period, and 0.3 for the second. An offsetting correction should be made in Table 2 to lower the growth rate of real GNP.

It may also be noted that while the French devaluation was immediately reflected in the price movement, the 5 percent appreciation of the Dutch and German currencies in 1961 apparently failed in one of its objectives; namely, to lower or at least to stabilize the price level.

Growth Rates of GNP

This pattern of price movements may be compared with the trend in production. Here also, and more surprisingly, the second five-year period is marked by acceleration, the only exception being Germany, where the reconstruction period, with its exceptional growth rates, was over by the middle fifties.

Since the acceleration has affected mostly the countries at the bottom of the table, the distinction, traditional in Europe, between fast and slow growers has lost most of its meaning in the last few years. After 1959, it is only the U.K. that falls significantly short of attaining a 5 percent growth rate.

Part of this phenomenon is accounted for by the fact that there was no recession in the second period, while the 1958 downswing had caused at best a slowdown, at worst an actual decline in GNP. In France its effects coincided with the deflationary measures taken concurrently with devaluation.

On the other hand, the full impact of the deflationary measures of 1963–64 is not yet reflected in Table 2, except in Italy, where the growth rate declined in 1963. In Belgium, France, and the U.K. the effect will show essentially in the 1965 figures, and the period 1960–65 is likely to show somewhat lower growth rates.

TABLE 2

AVERAGE ANNUAL GROWTH RATES OF GNP

Countries	*1954–59*	*1959–64*
Germany	7.1	5.4
Italy	5.5	5.9
France	4.4	5.9
Netherlands	3.7	5.2
Switzerland	3.5	5.4
Sweden	3.2	4.7
U.K.	2.5	3.7
Belgium*	2.5	5.0

*See second footnote (†) to Table 1.

Still, the timing of cyclical swings does not affect the main conclusion of Table 2. This is particularly true for the slow and medium growers of the first period. For each of them, the first three years of expansion (1954–57 and 1959–62) were marked by a higher growth rate in the second period than in the first.

The absence of a period of slack in demand thus offers only a partial explanation for the acceleration in growth. Factors from the supply side will be discussed later. A comparison of Tables 1 and 2 may also suggest that pressure of demand was not only more continuous but also stronger in the second period.

As already mentioned, there is a good, though lagged, correlation between demand and price changes on a year-to-year basis. But beyond that, the evidence is conflicting. Belgium, the Netherlands, and Switzerland seem to offer clear cases where increased demand pressure led simultaneously to higher growth rates and more rapid price increases. Discounting the French case, we still have Germany and the U.K., where the correlation is inverse. As will be shown later the explanation is to be sought, for Germany, in a deterioration on the supply side, and, for the U.K., in a change in the cost-price relationship. By and large, stronger demand pressure seems associated with faster increases both in production and prices.

This relation does not hold, however, in comparisons between countries. In the first period, prices rose slowly in two fast growers (Germany and Italy), and in a medium and a slow grower (Switzerland and Belgium). Here also, conditions on the supply side seem to have played a dominant role. The generalization may nevertheless remain valid, though qualified by an appropriate *ceteris paribus.*

The Foreign Trade Balance

Some confirmation of this generalization can be found in the consideration of the trade balance. By and large, this became more positive in the first period, indicating a slackening of internal pressures, while it deteriorated in the second period.

TABLE 3

NET EXPORTS, AS PERCENTAGE OF GNP*
(At Current Prices)

Year	*Belg.*	*France*	*Ger.*	*Italy*	*Neth.*	*Sweden*	*Switz.*	*U.K.*
1955	+2.0	+1.6	+2.3	−0.9	+2.6	−0.9	+2.8	−0.7
1956	+2.0	−1.8	+3.5	−1.2	−2.2	−0.2	+1.0	+1.2
1957	+1.2	−2.1	+4.2	−0.7	−1.5	−0.2	−0.3	+1.4
1958	+3.2	−0.9	+4.0	+1.1	+4.2	−0.2	+3.5	+1.9
1959	0.0	+1.4	+3.5	+1.9	+4.7	0.0	+2.9	+1.2
1960	+0.2	+1.7	+2.4	+0.3	+3.0	−0.8	+1.9	−0.6
1961	−0.1	+1.5	+2.1	+0.7	+1.5	+0.1	−1.0	+0.6
1962	+0.4	+0.8	+1.0	0.0	+1.3	−0.1	−1.7	+0.7
1963	−0.6	+0.4	+1.3	−2.1	+0.5	−0.2	−1.4	+0.8
1964	0.0	−0.1	+1.7	+0.7	−1.0	−0.1	−1.9	−0.5

*The concept used here is that of net exports of goods, services, and factor incomes. It differs from the current account in leaving out current transfers. Thus it is not the significant concept for balance of payments analysis (where it could be argued that private long-term capital movements should also be included). The current account of the U.K., for instance, is a good deal worse than the net exports shown here. Net exports appears, however, the more significant concept in terms of an analysis of inflationary pressures.

Year-to-year changes generally reflect increasing or decreasing domestic pressures. Thus the 1958 recession is attended by a general improvement, strongly marked in the cases of the Netherlands, Switzerland, and Belgium, where domestic demand declined, causing a sharp fall in imports while exports continued more or less sluggishly upward.

Again the recent inflationary bout is attended by a marked deterioration in 1963 and/or 1964. In Belgium and Italy, the situation is already reversed in 1964.

Sweden and the U.K. remain pretty [much] aloof from these movements and the German balance seems to respond as much to pressures outside the economy as on the domestic market. Thus in 1958, there is no improvement, as external and domestic demand slow down concurrently. The "überhitzung" of 1962 causes a decline in the surplus, but not a deficit, as exports still rise strongly. Thus the German case may provide the best example of the relative nature of the foreign balance indicator. This country's consistent surpluses do not mean that it has not been subjected to inflationary pressures, but only that they have generally been less violent than in the majority of trading partners. The only surprise is that the resulting inability to export one's excess demand has not led to an even faster rate of price increase.

This propagation mechanism explains that individual trade balances respond sometimes as much to the situation of the group as to domestic movements. But Western Europe does not constitute a closed economy, and the impression given by individual balances can be corrected by looking at the trade balance of this group of countries with the rest of the world. This reflects the extent to which they have transmitted collectively inflationary or deflationary impulses.

On merchandise trade alone, there was a negative swing of $1.5 billion as expansion accelerated from 1954 to 1957, then a positive one of $3 billion from 1957 to 1959. The first period as a whole is thus one of increasing surplus, or of resources rising faster than home demand.

The second period, on the other hand, is characterized by fairly regularly declining surpluses. The negative swing exceeds $5 billion between 1959 and 1964 (for 1964 the improvement in the Italian situation is more than offset by the deterioration in the British). These figures confirm the impression gained earlier that the acceleration of the second period is linked to an increase in the pressure of demand inside the group. The characteristic is one of gradually increasing domestic excess demand, or, through the spillover effect, of export-led inflation, which is still the leading force in Europe.

Money

A major difficulty for international comparisons in this field lies in the difference in institutional arrangements. What may be a liquid instrument in one country should not count as such in another. The simple way out has been taken in this paper. For all countries, currency plus sight deposits have been taken as money; "near-money" has simply been left out because of uncertain comparability.

This method, of course, distorts the picture somewhat. Belgium, France, and Italy are countries where the amount of time and savings deposits is far less than "money" as defined; the opposite is true in Germany, the Netherlands, and Sweden. The difference may not be significant where the concern lies only with rates of change. In most countries, however, time deposits have risen faster than sight deposits (though not in Italy), and the same may be true of other forms of "near-money."

Bearing in mind these qualifications, we shall speak here of "liquidity" as the ratio of money supply to GNP. Liquidity is thus the inverse of an income velocity of circulation. Comparisons between countries are not significant, but changes in liquidity—insofar as the index chosen does not distort the picture—are of course relevant for a discussion of inflation.

In the table below (Table 4), indices of the monthly averages of money supply have been divided into the indices of GNP at current prices.

TABLE 4

INDICES OF LIQUIDITY CHANGES
(Money Supply Divided by GNP)

Year	*Belg.*	*France*	*Ger.*	*Italy*	*Neth.*	*Sweden*	*Switz.*	*U.K.*
(1954 = 100)								
1955......	99	103	96	108	95	93	*	95
1956......	96	106	94	107	90	86	99	87
1957......	92	101	96	109	79	86	97	83
1958......	96	94	102	111	81	84	105	78
1959......	95	94	106	116	82	83	103	78
(1959 = 100)								
1960......	96	101	98	105	95	105	97	95
1961......	95	108	97	108	97	98	99	90
1962......	96	113	99	118	96	100	100	86
1963......	98	121	100	118	97	101	99	87
1964......	95	122	95	115	91	98	98	87

*1955 = 100.

The countries appear to fall into three groups: those who practiced active monetary restraint (Netherlands, Sweden, and the U.K. in the first period); those who had a more or less neutral monetary policy (Belgium, Germany, Sweden, and Switzerland in the second period); and France and Italy, who allowed liquidity to rise. The first period is, of course, not significant for France, since the great price increase which followed the devaluation was bound to reduce liquidity whatever the monetary policy.

This grouping of countries compares oddly with the figures in Table 1 on price increases. Leaving France aside, it is the three countries with active monetary restraint who experienced the most rapid rate of price increase in the first period, while Italy, at the time the country of least restraint, was enjoying relative price stability. Long-term cumulative effects may of course be invoked to explain that Italy was visited in the second period by her earlier sins, and thus to account for the inflationary push of 1963. But if the argument is valid, how is one to explain the bout of inflation which the Netherlands and the U.K. have undergone in 1964, after liquidity had declined over a ten-year period by nearly 30 percent in one case, and more than 30 percent in the other? And why should the Swiss, who are not usually classified as sinners in money matters, experience such strong inflationary pressures?

There are a few saving points for the quantity theorist: vigilance was relaxed somewhat in the Netherlands and Sweden in the second period, and prices rose faster. But then the opposite is true for Germany and the U.K. In the second period the chief sinner was France, and prices did rise substantially there—no more, however, than in the Netherlands, Sweden, or Switzerland, whose behavior was unimpeachable.

Of course, Table 4 does not present the whole picture, and a more sophisticated concept of liquidity may yield more satisfactory results. As the figures stand, it is hard to resist the impression that money supply was a rather passive element in the development. Causal relations are difficult to isolate. Is one to say that a recession and a slowdown in GNP increases liquidity (as in 1958), and that an inflationary rise in the value of the product causes liquidity to fall (as in 1964)? Or is one to say that monetary authorities have been so successfully "leaning against the wind" that changes in money supply have tended to counteract prevailing disequilibrium? As will be shown later, the latter view has a good deal to be said for it, at least for 1964, when restraint was everywhere the order of the day.

A comparison of Tables 3 and 4 provides a significant clue about year-to-year changes. The impact of the foreign balance is clearly discernible, superimposed on the action of the monetary authorities. Thus in the Netherlands (which provides a fine example owing to the amplitude of the swings), the large deficits of 1956 and 1957 helped the central bank to tighten up liquidity, while the even larger surpluses of the next two years arrested its decline; but the authorities did not allow an excess of exports of over 4 percent of GNP to increase liquidity significantly. In Germany and Switzerland also, the exceptional surpluses of 1958 and 1959 are clearly linked to the simultaneous increase in liquidity.

Other cases are not so clear, and the money supply seems to increase irrespective of the balance of payments. This can be explained by the fact that an external surplus is linked to a deficiency of home demand and, presumably, to a decline in investments and credits to finance them. An external deficit would be caused by rapidly rising investments and associated credits. Thus the banking system could maintain a fairly even rate of credit expansion, either internal, in the case of a boom, or external (exchange reserves), in the case of a slump. This is, of course, much too simple, as it leaves out government borrowing and repayments, as well as the actions of the central bank. But it may still provide an element of explanation.

The Cost Side

While demand inflation had clearly taken over in most countries in 1963–64, cost inflation had been there a long time, and its acceleration in the second period may well be a factor responsible for the reappearance of excess demand. The last five years are generally marked by a sharp increase in the rate of wage rises.

France again constitutes an exception. If, however, one looks at the figures expressed in dollars (that is, correcting for currency devaluation—these figures are given in parentheses in Table 5), even France falls into line.

TABLE 5

ANNUAL AVERAGE RATE OF INCREASE IN HOURLY EARNINGS*

Countries	*1954–59*	*1959–64*
Belgium	5.2	6.8
France	9.3 (2.3)†	7.9
Germany	7.3	9.2 (10.1)†
Italy	4.9	10.9
Netherlands	5.5	9.4 (10.5)†
Sweden	6.0	7.6
Switzerland	3.7	6.8
U.K.	5.9	6.2

*Figures refer to manufacturing in Italy, Netherlands, and the U.K.; to industry (mining included) in the other countries. In addition, utilities are included in Germany and construction in France.

†Figures in parentheses refer to changes as measured in dollars.

The genuine exception is the U.K. With only a modest degree of acceleration, it finds itself in the first half of the league in the first period, but right at the bottom in the second.

In Germany and the Netherlands, there was a bout of "überhitzung" in 1961–62. In France, the rise in earnings was almost perfectly regular; in all other countries, as well as in the Netherlands, there was a sharp acceleration of the trend in the last two years. Thus in 1964, the increase was more than 10 percent in Belgium, 16 percent in the Netherlands, and 12 percent in Italy (which had already registered a record 17 percent increase in 1963).

The reasons for this must be sought in the first place in the changing conditions on the labor market. A prolonged period of rapid expansion had gradually exhausted all the reserves of disguised and open unemployment. Labor shortage was often acute. The bargaining power of the unions increased, while the appearance of excess demand weakened the resistance of employers to wage increases. The latter felt that rising costs could safely be passed on to the purchaser or consumer.

The official data for unemployment vary considerably in quality and coverage. In some cases they mean little, but in some countries, at least, they are significant.

In some countries, the conditions in the labor market are better measured by a comparison between the number of vacancies and the number of unemployed. Thus in Germany in 1964, there were 600,000 registered vacancies for 170,000 unemployed; in the Netherlands, 140,000 against 30,000. More significant still, the number of jobs vacant had exceeded that of unemployed ever since 1959, and by a margin that steadily increased in both countries. In Switzerland, there are no unemployed. The conditions of the labor market are reflected in the number of foreign workers brought in to supplement the domestic labor force; by 1964 it was officially estimated that they made up one-third of all wage earners, and it is now official policy to slow this rate of immigration. The Swiss talk less of "überhitzung," and more of "überfremdung."

TABLE 6

REGISTERED UNEMPLOYED
(In Thousands)

Countries	*1959*	*1964*
Belgium	125	26
France	140	97
Germany	476	169
Italy	1,116	549
Netherlands	63	28
Sweden	37	21
U.K.	512	410

In Germany, the proportions are much lower. Nevertheless, it is estimated that the number of foreign workers rose from 775,000 in 1963 to 900,000 in 1964, both figures referring to yearly averages. Here immigration policy meets its limit in the inelasticity of supply.

The slowing down of cost inflation in the U.K. also seems to find its origin in the labor market. There was considerable tension in 1954 and 1955. Conditions eased in 1956, with the number of unemployed exceeding that of vacancies by the end of the year. The real slack occurred in 1958, then new tensions developed in 1960, but the unemployed remained more numerous than vacancies. Measures taken following the renewed threat of a balance of payments crisis then brought unemployment to a postwar peak early in 1963. As expansion was then resumed after 18 months of stagnation, the labor market tightened again and unemployment fell below vacancies early in 1965.

Through these alternations, the general impression is one of lesser pressure in the later years, particularly if the usual time lag is introduced. In the latter event four years out of five show either a substantial level of unemployment or conditions easing on the labor market. On these assumptions, 1965 should prove a difficult year in which to introduce incomes policy, as discussed below.

It also appears that the U.K. provides the most significant exception to the generalization put forward earlier that a higher growth rate has been associated with stronger pressures on the labor market.

Returning to cost inflation, if it can be traced back to excessive tightness on the labor market, it reduces simply to demand inflation. As already mentioned, this was certainly the dominant factor over the last couple of years. In earlier periods, however, cost inflation seems to have led an autonomous existence. At least this is suggested by a comparison of the trend in earnings (from Table 5) with that in output per man-hour, which is given in Table 7.

TABLE 7

OUTPUT PER MAN-HOUR IN MANUFACTURING
(Average Rates of Annual Increase)

Countries	*1954–59*	*1959–64*
Belgium	4.2	6.2
France	5.0	4.7*
Germany	6.3*	7.3*
Italy	2.4	7.4
Netherlands	3.7*	4.9*
Sweden	3.0	4.2
U.K.	3.4*	3.7*

*Official calculations. In the case of France, the figure is output per man-year in industry, corrected for changes in the work week.

These figures need a lot of qualification. In some cases, they result from official (and, one assumes, careful) calculations and can be directly compared with earnings. In other cases, a fairly rough method was used, based on employment indices, value added, and changes in the duration of the working week. In addition, the French figures for the two periods are not comparable, since in the first, only wage earners are included, but in the second, also salary earners. The Italian figures look very surprising. Both employment and hours per week are based on quarterly sample surveys of the Central Institute of Statistics. Perhaps the sample was not truly representative.

Most other figures appear fairly reasonable. The acceleration they show was to be expected from the parallel movement in GNP: changes in productivity have played a greater role than changes in employment. In Germany, acceleration in productivity has not proved sufficient to compensate for the narrowing possibilities of finding extra labor, and the rate of GNP growth has declined.

The next step would now be to compare trends in earnings and productivity, but first a few more statistical cautions are in order.

First, the data refer to the earnings of employees, not to the costs to the employers, and in some cases, the latter have risen substantially faster. Employers' contributions to legal systems of unemployment, sickness, or pension benefits have been increasing in relation to wages in every country on the continent. Data on wage costs (earnings plus indirect wages) are not, however, systematically reported, and accurate figures are scarce. Surveys made in 1961 and 1962 in two samples of industries for the Statistical Office of the Communities show that the percentage of indirect wages varies considerably from industry to industry in the same country; collective agreements often impose charges beyond the legal minima. Figures for earnings as given, and therefore also for costs per unit of output, thus understate the real rise.

Moreover, the productivity figures usually refer to wage earners, while it has been the common experience in recent years that the number of salary earners has risen faster, and this would be a second reason why the real trend in costs is understated.

A third point should be made. Manufacturing is usually the sector in the economy where, on the average, output per man-hour has risen fastest (agriculture provides the occasional exception). Since labor incomes tend to rise at similar rates throughout the economy, service inputs in manufacturing would have prices rising faster. This effect on costs would be partially offset in some cases, or more than offset in others, by the more stable trend in the price of imported raw materials and semifinished products. No hasty conclusions must therefore be drawn from a comparison of the price trends of Table 1 with the figures in Table 8.

TABLE 8

LABOR COSTS PER UNIT OF OUTPUT IN MANUFACTURING
(Average Rates of Annual Increase)

Countries	*1954–59*	*1959–64*
Belgium	1.0	0.8
France	4.3	3.2
Germany	1.0	1.9
Italy	2.5	3.5
Netherlands	1.7	4.7
Sweden	3.0	3.4
U.K.	2.5	2.5

Such as they are, the figures suggest that an element of cost inflation has been a universal feature in European manufacturing, and one may fairly assume that it has been even more significant in the economies taken as a whole.

Yet there does not appear to have been any dramatic increase in pressure from one period to the next, with the exception, of course, of the Netherlands, and with strong reservations about Italy. The same acceleration would probably also appear in Switzerland if production and employment data were available to make the calculations. Belgium, France, and the U.K. show no increases or actual declines.

One should not hastily conclude that demand inflation in the last few years has had little impact on costs. The figures shown are five-year averages, influenced as much by earlier stability as by later inflation. What is more significant is that costs have now been going up with some regularity and for a long period. This suggests that when European countries have gotten over the present phase of demand inflation (and many already have), they may remain faced with a far more intractable problem of increasing costs. As it has preceded excess demand, it may also survive it. As of the summer of 1965, the measures that have successfully curtailed demand in Belgium, France, and Italy have not brought the increase in wage rates down to the level of productivity improvement.

II. POLICIES

All European countries covered in this survey have experienced demand inflation in varying degrees in 1963–64. All have reacted through policy measures. An attempt will now be made to describe and classify these measures. Their effectiveness will be discussed in the next section when recent trends are shown.

Timing, of coure, has been far from uniform. The turning point at the peak occurred in Italy by the middle of 1963; in France, Switzerland, and Belgium, around the middle of 1964. Elsewhere the pressures may have abated somewhat, but demand remains strong in the beginning of 1965.

Policies can be classified under four headings: measures acting directly on demand, which have been widely used in one form or another; measures acting on supply, of which limited use has been made; the classical instruments of monetary policy, use of which has been universal; and finally, attempts to influence directly income formation, and to change the psychological climate through persuasion or other means.

All these have to be viewed against the international context of strong dependence on foreign trade and increasing freedom not only of merchandise trade but also of capital movements. In the European Community, for instance, no official restrictions could be placed on goods or capital imports; at the same time, little could be achieved on the supply side by further encouragement of imports. Germany had done so in the "überhitzung" period of 1961–62, but by 1964, with a further lowering of barriers, such measures had lost most of their significance, and only France made (a limited) use of them.

Restriction on Demand

Surprisingly enough, the most widely used measure has been quantitative restrictions imposed on credit. All except Sweden and Germany, where the pressures have been mildest, have resorted to this somewhat unusual method of curtailing demand.

Sometimes the quantitative ceilings applied to banks only, elsewhere they were extended to all or most types of lending institutions. Often they were attended by discriminatory features. For example, in the U.K. export credits were privileged (within the limits imposed) and in Switzerland complicated criteria about essential and not essential types of operations were established.

The classical measures acting on interest rates and bank liquidity were used at the same time (and will be described below), but it looks as if governments lacked confidence in their effectiveness. An increase in the rate of interest may have its effect offset by the expectation of rapidly rising prices, while a quantitative limit to credit expansion can be trusted to curb any excess, if the limit has been fixed, for instance, at half the rate of increase of the last 12 months. The preference for such measures may also reflect the fear that in a system of free capital movements, rising interest rates, while discouraging borrowers, might increase the liquidity of lenders.

Fiscal policy has also been a main talking point. The European Community had recommended that in 1964 public expenditure at current prices not increase beyond 5 percent; or if it did, any excess was to be offset by increasing tax rates.

As a matter of fact, only the Dutch raised tax rates in 1964, and, outside the Community, the British. The Italians had increased indirect taxation in 1963, with spectacular effects on the automobile market.

Yet no government succeeded in carrying out the Community policy to which it was committed: the minimum rise of budgetary outlays in the Community was 9 percent. But even this was quite an effort. The governments were caught in an inflationary nexus where costs were rising rapidly for public consumption, while transfers had to be adjusted to the higher price level. In addition, it was the common experience that most of current expenditure results from legal commitments which cannot be changed or from the working of an administrative machinery where the impact of new decisions is felt but slowly.

Still, the effort was made, and, among the Community members, it was only in France that there was no decline in 1964 in the real rate of increase of public consumption. In budgetary terms also, the balance improved everywhere (except in Italy, which was by then fighting deflation anyway) and government savings rose—quite markedly in France. Thus, despite a more than average increase in the price of public consumption, its share in GNP declined everywhere.

The same is true for the U.K. and Sweden, in the latter case for the central government only (the rise in local authority expenditure has maintained the share of public consumption in the total). At current prices, total outlays rose by 10 percent, as against 6.5 in the U.K.

While there is no denying that a serious effort, and sometimes a remarkable one, was made—as in the Netherlands, where public consumptions in real terms did not rise at all in 1964—the results, viewed statistically, do not encourage the view that fiscal policy can be used sharply and quickly as a means to control excess demand.

The story on government investment is no better. In a way it is worse, since one is here dealing essentially with discretionary expenditures which should provide an easy tool for policy. Strong restrictive measures were indeed announced, for instance in Belgium, the Netherlands, and (much later) in the U.K. The time lag between decision and execution seems, however, to have been so considerable that public investment was generally one of the most expansionary factors in the economies in 1964. The only exception is Italy, where the government, though alarmed at the spreading depression, reduced public investment in real terms.

Measures have also been taken to restrict private demand. On the consumption side, installment credit has been tightened up. The fiscal measures adopted in Italy in 1963 and in the U.K. in the autumn of 1964—but in most countries in April, 1965—will have their main incidence on consumers' disposable income.

Quantitative controls have also been in some cases imposed on investment through the system of building permits. This has been announced (rather than effectively used) in Belgium and the Netherlands, while the Swiss have announced that no new permits would be issued for nonessential construction. In the U.K. restrictions of this type were announced, but only in July, 1965.

If one considers the whole spectrum of such measures, it appears to be in Switzerland and in the U.K. that the strongest emphasis has been placed on quantitative restrictions on demand; in the U.K., however, this would be true only as of the summer of 1965.

Monetary Policy

This, of course, does not mean that monetary policy has not been used simultaneously. Its use has been universal.

The emphasis placed on the official discount rate has varied greatly. Italy never moved it at all (although interest rates both on short- and long-term securities rose substantially in response to other measures), Switzerland only went up to 2½ percent (coming from the traditional 2 percent), whereas the Bank of England went up to 7 percent (since reduced to 6 percent).

In some continental countries, where central banks rediscount commercial paper of the commercial banks, discrimination was also introduced according to the level of individual bank borrowings. For instance, the Swedes, following an earlier French practice, have given each bank a ceiling; if it needs to borrow beyond this figure, it can do so, but at twice the official discount rate.

At the same time that the rise in interest rates was supposed to discourage borrowers, numerous measures were taken to restrict the liquidity of lenders. Compulsory deposits with the central bank, bearing no interest, have been initiated or reinforced, liquidity coefficients have been raised, while in other cases limitations have been imposed on the duration or type of paper eligible for rediscount. Open-market operations, or operations on the national debt, have also been resorted to. Where external deficits occurred, as in the U.K., Netherlands, and Switzerland, they have been allowed their full play in reducing liquidity. (In the U.K., since the foreign exchange is held by the Treasury, the decrease in reserves finances government expenditure and enables it to reduce its offerings of Treasury bills, and thus to restrict bank liquidity).

A special problem arises in connection with foreign capital. Efforts to curtail domestic liquidity may readily be offset by borrowing abroad. Switzerland and Germany have taken strong measures in this respect. In both cases, banks have been compelled to deposit with the central bank the counterpart of nonresident sight deposits. No interest could be paid even on term deposits from foreigners. In addition, Germany has announced the imposition of a 25 percent withholding charge on interest paid abroad on German securities, and the threat has proved sufficient to stop the inflow of long-term funds. In Italy, the indebtedness of the commercial banks abroad had risen dramatically (it exceeded $1.5 billion for a period) during the period of inflation and the first restrictions on liquidity. The banks were subsequently requested to reduce the amounts outstanding.

In the U.K., the reverse problem has arisen. The British authorities assumed for a long time that they were dealing with a temporary balance of payments problem rather than with a straightforward case of excess demand at home. Being thus preoccupied with speculation against sterling, they put into effect measures to prevent capital exports, rather than imports. These applied both to short- and to long-term movements.

In all these cases, the question of disequilibrating capital movements has loomed very large, and all kinds of steps have been taken to avoid recourse to direct prohibition. The problem has often been complicated by the classical conflict between the demands of internal and external stability. Countries such as Germany or Switzerland who felt that the internal situation demanded a rise in interest rates have been chary of raising them for fear of attracting foreign capital. The widespread recourse to quantitative credit restrictions probably reflects to a large degree the fear that more classical types of measures not only could be offset by capital movements but could also react unfavorably on the international pattern of money rates.

Measures to Enlarge Supply

Far less has been done in this area, since short-term possibilities were far more limited.

Mention has already been made of policies on the labor market. Both the Swiss and the Germans, and, to a lesser extent, the French and the Belgians, tried to alleviate shortages through the importation of foreign workers. In the Swiss case, the policy met with such success that it became an embarrassment and had to be reversed.

In the U.K., the government has announced policies meant to promote efficient use of the existing labor force. The aim is to increase labor mobility by discouraging hoarding on the part of the employers and making job changes more acceptable to the employees. Simultaneously, training and retraining schemes should raise the levels of qualification. Productivity drives are initiated in various branches of industry. While similar policies have existed in some continental countries, most notably in Sweden, their concentrated impact could have significant results in the U.K., but in the medium term only. Thus they barely come under the heading of anti-inflation policies.

Measures to increase savings or to channel a greater proportion of them through the capital maket have also been tried in some cases, but without marked success.

On the external side, only the French have used the still extant limited margin of import liberalization to supplement domestic resources. This, however, is best regarded as a move in their psychological price policy.

The British import restrictions, which of course tended to increase the inflationary gap, can also be discussed under this heading. They proceeded from the assumption mentioned above that the problem was external in essence and that the first necessity was to gain time. The main effect appears to have been a postponement of some imports. The trade balance improved in the first quarter of 1965, but deteriorated again in the second as the surcharge was reduced from 15 to 10 percent.

One general remark should be made in concluding this section. While the fight against inflation has been the dominant preoccupation in 1963 or 1964 (and generally in both), policies have tried to avoid sacrificing the future to the exigencies of the present. Governments have generally attempted to shield productive investment from the impact of their restrictive measures; at least, it is only at a last resort that they have deliberately curtailed it. Where discriminatory credit policy has been in force, more tenderness has been shown to investment in industry. This, however, is in the realm of intentions. Since governments were usually incapable of acting quickly and effectively to curtail their own expenditure, and since their ability to affect private consumption was limited (excepting the violent automobile cycle generated in France and Italy), it is in the nature of the case that the main restrictions should fall on those expenditures financed from outside sources—namely on investment, productive or otherwise.

Income and Price Policies

Only one country in Europe had systematically used an incomes policy to control the total volume of demand. In the Netherlands, ever since the end of the war, wages and most prices were strictly controlled by the government, and earnings were allowed to rise only insofar as their increase did not threaten the internal stability or the competitive position of the economy. Since, moreover, the Dutch wanted a rapid industrialization of their country, the aim was to maintain the wage level substantially below that prevailing in neighboring countries. In this way an easy outlet could be found for Dutch products on the export markets. It must be stressed that imports or exports of goods and services account for over 50 percent of Dutch GNP, the highest proportion in Europe.

Thus, successful industrialization demanded the ability to export a large proportion of the additional output (the marginal import coefficient is even higher than the average).

The machinery of wage control in the Netherlands was modified time and again, usually to decrease the powers of the government. Its operation in the last few years can be summarized as follows. The Employers' Federation and the Trades Unions met in the Economic and Social Council to discuss the projections of the Central Planning Bureau for the coming year. Agreed conclusions as to the possible rate of wage increase received practical elaboration in bilateral discussions in the Foundation for Labor. The government no longer dictated, but could veto, any draft collective agreement that emerged from this process.

These methods had proved highly successful in the past, to the extent of gaining acceptance for reductions in wages and salaries in periods of inflationary tensions and external deficits.

The system broke down at the end of 1963 for a set of interrelated reasons. While the Unions' leadership had been educated to identify their members' interest with the long-term advantage of the country, the rank and file (as well as many of the employers) became increasingly irritated at the lack of bargaining freedom. Since the greater part of industrial output was exported at prices over which the government had no control, low domestic costs meant high profit margins. The conviction on the part of the Unions that the employers could pay more was borne out by many employers' paying "black" wages. Finally, the Central Planning Bureau had been overcautious in its estimates, and consistently failed to take into account rising labor costs in the neighboring countries. As a result, the competitive advantage of the Dutch economy was too great, the industrialization policy too successful, and an acute tension developed in the labor market and went on increasing for four years.

The break occurred when some important firms left the Employers' Federation and granted substantial wage increases to aid the recruiting of manpower. Once the breach was made, a general increase of 16 percent in wages was granted for 1964. It was absorbed with surprising ease. The resulting inflationary pressure is already abating, merchandise exports rose 14 percent in 1964, and the balance of payments looks as if it will be back in equilibrium in 1965.

Incomes policy has not been renounced after this failure, but a somewhat unreal air hangs over its proceedings. The various bodies concerned continue going through the motions, but a little like actors who are not sure that anybody is listening. The long-established Dutch tradition of cooperation and discipline may well reassert itself, but it is clear that incomes policy is never going to be the same again. The greatest danger to its future arises from the lack of damaging consequences of the 1964 wage inflation: the competitive position of the economy does not appear to be impaired, and no recession and unemployment has been necessary (as in the case of Italy) to bring the economy back into balance. Though the tension has slackened somewhat on the labor market, expansion continues unabated.

While the main emphasis of Dutch policy has been on wage formation, a parallel function has been given to control over other prices. Thus farm prices have been kept at a low level, both to facilitate exports and to insure a decent standard of living to wage earners despite the low wage level. The important agricultural budget has been used partly to subsidize farm output, but even more to keep production costs low on the farms. A comprehensive system has covered farm inputs, extension services, and even agricultural investment.

Other types of price control have also served as income regulators. Thus retail margins were set to prevent excessive profits in conditions of inflationary pressure. Rents were also fixed at a low level. Here, as in most of the price field, the policy had been to allow a regular rise that would gradually bring levels more in conformity with costs, as well as closer to prices prevailing in neighboring countries.

In 1964 the Dutch government was the only one to use price rises systematically to absorb inflation. Since it was decided at the end of 1963 that money wages would rise by 15 percent at least, the concern was to limit the increase in real consumption and this was done through price increases. Thus food prices were raised by 8 percent and controlled rents by a substantial amount. A large proportion of low-cost housing belongs to the local authorities, and the increase in farm prices permitted a reduction of subsidies. Thus these price rises had no multiplier effect.

As a result, consumption in real terms rose less in 1964 than it had in 1963, despite the "wage explosion" of the latter year. Such a policy is possible only if there is a margin in hand with respect to foreign prices and if there is no danger of creating thereby an autonomous price spiral.

This latter danger had, on the contrary, been the main preoccupation in France and Belgium. In both countries, wages are linked to the cost-of-living index (in France, only the minimum wage is so linked, but higher rates tend to move in sympathy). Under such circumstances, price policies become an important element of wage policy, and both the French and the Belgians made a major effort to prevent the development of a psychology of inflation. The French were both more imaginative and more successful. Not only did they use controls, but they sought to enlist the cooperation of wholesalers and retailers in their stabilization policy. The effective measures of deflation were, of course, a powerful help in changing the climate, but one must still count the policy a success. The GNP price deflator, which had risen by 5.6 percent in 1963, rose by only 3.6 in 1964, and the retail price index shows the same trends. Comparing first quarters of successive years, the rise was 2.5 percent in the course of 1964 as against 4.5 in 1963. Even the pace of the advance of wages has slackened a bit.

The same cannot be said for Belgium. The change in business climate occurred toward the middle of 1964 (somewhat later than in France), and the external account was balanced for the year, a large surplus in the second half having succeeded an equally large deficit in the first half. But wages and prices nevertheless went on rising, and even accelerating. In the 12 months ending with the first quarters, the rise in wages went from 10 to 11 percent from 1964 to 1965, and retail prices from 3.5 to 4.

In both countries, the government also tried (somewhat belatedly) to get industry and the unions to agree to a wage policy. The French attempt was pushed further and with more determination but was no more successful. The hope of an improved income distribution in the long run did not prove sufficient to offset the drawbacks to moderation in the short run. In Belgium, the employers helped the reluctant unions by saying "No," for fear that dividend limitation would form the counterpart to wage moderation.

Switzerland has developed an original method of alleviating wage pressures without an incomes policy: direct controls have been used to change the balance of the labor market. Each enterprise (both industrial and commercial) has received an employment quota and is forbidden to try to hire labor beyond this fixed ceiling. If labor supply is completely inelastic, this forcible curtailment of demand need not entail any decrease of production. Partly as a result of this measure, and partly because of quantitative controls over construction, the labor market appears to be more nearly balanced in 1965, although no effect is as yet apparent on the rate of wage increase.

In Sweden, there is no official incomes policy, and government pressure for moderation in wage increases seems to have been largely offset by an unusually large wage drift. There are, however, agreements regulating the level of agricultural prices and therefore incomes. These agreements move according to a complicated formula involving two types of parity: the one brings in the index of farm costs and international agricultural prices, the other the movements of other incomes. No changes in these policies were made in 1964, and, as a matter of fact, prices rose no faster in 1964 than they had in 1963, despite the considerable acceleration of growth in real terms.

In the U.K., on the other hand, a fresh start was made with incomes policy after the Labor government came into office. The first negotiations produced an Agreed Statement with the Employers' Federations and the Trades Unions. This was followed by the setting up of machinery to review both wage agreements and prices. Directives as to acceptable movements were also agreed upon. This constitutes a fine beginning, but there is as yet insufficient experience of operation. Apart from a great deal of general propaganda, any agreements of this type are by necessity negotiated with a small number of responsible leaders. It remains to be seen how far down the line the people who negotiate actual contracts are really "persuaded."

Development of inflationary pressures in Italy came earlier and followed a pattern different from all other countries. From 1954 to 1962, an exceptional rate of growth of GNP (6.3 percent compounded in real terms) had been paced by investment (9.3 percent), and even more by exports (14.1 percent). Over this period, consumption had fallen from 70.5 percent of GNP to 60.5; despite a rapid rise, the standard of living was not increasing as fast as prosperity. Rapid expansion had meanwhile radically changed the employment situation. Unemployment, which had fallen below the million mark for the first time in 1960, reached less than half that amount early in 1963. Simultaneously, the political climate had changed with "l'appertura a sinistra."

A wave of wage demands swept the country. The index of industrial wages rose by 20 percent in the course of 1962, and by another 15 percent in the course of 1963. Salary readjustments were even sharper in the public service. Consumption followed with a slight timelag: the increases (in current prices) were 13 and 16.5 percent in 1962 and 1963. Prices, of course, moved up. Still the share of wages and salaries in the national income rose from 52 to 58 percent in two years. The change in income distribution was marked enough to bring about an absolute decline in private net savings at current prices.

The investment boom continued, meanwhile, on the basis of previous orders, although business confidence was already on the wane at the end of 1962, largely because of the decline in profit margins. Thus, when severe credit restrictions were imposed in 1963 to curb what looked like a developing runaway inflation, a number of firms were caught off balance, and could meet their extensive commitments neither through internal cash flow nor through external finance.

The reversal was then brutal. Production of investment goods declined by 11 percent, and imports by 21 percent between the third quarters of 1963 and of 1964. Despite rising unemployment, wage rates still rose by 14 percent during the same period.

The government was thus faced with the double problem of reviving investment, while at the same time moderating wage claims. Discussions around an agreed wage policy failed, however, apparently for political reasons.

Fortunately, the Italian economy (like the Dutch) possessed a substantial margin of cost advantage. Despite increased labor costs, the recovery was led by exports. They rose by 24 percent (in value) between the first halves of 1964 and 1965, which is a remarkable response to the decline in home demand.

Although demand inflation disappeared at the end of 1963, the problem of cost inflation is still present. In the 12 months ending in June, 1965, wage rates still rose by 8 percent, although the trend is flattening out. Meanwhile, unemployment and short-time working are still rising, despite some signs of revival in production.

III. RECENT TRENDS

The effect of the policies discussed can now be viewed in terms of the recent movements in the components of GNP. Rates of change in real terms are presented in Table 9, and changes in the composition of expenditure at current prices in Table 10.

Increased demand pressure in the last couple of years has pushed up the rate of growth of GNP everywhere (except, of course, in Italy, where 1964 already belongs to the recession phase). Also, this acceleration was accompanied by a more rapid rate of price increase. Here France provides one exception: the comparison of changes in GNP at constant and at current prices shows that the price deflator rose less in 1964 than in 1963. This appears as a major success for the stabilization policy. To maintain the growth rate, while cutting down the speed of price increase, indicates good management indeed. There was also a bit of luck involved.

In Western Europe the winter was particularly severe in 1963, but exceptionally mild in 1964. As a result, the construction industry could work in 1964 from one to two months more than in 1963. This factor accounts for the apparent investment boom of 1964 in the "middle-

TABLE 9

Rates of Changes in Expenditure and GNP (Constant Prices)

	Private Consumption	Government Expenditure	Gross Domestic Investment (fixed)	Exports of Goods, Services, and Factor Incomes	Imports of Goods, Services, and Factor Incomes	GNP	GNP Current Prices
Belgium							
1962	4.5	9.4	1.4	9.4	8.1	4.9	6.8
1963	5.5	11.5	1.2	7.3	8.6	4.8	7.8
1964	4.2	2.9	8.9	13.0	12.6	5.0	10.0
France							
1962	6.9	4.2	11.5	2.7	8.6	6.6	11.4
1963	6.8	2.5	4.7	8.6	12.8	5.1	11.0
1964	4.3	3.0	13.5	7.2	11.9	5.4	9.2
Germany							
1962	5.8	11.5	5.6	3.9	11.4	4.2	8.7
1963	2.7	6.4	2.1	9.0	8.0	3.2	6.2
1964	5.4	3.3	9.4	10.4	8.4	6.5	9.5
Italy							
1962	7.4	4.3	8.8	10.7	15.1	6.3	12.5
1963	9.7	5.7	5.7	6.3	20.7	4.8	13.7
1964	2.7	2.4	−10.1	10.9	− 5.9	2.7	9.3
Netherlands							
1962	4.9	6.7	3.1	6.3	7.5	2.6	6.2
1963	7.1	2.8	3.9	6.4	9.6	3.6	8.5
1964	6.0	0.0	20.5	11.0	14.5	7.5	15.0
Sweden							
1962	3.6	5.2	5.1	6.9	6.4	3.5	8.4
1963	5.0	4.8	5.2	7.8	6.5	4.8	8.4
1964	5.2	4.7	5.6	11.0	10.3	6.4	10.1
U.K.							
1962	2.0	2.6	− 1.0	1.8	1.8	0.7	4.6
1963	4.4	2.1	3.1	4.3	3.6	4.1	5.7
1964	3.6	2.3	16.2	3.4	8.9	5.8	8.3

TABLE 10

DISTRIBUTION OF EXPENDITURE ON GNP (Percentages of GNP at Current Prices)

	Private Consumption	*Government Expenditure*	*Gross Domestic Investment (fixed)*	*Change in Inventories*	*Internal Demand*	*Exports of Goods, Services, and Factor Incomes*	*Imports of Goods, Services, and Factor Incomes*
Belgium							
1962	67.1	12.4	19.8	0.2	99.5	36.1	35.6
1963	67.9	13.1	19.4	0.2	100.6	36.5	37.1
1964	66.7	12.7	20.1	0.5	100.0	38.6	38.6
France							
1962	64.5	13.5	19.6	1.6	99.2	14.4	13.6
1963	64.9	13.6	20.0	1.1	99.6	14.3	13.9
1964	64.2	13.3	21.1	1.5	100.1	14.5	14.6
Germany							
1962	57.5	15.0	25.4	1.1	99.0	19.4	18.4
1963	57.1	15.5	25.2	0.9	98.7	19.9	18.6
1964	56.1	15.2	26.1	0.9	98.3	20.3	18.6
Italy							
1962	60.5	14.7	23.6	1.2	100.0	17.6	17.6
1963	62.3	15.8	23.2	0.8	102.1	17.1	19.2
1964	61.2	16.5	21.6	0.0	99.3	17.9	17.2
Netherlands							
1962	58.2	15.0	24.0	1.5	98.7	50.5	49.2
1963	59.0	15.2	24.0	1.3	99.5	50.8	50.3
1964	57.8	15.1	25.5	2.6	101.0	50.0	51.0
Sweden							
1962	54.3	13.4	32.0	0.5	100.2	19.7	19.9
1963	54.2	14.0	32.1	−0.2	100.1	19.8	19.9
1964	53.1	14.1	32.2	0.7	100.1	20.4	10.5
Switzerland							
1962	60.2	11.6	27.4	2.5	101.7	31.1	32.8
1963	59.9	11.6	28.5	1.4	101.4	31.0	32.4
1964	58.5	12.0	29.8	1.6	101.9	30.8	32.7
U.K.							
1962	65.8	16.9	16.3	0.3	99.3	20.4	19.7
1963	65.5	16.9	16.3	0.5	99.2	20.5	19.7
1964	64.5	16.6	17.8	1.6	100.5	20.1	20.6

Atlantic" area (that is, everywhere except Sweden and Italy). In the extreme case of the Netherlands, the volume of construction rose by 27 percent from one year to the next. In Belgium, the demand for investment goods was leveling off in 1964, whereas it was strong in 1963, but weather vagaries reverse this picture. In France, finally, it was the improvement in the weather which hid the depressing effects the stabilization policy would otherwise already have exercised on the growth of the economy.

Yet, if the picture of cost inflation is general, that of demand inflation is far less so. In addition to Italy, Belgium and Germany improved their foreign balance, and in Sweden it remained unchanged. This, of course, is but a relative measure. France, the Netherlands, and the U.K. were more inflationary than the average of their trading partners; the others, less so.

There are other signs, however, that demand inflation was tailing off. In every country, cost inflation in 1962 and 1963 had led to a strong pressure of demand: consumption everywhere rose faster than GNP. By 1964, the picture is reversed. While in many countries wage increases were still accelerating, consumption in real terms was rising less than GNP, and, at current prices, its share was falling everywhere. This is particularly surprising in the Netherlands, where the "wage explosion" was specifically a 1964 phenomenon. Thus the rapid increase in incomes, while it caused a general price rise, did not turn into a classical inflationary spiral.

It is very hard to assess the impact of public policy on this score. By and large, one would assume that if the authorities have failed to prevent a rapid rise in incomes, their influence on curtailing consumption would be quite limited. Thus, the saving grace of a declining share of consumption may appear more a result of luck than of good management. While automobile sales in France and Italy have proved highly responsive to government action, the much more widespread slump in the textile industry bears the marks of an autonomous cycle.

The effort to limit public consumption is more significant. In real terms, its rate of increase declined in all countries except France and the U.K. At current prices, however, the effect is far less spectacular. The implicit price rise for public consumption was high in most countries (in the extreme case, 15 percent in the Netherlands, and even 21 percent for included salaries alone). Thus, at current prices, the share of public consumption nowhere declined significantly. The importance of the price rise, of course, made nonsense of the recommendation of the European Community that public expenditure should not be allowed to rise by more than 5 percent in 1964. Still, some effort was made, and public finance, which had been a dynamic factor in demand in 1963, nowhere gave active support to inflation in 1964.

Surprisingly enough, it is investment, both fixed and in inventories, which appears primarily responsible for the inflationary pressures of 1964 (with, once more, the exception of Italy). As mentioned earlier, allowance must be made for weather favorable to a rapid development of house building. But even if one considers only the other forms of investment, they remain the component of demand which shows the most rapid rate of increase. It may be a comforting thought to some theorist to see the accelerator thus firmly in the saddle, turning a typical case of cost-push into demand-pull inflation. From the policy-making point of view, it is, however, disconcerting. Restrictive policies may not be easy to enforce in the public sector. Time lags and structural rigidities may prevent actual decline or even a rapid slowing down in government consumption. But severe monetary restrictions should bite deeply into that part of expenditure which is financed through credit, and that means, in the first place, fixed business investment and inventory accumulation. Yet the statistical picture shows the opposite.

It may, of course, also be the consequence of lag factors, as already suggested by the collapse of investment in Italy. It is very likely that in France, Belgium, and the U.K. the 1965 picture will be very different, and that the slowdown consequent upon the restrictive measures will bear most heavily on capital formation.

TABLE 11

Share of Wages and Salaries in National Income
(Percentages)

Countries	*1961*	*1962*	*1963*	*1964*
Belgium	57.0	58.5	60.3	61.7
France	60.5	60.7	63.0	64.0
Germany	62.5	64.0	64.8	64.8*
Italy	52.3	54.6	58.5	60.0
Netherlands†	69.4	71.4	72.5	74.3
Sweden‡	61.6	64.3	65.7	65.0
U.K.‡	67.8	68.2	68.0	67.9

*Estimated.

†Includes an imputed wage for self-employed. This correction eliminates that part of the rise in the share of wages which is due to the transfer of labor from self-employment to wage earning.

‡Shares in gross, rather than net, product at factor costs

Meanwhile we have the surprising combination of an increasing share of wages in national income (as shown in Table 11, this form of cost-push inflation has spared the U.K. and, possibly, Germany) and a decreasing share of consumption in national expenditure. In addition, we have a declining rate of profit coupled with an investment boom. It is thus clear that the Kaldor equilibrating mechanism has broken down, and apparently in two places: the savings pattern and the wage-price link. (The latter may be an unfair comment since Kaldor's model was a closed one, and the failure of his mechanism is likely due to the importance of both imports and exports.)

The other striking feature of 1964 is that, for all continental countries, exports rose more than GNP, both at current and at constant prices. This, of course, would be expected in the case of Italy or Germany. It is also true of Belgium, France, and the Netherlands, where internal demand inflation prevailed for at least part of the year. In Belgium, Germany, Italy, and Sweden, exports appear in fact to have been the mainspring of accelerated growth. The U.K. stands apart from this phenomenon of imported inflation. Exports there rose less than GNP, and this lack of buoyancy, when external demand was at a peak, is obviously a causal factor in the persistent balance of payments problem.

Elsewhere it appears that exports can continue to rise, even in the presence of excess demand on the home market, which suggests a far advanced process of international specialization. It also indicates the importance of handling the policy problem of inflation on a wider than national basis. The great responsiveness of imports to domestic situations make it a truly international problem. Any excess or shortfall of home demand is rapidly (though only partly) offset through the external account and does not have its full impact on production or employment. More important still, external deficits in the European setting (and excluding the U.K.) can disappear as quickly as they arose thanks to the rapidly rising trend in exports, and this offers far greater leeway for expansionary policies.

Some features of the 1964 situations still remain paradoxical. Policies (on the continent) were dominated by the fears that rising costs and wages would both endanger competitive positions and cause too rapid a rise in consumption. Yet, excess demand was largely the result of rapid growth in exports and investment. It appears typical in this respect that each successive revision of the Dutch accounts for 1964 has had a higher figure for these two components, together with a decline in the external deficit. This change, as one goes from forecast to estimate, and finally to actual accounts, gives a measure of the element of surprise in the type of development which occurred.

The figures available for the first few months of 1965 confirm this trend. In all countries, except the U.K. and perhaps Germany, they seem to announce the swing back to a surplus on the external account. Exports everywhere are still rising at more than 10 percent per annum, and only in Germany (which had a large surplus in 1964) are imports rising faster.

CONCLUSION

Two types of conclusions appear to emerge from this confusing mass of figures and interpretations: the first group on the level of facts, the second on the level of policy.

1. The acute phase of demand inflation appears to be over in Western Europe, and this experience suggests that internal demand can be controlled, though not always in the ways anticipated. Also, the downward spiral of deflation need not be as painful as could be feared, because of the cushion of exports. Production will be partly maintained and the spiral arrested by their rapid rise. Thus the balance of payments is a major constraint in the short run only. Both imports and exports are highly responsive to a little bout of deflation.

This optimistic view of the positions of individual countries is, of course, valid only against the background of a group where demand is maintained at a high, and perhaps an excessive, level. The easy elimination of a substantial deficit in any one country may depend on the group as a whole maintaining an external deficit with the rest of the world.

Cost inflation appears far more intractable. Here also a lag phenomenon is probably at work, and one may expect that the rise in wages will slow down some time after excess demand has disappeared. However, it was noted earlier that productivity also rose rapidly as a result of pressure on the labor market. Thus, the deceleration in output per man-hour may partly offset that in wage rates, and costs per unit of output may well go on rising. In the last few years, the competitive position of European manufactures has substantially deteriorated in relation to that of the U.S.A. While this is to be welcomed as a contribution to better international equilibrium, the continuation of this trend may in time slow down the growth rate in Europe. That is, if exports lose their buoyancy, problems of internal as well as external equilibrium become far more difficult to cope with, as can be seen in the case of the U.K. It must be added that, so far, experience does not bear out these fears for the future.

2. On policy, the conclusions are perhaps less optimistic. No doubt, demand inflation can be overcome successfully. The time lags are, however, longer than one would expect, and the contribution of public finance less decisive. Owing to the time lag, one would be tempted to say policy was put into action too late, and this was certainly true in the U.K. in 1964, as well as in Italy in 1962. It is, however, more doubtful in other countries, where governments react fairly promptly (and central banks even more promptly) to the danger of inflation. At the beginning, it is a small menace, dealt with by mild measures. Then the menace grows and the measures get tougher, and so the escalation continues, until a point of rather sudden and sometimes violent reversal is reached. The real trouble may be impatience; that is, fairly mild measures may have been adequate if they had been given time to work themselves out. But the lack of immediate response encourages the authorities to get tougher and often to go beyond the requirements of the case.

This combination of too late and too much in the later stages is most obvious in the British case. Having started too late, time was lacking to allow a mild dose of deflation to produce its effects, and it is likely that the dose will be unduly heavy. But this is not the only case, and one may wonder whether it was really necessary to produce a decline in industrial production in Italy and France and a stagnation that could turn into a decline in Belgium.

On cost inflation, the picture is even less promising, since effective policies to control the development of incomes hardly exist. Even the exceptional Dutch discipline broke when too heavy a stress was placed on it; and the difficulties encountered in France and in the U.K. suggest that conditions may be less favorable elsewhere. Yet some such policies may be indispensable for combining growth with stability. If the Dutch inflation of 1964 was not directly caused by consumption, the Italian inflation of 1963 certainly was. And elsewhere the proximate cause of excess demand, the investment boom, may well trace its origin to the rapid increase in consumption, both past and expected.

Still, the European experience shows that a group of countries can get along quite happily for a time with a modest degree of price inflation. If everybody remains more or less in step (taking into account differences in level as well as in rates of change), no great external difficulties need arise. The problem is rather one of stability. Two percent per annum may be tolerable, but tends to degenerate; and when the rate of price increase reaches 4 or 5 percent, it creates destabilizing expectations, where cost-push turns into demand-pull inflation.

This may well remain the main unsolved problem for future policies.

APPENDIX TABLES

TABLE A–1

INDEX OF PRICE DEFLATORS OF GNP

Years	*Belg.*	*France*	*Ger.*	*Italy*	*Neth.*	*Sweden*	*Switz.*	*U.K.*
(1954 = 100)								
1955	101	101	102	103	104	104	102	104
1956	105	106	105	106	107	109	103	110
1957	108	112	109	108	113	113	105	114
1958	110	126	112	111	115	117	110	118
1959	110	134	113	111	118	118	110	119
(1959 = 100)								
1960	101	103	103	102	102	104	104	101
1961	102	106	107	104	104	107	108	104
1962	104	111	112	110	108	113	114	108
1963	107	117	115	119	113	117	119	110
1964	112	122	118	127	121	122	123	112

TABLE A–2

VOLUME INDICES OF GNP AT MARKET PRICES

Years	*Belg.*	*France*	*Ger.*	*Italy*	*Neth.*	*Sweden*	*Switz.*	*U.K.*
(1954 = 100)								
1955	105	106	112	106.5	107.5	103	106	103
1956	108	111	120	110	111	106	110	105
1957	111	118	128	117	114	110	113	107
1958	110	120	132	122	114	111	111	108
1959	113	124	141	131	120	117	119	113
(1959 = 100)								
1960	106	108	108.5	107	109	104	105	105
1961	111	112	114	116	113	110	114	109
1962	116	120	119	123	116	113	119	110
1963	122	126	122	129	120	119	125	114
1964	128	133	130	133	129	126	130	120

TABLE A–3

HOURLY EARNINGS IN MANUFACTURING

	*Belg.**	*France*†*	*Ger.**	*Italy*	*Neth.†*	*Sweden**	*Switz.*	*U.K.*
(1954 = 100)								
1955	103	107	108	107	104	108	104	108
1956	111	120	116	113	110	115	108	116
1957	121	132	127	118	123	123	113	124
1958	127	146	135	124	129	130	118	128
1959	129	156	142	127	131	134	120	133
(1959 = 100)								
1960	104	108	109	105	109	107	106	108
1961	108	117	120	112	115	116	112	115
1962	116	127	133	129	125	124	121	120
1963	126	137	143	151	136	135	131	125
1964	139	146	155	168	158	144	139	135

*Industry (mining included; in Germany, utilities; in France, construction).

†Wage rates.

SOURCES: OECD; General statistics,; November, 1964 and January, 1965; Main Economic Indicators, August, 1965. Office Statistique des Communautés Européennes: Bulletin Général de Statistiques, 1964, N° II.

National sources for 1964:

Belgium: Bulletin de statistiques, Institut National de Statistique, Aout, 1965.
France: Les comptes de la Nation, Etudes et conjoncture, Juillet, 1965.
Italy: Relazione Generale sulla situazione economica del paese, Ministero del Bilancio, 1965.
Germany: Monatsbericht der Bundesbank, March, 1965.
Netherlands: Centraal Economisch Plan 1965, Centraal Planbureau, April, 1965.
Sweden: The Swedish economy 1965, Revised National Budget, Ministry of Finance.
Switzerland: Memorandum to OECD, September, 1965.
United Kingdom: Economic Trends, Central Statistical Office, April, 1965.

DISCUSSION

Trade Unionism, Inflation, and Unemployment

Lowell E. Gallaway

Let me say at the outset that I am in fundamental agreement with the general conclusion advanced by Professor Hildebrand, namely, that trade union wage policies have made a fundamental contribution to both inflationary pressure and high levels of unemployment in the United States in recent years. To buttress this conclusion he advances a theoretical explanation which attempts to reconcile the existence of trade union market power with empirical evidence which indicates that wages in the union sector have not increased relative to those in the nonunion sector.

Despite my basic agreement with Hildebrand's conclusion, I must confess that I feel somewhat uneasy in the presence of his explanation in that it depends upon workers in the nonunion sector somehow acquiring market power that is equivalent to that of workers in the union sector. This bothers me on two counts: (1) I find it difficult to justify as a logical concept and (2) it presents problems from the empirical standpoint, in that it is very difficult to discriminate between it and the alternative hypothesis that trade unions have had no marked effect on wage rates. Yet, I do agree with the conclusions drawn from the analysis. How can this be? Very simple: I feel that Hildebrand has conceded too much in assuming that he must explain away the evidence of stability in the relative wage structure in order to demonstrate the presence of trade union market power. And, in conceding too much he has so constrained himself that it is difficult for him to make a strong case for his general conclusion.

Now, these are strong statements on my part and require further elaboration before they can be accepted. Essentially, I question whether the impact of trade unions in the marketplace can be properly evaluated by reference to the behavior of the relative wage structure. My own view is that relative wages are not the appropriate variable to consider, but that absolute differences in real wages are. I expect that the past tendency to focus on relative wages is a product of economists' general concern with relative prices, to wit, the role that relative factor prices play in the theory of production. However, when the object of analysis is the behavior of wage differentials through time, it is by no means clear that relative wages are the appropriate magnitude to consider.

Starting with the formal theory of consumer demand and applying it to worker behavior in labor markets, we can develop an argument to the effect that in a competitive labor market there will be a tendency toward an equilibrium wage structure which reflects two types of opportunity costs of mobility between markets: objective ones involving explicit money costs, and subjective ones which reflect a variety of psychological considerations. Space limitations do not permit a full development of the rationale of this statement, but I doubt that much disagreement will arise over this point.

Given a tendency toward some equilibrium wage structure in a competitive market, the pertinent question now is how this wage structure will behave through time in the presence of such normal economic changes as growth in real output and wage levels. In effect, the use of the relative wage structure as a norm for evaluating the impact of unions in the marketplace assumes that over time a competitive market wage structure would respond to economic growth by showing equal percentage rate increases in wages in all sectors. Now, this certainly sounds appealing enough at first glance. However, I myself have not been able to find in the formal theory of consumer behavior evidence which is strongly suggestive that this would be the case in a true competitive labor market.

As noted, the equilibrium wage structure in a competitive market reflects both the objective and subjective costs of movement between sectors of the market. Now, the contention that in the face of economic growth the whole wage structure shifts upward by the same percentage rate implies that these opportunity costs of movement also shift upward by that same percentage. Thus, if the general level of money wages rose by, say, 10 percent, this argument would seem to hold that the costs of movement between sectors would also rise by 10 percent. To the extent that increases in the general wage level reflect pure price inflation this would seem to be defensible. However, if the increase in the general wage level represents an increase in real wages, I see no compelling reason to expect the wage structure to respond in the fashion suggested by the advocates of relative wages as a criterion for evaluating the impact of trade unions in the market. Rather, I would surely expect certain of the objective costs of movement, such as relocation costs and out-of-pocket retraining costs, to remain fairly constant in real terms. Admittedly, it may be argued that some of the objective costs should properly be expressed in terms of "work time" lost in making the transition between jobs. This would be the case with respect to time spent in retraining or time spent in relocating the worker and his family. To the extent that this is the case and to the extent that these time intervals are intertemporally invariant, the real costs of these factors will increase in proportion to increases in the general level of real wages. However, it is by no means clear that the amount of "downtime" between jobs is invariant through time. As the real cost of such time increases, it is not unreasonable to anticipate that workers might make attempts to reduce the amount of it.

Turning now to the subjective costs of mobility, I really can see no obvious reason for expecting anything other than constancy on the part of the real wage equivalent of such costs. To argue otherwise, and in particular to argue that such costs would change in direct proportion to changes in the general level of real wage rates, would seem to involve some very special assumptions regarding either the nature of workers' "leisure-income" preferences or the character of the subjective factors which gave rise to these costs in the first place.

To sum up, I have suggested that there are good reasons to expect substantial portions of the real wage equivalent of the costs of labor mobility between sectors of the economy to remain fairly constant over time. If this line of argument is accepted, then it is not clear that it is appropriate to expect to find a constant relative wage structure over time in a competitive labor market. At the same time, the discussion to this point does not conclusively demonstrate that a wage structure which exhibits constant real wage differentials is the appropriate norm to employ in evaluating the impact of trade unions in the marketplace. Thus, we face a dilemma. In order to provide some assistance in resolving this difficulty, I wish to propose a modest empirical test which may be helpful. Essentially, the test consists of selecting a time period prior to the granting of exclusive bargaining rights to trade unions (that is, prior to the mid-1930s) and observing the behavior of the wage structure in this interval. If the wage structure in such a period exhibits fairly constant real wage differentials, this would seem to argue against the relative wage structure criterion. I would submit that the test I am proposing is a strong one in that trade union activity was sizable in the period prior to unions receiving the grant of exclusive bargaining rights. Thus, if the test is biased in any one direction, it is toward refuting the argument I have advanced.

If we arbitrarily set the date of unions' receiving their grant of bargaining rights at 1935 (passage of the Wagner Act), we can observe the behavior of the wage structure over a 17-year period (1919–35) prior to the receipt of that grant. In Table 1 data are presented which show

TABLE 1

COMPENSATION PER FULL-TIME EQUIVALENT EMPLOYEE* (COLUMN A), AND DIFFERENCE IN COMPENSATION PER FULL-TIME EQUIVALENT EMPLOYEE BETWEEN UNION AND NON-UNION SECTOR (COLUMN B), UNITED STATES, 1919–1960 (1957–59 Prices)

Year	*Column A*	*Column B*
1919	$2,037	$ 147
1921	2,098	121
1922	2,306	− 44
1923	2,319	131
1924	2,318	150
1925	2,319	92
1926	2,383	76
1927	2,386	158
1928	2,446	175
1929	2,624	147
1930	2,479	96
1931	2,586	− 6
1932	2,560	−151
1933	2,466	− 18
1934	2,455	26
1935	2,467	90
1936	2,499	201
1937	2,520	264
1938	2,556	149
1939	2,607	269
1940	2,611	369
1941	2,641	612
1946	3,274	484
1947	3,341	625
1948	3,192	704
1949	3,314	711
1950	3,431	839
1951	3,348	993
1952	3,431	1,068
1953	3,570	1,122
1954	3,700	1,107
1955	3,856	1,225
1956	3,992	1,323
1957	4,009	1,369
1958	4,038	1,388
1959	4,216	1,478
1960	4,348	1,437

SOURCE: U.S. Department of Commerce, Bureau of the Census *Historical Statistics of the United States, Colonial Times to 1957*, Series D-685–D-719; and U.S. Department of Commerce, *Survey of Current Business*, July, 1961.

*In order to take account of changes in industrial mix through time, 1954 weights were used throughout to standardize the estimates of compensation per full-time equivalent employee. Thus, these estimates abstract from shifts in industrial structure.

compensation of full-time equivalent employees for union and nonunion sectors of the economy for such a period.[1] From these data the wage differential (in real terms) between the union and nonunion sectors can be estimated and then regressed against the level of real wages for the economy as a whole. If the position taken by the advocates of the relative wage criterion is borne out, the real wage differential should be significantly related in a positive fashion to the overall level of real wages. On the other hand, if no significant relationship exists between these variables, support is accorded to the belief that absolute differentials, rather than relative ones, are the appropriate criterion to employ in evaluating the impact of trade union behavior in the marketplace. The results of the regression analysis are:

$$D = 569.3815 - \underset{(.1412)}{.2069W}, \quad R^2 = .13 \tag{1}$$

where D denotes the wage differential and W the general level of wages. Clearly, the regression coefficient associated with W is not significantly different from zero at the 5 percent level. Further, the negative sign of the coefficient suggests a tendency toward a reversal of the differential. However, the latter phenomenon is apparently a result of the behavior of the wage differential during the deep depression years of 1931–33. In these years the differential reversed itself so that it was in favor of the nonunion sector. By 1935, though, this differential is again in favor of the union sector. If the observations from the deep depression years are eliminated from consideration, any semblance of a relationship between D and W disappears, as is shown by the following regression:

$$D = 143.2609 - \underset{(.1167)}{.0162W}, \quad R^2 = .002 \tag{2}$$

What this suggests is that if we abstract from cyclical impacts on the union–nonunion wage differential, there is no relationship at all between the level of the wage differential and the level of wages in this period. Also, the distribution of the union–nonunion wage differential (excluding the 1931–33 period) shows a mean of $105 and a standard deviation of $55. Thus, the variable D seems to fluctuate within a fairly narrow range irrespective of the level of overall real wages in the period under consideration. This is certainly consistent with the proposition that the appropriate criterion to use in evaluating the impact of trade unions in the marketplace is that of constancy of absolute differentials in real wages.

---

[1]The union sector is defined as including the mining, construction, manufacturing, and transportation and public utilities industries, while the nonunion sector consists of the wholesale and retail trade, services, and finance, insurance, and real estate industries.

On the basis of the argument that has been presented to this point, we are in a position to say that Hildebrand need not be concerned with reconciling a theoretical explanation of the workings of trade union market power with the empirical evidence of a stable relative wage structure. Once this is recognized it is possible to demonstrate in a fairly straightforward fashion that trade unions do have an impact on wage levels in their sector of the market. Space limitations do not permit me to describe in detail the theory which underlies this conclusion but, building on the work of Fellner and Cartter with respect to the economic behavior of trade unions in the marketplace,[2] it is possible to construct a model of the labor market which produces the following results: (1) a tendency toward "creeping" unemployment in the United States, (2) a finding that the use of aggregate-demand policy solutions can alleviate the unemployment but at the cost of a widening spread of the real wage structure, and (3) the further conclusion that aggregate-demand policy techniques will tend to generate price inflation in the economy.

While the theory which generates these conclusions is interesting in and of itself, it also has the distinct advantage of being susceptible to a sizable degree of empirical testing. Among other things, it suggests that real wages in the trade union sector will increase more rapidly in absolute terms than real wages in the nonunion sector.[3] Now, this actually occurs. In the post-1935 period in the United States the difference in real wages (again measured by annual compensation of full time equivalent employees) between the union sector and the nonunion sector has consistently increased as the overall wage level has risen. When a regression similar to that fitted for the 1919–35 period is fitted to data for 1936–40 (excluding the World War II years of 1941–45) the following results are obtained:

$$D = -81.2975 + \underset{(.0498)}{.7118}W, \; R^2 = .91 \qquad (3)$$

The differences between these results and those shown in regressions (1) and (2) are quite striking and suggest a fundamental alteration in the relationship between the union-nonunion wage differential and the overall level of real wages. This is quite consistent with the premise that trade unions are able to exert meaningful pressure on wage levels in the union sector of the market, pressure which produces a widening real wage differential in favor of the union sector. Now, the employment

[2]Allan Cartter, *Theory of Wages and Employment* (Homewood, Illinois: Richard D. Irwin, Inc., 1959), pp. 86–94; and William Fellner, *Competition Among the Few* (Rev. ed.; New York: Augustus M. Kelley, Publisher, 1949), pp. 252–76.

[3]The model also suggests certain specific patterns of behavior for the wage differential and levels of employment by sectors, which should take place in the course of the business cycle. Such patterns do actually occur, although space limitations do not permit a discussion of them is this paper.

effects of wage pressure of this sort in the union sector will serve to shift the burden of overall labor market adjustment to the nonunion sector. But, if wages in the nonunion sector are not sufficiently flexible to accommodate this pressure, unemployment will result. Thus, the incorporation into the theoretical structure of some concept of a "social" minimum wage (not necessarily the legal one), à la Long,[4] will produce a mechanism which can account for the rise in the unemployment rate that has occurred in recent years. And, of course, the presence of such trade union induced unemployment has inflationary overtones for the economy as a whole in that it implies a less favorable Phillips curve.

To summarize, I must say that I am in basic agreement with Professor Hildebrand's contention that trade union market power is a significant factor in explaining recent developments in the American economy, although my rationale for this conclusion is somewhat different than his since I reject the evidence of a stable relative wage structure as being pertinent to this question. Consequently, I must close with a somewhat negative comment to the effect that I am not fully satisfied with the theoretical mechanism Professor Hildebrand suggests. Nevertheless, he has made a significant contribution in raising again an issue which has been somewhat buried by the evidence of a stable relative wage structure. Hopefully, we may now proceed toward a more satisfactory evaluation of the economic impact of trade unions in the marketplace.

[4]Clarence Long employs such a device in his "A Theory of Creeping Unemployment and Labor Force Replacement" (Catholic Economic Association, Annual Meeting, Dec. 27, 1960), reprinted in 107 Cong. Rec. 12455 (daily ed. July 25, 1961).

DISCUSSION

Comments on Hildebrand Paper

Arthur M. Ross

The significance of wage rates for the problem of unemployment in the United States has been a neglected question in recent years. Professor Hildebrand has performed a real service by recalling our attention to this issue.

His paper deals with wages in two aspects—movements in the general wage level and changes in the structure of wage differentials.

1. *The general wage level.* Cost-push inflation, and the pros and cons of "creeping inflation," were debated extensively in the late 1950s, but the balance of payments deficit was not then such a preoccupying concern as it has since become. From today's vantage point, how much weight should be given to movements in the general wage level as a factor in the persistent excessive unemployment of the 1960s?

Concern over the balance of payments has certainly been a major constraint limiting the exercise of fiscal and monetary policies which might have produced higher growth rates and a closer approximation to full employment. But it seems to me that the facts do not warrant an indictment of wage-setting institutions in the United States as a major cause of the payments problem. First, wage increases in the United States have been much smaller than those in the other major industrial nations. Second, labor costs per unit of output have risen very little in this country, while they have increased substantially in the competing economies. Likewise, our wholesale price level has been much more stable than those abroad; and while we do not have very good statistics on comparative export and import prices, it can safely be asserted that relative price movements have aided the American position in world markets.

Consistent with these facts, our balance of current transactions has been very favorable in recent years. Were it not for the noncommercial obligations and activities of the United States in other parts of the world, there would be little ground for concern over foreign dollar holdings and the outflow of gold. This is not to disparage the essentiality of foreign economic and military aid nor of our own overseas military operations. But it may certainly be questioned whether we can fairly demand of our wage- and price-making institutions that they produce such a favorable balance on the commercial account as to offset not only tourist expenditures, overseas investment, and short-term capital flows but also any amount of noncommercial transactions which may be in the interests of the United States and/or the world community. This is not the place for an extended discussion of international finance. Suffice it to say that *ad hoc* remedies must be found for these extraordinary demands on our international accounts. From a policy standpoint, a $700 billion economy should not be thrown in reverse because of foreign exchange difficulties involving two or three billions. From an analytical standpoint, movements in the domestic wage level cannot fairly be regarded as a major cause of the problem.

2. *The structure of relative wages.* I must observe that recent developments do not support Professor Hildebrand's judgment that lower skilled workers are overpriced to such an extent as to burden them with an increasing share of total unemployment. In the first place, the unskilled workers (and the manual workers in general) have not had the greatest increases in compensation during recent years. (Salary increases for college teachers, for example, have not only regularly broken through the wage guidelines but have considerably exceeded the wage increases of manual workers.) In the second place, the relative unemployment of the unskilled has not been worsening. On the contrary, it has been improving for most groups of the unskilled, with the notable exception of those lacking previous work experience. For unskilled labor as a whole, omitting the inexperienced, their relative share of total unemployment is less than it was in 1950.

Now there is a considerable overlap between the inexperienced and the teen-agers. As is well known, teen-age unemployment has been chronically excessive and has represented an increasing proportion of total unemployment. I think that Professor Hildebrand, in arguing the relevance of wage structure as a factor in sectoral unemployment, makes his strongest case with respect to inexperienced youth. It is interesting to compare the situation in the United States, where teen-agers have experienced chronic difficulties in gaining a foothold in the labor market, with that of Japan, where new graduates of high schools and junior high schools have been the scarcest item on the market. The Japanese youngsters are paid very little and often do not do a great deal of work; but they are connected with an enterprise and they are beginning to make their way slowly up the ladder of increasing seniority, work assignments, and compensation. In the United States, young and inexperienced workers are generally expected to do a full job and earn the full rate within a very brief period after being hired.

Of course, there are the formal apprenticeship plans, but they cover only a small proportion of the young workers. In some other activities there are gradations of status and compensation roughly equivalent to the higher qualifications of young workers as they gain experience. But in many establishments, a new employee must either "make out" from the beginning, in which case he deserves the full rate for all workers in the occupation, or else it is uneconomical to hire him in competition with experienced persons.

A sensible youth-progression rate might play a legitimate part in a comprehensive set of institutions which would build a bridge, or serve as rites of passage, between the world of school and the world of work.

POSSIBLE INSTABILITY OF THE FINANCIAL STRUCTURE

IS THE GROWTH OF PRIVATE DEBT A CAUSE FOR CONCERN?

Warren L. Smith

I. INTRODUCTION

There has recently been considerable apprehension about the growth of private debt in the United States. Indeed, to a considerable extent, private debt seems to have superseded the federal debt as a matter of public concern. This concern, it might be added, is not entirely new: similar misgivings were expressed during the 1958–60 expansion and, on occasion, earlier in the postwar period. Although the sources of anxiety about the growth of private debt have not always been made entirely clear by commentators who have addressed themselves to the subject, it is possible to distinguish several different strands in discussion.

1. There is a view that the pace of debt growth in recent years has been so rapid that it cannot possibly continue indefinitely.[1] This view is most frequently expressed with respect to the growth of household indebtedness—mainly consumer installment and mortgage debt. Consumers, it is said, will at some point have to take a pause in incurring new debt and concentrate on the repayment of their existing debts. When this happens the stimulus to economic expansion stemming from debt growth will weaken, and a decline in economic activity—or at least a slowing down of the growth of actual output relative to productive capacity—may set in, unless some means can be found to head off such a development. According to this view, our present prosperity rests to some

[1]The fact that "an increase in private debt that is faster than the increase in GNP cannot continue indefinitely" has been cited by Robert Turner as a possible impediment to economic expansion during the years to come. See "Long-Run Economic Growth: Identifiable Trends of Significance to Business," in *The Economic Outlook for 1965* (Papers presented to the Twelfth Annual Conference on the Economic Outlook) (University of Michigan, 1965), pp. 95–98.

extent on an insubstantial foundation, since it is in part being induced by an unsustainable expansion of private debt.[2]

2. There is fear that the burden of debt repayments would considerably accentuate the effect of a decline in income if such a decline should occur for any reason. Debt repayments represent a contractual commitment that would have to be met and would cut into the amount of discretionary income available for current consumption spending. As a result, the marginal response of consumer expenditures to a decline in income might be large, thus raising the multiplier and strengthening the cumulative process of contraction. And beyond this immediate destabilizing effect, if the decline in income should be large, there would be a further danger of cumulative defaults on outstanding debt as a result of unemployment and reduced incomes. This, in turn, could undermine the financial structure of the economy, leading to a collapse of financial institutions such as occurred in the early 1930s.[3]

3. A third concern has to do with so-called quality of credit, as reflected in an increased frequency of defaults, foreclosures, repossessions of collateral, and so on.[4] The deterioration of credit quality is presumably of primary significance, because it accentuates the possible tendency for a decline in income to produce a financial collapse ([2] above).

4. There is a further question which is not as frequently raised as the other three, but which seems to me to be perhaps the essence of the problem of debt growth: Do our financial institutions and financial markets possess sufficient flexibility to enable them to adjust readily to major shifts in the composition of credit demand if such shifts should occur?[5]

As far as I can discover, economists have made few attempts to analyze

---

[2]This particular view was expressed by Seymour Harris with reference to an earlier period of rapid expansion in 1954–55, when he expressed doubt concerning the sustainability of the rapid growth of consumer installment and mortgage debt and questioned whether the prosperity was not in part a "sham prosperity" because it was built on excessive credit growth. See "The Economics of Eisenhower: A Symposium," *Review of Economics and Statistics,* Vol. XXXVIII, (November, 1956), p. 358. A similar view was expressed by Harold Groves in the same symposium (p. 378).

[3]For a classic exposition of the way in which deflationary pressure may cumulate into a major decline in an economy that is "overburdened" with debt, see Irving Fisher, "The Debt-Deflation Theory of Great Depressions," *Econometrica,* Vol. I (October, 1933), pp. 337–57.

[4]See, for example, J. S. Earley, "The Quality of Credit in Residential Financing," in *Proceedings of the 1963 Conference on Savings and Residential Financing* (Chicago: United States Savings and Loan League, 1963), pp. 127–41.

[5]Some have questioned the rapid growth of debt on the ground that excessive debt-financed private spending may cause inflation. This view is outside the scope of my discussion, since it presumably relates to the posture of overall stabilization policy, including fiscal as well as monetary policy, in relation to the underlying strength of private demand and the availability of productive resources to satisfy that demand. Another argument is that unduly rapid credit expansion and associated low levels of interest rates may lead to capital outflows and an increase in the U.S. balance of payments deficit. This question, too, is outside the purview of the present paper.

the problems that may arise as a result of the growth of private debt.[6] After having struggled with the subject in writing this paper, I can easily understand why. The issues raised are often difficult to define precisely. Data, especially for the period covered by the Federal Reserve flow of funds accounts, are available in great detail but are extremely difficult to interpret. Despite the difficulties, however, I believe the subject deserves more attention than it has received from economists—if for no other reason, in order to quiet the fears that have been expressed.

II. SOME GENERAL OBSERVATIONS ON DEBT GROWTH

Over the 35-year period 1929–64, net public and private debt—that is, primary debt owed by nonfinancial spending units, including households, businesses, and governments—grew at an average annual rate of 5.2 percent, in very close alignment with the 5.3 percent average rate of growth of current-dollar GNP.[7] During the postwar period from 1947 to 1964, total primary debt, as measured by the outstanding liabilities of the household, business, and government sectors of the Federal Reserve flow of funds accounts, grew at an average annual rate of 6.2 percent, only slightly higher than the 5.9 percent rate of growth of current-dollar GNP. As a result, the ratio of primary debt to GNP rose slightly from 1.822 in 1947 to 1.895 in 1964. But while debt growth has roughly paralleled GNP growth during the postwar period as a whole, it should be noted that debt grew noticeably less rapidly than GNP up to 1951 so that the ratio of outstanding debt to GNP declined during this period. Since 1951, debt has been rising substantially more rapidly than GNP, and the ratio has been rising. This tendency is especially noticeable since 1957: from 1957 to 1964, total outstanding primary debt rose at a rate of 6.5 percent per annum, while current-dollar GNP grew at a rate of only 5.0 percent. As a result, the debt-to-GNP ratio rose quite sharply from 1.715 in 1957 to 1.895 in 1964.

The growth of total primary debt during the postwar period is, of

---

[6]Substantial work on the relation of the financial structure to economic instability has, however, been done recently by Hyman Minsky. See his papers, "Financial Crisis, Financial Systems, and the Performance of the Economy," in *Private Capital Markets* (Englewood Cliffs, N.J.: Prentice-Hall, Inc., 1964), pp. 173–380; "Can 'It' Happen Again?" in Dean Carson (ed.), *Banking and Monetary Studies* (Homewood, Illinois: Richard D. Irwin, Inc., 1963), pp. 101–11; and "Longer Waves in Financial Relations: Financial Factors in the More Severe Depressions," *American Economic Review Papers and Proceedings,* Vol. LIV (May, 1964), pp. 324–35, together with comments by James Duesenberry, J. G. Gurley, and A. H. Meltzer, *op. cit.*, pp. 336–43.

[7]This calculation of the growth of debt is based on the Commerce Department series for net public and private debt. See *Historical Statistics of the United States; Colonial Times to 1957,* Series X 423–434, p. 664; and *Economic Report of the President,* January, 1965, Table B–54, p. 254.

course, the result of quite divergent growth patterns for the debt of the federal government and the debt of other sectors. The liabilities of the federal government as shown in the flow of funds accounts (which include some liabilities in addition to the public debt) grew at an average rate of 1.2 percent from 1946 to 1964, while the total liabilities of the other nonfinancial sectors grew at an average rate of 9.8 percent. The growth of debt has been rapid during the postwar period for each of the major sectors of the economy other than the federal government. From 1947 to 1964, total liabilities, as recorded in the flow of funds accounts, grew at average rates of 12.4 percent for the household sector, 7.8 percent for the business sector, and 11.2 percent for the state and local government sector.

The fact that over a long period of time total primary debt and income have grown at about the same rate suggests the existence of a mechanism that works to produce this result, at least approximately. Since debt is issued mainly by deficit spending units and is absorbed (either directly or through financial intermediation) mainly by surplus units, debt would tend to grow roughly in pace with income if aggregate deficits (and surpluses) represented a constant fraction of income. This seems to me to be a plausible hypothesis, but it is extremely difficult to verify. Data are available in the Federal Reserve flow-of-funds accounts for the deficits and surpluses of various sectors of the economy. But while, apart from statistical discrepancy, each sector's surplus or deficit must equal the increase or decrease in its net financial assets (financial assets minus liabilities), there is no simple relation between a sector's deficit or surplus, on the one hand, and its total borrowing and total accumulation of financial assets, on the other.[8] For example, the household sector, which is consistently a surplus sector, exhibits a steady growth of outstanding debt (more than offset, of course, by growth of financial assets).

[8] There are three main reasons for these "loose connections." (1) The sectors other than the federal government in the flow of funds are consolidated sectors containing many spending units. During any period, some of the units in a sector will have surpluses and others will have deficits, the deficit or surplus of the sector being the algebraic sum of the deficits and surpluses of the individual units. If the deficit units finance their deficits by borrowing, and the surplus units use their surpluses to accumulate financial assets, both the debt and the financial assets of the sector will grow. (2) Spending units may finance deficits by liquidating financial assets rather than by borrowing and may use surpluses to pay off debt rather than to accumulate financial assets. There are limits on the cumulative magnitude of such possibilities, but they are undoubtedly important at times. (3) The same spending unit may both borrow and accumulate financial assets or may repay debt and reduce financial assets. In effect, this amounts to borrowing to accumulate financial assets or using the proceeds from the sale of financial assets to repay borrowing. There is evidence—for example from the Surveys of Consumer Finances—that such behavior is not uncommon.

If there is an underlying tendency for total primary debt, including federal government debt, to grow more or less in pace with income and if the fiscal policy followed is such as to cause the federal debt to grow less rapidly than income, it is clear that the rate of growth of private debt must exceed that of income. However, as private debt grows relative to income and the federal debt, a convergence will begin to occur in which the growth of private debt will gradually slow down and come more and more closely into line with the growth of income.

I believe some such tendency as this is at work, but, in view of the complex nature of the relationships, a general explanation of patterns of debt growth is beyond the reach of this paper. Accordingly, I shall focus my attention on the growth of the debt of the household sector. One thing I hope to show is that, even though household debt has been growing much more rapidly than disposable income in recent years, the relationships are such that a convergence between the growth of debt and the growth of income either could come about rather quickly (in the case of installment debt) or may be in the gradual process of development already (in the case of mortgage debt). Even if the growth of private debt does eventually come into line with the growth of income, however, this result will occur at a considerably higher ratio of private debt to income than now exists. Accordingly, in the concluding sections, I shall have some comments to make concerning questions of public policy that are related to the problems associated with rising ratios of private debt to income.

III. GROWTH OF HOUSEHOLD SECTOR DEBT

Household borrowing consists almost entirely of short- and intermediate-term consumer debt and mortgage debt, and I shall discuss each of these in turn.

Consumer Debt

Short- and intermediate-term consumer debt includes installment debt and noninstallment debt. Both of these components have grown rapidly during the postwar period. As a result of shortages of consumer goods and the prosperous conditions that prevailed, consumer debt was reduced during World War II. At the end of 1945, such debt amounted to only $5.7 billion or only about 3.8 percent of the disposable personal income of that year. During the 19-year period to the end of 1964, consumer debt increased at an average rate of 14.8 percent per year, reaching a total of $76.8 billion or 17.8 percent of the disposable personal income of 1964. Consumer installment debt has grown even more rapidly than total consumer debt—at an average rate of 18.2 percent from the end of 1945 to the end of 1964. As a result, the ratio of outstanding installment debt to annual disposable personal income rose from 1.6 percent in 1945 to 13.8 percent in 1964. While installment debt grew substantially more rapidly than noninstallment debt during the early postwar period, the ratio of noninstallment debt to installment debt has been approximately one-third for the last decade.

An effort has been made by Alain Enthoven to explain the growth of consumer installment debt.[9] However, while the life-cycle hypothesis underlying Enthoven's model is supported by the findings of the Survey Research Center, F. R. Oliver has pointed out a technical defect in the model, which, in my opinion, renders it unsatisfactory.[10] I shall therefore attempt to develop an alternative model that is more closely tied to the process of debt generation.

In analyzing the growth of consumer debt, it is important to recognize that the demand for consumer credit is derived from the demand for the goods whose purchase the credit is used to finance. Any change in the supply conditions of either the goods or the credit will have an effect on the quantities of both goods purchased and credit extended. In my model, I shall take account in a simple way of this interdependence between the demand for goods and the demand for credit.

Since consumer installment debt is liquidated through monthly payments, it will be useful to begin by measuring the relevant flow variables (income, expenditures on consumer durable goods, credit extensions, and credit repayments) at monthly rates. We can then translate to annual levels, where this seems appropriate, at a later stage in our analysis.

Let us suppose that disposable personal income (Y) grows at a steady rate of $100r$ percent per month in accordance with the following equation:

$$Y_m = Y_o (1 + r)^m \qquad (1)$$

We shall express expenditures on consumer durable goods (A) in any month (m) as a proportion of disposable personal income in that month. Thus,

$$A_m = \alpha Y_m \qquad (2)$$

Moreover, extensions of installment credit (E) in any month are ex-

[9]Alain Enthoven, "The Growth of Installment Credit and the Future of Prosperity," *American Economic Review*, Vol. XLVII (December, 1957), pp. 911–29.

[10]F. R. Oliver, "On a Debt-Income Model of Consumer Installment Credit Growth: Comment," and Alain Enthoven, "On a Debt-Income Model of Consumer Installment Credit Growth: Reply," *American Economic Review*, Vol. LIV (June, 1964), pp. 415–23.

pressed as a proportion of expenditures on durable goods in that month; that is,

$$E_m = \beta A_m \tag{3}$$

It may be noted that installment credit has recently been used increasingly for the purchase of nondurable goods and services, such as vacations and college education. Nevertheless, since installment credit is still used predominantly to finance purchases of durable goods, it seems reasonably appropriate to relate it to expenditures on such goods. Substituting equations (2) and (3) into equation (1), we obtain the following expression:

$$E_m = \alpha\beta Y_o\,(1 + r)^m \tag{4}$$

For simplicity and precision, we shall assume that all installment contracts have the same initial maturity, which is equal to n months, and that they are repaid in equal installments of E/n per month.[11] Then the total amount of outstanding debt at the end of any month is given by

$$D_m = \sum_{i=0}^{n-1} \frac{n-i}{n} E_{m-i} \tag{5}$$

All credit that was extended prior to month m-n+1 has already been fully liquidated and therefore does not affect the stock of debt outstanding in month m in any way.[12]

Substituting values of E given by equation (4) into equation (5), we obtain

$$D_m = \alpha\beta Y_o \sum_{i=0}^{n-1} \frac{n-i}{n} (1 + r)^{m-i} \tag{6}$$

Since

$$\sum_{i=0}^{n-1} \frac{n-i}{n} (1 + r)^{m-i} = \frac{(1 + r)^{m+1}}{r}\left[1 - \frac{1}{n}\left(\frac{1 - (1 + r)^{-n}}{r}\right)\right]$$

---

[11]When, as is the usual practice, debt is paid off in equal installments which include interest, the proportion of the installments that represent repayment of the principal will rise during the life of the contract, and the assumption of repayment in equal installments will not be precisely satisfied. In view of the short maturities of installment debt, however, this qualification is not great enough to be important.

[12]The basic mathematical relations between installment credit extensions and repayments and the stock of outstanding debt are set forth in F. R. Oliver, *The Control of Hire-Purchase* (London: George Allen and Unwin, Ltd., 1961), chap. iv; and in P. A. Samuelson, "A Mathematical Analysis of the Relationship of New Credits, Total Credits Outstanding and Net Credit Change," Appendix B of G. Haberler, *Consumer Installment Credit and Economic Fluctuations* (New York: National Bureau of Economic Research, 1942).

D_m can be expressed as

$$D_m = \frac{\alpha\beta Y_o\,(1+r)^{m+1}}{r}\left[1 - \frac{1}{n}\left(\frac{1-(1+r)^{-n}}{r}\right)\right] \tag{7}$$

If we divide the stock of debt at the end of one month by the stock at the end of the previous month, we obtain

$$\frac{D_m}{D_{m-1}} = 1 + r$$

Thus, the stock of debt grows at a rate of 100*r* percent per month, the same as the rate of growth of income.

Dividing the stock of debt (as given in equation [7]) by income (using equation [1]), we obtain

$$\frac{D_m}{Y_m} = \alpha\beta\,\frac{1+r}{r}\left[1 - \frac{1}{n}\left(\frac{1-(1+r)^{-n}}{r}\right)\right] \tag{8}$$

In this equation, Y_m is *monthly* disposable personal income. In order to change the dimension to *annual rate*, the equation must be divided through by 12. Thus, if Y_{am} is disposable personal income at annual rate, the equation becomes

$$\frac{D_m}{Y_{am}} = \alpha\beta\,\frac{1+r}{12r}\left[1 - \frac{1}{n}\left(\frac{1-(1+r)^{-n}}{r}\right)\right] \tag{9}$$

There is still a further correction that needs to be made in this equation to put it in a form in which it can be applied to the relation between annual income (Y_a) and stocks of outstanding debt at the end of the year (D). When income is growing steadily, income for a year (Y_a) is related to income in the last month of the year expressed at an annual rate (Y_{am}) by the following equation:[13]

$$Y_a = kY_{am}$$

[13]If income for the month of December of year 1 (expressed at annual rate) is $Y_{ao}\,(1+r)^m$, income for December of year 2 will be $Y_{ao}\,(1+r)^{m+12}$, and average income for the 12 months of year 2 will be

$$Y_a = \frac{Y_{ao}}{12}\sum_{i=1}^{12}(1+r)^{m+i} = \frac{Y_{ao}}{12r}\left[(1+r)^{m+13} - (1+r)^{m+1}\right]$$

and the necessary adjustment factor to be applied to December income to convert it to annual average income will be

$$k = \frac{Y_a}{Y_{ao}\,(1+r)^{m+12}} = \frac{1+r}{12r}\left[1 - (1+r)^{-12}\right]$$

where

$$k = \frac{1+r}{12}\left(\frac{1-(1+r)^{-12}}{r}\right)$$

When this correction is allowed for, equation (9) becomes

$$\frac{D}{Y_a} = \alpha\beta\frac{1+r}{12rk}\left[1 - \frac{1}{n}\left(\frac{1-(1+r)^{-n}}{r}\right)\right] \tag{10}$$

It is apparent from equation (10) that for given values of the parameters of the system—α, β, r, and n—the debt-to-income ratio is a constant. Any change in the parameters will change the ratio.

The ratio of the stock of outstanding debt at the end of the year (D) to annual credit extensions (E_a) is given by the following equation, which is obtained by dividing (7) by (4) and introducing a correction factor of $12k$ to convert extensions to an annual basis:

$$\frac{D}{E_a} = \frac{1+r}{12rk}\left[1 - \frac{1}{n}\left(\frac{1-(1+r)^{-n}}{r}\right)\right] \tag{11}$$

The ratio D/E_a thus depends only on the rate of growth of income, r, and the maturity of debt contracts, n. Table 1 shows values of D/E_a for rates of growth of income of approximately 4 percent, 6 percent, and 8 percent per year,[14] combined with various contract maturities ranging from 12 to 28 months. It is apparent from the table that the ratio is very

TABLE 1

EQUILIBRIUM VALUES OF THE RATIO (D/E_a) OF INSTALLMENT DEBT TO ANNUAL REPAYMENTS FOR VARIOUS VALUES OF r AND n

Value of n *(months)*	*Value of* r *(percent per month)*		
	1/3	*1/2*	*2/3*
12	.5449	.5467	.5483
18	.7914	.7911	.7909
20	.8726	.8715	.8703
21	.9132	.9114	.9098
22	.9537	.9514	.9491
24	1.0343	1.0309	1.0273
28	1.1945	1.1879	1.1550

Calculated from: $\frac{D}{E_a} = \frac{1+r}{12rk}\left[1 - \frac{1}{n}\left(\frac{1-(1+r)^{-n}}{r}\right)\right]$

where $k = \frac{1+r}{12}\left(\frac{1-(1+r)^{-12}}{r}\right)$

[14]The rates of ⅓ percent, ½ percent, and ⅔ percent per month are equivalent to rates per year of 4.07 percent, 6.17 percent, and 8.30 percent, respectively.

insensitive to changes in the rate of growth of income (within the relevant range) but increases strongly as the debt maturity increases.

Since the excess of credit extensions over repayments—the net increase in credit outstanding—is often used as an index of the contribution of consumer credit to aggregate demand, it will be useful to develop an equation for extensions minus repayments.[15] The basic equation for repayments is

$$R_m = \frac{1}{n} \sum_{i=1}^{n} E_{m-i}$$

Substituting for the Es the values given by (4), we obtain

$$R_m = \alpha\beta Y_o \frac{1}{n} \sum_{i=1}^{n} (1+r)^{m-i}$$

Since

$$\sum_{i=1}^{n} (1+r)^{m-i} = \frac{1}{r}[(1+r)^m - (1+r)^{m-n}]$$

we have

$$R_m = \alpha\beta Y_o \frac{1}{n}\left[\frac{(1+r)^m - (1+r)^{m-n}}{r}\right]$$

Thus, by use of equation (4),

$$E_m - R_m = \alpha\beta Y_o (1+r)^m - \alpha\beta Y_o \frac{1}{n}\left[\frac{(1+r)^m - (1+r)^{m-n}}{r}\right] \quad (12)$$

It is useful to express the excess of extensions over repayments—or the net increase in credit outstanding—as a ratio to disposable income. Dividing (12) by (1) and designating this ratio as K, we obtain

$$K = \alpha\beta\left[1 - \frac{1}{n}\left(\frac{1-(1+r)^{-n}}{r}\right)\right] \quad (13)$$

Of course, the conditions assumed in this model are not fully satisfied in reality. In particular, income does not grow at a steady rate either from month to month or from year to year, and all installment debt contracts do not have the same maturity. Moreover, the conditions described in the

[15]The net increase in credit outstanding is used as a measure of the direct effect of installment credit on aggregate demand by D. D. Humphrey, in "Instalment Credit and Business Cycles," *Consumer Instalment Credit*, Part II, Vol. 2 (Board of Governors of the Federal Reserve System, 1957), pp. 3–55. Since some of the expenditures financed by new credit extensions would probably have been made even if credit had not been available and some of the debt repayments probably come at the expense of other forms of saving, it is very doubtful whether the net increase in credit outstanding contributes dollar for dollar to consumer spending, as portions of Humphrey's analysis imply. See W. L. Smith, "Consumer Instalment Credit: A Review Article," *American Economic Review*, Vol. XLVII (December, 1957), pp. 972–73.

above equations are those that would prevail in equilibrium with constant values of the parameters; in reality, of course, the system is never in equilibrium. Fortunately, however, since it appears that maturities of installment contracts rarely exceed three years, the system is never likely to be very far out of equilibrium. If the parameters were to remain constant long enough for existing contracts to mature, equilibrium would be reached. On the whole, I believe the model is an appropriate one to use in analyzing the growth of consumer installment debt.

Clearly the driving force that has led to rapid growth of debt during the postwar period has been the steady rise in the ratio of credit extensions to disposable personal income—the composite ratio $\alpha\beta$. This ratio rose from a little over 5 percent in 1946 to more than 15 percent in 1964. The increase was rapid up to 1952, when it exceeded 12 percent for the first time. Since 1952 the rate of increase has been much less rapid, although it has been quite persistent despite some mild declines in the recession years 1954, 1958, and 1960–61. The rise in $\alpha\beta$ is not accounted for by any persistent rise in α, the fraction of disposable personal income spent on consumer durable goods. While there has been year-to-year variations in this ratio, it has shown no trend and has remained approximately in the range of 11–13 percent in every year since 1949, with the exceptions of 1950 and 1955 when it exceeded 14 percent due to unusual circumstances.

The primary reason for the rise in credit extensions in relation to income is the rise in β, the ratio of credit extensions to durable goods expenditures. This ratio has risen with very few interruptions from about 53 percent in 1946 to 116 percent in 1964. While the rise was particularly rapid up to 1952, it has continued since that year. Undoubtedly this increase is due both to a greater use of credit to finance purchases of durable goods and to the increasing spread of its use to the financing of nondurable goods and services.

The rise in β is almost surely attributable in part to an easing of credit terms, particularly a lengthening of maturities. It is possible to get some clues as to what has been happening in this respect by studying changes in the ratio of the outstanding stock of debt to credit extensions. This ratio has risen over the postwar period from 49 percent in 1946 to 90 percent in 1964. In equilibrium, as indicated by equation (11), this ratio is independent of α and β. Moreover, as the calculations presented in Table 1 show, it is virtually a function of the maturity of debt contracts, n, alone, and equation (11) can therefore be used to estimate average debt maturities. Thus, according to Table 1, the fact that D/E averaged about 90 percent from 1961 to 1964 suggests that the average maturity of contracts was in the neighborhood of 20 to 21 months during that period. In 1956–59, the ratio averaged in the neighborhood of 80 percent, suggesting an average maturity of about 18 months. Of course, this interpretation is necessarily crude, because the calculations shown in Table 1 are based on the assumption that the system was in equilibrium and because it involves the application of a relationship derived from a model in which all debt has the same maturity to the *average* maturity of a stock containing debt of varying maturities.

As equation (10) shows, the ratio of the stock of outstanding debt to income depends on α, β, r, and n. However, it is apparent from equations (10) and (11) that the ratio of debt to income is related to the ratio of debt to credit extensions by the equation

$$\frac{D}{Y_a} = \alpha\beta \frac{D}{E_a}$$

Since, as we have just seen, D/E_a is virtually independent of r, so is D/Y_a. For a given value of $\alpha\beta$, the equilibrium value of the ratio of debt to income will be greater the longer is the maturity of the debt. This ratio has risen steadily during the postwar period from 2.6 percent in 1946 to 13.8 percent in 1964. Undoubtedly, the rise in the debt-to-income ratio has been caused by a combination of substantial rises in β and in n.

The studies of the Survey Research Center support the idea that the use of consumer installment credit is associated with the family life-cycle stage. The life-cycle concept is a rather complex one having several dimensions; moreover, there are many other variables which operate simultaneously to influence the use of credit. However, a multivariate analysis of the returns from the 1964 Survey of Consumer Finances led to the following conclusion regarding the effects of life-cycle variables:[16]

> Single families are less likely to have installment debt than married families, even when the effects of income, financial reserves, and other variables are also considered. Married families with children are more likely to have debt than their counterparts with no children, and families with four or more children are much more likely to have installment debt. In addition, recently married families are more likely to have debt than longer married families.

The conclusions concerning the life-cycle hypothesis are consistent with the other findings of the Surveys of Consumer Finances. According to Survey estimates, the proportion of spending units having some debt outstanding rose from 38 percent in 1952 to 48 percent in 1958, at which point it stabilized for several years before rising to 50 percent in 1963. Beginning with the 1964 Survey of Consumer Finances, reporting was changed from a spending unit to a family basis; the proportion of families reporting outstanding installment debt was 47 percent in 1964 and rose

[16] George Katona, C. A. Lininger, and Eva Mueller, *1964 Survey of Consumer Finances* (Monograph No. 39, Survey Research Center, Institute for Social Research, University of Michigan, 1965), p. 68.

to 49 percent in 1965.[17] Thus, a primary explanation of the growth of installment debt is that more families are using such debt now than formerly.

The median ratio of payments on installment debt to the previous year's disposable income for debtor spending units was estimated at 14 percent in 1955. The ratio has shown no tendency to rise since that time; indeed, it was 13 percent in 1963, and 12 percent (for families) in 1964 and 1965.[18] Moreover, the proportion of debtors having debt-payment-to-income ratios in excess of 20 percent of income does not appear to have changed significantly; in 1965 it was estimated at 13 percent (for families) compared with 12 percent (for spending units) a decade earlier.[19] In other words, debt appears to have been rising primarily because the number of borrowers has been increasing rather than because the same borrowers have been getting more deeply into debt. In appraising the burden of installment debt, it is also worthy of note that debtors tend to have substantially higher incomes than nondebtors; for persons having debt outstanding at the time of the 1965 Survey, the median income in 1964 was $7,000, while the median income of nondebtors was only $5,250. And there are indications that the income of debtors has been rising relative to that of nondebtors.[20]

According to the population projections of the Bureau of the Census,

---

[17]Katona, Lininger, and Mueller, *1963 Survey of Consumer Finances* (Monograph No. 34, Survey Research Center, 1964), Table 4–1, p. 65; *1964 Survey of Consumer Finances, op. cit.*, Table 4–1, p. 71; and Statistical Report No. II, 1965 Survey of Consumer Finances (mimeographed) (Survey Research Center, 1965).

[18]The reader may be puzzled by the fact that the median ratio of debt repayments to the previous year's disposable income of debtors is lower than the aggregate ratio of debt repayments (as reported by the Federal Reserve) to total personal disposable income (which was 15.3 percent in 1964). The main explanation is undoubtedly the fact that debt is understated by some Survey respondents, together with inclusion of some components of debt in the Federal Reserve series that are not regarded as installment debt in the Surveys. Estimates of aggregate installment debt derived from Survey data are substantially smaller than the amounts reported by the Federal Reserve, although the year-to-year changes are in substantial agreement (see George Katona, C. A. Lininger, and R. F. Kosobud, *1962 Survey of Consumer Finances* [Monograph No. 32, Survey Research Center], p. 62). Another reason for a discrepancy between the two ratios is that one is a median and the other a weighted arithmetic mean. If both ratios were calculated on the same basis, one would, of course, expect the ratio of debt payments to *debtors'* income to be higher than the ratio of debt payments to *total* income, although this tendency would be substantially reduced by the fact that, as indicated above, debtors tend to have above-average incomes. In any case, it is the stability over time of the median ratio of debt payments to income of debtors rather than its level that is of primary signficance, and there is no reason to think that the trend of the ratio has been distorted by any of the factors referred to.

[19]Katona, Lininger, and Mueller, *1963 Survey of Consumer Finances, op. cit.*, Table 4–4, p. 68; *1964 Survey of Consumer Finances, op. cit.*, Table 4–4, p. 74; and Statistical Report No. II, *1965 Survey of Consumer Finances, op. cit.*

[20]Statistical Report No. II, *1965 Survey of Consumer Finances, op. cit.*

the number of persons between the ages of 20 and 34 will increase from 35.4 million or 18.4 percent of the total population in 1964, to 42.3 million or 20.3 percent of population in 1970, and to 50.2 million or 22.2 percent of population in 1975.[21] Since these are the prime age brackets for the formation of households, the raising of young children, and the use of installment credit to finance purchases of automobiles and household durable goods, the projections suggest some further continuation of the relatively slow rise in $\alpha\beta$ that has occurred during the last decade. But it is important to note that, according to the life-cycle hypothesis, the rise in $\alpha\beta$ will not necessarily mean that individual families are getting more and more deeply into debt. Rather the debt will, to a considerable extent, be rolled over from one "cadre" of families in the prime debt-incurring stage to another, with $\alpha\beta$ rising slowly because the successive "cadres" are increasing in size.

Table 2 shows equilibrium values of the debt-to-income ratio (D/Y_a) associated with various values of the ratio of credit extensions to disposable income ($\alpha\beta$) and of average debt maturity (n). The table was constructed on the assumption of steady growth of income at a rate of 0.5 percent per month or 6.2 percent per year, but the results would be practically identical for other growth rates between 4 and 8 percent per year.

I believe this analysis should be encouraging to those who have been worried about excessively rapid growth of consumer installment debt. The last few years have been a period of innovation in the field of installment credit, during which the use of credit has been extended outside its traditional domain. In spite of this, $\alpha\beta$, the ratio of new credit extensions to personal disposable income, rose by only about one percentage point from an average of 13.8 percent in 1955–57 to an average of 14.9 percent in 1962–64. It is true that population trends were, on the whole, less favorable to the expansion of consumer debt than they are likely to be in the years ahead: the proportion of the population in the age range 20–34 declined from 20.1 percent in 1957 to 18.4 percent in 1964.[22] Thus, with continuing innovations in credit use—which can,

---

[21]See *Projections of the Population of the United States, by Age and Sex: 1964 to 1985* (Current Population Reports, Population Estimates, Series P-25, No. 286), July, 1964, Table 4, pp. 47–49. These particular projections are based on Series B, one of four series which employ different fertility assumptions. However, the choice of fertility assumptions has no effect on the projections of numbers of persons in the 20–34-year age brackets in 1970 and 1975, since all of these persons were born prior to 1964.

[22]The 1957 data are taken from the Census Bureau publication, *Estimates of the Population of the United States by Single Years of Age, Color, and Sex, 1950 to 1959* (Current Population Reports, Population Estimates, Series P-25, No. 311), July 2, 1965, pp. 8–9. It may be noted that the proportion of the population in the 15–19-year age bracket, which seems to be an important factor in the demand for automobiles and perhaps some other kinds of durable goods, increased from 6.9 percent in 1957 to 8.5 percent in 1964. This proportion is projected to rise much less rapidly in the next few years, reaching 9.1 percent in 1970 and 1975.

however, probably be expected to encounter diminishing marginal returns—and with population shifts that will be favorable to the use of credit, $\alpha\beta$ can be expected to continue its slow rise for a few more years. Precise prediction is obviously impossible, but, to illustrate the possibilities, if $\alpha\beta$ should ultimately stabilize at 18 percent and if n should also stabilize at 22 months, the debt-to-income ratio should rapidly adjust to its equilibrium value of about 17 percent, as shown in Table 2. From then on, in the absence of further changes in $\alpha\beta$ or n, extensions (E), repayments (R), and the stock of debt (D) would all grow at the same rate as income. In other words, the tendency for debt to grow persistently at a considerably more rapid rate than income, as has occurred in recent years, is characteristic of a situation in which either $\alpha\beta$ or n or both are increasing. When and if these parameters stabilize, debt growth will quickly fall into line with income growth.

TABLE 2

EQUILIBRIUM VALUES OF THE RATIO (D/Y_a) OF INSTALLMENT DEBT TO ANNUAL DISPOSABLE PERSONAL INCOME FOR ALTERNATIVE VALUES OF $\alpha\beta$ AND n

Value of n *(months)*	*Value of $\alpha\beta$ (percent)*			
	17	*18*	*19*	*20*
20	.148	.157	.166	.174
22	.162	.171	.181	.190
24	.175	.186	.196	.206
26	.189	.200	.211	.222

Calculated from: $\frac{D}{Y_a} = \alpha\beta \frac{1+r}{12rk}\left[1 - \frac{1}{n}\left(\frac{1-(1+r)^{-n}}{r}\right)\right]$

where $k = \frac{1+r}{12}\left(\frac{1-(1+r)^{-12}}{r}\right)$,

$r = 0.5$ percent per month (equivalent to 6.2 percent per year)

Table 3 shows equilibrium values of the ratio (K) of the net increase in debt outstanding to disposable personal income for various values of $\alpha\beta$, n, and r. Unlike D/Y_a, K depends to some extent on the rate of growth of income. In the case referred to above, in which $\alpha\beta$ and n stabilize at values of 18 percent and 22 months, respectively, the equilibrium value of K will be approximately 0.8 percent if income grows at about 5 percent per year and approximately 0.9 percent if the growth rate is in the neighborhood of 6 percent. It will be noted, however, that the values of K do not vary a great deal with moderate changes in any of the variables. Over a considerable range of reasonable values of $\alpha\beta$, n, and r, the equilibrium value of K will be in the neighborhood of 1 percent. That is, the contribution of consumer installment credit to consumer purchasing power will grow in absolute magnitude at the same rate as disposable income and will amount to about 1 percent of such income.

It is interesting to compare this equilibrium ratio of roughly 1 percent with the actual ratios of net increase in debt to disposable income that have prevailed in recent years. Since this ratio is the difference between two much larger magnitudes, extensions and repayments, it is very sensitive to fluctuations in extensions and has therefore varied considerably in recent years, ranging from nearly 2 percent in 1955 to slightly less than zero in 1958. It averaged 0.9 percent from 1957 to 1964 and 1.0 percent from 1960 to 1964. Thus, although the equilibrium values of roughly 1 percent suggested by Table 3 are somewhat smaller than the values of 1.4 percent and 1.3 percent experienced in 1963 and 1964 when K was being pulled up by rapidly rising extensions with the adjustment of repayments lagging behind, they are about in line with the average values of K experienced over the last few years.

TABLE 3

EQUILIBRIUM VALUES OF THE RATIO (K) OF NET INCREASE IN INSTALLMENT DEBT TO DISPOSABLE PERSONAL INCOME FOR ALTERNATIVE VALUES OF $\alpha\beta$, n, AND r

Value of n (months)	Value of αβ (percent): 17		18		19		20	
	r = 5.1%	r = 6.2%	r = 5.1%	r = 6.2%	r = 5.1%	r = 6.2%	r = 5.1%	r = 6.2%
20	.007	.009	.008	.009	.008	.010	.008	.010
22	.008	.009	.008	.010	.009	.010	.009	.011
24	.009	.010	.009	.011	.010	.011	.010	.012
26	.009	.011	.010	.012	.010	.012	.011	.013

Calculated from: $K = \alpha\beta\left[1 - \frac{1}{n}\left(\frac{1-(1+r)^{-n}}{r}\right)\right]$

r in units of percent per year

Mortgage Debt

The mortgage indebtedness of the household sector has grown at about the same rate as installment debt during the postwar period. The stock of household mortgage debt increased at an average rate of 14.7 percent from the end of 1945 to 1964, and, as a result, the ratio of year-end outstanding debt to annual disposable personal income rose from 9.3 percent in 1945 to 43.7 percent in 1964. Although the growth moderated somewhat after the steep rise of the immediate postwar years, it has continued to be very rapid, amounting to an average of 9.4 percent per year from 1957 to 1964 and 9.0 percent per year from 1960 to 1964. The debt-to-income ratio stood at 32.5 percent in 1957 and 35.3 percent in 1960.

The same model that was used above in analyzing the growth of consumer installment debt could, in principle, be applied to mortgage debt as well, although some modifications would need to be made in it. As indicated earlier, the maturities of installment debt are so short that it seems unlikely that the model would ever be very far from equilibrium. This is not, however, the case for mortgage debt, which is characterized by much longer maturities. Consequently, if the model were to be applied to mortgage debt, it would be necessary to work out the dynamic process by which equilibrium is established. And, in working through the dynamics, allowance would have to be made for the fact that the conditions which govern repayments are dependent on the variable mortgage maturities that prevailed at various times in the past when the components of the existing debt were first issued. Moreover, satisfactory data on mortgage extensions and repayments paralleling the Federal Reserve installment credit statistics are not available; and there would therefore be little basis for the use of such a model to make even tentative projections of future debt growth.

In view of these difficulties, I shall use an approach similar to that employed by Enthoven in his analysis of consumer credit.[23] Let us suppose that disposable income (Y) grows at a steady rate of $100r$ percent per year. Then

$$Y_t = Y_o (1 + r)^t \tag{14}$$

where Y_0 is income in the initial year and t indicates time, in years in this case. Suppose also that the net increase in outstanding mortgage debt (ΔD)—that is, the difference between mortgage credit extensions and repayments—is a constant fraction, a, of income. That is,

$$\Delta D_t = D_t - D_{t-1} = aY_t \tag{15}$$

By combining (14) and (15), the following expression for the outstanding stock of debt can be derived:

$$D_t = a(1 + r)\, Y_o \frac{(1 + r)^t - 1}{r} + D_o \tag{16}$$

where D_0 is the amount of debt outstanding at the end of the initial year. Dividing (16) by (14), the following expression for the ratio of outstanding debt to disposable income is obtained:

$$\frac{D_t}{Y_t} = \frac{a(1 + r)}{r} + \left(\frac{D_o}{Y_o} - \frac{a(1 + r)}{r}\right)(1 + r)^{-t} \tag{17}$$

As time passes and income grows, the second term in (17) becomes steadily smaller, and we have

$$\lim_{t\to\infty} \frac{D_t}{Y_t} = \frac{a(1 + r)}{r} \tag{18}$$

[23]In view of the defect in Enthoven's original model as pointed out by Oliver, the model I am using corresponds to the simplified version defended by Enthoven in his reply to Oliver. See Enthoven's original article and his exchange with Oliver cited in footnotes 9 and 10 above.

In order to make projections of future debt growth with this model, it is necessary to make assumptions about a, the ratio of the annual net increase in debt to disposable income, and r, the rate of growth of income. Table 4 shows the relation between debt increments and disposable personal income from 1954 to 1964. While this ratio has varied considerably from year to year, it has shown no particular trend, and, as the table shows, it averaged 3.5 percent from 1954–64 and 3.4 percent from 1960–64.

TABLE 4

INCREASE IN HOUSEHOLD MORTGAGE DEBT OUTSTANDING IN RELATION TO DISPOSABLE PERSONAL INCOME, 1954–64
(In Billions of Dollars)

Year	*Disposable Personal Income*	*Increase in Household Mortgage Debt Outstanding*	$\frac{\Delta D}{Y}$ *(Percent)*
1954	$256.9	$ 8.7	3.4
1955	274.4	12.2	4.4
1956	292.9	11.1	3.8
1957	308.8	8.8	2.8
1958	317.9	9.2	2.9
1959	337.1	12.9	3.8
1960	349.9	11.0	3.1
1961	364.7	11.1	3.0
1962	384.6	12.8	3.3
1963	402.5	14.9	3.7
1964	431.8	16.2	3.8
Average, 1954–64			3.5
Average, 1960–64			3.4

SOURCE: Federal Reserve System and Department of Commerce.

Table 5 shows equilibrium values of the ratio of mortgage debt to disposable income for various values of a and r. The debt-to-income ratio would approach the indicated value asymptotically if the ratio of annual net credit increase to disposable income remained constant at the specified value and income grew steadily at the specified rate. This suggests, for example, that if the ratio of debt increase to income averaged the 3.5 percent value of 1954–64 and income grew at an average rate of 5½ percent per year, the ratio of debt to income should gradually approach 67 percent as an upper limit. Thus, the growth of debt would gradually come into alignment with the growth of income.

The process by which the mortgage debt would approach its ultimate relation to income would, however, work very slowly. It is therefore interesting to see what would happen in the course of a decade or so. Table 6 shows the ratios of debt to income that would prevail in 1975 for various values of a and r with the system starting from the actual values of mortgage debt and disposable income that prevailed in 1964.

This table suggests that if the ratio of debt increase to income should average 3.5 percent and income should grow at an average rate of 5½ percent, the ratio of outstanding debt to income would be about 54 percent in 1975. This would represent an increase of ten percentage points

TABLE 5

LIMITING VALUES OF THE RATIO (D/Y) OF MORTGAGE DEBT TO PERSONAL DISPOSABLE INCOME FOR VARIOUS VALUES OF a AND r

Value of a *(Percent)*	*Value of* r *(Percent per Year)*		
	5.0	*5.5*	*6.0*
3.1	.651	.595	.548
3.3	.693	.633	.583
3.5	.735	.671	.618
3.7	.777	.710	.654
3.9	.819	.748	.689
4.1	.861	.786	.724

Calculated from: $\lim_{t\to\infty} \frac{D_t}{Y_t} = \frac{a(1+r)}{r}$

TABLE 6

PROJECTIONS OF THE RATIO (D/Y) OF MORTGAGE DEBT TO PERSONAL DISPOSABLE INCOME TO 1975 FOR VARIOUS VALUES OF r AND a

Value of a *(Percent)*	*Value of* r *(Percent per Year)*		
	5.0	*5.5*	*6.0*
3.1	.526	.507	.489
3.3	.543	.524	.506
3.5	.563	.541	.522
3.7	.578	.558	.539
3.9	.595	.575	.556
4.1	.613	.592	.573

Calculated from: $\frac{D_t}{Y_t} = \frac{a(1+r)}{r} + \left(\frac{D_o}{Y_o} - \frac{a(1+r)}{r}\right)(1+r)^{-t}$

where

D_o = \$188.5 billion (1964) value),

Y_o = \$431.8 billion (1964 value),

t = 11 years.

over the ratio of 44 percent that prevailed in 1964. The rate of increase in debt would still be greater than the rate of increase in income, although the margin would be considerably reduced. If the steady growth path was followed, the outstanding mortgage debt would be \$394 billion in 1974 and would rise by 6.9 percent to \$421 billion in 1975.

What this analysis shows is that mortgage credit can continue to make the same proportionate contribution to aggregate demand that it has made on the average in the last few years—assuming this contribution is measured by the excess of credit extensions over repayments—while at the same time there are forces at work which will in the long run tend to bring the growth of mortgage debt into alignment with the growth of income. Whether or not mortgage debt will in fact expand in the indicated fashion is, of course, a complex question, the answer to which depends on demographic factors, on the kinds of monetary and fiscal policies that are followed, and on a host of other factors which are far beyond the scope of this paper. The point is, however, that recent trends in the expansion of household mortgage debt—at least as measured by the net increase in credit outstanding—if they continue, do not imply that the growth of such debt will continue indefinitely at the recent rapid rates that have exceeded the growth of income by a considerable margin.

Financial Assets and Liabilities of Households

In assessing the financial soundness of households, it is necessary to consider their assets and net worth in relation to their liabilities. The household sector was a surplus sector in every year from 1946 through 1963 in the sense that its disposable income exceeded its expenditures on currently produced goods and services, including residential construction, as recorded in the Federal Reserve flow of funds accounts. As a result of these surpluses, the aggregate excess of the sector's financial assets over its liabilities has grown steadily from a third of a trillion dollars in 1945 to over a trillion in 1964. However, roughly $475 billion of the increase in its margin of financial assets over liabilities is accounted for by a rise in the value of its holdings of corporate stock which are included in financial assets at market value. But even when the value of holdings of corporate stock is removed from total financial assets, the excess of the remaining household assets over liabilities increased from $220 billion in 1945 to nearly $450 billion in 1964. Sector holdings of fixed-value claims—including currency, demand deposits, time and savings deposits, savings and loan shares, and U.S. savings bonds—exceeded total liabilities by $81 billion in 1964.

The findings of the Surveys of Consumer Finances, some of which are referred to above, have generally favorable connotations with respect to the financial condition of individual households insofar as consumer installment debt is concerned. As already indicated, the Surveys suggest that debt has been rising primarily because more households are borrowing rather than because the same households are getting more deeply into debt. And although Survey findings show that the larger a family's liquid assets the less likely it is to be in debt, there is nevertheless evidence that many families that are installment debtors have substantial liquid assets. Indeed, at the time of the 1965 Survey, about 30 percent of the families that were in debt reported liquid assets that exceeded their outstanding debt, and approximately another 10 percent reported liquid assets about equal to their debt. Many families having fairly substantial amounts of liquid assets make use of installment credit: 63 percent of the families having $500–$999 of liquid assets, 60 percent of those having $1,000–$1,999 of liquid assets, and 38 percent of those having $2,000–$4,999 of liquid assets had debt outstanding at the time of the 1965 Survey of Consumer Finances.[24]

III. SOME COMMENTS ON POLICY ISSUES RELATED TO THE GROWTH OF PRIVATE DEBT

I have tried to suggest that, at least as far as the household sector is concerned, there is no cause for panic with respect to the growth of debt. Maintenance of the contribution of credit to household aggregate demand does not necessarily imply that such debt will have to expand at the rates that have prevailed recently for the indefinite future. The margin of household financial assets over household debt has widened at the same time that debt has been increasing rapidly. And the fragmentary data that are available do not suggest that an increasing fraction of households are incurring excessive debt commitments.

There are, nevertheless, some aspects of the growth of private debt which raise questions of economic policy concerning which I would like to comment briefly.

The "Quality of Credit" Issue

There has been much apprehension recently concerning the so-called deterioration of the "quality of credit," especially in the residential mortgage field. The primary evidence cited to support the contention that credit quality has deteriorated is the rising level of mortgage foreclosures. There can be no question that foreclosures have risen substantially in recent years, both absolutely and relative to the volume of mortgages outstanding. From 1950 to 1957, annual mortgage foreclosures on one- to four-family nonfarm homes averaged 24.9 thousand or 1.65 per thousand units under mortgage. Since that time foreclosures have risen steadily and fairly rapidly, reaching 98,195 units or 4.40 per thousand mortgaged homes in 1963.[25] This rise in mortgage foreclosures should be viewed in historical perspective. It will hardly surprise anyone to find

[24]Statistical Report No. II, *1965 Survey of Consumer Finances, op. cit.*

[25]*1963 Annual Report of the Housing and Home Finance Agency,* Table B–57, p. 474. Foreclosures rose further to 108,620 in 1964 (*Housing Statistics,* July, 1965, Table D–4, p. 24).

that foreclosure rates are far lower than they were during the depression years of the 1930s. But it is worthy of note that they are also substantially lower than the rates that prevailed in the prosperous period of the late 1920s.[26]

That the easing of credit terms has had a good deal to do with the rise in foreclosures is strongly indicated by the particularly sharp rise in the foreclosure rate for FHA-insured mortgages. This rate averaged 1.53 per thousand mortgaged houses from 1950–57—somewhat below the foreclosure rate for conventional mortgages. By 1963, the foreclosure rate for FHA-insured mortgages had risen to 10.89 per thousand, or over four times the rate of 2.47 per thousand for conventional mortgages.[27] After 1957, the terms of FHA-insured mortgages became progressively more liberal. The median loan-value ratio for transactions involving new one-family homes financed by FHA-insured mortgages under Section 203 of the National Housing Act, as estimated from samples of transactions, increased steadily from 85.1 percent in 1957 to 94.5 percent in 1963. As a result of rising incomes and an increase in the average maturity of mortgages from 25.5 years in 1957 to 31.0 years in 1963, the average ratio of housing expense to borrower's income rose only from 19.7 percent to 20.8 percent, despite the lower down payments and an increase of 9.2 percent in the average selling price of houses. Similar developments occurred in the financing of transactions in existing houses under the FHA program.[28]

The sharp rise in foreclosure rates is thus a clearly established fact. The question is what interpretation should be given to it. Is it a development about which we should be seriously concerned? To begin with, it should be recognized that complete absence of defaults on loans—or even of failures among financial institutions—is evidence that the financial system is not performing adequately its function of risk-bearing. It is one of the functions of the management of financial institutions to be able to judge risks and to be willing to undertake them, provided yields are sufficient to enable the institutions to set aside sufficient reserves to provide protection against losses. This is as true in the field of mortgage lending as it is elsewhere. Occasional miscalculations can be expected to lead to failures of individual institutions from time to time. It is the function of deposit and share insurance to provide protection to holders of financial assets in such cases. Occasional failures of financial institutions

[26]Foreclosures averaged 102,500 per year from 1926 to 1929—and were rising steadily from year to year—at a time when the volume of nonfarm residential mortgage debt was less than $30 billion. *Historical Statistics of the United States: Colonial Times to 1957,* Series N 189, p. 398, and Series N 150–160, p. 396.

[27]*1963 Annual Report of the Housing and Home Finance Agency,* Tables B–57 and B–58, pp. 474–75.

[28]The calculations are based on data from the *1963 Annual Report of the Housing and Home Finance Agency,* Table III–35, p. 127.

are no more a cause for concern than are failures of other busines enterprises. Failures on a massive scale such as we experienced in the 1930s can hardly occur unless the authorities responsible for monetary and fiscal policy fail to fulfill their functions properly and permit a drastic decline in aggregate demand and economic activity.

There are two aspects of the mortgage market, however, which may make defaults—that is, foreclosures—more a matter of concern than they should be in other financial markets. The first is the existence of FHA mortgage insurance. The fact that such insurance substantially reduces his risk of loss may make the lender less inclined to adjust the yields on such loans to the risks he associates with the particular characteristics of the individual mortgage contract. This may easily lead to a misallocation of capital, as high-risk borrowers obtain funds at interest rates that are lower relative to those paid on lower risk loans than would be established by the market. Obviously, to some degree, just such a distortion in the allocation of capital is the very purpose of such a program as FHA mortgage insurance. However, beyond some point, one may certainly question the wisdom of a government program which allocates large amounts of scarce capital to the construction of relatively expensive homes for middle-class people on such easy terms as to encourage foreclosures. This is an especially questionable use of resources in a society in which large numbers of low-income persons lack adequate shelter.

A second question has to do with the flexibility and adaptability of the financial system. Savings and loan associations, which have in the postwar period been the most rapidly growing component of that system, are very heavily specialized mortgage lenders, partly as a result of legal restrictions on their portfolios and partly as a result of the custom which causes them to regard themselves as the apostles of home ownership. Mutual savings banks are also, in the sections of the country where they are concentrated, heavily committed to the mortgage market, though less so than savings and loan associations. One wonders how a financial structure which includes such a large component of specialized institutions would adjust to a sharp decline in the demand for houses—or to a sharp increase in demands in other segments of the capital market. To be sure, there are some channels through which an adjustment to a decline in housing demand would occur. As interest rates on mortgages declined, savings and loan associations could be expected to reduce the yields on their shares, thus leading to a diversion of funds to other institutions with more flexible portfolio arrangements. And other institutions—such as commercial banks and insurance companies—would shift their funds away from mortgages toward more remunerative assets, leaving a larger share of the mortgage market to the specialized institutions of housing finance. Mobility of capital does not require that all institutions have completely flexible portfolio policies, but only that there be a flexible component in the system of sufficient magnitude to permit the reallocation. Nevertheless, one wonders whether these adjustments would be sufficient to permit the readjustment in the flow of capital that would be required to achieve efficient allocation.

Fortunately, the outlook for household formation and housing demand in the next few years is sufficiently promising so that there is unlikely to be a need for a major diversion of funds to other markets. Nevertheless, it seems to me that it would be highly desirable to relax substantially the portfolio restrictions that now apply to savings and loan associations and to encourage these institutions to diversify their portfolios. This should have the incidental advantages of making savings and loan associations less vulnerable to mishaps that may be peculiar to the housing market and of increasing competition in other segments of the capital market.

Monetary-Fiscal Policy and the Growth of Private Debt

Of the reasons for concern about the growth of private debt referred to at the beginning of this paper, the one that seems to me to be the most serious is the second: that the increased burden of debt may increase the sensitivity of the economy to deflationary shocks. I suspect that there are forces at work which will gradually bring the growth of private debt into line with the growth of income, and I have tried to illustrate the possible nature of such forces in the fields of consumer installment and mortgage debt. But it seems clear that when the economy starts from a position in which the financial system is as extensively dependent on federal debt, as was the case at the end of World War II, and a fiscal-monetary policy is pursued which holds down the growth of federal debt, a long period of growth of private debt at high but slowly diminishing rates is inevitable. Thus it seems certain that private debt will continue to grow more rapidly than income for some time to come and that ratios of private debt to income will reach substantially higher levels than presently prevail before an equilibrium is reached in which growth of debt and growth of income are brought into a rough balance.

Hyman Minsky has argued convincingly that in the course of an extended period of expansion in which the ratio of private debt to income rises, the danger of financial crisis steadily increases.[29] Discussion of financial panics has long since gone out of style, and it would certainly be unwise to exaggerate the dangers. There have been many innovations in the past 30 years which have greatly reduced the vulnerability of the U.S. economy to financial collapse, among the most important being the introduction of deposit and mortgage insurance and the development and widespread use of amortized mortgages. Nevertheless, it seems likely

[29] See Minsky's papers cited in footnote 6.

that as the burden of private debt and debt repayments grows relative to income, the size of the deflationary shock that the economy can absorb under any given set of institutional arrangements, without creating financial repercussions that might lead to a serious depression, becomes progressively smaller.

The most effective way to protect the economy against these dangers is the vigorous use of flexible fiscal and monetary policies to maintain continuing economic expansion and, particularly, to prevent serious declines from occurring. It might be well, however, to seek possible further protections that might be built into the financial system. The possibility that seems to me to be especially worthy of consideration is the development of arrangements by which financial institutions other than member commercial banks might be given emergency access to Federal Reserve credit. Savings and loan shares and time deposits in mutual savings banks are already greater relative to demand deposits than was the case in 1929, and they seem destined to continue to grow rapidly. It might be wise to take steps to protect the ultimate liquidity of these claims and to clarify the responsibility of the Federal Reserve System for the support and protection of the entire financial system if a financial crisis should threaten.[30]

If there should be concern about an excessive expansion of private debt, the worst possible way of counteracting it would be the adoption of a sharply restrictive monetary policy. While such a policy would curtail further growth of debt—at a heavy cost in terms of output and employment—it would actually increase the burden of the existing debt and the risk of a financial collapse. The appropriate way to slow down the growth of private debt, if this should seem necessary, would be a shift in the mix of fiscal and monetary policies. More specifically, the federal government could adopt a more restrictive monetary policy, which would slow the growth of private debt, accompanied by a compensating shift to a more expansionary fiscal policy to maintain aggregate demand at the target level. Thus, growth of the public debt would be substituted for growth of private debt with some possible benefit to the stability of the economy.[31]

To get some idea of the orders of magnitude that might be involved,

[30]Minsky ("Financial Crisis, Financial Systems, and the Performance of the Economy," *op. cit.*, pp. 370–80) argues for a drastic reorientation of Federal Reserve policy under which primary emphasis would be placed on the lender of last resort function in the interest of maintaining the stability of the entire financial system.

[31]The fact that if we are to have less rapid growth of private debt, the maintenance of a healthy economy will require a shift toward a fiscal policy which will provide for more rapid growth of public debt was pointed out some years ago by Paul McCracken. See his paper, "The Debt Problem and Economic Growth," *Michigan Business Review*, Vol. VIII (November, 1956), pp. 11–15. Minsky ("Financial Crisis, Financial Systems, and the Performance of the Economy," *op. cit.*, pp. 372–73) argues that a tight monetary policy and an easy fiscal policy would lead to a smaller money

(*Continued on next page*)

suppose that the maintenance of the target level of employment requires that current-dollar GNP grow at 5½ percent per year and that the configuration of deficits and surpluses at the target level of GNP is such that total primary debt—public and private—must grow at the same rate as GNP. In this case, in order to bring the growth of private debt promptly into line with the growth of GNP and stabilize the ratios of private debt to income, growth of the public debt would have to be stepped up to 5½ percent per year. At the present level of the publicly held federal debt, this would require a deficit of about $12 billion a year under conditions of full employment and a sufficiently drastic restrictive shift in monetary policy to cut private investment by roughly the amount of the shift toward a full-employment deficit. A change in the policy mix of this magnitude would be likely to have a strongly unfavorable effect on the long-term rate of growth of the economy.[32]

Of course, such a shift in the policy mix would not have to be applied as drastically as this example suggests. Even a moderate shift toward a tighter monetary policy offset by an easier fiscal policy would slow down the growth of private debt to some extent. But such a shift would be very likely to have some adverse effect on the rate of investment and growth. The basic policy issue with respect to growth of private debt, then, seems to be this: Is there sufficient cause for concern about excessively rapid growth of private debt to justify a distortion of monetary-fiscal policies away from the mix that is judged to be optimal from the standpoint of growth? In my judgment, the answer to this question at the present time is decidedly in the negative.

---

stock and a larger volume of government debt than would the opposite combination of policies. Since both money and riskless government debt are conducive to financial stability, he concludes that it is not clear which mix of policies should be preferred. What he appears to overlook is the fact that a policy mix involving tight money and budget deficits could presumably be expected to result in a *lower* ratio of *private* debt to income than would a mix involving easy money and budget surpluses.

[32]Actually the increase in public debt needed to offset each dollar of reduction in private debt would be unlikely to be precisely one dollar. The outcome would seem to depend on the balance of opposing forces. On the one hand, a tightening of monetary policy would be likely to reduce not only the investment of deficit units which finance their investment externally but also, to some extent, the investment of surplus units which finance their investment internally. Thus, the deficits and private debt offerings of deficit units would be reduced and the surpluses and demands for financial assets of surplus units would be increased (at the target level of GNP, of course). In order to reduce the increment to private debt by a given amount, private investment would have to be reduced by an even larger amount. And government expenditures and government borrowing would have to be increased by as much as private investment declined in order to sustain aggregate demand. In financial terms, the public debt would have to increase by an amount equal to the sum of the decline in private deficits and the increase in private surpluses, or by more than the decline in the increment to private debt. On the other hand, the increase in government debt would be an addition to the wealth of the private sector and might lead to an increase in consumption and investment demand, thereby calling for a further rise in interest rates which would lead to a further reduction in private debt.

FINANCIAL INNOVATIONS AND THE EFFICIENCY OF FEDERAL RESERVE POLICY

Tilford C. Gaines

Commercial banking in the past few years has been affected by revolutionary changes. The financial innovations that have brought about the revolution in banking have simultaneously raised questions as to the efficiency of monetary policies that rest upon earlier and perhaps obsolete concepts of the nature of the banking system. It is the purpose of this paper to describe the innovations that have so radically altered banking and to appraise their effect upon the efficiency of Federal Reserve policy.

Innovation as used here refers to changes in techniques, institutions, or operating policies that have the effect of altering the way the industry functions. In some cases the innovations have arisen outside the industry, but have influenced the way banks operate. In other cases they have been generated within the industry as reflections of an ever more intense competitive drive. The source of the innovation is irrelevant so long as it has played a part in reshaping commercial banking.

I. TYPES OF INNOVATION

A. Corporate Cash Management

The business customers of commercial banks have contributed importantly to banking change through the greater precision they have developed in managing their cash balances. Probably the movement toward better cash management got its principal impetus from the emergence of more attractive short-term rates of interest in the years immediately after World War II. But the development, once started, has continued through years of rising and falling rates and has produced results that could scarcely have been visualized only a few years ago.

Money is a valuable inventory item to the corporate treasurer and the development of improved efficiency in managing money has paralleled the similar development in inventory management. Modern funds mobilization processes enable the corporate treasurer to know at all times precisely where and when he will have collected funds, and the Federal Reserve wire transfer system makes it possible for him to move those funds speedily to the point where they are needed to cover drafts. The banks have assisted their customers through such arrangements as lockboxes, which centralize and expedite the collection of cash items. Today, the treasurers of almost all businesses of any size maintain with their banks only those collected balances that are necessary to compensate the bank for the services it is providing; funds in excess of this amount are employed in short-term investments.

More precise corporate cash management has resulted in new forms of financial intermediation. Part of the reduction in cash balances relative to transactions has been employed internally in corporations as part of working capital. Much of this employment has been in vastly increased trade credits, with the nonfinancial corporation providing its own intermediation. The balance has gone into marketable investments at competitively attractive rates of return. Because commercial banks until recently did not attempt to compete for these funds, finance companies and other financial institutions found it possible to grow rapidly into areas of lending that formerly had been dominated by commercial banks. In this context, the decision of banks to issue certificates of deposit (and later, short-term negotiable notes) was no more than belated recognition that the old order had changed and that banks could no longer rely upon demand deposit growth to supply the resources required to hold their own in the financial system. Total credit growth probably would not have been significantly different if C.D.s had not been developed, but the relative growth rates of the different types of intermediaries would have been different.

B. Internal Bank Management and Pricing

The consequences of tighter corporate cash management have been quite profound for banks. Faced with customers who insisted that they would pay no more for banking services than they were worth, and less if they could get away with it, banks have found it necessary to determine just how much these services are worth. Out of this is emerging, for the first time, a workable system of cost accounting for banks. Banks also have learned that "free" demand balances are not the only source of bank income; where balances are not adequate to cover the price of bank services, fees may be levied. And the most important lesson banks have learned is that they must buy their raw material through one form of payment or another, and that their function is to convert this raw material into credit forms which, after balancing risks, return a profit.

The importance of the management changes that are occurring in banking cannot be overemphasized. It is almost unbelievable, but true, that most banks until recently did not have adequate cost accounting systems and did not, therefore, know how to price their services. Activated by their improved knowledge of costs and returns, modern banks have found it possible to operate safely with lower liquidity ratios, have become more willing to innovate where innovation is profitable, and in general have replaced rational risk appraisal for arbitrary rules of thumb. The consequences for Federal Reserve policy have been far-reaching, since the effectiveness of central bank policy in the past has rested to an important degree upon the existence of a banking system that responded passively to the changes in its environment wrought by Fed policy.

C. Development of "Discretionary Resources" for Banks

The principal banks in the past five years have added $16 billion to their resources by "buying" money in the certificate of deposit market. What is particularly significant in this development is not the amount involved—total bank resources in the same period grew by $85 billion—but the fact that banks for the first time have had access to a type of liability that could be expanded or reduced at their own initiative in precise adjustment to their needs for funds. As more and more banks have reduced their liquid assets to minimum levels consistent with a conservative hedge against the unknown, they have increasingly relied upon the liability side of their balance sheets—through C.D.s—rather than the asset side, for discretionary adjustments to changing needs for funds. In at least a routine seasonal sense, C.D.s have become the primary source of liquidity for many banks.[1]

The emergence of certificates of deposit has created uncertainties for monetary policy that will be discussed later. Their immediate effect upon commercial banking has been to make the industry more flexible in adjusting to changes in the demand for bank credit. A useful adjunct to the money market has been developed that permits banks to be more

[1]It is likely that certificates of deposit are only a transitional instrument in developing discretionary sources of bank funds. Banks moved to C.D.s because this was a type of liability with which they were familiar, and in spite of the fact that reserve requirements and FDIC assessments added some 20 basis points to the cost of this type of money as compared with other types of debt. The gradual development of short notes represents the next step, although obsolete laws for banks chartered in New York State and legal ceilings upon direct debt that national banks may incur place limits upon the issuance of negotiable short-term notes. It is predictable that banks will develop instruments that will provide broader and less expensive access to the money market.

competitive in reaching for new business and that helps to channel funds to those banks and regions where they are most needed.

D. Competitive Interrelationships among Markets

Recent years have seen the growth of closer linkages among financial markets, fostered by greater willingness and ability of commercial banks to be competitive. Increased bank competition for resources in the financial intermediation process is reflected in the improved growth rate for commercial banks relative to other financial intermediaries. For example, between 1953 and 1960 the proportion of time and savings deposits of commercial banks in total intermediation of financial institutions, excluding demand deposits, fell from 48 percent to 41 percent, while savings and loan associations increased their share from 24 percent to 35 percent. This trend has since been reversed, and between 1960 and 1964 the commercial bank share has risen to 44 percent.[2] Total intermediation of commercial banks has continued to decline as a proportion of the total, as the result of a continued slow growth rate of demand deposits relative to other financial claims, but here too the rate of decline has been slowed significantly. Both through the higher rates of interest paid by commercial banks on savings deposits and through the development of C.D.s, commercial banks have substantially checked the trend toward a reduced role in the financial system that has prevailed at least since the early years of this century.

The development of negotiable certificates of deposit has involved banks in competition with forms of financial intermediation that are not usually included in the analyses of the intermediation process. Competition by banks in the C.D. market is with finance paper, bankers' acceptances, short governments and the like, rather than with savings and loan shares, deposits with mutual savings banks, and so forth. What is involved here is a redirection of money market funds—as opposed to savings funds—into forms of credit that might not have been serviced by this market—at least not as efficiently—if commercial banks had not chosen to compete.

Innovation on the liability side of bank balance sheets, resulting from the newly competitive attitudes of commercial banks, has been matched by innovation on the asset side. Certain elements of this competitive innovation are evident in the published data. Banks, for example, have become more aggressive in the real estate mortgage market. The sharp growth in bank-owned mortgages has been due partly to the enlarged

---

[2]This paper emphasizes the role of C.D.s in this development, but commercial bank competition for small savings deposits has actually brought in more funds than has the use of C.D.s. And perhaps over the longer run this type of competitive innovation will prove to have been more important.

flow of these instruments. But the fact that mortgage rates have declined, in spite of the expanding demand for such credit, suggests another answer —that banks, having access to new sources of funds, have employed part of their excess funds in this market. Similarly, the large purchases of tax-exempt securities by banks in recent years are due partly to the supply of such bonds, but also to the fact that banks, after servicing their traditional credit demands, have had resources available for investment in high-yielding securities.

Many other forms of innovation in competition have emerged, in addition to those that are visible in the published statistics. Banks today are competing more aggressively and more effectively than ever before with lenders of longer term credit. Part of this competition is in the form of ordinary term lending that banks have long been involved in. But part takes the form of direct equipment leasing and other types of credit that involve longer maturities and different terms or conditions than banks have customarily accepted on term loans.

The increased competitiveness of commercial banks has not been a one-way street. Other financial intermediaries have simultaneously entered more aggressively into competition with banks in types of credit that had formerly been more or less reserved to banks. Long-term lenders have adapted their terms to make them attractive vis-à-vis bank term loans. Finance companies have moved increasingly into short-term business finance, a hallowed preserve of the commercial banks. And more and more industrial and commercial corporations have turned to the commercial paper market as an important source of funds to supplement their bank lines, in many cases establishing captive finance companies for this purpose.

E. Summary of the "Revolution"

The revolution I have attempted to outline is multifaceted, encompassing the entire financial market, and more profound than the specific details can convey. In brief, it constitutes a breaking down of older concepts of the respective roles of different financial intermediaries and a discarding of notions on the proper functions of these intermediaries. Today, the person or institution with available funds, or seeking funds, has a range of equally acceptable alternatives, allowing for risk differentials, for depositing, investing, or borrowing. Reasoned judgment has, by and large, replaced irrational prejudice in directing the savings flow through the financial intermediation process into credit uses. The guiding criterion is risk-adjusted rate of return or cost.

Changes in commercial bank practices and attitudes have been the principal generative force in bringing into existence this more fluid, viable financial system, since banks have greater latitude for competing both in attracting and lending funds. The result, however, has been a most significant change in the nature of commercial banking. On the one hand, banks today are less liquid than at any time since the late 1920s. In the period between December, 1960, and May, 1965, the total of loans and "other" securities (mostly municipals) in bank portfolios expanded from 69 to 79 percent of total earning assets, while holdings of government securities fell from 31 to 21 percent. And within these asset categories, there was a pronounced shift toward longer term, less liquid loans and investments. In becoming more competitive, banks have become less conservative.

On the liability side of their balance sheets, banks have experienced a similar radical realignment. The combined growth of time deposits and demand deposits adjusted between December, 1960, and May, 1965, has been some $73 billion, of which 84 percent has been time money. Since loans have increased by $65 billion in this period, it is likely that perhaps one-half of the roughly $12 billion growth in demand deposits has been in the form of compensating balances required to be held against loans. Only a very small part of total new banking resources has derived from growth in demand deposits held by depositors solely because of transaction needs.

II. UNCERTAINTIES FOR FEDERAL RESERVE POLICY

The course along which banking has developed in recent years has posed some very perplexing problems for the central bank. These problems have centered principally upon three overlapping questions: (1) how has the shifting composition of banks' assets and liabilities affected the soundness of the banking system; (2) have recent innovations undermined the effectiveness of Federal Reserve policy in regulating credit and money supply; and (3) have these innovations created a banking structure in which Federal Reserve policy actions will have uneven impact upon different groups of banks?

A. Soundness of the Banking System

The shifts in bank assets and liabilities have created serious uncertainties in the minds of independent analysts and among monetary policy officials as to the soundness of the commercial banking system. There are no magic touchstones to which the monetary authorities might refer in judging whether an individual bank or the entire banking system has developed a condition of liquidity or a risk asset structure that might prove dangerous to its continued functioning. Rules of thumb are employed to judge risk asset ratios, capital adequacy, and the like, but these rules of thumb are nothing more than the distillation of experience in previous periods when far different institutional arrangements existed.

The beneficial consequence of the decline in liquidity and increase in risk asset ratios among commercial banks has been a growing recognition that protection of banks from unreasonable vulnerability properly falls under the examination function of the monetary authorities, rather than in the area of broad policy. While it is scarcely possible to establish limitations or restraints upon the banking system that would be equally relevant to all banks in preventing excess, it is usually possible in examining the individual bank to determine whether or not sufficient thought has been given to credit risks and to proper provision for liquidity. To the extent that examination replaces regulation, a great many significant regulatory changes affecting types of loans banks may make, rates of interest they may pay, and reserves they must keep, should be possible.

But, from the point of view of the monetary officials, the nagging concern is that the reduced liquidity and increased risk in bank assets, and the increased reliance upon "hot money" to support these assets, may increase the vulnerability of the entire banking system to a degree that will not be evident until a crisis actually emerges. Most policy officials would agree that for many years commercial banks have limited their profit potential through a needlessly conservative approach to asset and deposit management. But has the process of reaching for income in a fiercely competitive, fast-moving financial market gone too far? The examination process reveals individual banks that have exceeded the limits of prudence, as measured against standard practice in banking. But it is the responsibility of the authorities to judge whether the standard against which the individual bank is measured is itself sound. Here there are no wholly usable guideposts either in past experience or, most particularly, in the theoretical concepts of banking that have helped to shape legislation and regulation in the past.

B. Effects upon Policy Efficiency

In the development and execution of Federal Reserve policy since the early 1950s, the commercial banks generally have had access to a liquidity cushion in periods of monetary restraint through their government bond portfolios. As the Federal Reserve has increased pressures upon banking reserves, banks have been able to liquidate government securities, transferring ownership to nonbank investors and thus freeing reserves to meet customer credit demands. In spite of this cushion, the Federal Reserve, at the peak of its restraining efforts in 1953, 1957, and 1959, has been able to create a condition of significant restraint upon the availability of bank credit. This restraint resulted either from the fact that further liquidation of governments by banks could have been effected only at prohibitive capital losses, or from the fact that the total liquidity position of banks had reached minimum levels consistent with then prevailing notions of what was adequate liquidity.

In the commercial banking structure that has evolved during the past few years, there is serious doubt that a severely restrictive policy similar to those pursued from time to time in the 1950s could be made effective. The fact that large commercial banks have turned to the liability side of their balance sheets, through certificates of deposit, for their principal source of liquidity offers a form of protection against monetary restraint that they have not had before. In a money market where the total supply of short-term investment instruments amounts to not much less than $200 billion, the individual bank has reason to feel confident that, at a price, it would be able to raise the funds it needed to service its customers' credit requests in all but the most unusually tight conditions. If these conditions should arise temporarily, there is always the Federal Reserve discount window to carry the bank over the period of most severe strain. In these circumstances, how confident can the Federal Reserve be that a policy of monetary restraint would be successful, if such a policy were to be called for?

Two answers immediately suggest themselves. First, the Federal Reserve Board has the authority, after all, either to raise or not to raise permissible time deposit rates under Regulation Q so as to enable banks to continue to compete in the money market. If, as a consequence of severe monetary restraint, short-term rates of interest were to rise to levels at which banks could no longer compete for C.D. money, the result might be not only restraint upon banks' ability to expand their loan credit further but, in the absence of liquid marketable assets, forced liquidation of existing loans as C.D.s ran down. But it is precisely this potential for sudden and extreme restraint upon bank lending that probably would inhibit the Federal Reserve Board from refusing to amend Regulation Q at such a time. It is one thing for the Federal Reserve to pursue an aggressively restrictive policy when the banking system has a liquid asset cushion that permits gradual adjustment to the effects of this policy. It is quite another matter to adopt such a policy at a time when it is known that there is very little liquidity cushion left on the asset side of bank balance sheets and when, therefore, such a policy could be almost immediately and unpredictably severe. In other words, the Federal Reserve might find itself in the dilemma of either amending Regulation Q, and by so doing, lessening its capacity to achieve its policy objectives, or of refusing to amend Regulation Q and thus running the risk of precipitating the bank crisis potentially inherent in the new asset and liability structures of the banking system.

A second and obvious response to the line of reasoning which suggests that recent innovations have lessened the efficiency of Fed policy is that restraint on the reserve base alone would, in time, force the commercial banking system to limit its additions to time deposits. Even though the reserve requirement on time deposits is only a fraction of that on demand deposits, each addition to time deposits does eat into the available supply of reserves; and therefore at some point, assuming a reserve limit imposed by the Fed, the process of bank credit expansion could be brought to a halt. There are two difficulties with this line of reasoning. First, there is still a considerable amount of slack in the demand deposits of commercial banks, which thus could be released to support a much larger volume of time deposits. This slack exists in large part in the compensating balances banks requires from their customers. It is reasonably certain that a new period of monetary restraint would set into motion a more or less rapid conversion of these compensating balances into noninterest-bearing time deposits. Again, we find that the adjustment would occur on the liability side of bank balance sheets. The second weakness with the argument that regulation of total reserves still permits efficient Federal Reserve operation relates to the incidence of restraint, which is treated below as the third area of Federal Reserve concern.

C. Incidence of Policy Effects

During the postwar period through 1960, there was a tendency for smaller banks and banks outside the money centers to grow at a faster rate than the money market banks. This was due partly to the fact that the corporations that were learning more efficient ways to manage their funds hold their principal balances at the money market banks. Partly it was due to the fact that among the smaller or nonmoney market banks are those located in the fastest growing suburban or regional areas. Between December, 1947, and December, 1960, total loans and investments of country banks rose by 87 percent, of "other" reserve city banks by 75 percent, of Chicago banks by 39 percent, and of New York banks by 36 percent. This tendency for slower growth at city banks has been sharply reversed during the most recent years. From December, 1960, through June, 1965, growth of loans and investments at country banks was 43 percent; at other reserve city banks, 39 percent; at Chicago banks, 53 percent; and at New York banks, 49 percent. There has been virtually no growth in demand deposits in the New York and Chicago banks during the most recent period; the increased rate of growth in available funds to support the expanding growth in asset holdings has come from time deposits and, in particular, from negotiable time certificates of deposit. The development of discretionary access to deposits in the form of certificates of deposit has given a decided advantage to the prime banks in access to loanable funds.

This recent shift in the big bank/small bank competitive position has important implications for the distributional effects of a restrictive Federal Reserve policy. As noted earlier, were such a policy to be adopted, there could be considerable slippage between the impact of the policy on bank reserves and its effects upon bank credit. This slippage would result from commercial bank access to the money market through certificates of deposit. But in a period of tight money it is likely that only the prime banks would find it possible to raise C.D. money at rates of interest permitted under Regulation Q. The very real danger would arise that smaller, nonprime banks would find their time funds drained off into the money market banks. The result would be a condition of little or no restraint upon the credit granting capacity of big banks and extreme restraint upon the ability of other banks to service their customers. For a good many reasons, this is an outcome that the monetary authorities would deplore.

III. FEDERAL RESERVE POLICY

The influence of recent innovations in commercial banking upon the efficiency of Federal Reserve policy has thus far been only potential rather than real. Economic and credit conditions of the past four and a half years have not made it necessary that the Federal Reserve impose restraints upon bank credit of a type that would test whether its efficiency has in fact been reduced. Total bank credit has grown at an unprecedented rate, but throughout there have been available resources in the economy to employ this credit in productive rather than inflationary ways. Monetary policy has aimed at two objectives. First, it has supplied the necessary reserves to permit bank credit to flow freely into the domestic economy to promote domestic economic advance. Second, it has adjusted discount rate, Regulation Q, and open market operations (in concert with Treasury debt management) so as to bring about and maintain a structure of short-term rates in the money market that would inhibit transfers of short-term funds to foreign money markets. Both policies presumably have been successful.[3]

Even though the financial innovations of recent years have not yet created actual problems for monetary policy, it should be asked whether they are likely to create problems in the future. Are the potential inhibitions upon the efficiency of monetary policy real? In approaching this question, it is first necessary to raise some questions as to the usefulness for analysis of real conditions of some of the accepted concepts on bank-

---

[3]The increased competitiveness of commercial banks in the various domestic financial markets was also extended to the international markets, with a resulting increase in bank loans abroad. For the time being, at least, this balance of payments difficulty resulting from the new banking climate has been brought under control by the President's "voluntary" program of restraint on foreign lending.

ing and monetary policy. This paper is intended as an impressionistic description of what has happened in banking and monetary policy, rather than as an excursion into monetary and banking "theory." But such an excursion is unavoidable. The line of analysis developed here is certainly not new, but it will do no harm to restate it.

Commercial banks were, historically, the earliest important financial intermediaries. They innovated in supplying their own notes as a circulating medium to supplement specie; and later, with the development of regional clearing houses and then the Federal Reserve wire transfer system, their demand deposit liabilities became the most important part of the active money supply. A long series of financial crises created by unrestrained note or deposit generation by commercial banks led to various requirements that liquid reserves be maintained to assure the safety of these liabilities. When the Federal Reserve Act was written, it was natural that safety reserves against notes and deposits should be included. It was only some ten years or more later that the Federal Reserve became aware that by manipulating the reserve base it was possible to regulate commercial bank credit and, presumably, the money supply. Out of this awareness, in a process of fitting theory to institutional peculiarities, has grown some most unusual concepts. So much for historical background.

It is probably understandable that the long history of banking and the financial crises caused by banking excesses should have resulted over the years in a body of legislation aimed at regulating banking. The analogy with railroads in the transportation industry is obvious. It also is understandable that, since banks carry as liabilities the major part of the money supply, monetary theorists have been particularly concerned with banks, and monetary policy should have been developed to have its effect through banks. But it is difficult to understand—granting the ways in which commercial banks may be unique among financial intermediaries—the reason for some of the notions held by many economists and others on the way the financial system operates and on the unique significance of commercial bank credit.[4]

The typical textbook description of the way the banking system works involves something called the "multiple expansion of bank credit" or the "deposit creation process." The Federal Reserve System is pictured as the prime mover, with commercial banks and the deposit-holding public the passive responders to forces set in motion by the central bank. In this analysis, reserves are supplied to "Bank A," pass on to "Bank B,"

[4]I think it is necessary at this point to insert an apology to my economist colleagues for any implication that they might subscribe to the positions that are "demolished" in the next few paragraphs. Most academic economists have long since moved away from these notions, as have the great majority of commercial bank and Federal Reserve economists. Still, I am constantly amazed at how often the old ideas continue to crop up among economists and, probably more important, the reverent attachment that many practicing bankers still have for them.

and so forth, generating a growth in deposits equal to a multiple of the original injection of reserves, the multiple being the reciprocal of the reserve requirement ratio.

This description probably is a useful teaching device, but it is unfortunate that it has created among a generation of students an erroneous impression of the relationship between the central bank and commercial banks. Assuming that banks employ their reserves efficiently, there will obviously be a multiple relationship at all times between reserves and deposits. But this necessary arithmetic connection scarcely establishes the causal force. For the past several years the Federal Reserve, through its open market operations, has supplied reserves to banks as they were needed to support deposit growth, rather than on independent initiative aimed at creating, through a multiple process, a given increase in bank credits or deposits. In other words, the Federal Reserve, rather than the banks and the public, has been the passive unit in the bank credit expansion process.

In the banking systems of other developed countries, reserve requirements generally are recognized as a means by which the monetary authorities siphon off some part of the credit supply (savings ? cash throw-off ?)generated by a growing economy. This point of entry into the financial markets gives the authorities the option of replacing in the market an amount of funds either greater or less than the amount of funds that was siphoned off. There is no suggestion that the central bank, by replacing these funds (reserves), is thereby "creating high-powered money."[5]

A closely related line of reasoning holds that the central bank, working through the commercial banks, is able to determine the size of the money supply and its rate of growth. Surely, the central bank influences the conditions that help to shape decisions to hold money, rather than income-earning assets. Through management of banking reserves, the Federal Reserves determines the ability of commercial banks to share in credit growth and by so doing affects market rates of interest. However, in the hierarchy of influences that shape decisions to hold money, interest rates do not bulk particularly large except in the extreme case of their being pushed so low that the diflerence between holding money and income-earning assets becomes a matter of indifference.

It is rather difficult to understand why, in much of the writing on monetary and banking matters, demand deposits have been treated as an asset not subject to the usual economic principles of portfolio selection. Logically, an increase in money supply reflects the composite decisions of money holders, usually based on transaction needs, rather than the

[5]Committee on the Working of the Monetary System, *Report* (London: Her Majesty's Stationery Office, August, 1959), pp. 125–29.

unilateral decision of the central bank or changes in the amount of credit granted by commercial banks. At extremely low rates of interest, a sterile addition to the money supply may be forced by the central bank. Short of this extreme, additions to money supply represent conscious decisions of money holders to forego income because they require additional cash. Precautionary and expectational reasons for this need do not apply in the modern money market because of the availability of interest-bearing near-money substitutes. And inertia is probably a minor and certainly a logically unacceptable reason. Transactions requirements no doubt dictate the bulk of money supply changes.

Just as the central bank is unable to force money supply growth except by forcing short-term interest rates close to zero, it is unable to prevent money supply growth except by forcing interest rates sharply higher. The interest elasticity of demand for money varies with the extent to which there are idle balances. Given the current relationship between money supply and transaction needs for money, the volume of idle balances probably is quite low, suggesting that money demand is highly interest inelastic over a band of rate levels stretching from close to zero, at one extreme, to a relatively high level at the other. The most important body of "idle" demand balances at the present time is in the compensating balances banks require against credit lines or as compensation for other services. At some point in a period of rising interest rates, it is likely that strong pressures would develop to transfer these balances to non-interest-bearing time accounts, thus economizing on reserves. Statistically, this shift would appear to reduce or limit the growth of money supply, but it would be a matter of appearance only, not of substance.

The inability of the central bank to regulate money supply growth, except at interest rate extremes, derives from the inescapable fact that money holders have full discretion as to the allocation of their assets. The public at all times holds noncash assets, or has access to credit that is convertible into money at the individual's option. The central bank and commercial banks have no direct control over this process. To attempt to create circumstances in which free movement between money and other assets would be impeded would create an old-fashioned money panic. This option need not be considered in an analysis of the effectiveness of Federal Reserve policy.

Another notion about the operation of the banking system that apparently is fairly widely held is that bank deposits are peculiar financial assets which belong to commercial banks and which the owner is powerless to transfer to other forms of financial asset. An illustration of this type of reasoning has appeared in recent years in connection with certificates of deposit. The line of reasoning premises that corporate funds that have gone into certificates of deposit must have come out of demand balances. This transfer from demand to time, by releasing reserves, has promoted an easy reserve position in the banking system. The reasoning then goes on that if interest rates on competitive money market instruments were to rise above permissible C.D. rates under Regulation Q, these funds would move out of C.D.s—since the rate was no longer competitive—*but back into noninterest-bearing demand deposits,* thus tightening bank reserve supply.

The interplay of market forces, relative rates of return, and depositor preference play no part in the analysis. Commercial banks are unique and their deposits exist in an airtight cubicle protected from outside influence. It is obvious that a shift of investor funds out of C.D.s because their rates were too low could not possibly result in an increase in noninterest-bearing demand deposits. The very fact that such an analysis could have been developed, however, is indicative of the way in which acceptance of the older ideas on banking can lead even sound analysts to illogical conclusions.

Still another illustration of old attitudes that are unrelated to today's reality is the impression that commercial bank credit differs in some important way from other types of credit. One finds constant reference to changes in bank credit outstanding, but only seldom are references made to total credit. For example, during the first half of 1965 commercial bank loans grew very rapidly, and this led to numerous expressions of concern, from official and unofficial sources, of the inflationary consequences of bank credit growth. A similar rapid expansion of credit through other financial intermediaries in recent years has not created the same alarm.

It is difficult to see the way in which bank credit is supposed to differ from other credit. If one could argue that bank credit automatically generates demand deposits, adding to money supply and thus creating an inflationary danger, it might be possible to distinguish bank from other types of credit. But the financial system simply does not work in this way. The funds loaned by banks thus far in 1965 have been made available by growth in time and savings deposits, and these deposits in turn have derived from personal savings and corporate cash flow and have been acquired by banks in competition with other financial intermediaries. The intermediation route that funds follow from savings into credit may have economic consequences with respect to the relative availability of credit for different types of borrowers—to be sure. Since banks operate across a broader band of credit markets than other lenders, however, the expanded intermediation role of banks should be encouraging, suggesting an improved allocation of credit, rather than something to be viewed with alarm.

It seems to me that we have developed an analytical apparatus to describe the way our banking and monetary system has worked, given the particular institutional arrangements of that system—reserve requirements, demand balances used to settle claims, and the rest—and we have then elevated this analysis to doctrine, forgetting that institutional arrangements are subject to change. In particular, the analysis has rested upon a commercial banking system that was willing to submit itself to central bank constraints and upon a deposit-owning public that did not manage its cash economically. Both circumstances have changed.

To test the validity of the positions taken in this paper, let us attempt a hypothetical reconstruction of the past four years. Imagine a situation in which Federal Reserve policy objectives had been just what they have actually been in terms of net availability of reserves to the banking system and of interest rate objectives dictated by the balance of payments. Suppose then that Regulation Q had not been amended to permit commercial banks to compete with other financial intermediaries for savings and that commercial banks had not innovated in offering certificates of deposit to business customers. Would the history of the past four years have been different in any important way?

Under these hypothetical conditions, it seem likely that total bank deposit and credit growth would have been less than it has been and that, as a consequence, reserves supplied by the Fed would have been less. But is there any reason to believe that *total* credit extension through the financial system or the *total* increase in claims on financial intermediaries would have been different? To conclude that these totals would have been smaller would require an assumption that economic activity and income would have increased by less than it actually did, for the growth in net claims upon financial intermediaries reflects savings flow out of income and net throw-off of funds from corporate cash flow. This assumption, in turn, assumes that the intermediation of other financial institutions is somehow less efficient than bank intermediation.

If we may conclude that total credit extended would have been about what it actually was, although commercial bank and Federal Reserve participation was less, is it not possible that there would have been important distributional differences in the credit flow? In view of the record of the financial market in adapting to shifting credit demands, this outcome appears unlikely. Or might the extension of credit by intermediaries other than banks have been less inflationary? If so, it is hard to see why.

Finally, what about demand deposits? Is it possible that with the Federal Reserve prepared to supply reserves as needed, growth in banking resources would have occurred through demand deposits if the banks had not set out to compete for time and savings money? To argue this position would require the unlikely assumption that demand deposits may be created at will by the monetary authorities and the banking system, without concern for the asset preferences of the public. Assuming the balance of payments constraint upon market rates of interest, what would have been the inducement for individuals and businesses to have carried voluntarily larger demand balances with banks?

In my judgment, the only important difference between what would have happened in my hypothetical situation and what actually happened was that banks innovated. The fact that bank liabilities and assets grew faster than they would have in the absence of innovation, and that as a consequence the Federal Reserve found it necessary to supply more reserves, is irrelevant to any important economic consequence.

What then has been the effect of banking innovation upon the efficiency of Federal Reserve policy? My remarks might suggest that monetary policy has become purposeless. I have argued that the growth of demand deposits, within a reasonable range of interest rates, is a function of the public's desire to hold cash, rather than a function of either Federal Reserve or commercial bank credit practices. I have also argued that the time and savings balances at commercial banks are simply that portion of the savings flow that depositors have voluntarily chosen to retain at commercial banks because of interest rate advantage or other reasons. Similarly, I have argued that the intermediation process of commercial banks in granting credit does not differ in economic effect from the credit granting of other intermediaries. Having eliminated Federal Reserve control over the money supply and the peculiar characteristics of commercial banking that have been used to justify our monetary policies, just what is left for monetary policy?

The efficiency of monetary policy, as it was applied in the 1950s, has been much reduced, if not destroyed, by recent financial innovation. Its success—if in fact it did accomplish anything—depended upon a banking system whose asset growth responded predictably to changes in net reserve availability and upon a nonbank financial market that, while growing rapidly, had not yet developed to the point where it could promptly pick up the slack created by retarded bank participation. But both of these foundations for the old policies were self-destroying.

In the case of the commercial banking sector, there were three important circumstances supporting Federal Reserve policies, so that restraints on bank reserves led more or less smoothly to a reduced rate of growth for bank deposits and credit. First, and probably most important, was the willingness of bank management to permit commercial banking to be used as the instrument of monetary policy. Second was the movement toward more efficient cash management by bank depositors. Third was the excessive liquidity of the banking system, particularly in holdings of government securities. As reserve pressures bore down upon them, banks were able to sell off government securities to raise funds to service loan demands. This net liquidation of governments meshed with the shift of corporate liquid assets from demand deposits to short-term investments. No one of these three circumstances would now be available to the same degree to support Federal Reserve efforts to restrain credit growth through restraint on bank reserves.

Meanwhile, the nonbank financial sector has matured to the point where, even if banks were not to compete to hold their share of the credit market, as they did in the 1950s, the net result would probably be a redirection of intermediation with little appreciable effect upon total credit extensions. In fact, by 1959, nonbank intermediation had grown to a point where it was possible for total credit funds raised to climb to a record level while bank credit grew scarcely at all. Innovation by nonbank intermediaries since then guarantees that, with very little lag, the nonbank sector would be able to pick up any slack in the credit flow resulting from reduced competition by banks.

The analysis thus far has dealt only with efforts by the central bank to restrain growth in bank credit and money supply. It does not treat efforts to force money supply growth of the sort that were effective in 1954 and again in 1958. The easy money policies in these two years were successful in increasing demand deposits and bank assets by forcing short-term interest rates below the indifference threshold between money and interest-earning investments. This in turn was made possible by the fact that there was, for all practical purposes, no international money market at that time. The subsequent movement to convertibility of all major currencies and development of a broad international money market has probably destroyed the ability of a national central bank to impose interest rates so low as would be necessary to force demand deposit growth in a business recession.

In my judgment, the Federal Reserve System at this time would be unable to regulate bank credit or total credit through restraints upon bank reserves as it did in the 1950s. To be successful, such general reserve restraints would have to be accompanied by an application of time deposit interest rate ceilings under Regulation Q that would make even the largest banks unable to compete for funds in the money market. The resulting squeeze upon already illiquid banks, as they were forced to reduce assets in line with their falling deposit liabilities, could be most serious if the policy were persisted in. At the same time, if reserve restraints were to be applied in tandem with a Regulation Q policy of the sort followed in recent years—which has set maximum time deposit rates only a shade above market rates on prime paper—it is more than likely that serious distributional inequities would arise between large and small banks. The large banks would more than likely be able to continue to raise the funds—that is, reserves—needed to meet credit demands, while the full impact of the reserve restraint would be thrown back upon the nonprime banks. Of course, a variety of more or less direct controls might be devised to allocate reserves among banks, but is this really necessary? Does it unavoidably follow that the potential for efficient monetary policy is destroyed because the circumstances have changed that made a particular type of policy effective in an earlier period?

In fact, quite the reverse is true. The new-found imagination and competitiveness of commercial banks in the financial markets has helped to create an environment in which more rational and more efficient monetary policies might be developed. These more powerful policies would require recognition that credit supplied through commercial bank intermediation does not differ from other types of credit and that there is no reason, therefore, for either reserve requirements against time deposits or ceilings upon rates of interest banks may pay for such deposits. These changes would eliminate the present inequity in the cost of money market funds to banks versus other intermediaries and would give some protection against unwanted shifts of funds from small to large banks. It would also require recognition that the only avenue other than direct controls through which monetary policy can influence total credit generation is interest rates.

From the point of view of Federal Reserve policy, the most important consequence of the financial innovations of recent years has been that the commercial banking system has become more intimately involved with the full spectrum of financial intermediaries. Commercial banks have traditionally been the avenue through which public policy has attempted to influence the credit markets, and there is no particular reason why policy should not continue to use banks as the medium through which policy influence is brought to bear upon the market. The point of contact, however, need be only the reserve requirement against demand deposits.[6] Reserve requirements against time and savings deposits, and interest rate ceilings on these deposits, serve no useful policy pur-

---

[6]Professor Carson of Northwestern University has raised a question as to whether the logic of my argument should not also suggest elimination of reserve requirements on demand deposits. His point is well taken. Reserve requirements provide a point of entry into the financial markets for public credit policy by siphoning off a portion of the savings (cash throw-off) generated in the economy. Public policy then has the option of replacing these funds by taking off the market an equivalent dollar amount of financial claims, or of replacing a larger or smaller amount of funds than was siphoned off. But the net effect upon the availability of credit to private borrowers has a one-for-one, not a multiple, relationship to the net funds absorbed or supplied by the central bank. Since both the asset and liability sides of bank balance sheets are equally affected by the multiple adjustment to the change in reserves, it is obvious that the *stock* of financial claims in the total economy is unaffected, that the only effect is upon the *flow,* and that this effect is exactly equal to the amount of the Fed's net addition to, or absorption of, funds.

Elimination of all cash reserve requirements would be economically beneficial in at least two ways. First, by working directly upon credit flows, rather than relying upon commerical banks to intermediate, responses to policy would be more immediate, more precise, and more predictable. Second, elimination of reserve requirements would remove a wholly unjustifiable special tax upon banks. If reserve requirements were to be done away with, the Federal Reserve would then have to assess charges for the services it provides to banks, and still further responsibility would be thrown upon the examination function to assure a sound banking system. But these and other minor adjustments could be easily made if once the principle were recognized that reserve requirements serve no useful purpose and, in fact, probably impede the development of effective credit policies.

pose and, in fact, tend to interfere with the rational functioning of the credit markets.

Through a combination of discount rate policy and variations in the net availability of reserves behind demand deposits, the Federal Reserve should be able to achieve a rather immediate effect upon interest rates. Competition among banks for the available supply of reserves through the C.D. market and savings accounts should promptly translate Federal Reserve policy intentions into higher or lower rates on a wide spectrum of credit instruments. For example, an increase in discount rate and/or reduced net availability of reserves would lead banks to offer higher rates for C.D. money, leading to higher rates on all short-term instruments. The banks might also raise interest rates on savings accounts, thus causing a redirection of savings flow from other institutions and, indirectly, upward pressure upon mortgage rates and other long-term interest rates. Assuming some interest elasticity of demand for credit, the net result would be restraint upon credit of all types.

The difference between this outcome and that achieved in the 1950s is that the restraining influence would bear upon the entire credit market and would not be centered upon the commercial banks. The policy instruments used would be the same, except for the elimination of rate ceilings and reserve requirements upon time deposits. But the purpose of policy would be to achieve an interest rate structure that would have the desired effect upon *total* credit, rather than to achieve a specific restraining or expansive influence upon *bank* credit. In fact, depending upon the intensity of demand for different types of credit and the degree of participation of banks in the various credit markets, bank credit under any given policy might expand at either a faster or slower rate than the total of all credit. But the rate of bank credit expansion would be irrelevant so long as total credit was expanding at a rate consistent with policy objectives.

In short, recent financial innovations have created a more rational financial system in which Federal Reserve policy can be effective in promoting the most efficient allocation of credit resources. The policies of the 1950s, in the institutional setting of that period, did not promote efficient resource allocation. But to develop these policies requires a new understanding of the commercial banking process and the discarding of obsolete notions of banking and money.

One aspect of the new policies would be indifference toward changes in the money supply. New growth in the money supply will reflect changing transaction needs as modified by further innovations in cash management. Assuming interest rates within some "normal" range, it is impossible to conceive of a set of circumstances that would cause the public to stockpile money rather than interest-earning assets. At the same time, within such a range of interest rates it would not be possible for the central bank to impose a slower rate of growth in money supply than that required for transaction purposes. There should be no need for concern if money supply does not grow in pace with some preconceived "normal" rate of growth. And there should be no need for alarm at a faster than "normal" growth rate.

In summary, recent innovations in commercial banking have outmoded the credit policies of the 1950s, but have created a setting in which credit policy could be more effective. Policies of the 1950s required for their success (a) a banking system that responded predictably to changes in reserve availability and (b) a nonbank financial sector that adjusted only with a lag to fill the gap created by restraint upon bank credit. Circumstances have changed, and policies aimed specifically at regulating bank credit would be unlikely to be effective. At the same time, the better integrated, more rational financial market that has emerged in recent years gives the central bank a mechanism through which its policies can be made promptly and powerfully effective. All that is required is a shift of emphasis away from commercial bank credit, money supply, and other such partial objectives, and a shift to emphasis upon regulation of total credit through conscious influence upon interest rates.

DISCUSSION

Comment on Gaines and Smith Papers

Jacob Cohen

Gaines sees the banking innovation of negotiable time certificates of deposit as constituting a revolution in commercial banking and, in the process, affecting the role of the Federal Reserve. Commercial banks are now masters of their own destinies. If they wish to increase their reserves they issue certificates of deposit bearing a competitive interest rate. Their ability to acquire or not to acquire assets is at their own discretion. By this innovation the resemblance of banks to other financial institutions has increased. They must "buy" their raw material like other institutions. The credit they extend is no different from the credit extended by other institutions.

The revolution in banking is the joint product of more alert banking policies, more efficient corporate cash management, and amendments to the interest rate ceiling under Regulation Q. For Gaines this means that traditional thinking about the Fed's control of the money supply is wrong. The Fed is unable to control the money supply because if money holders do not wish to hold money balances they needn't do so. Money holders will hold just the amount of money that they want to hold. If they find themselves holding more than the desired amount they will buy interest-yielding assets with the result that the money stock declines. Money demand determines the stock of money.

This lack of control over the money supply must be qualified in the case of extreme variations in the interest rate. By keeping interest rates close to zero, the public can be induced to increase its holdings of money. On the other hand, growth in the money supply can be prevented by forcing interest rates sharply higher.[1] By controlling rates within a "nor-

[1]Gaines's paper, with its defense of an antiprinciple—that the Federal Reserve cannot control the money supply—is an expression of the "new view" in monetary economics. The best theoretical exposition is probably to be found in Lyle E. Gramley and Samuel B. Chase, Jr., "Time Deposits in Monetary Analysis," *Federal Reserve Bulletin*, October, 1965, pp. 1380 ff. Unlike these authors' and other "new view" writings, however, Gaines espouses a demand for money curve that is discontinuous with respect to interest rates.

mal" range, the central bank can exert its most important influence: control of the total volume of credit including credit extended by nonbank intermediaries.

How does the Fed influence interest rates without influencing the money supply? It does this through variations in the net availability of reserves. In this way, it can control commercial bank competition for reserves via the interest rate offered by banks on certificates of deposit. Ultimately the entire short-term interest rate structure can be made to feel the effect of reserve restraint. Given some interest elasticity in the demand for credit, the result will be overall credit restraint.

To tackle Gaines's argument, one must first overlook its ambivalence. On several occasions he sees the central bank as passive, only supplying reserves as required by deposit growth (pp. 110, 117–18). This view is less acceptable than the view shared by both the old and new looks in monetary theory—that reserves are determined exogenously by the central bank.

But what is the process whereby reserves affect bank competition and thereby interest rates? Gaines does not spell this out. It may be that he fears mentioning the inevitable connection with bank credit and demand deposit growth. Given an increase in excess reserves, one would suggest that the banking system will ordinarily increase its earning assets, financing such increases by crediting the checking accounts of asset sellers. The greater the possibilities of credit expansion via increases in the money stock the less need for banks to attract time deposits by paying higher interest rates.

Credit restriction then does not take place by some mystical effect of interest rates on the amount of credit demanded. As we see the process, a decrease in available reserves will shift the supply curve of bank credit to the left faster than the demand for credit is expanding, so that total credit flows are contracted. Gaines's analysis provides no such mechanism for reduced credit flows. The process of spiraling interest rates that he describes is consistent with a demand curve for credit shifting to the right and intersecting an interest-sensitive supply curve of credit at ever higher levels of interest rates and credit flows.

Credit expansion takes place in the same unmysterious way. The growth in bank credit in the first half of the 1960s was the outcome of a tremendous upsurge in reserve bank credit. Gaines puts his emphasis on the comparative expansion of time deposits without facing the more fundamental question as to the generating force behind total (demand and time) deposits. Increases in demand deposits and leakages into time deposits were both made possible by increases in reserve credit. The central bank provided not only the necessary condition for the increase in time deposits—amendments to Regulation Q—but also provided the necessary and sufficient condition for the expansion in total deposits.[2]

On the basis of his analysis, Gaines urges a shift of policy away from commercial bank credit, money supply, and "other such partial objectives" toward emphasis on "regulation of all credit through conscious influence upon interest rates" (p. 118). We would agree that the regulation of total credit flows should be the central objective of policy. But we are not agreed on interest rates as the appropriate instrument. The central bank must focus on the quantity of money and its velocity since these are the variables that lie behind changes in total credit flows. The central bank should therefore aim at controlling the money stock and, where possible, the demand for money. Gaines would of course reply that such control of the money stock is not possible. His identification of contemporary money supply analysis with the simplest kind of textbook multipliers does a disservice not only to recent sophisticated studies of the money supply function[3] but to the typical money and banking textbook. The determinants of the money supply are complex, but allowing for the necessary functional relationship (including the dependence of time deposits on interest rates), it should be possible to make fairly good predictions of changes in *M* associated with changes in the reserve base.[4]

If the public's desire for interest-bearing assets in general had the same effect on the money supply as on time deposits in commercial banks, this would cast doubt on the validity or usefulness of an independent money supply function. The "monetary equation," however, suggests that this is not the case. Assume financial market transactions among the nonbank public, or that the nonbank public transfers demand deposits into the liabilities of nonbank intermediaries. In neither case will the money supply, as conventionally defined, be affected.[5]

---

[2]Gaines is reluctant to admit that commercial banks "owe" anything to the central bank for their current high activity—apart from upward revisions in Regulation Q. Frequently the impression is conveyed that if the central bank simply spent its time in weeding out the odd case of bank illiquidity, the commercial banking system could look after itself, thank you. This ignores the tremendous expansion in the reserve base contemporaneous with the growth in C.D.s.

[3]See, for example, Karl Brunner and Allan H. Meltzer, "Some Further Investigations of Demand and Supply Functions for Money," *Journal of Finance*, Vol. XIX (May, 1964), pp. 240 ff.

[4]*Ibid.*, p. 253.

[5]If demand deposits kept as reserves by financial intermediaries against their liabilities are segregated from other demand deposits, "private" demand deposits will decline as financial intermediary liabilities increase. See, for example, James P. Yohe, "Financial Institutions in Aggregative Models," *Statsøkonomisk Tidskrift*, No. 4 (1963), p. 216.

An argument less dependent on taxonomy is that increased competition from nonbank institutions forces yields so low that banks can no longer afford their demand deposit liabilities, resulting in the sell-off of assets. See James Tobin, "Commercial Banks as Creators of Money," in Dean Carson (ed.), *Banking and Monetary Studies* (Homewood, Illinois: Richard D. Irwin, Inc., 1963), pp. 408 ff. This is an interesting

(Continued on next page)

Velocity considerations have always plagued policy decisions and they will continue to do so. Gaines exaggerates the banking revolution of the 1960s. Since 1946 the trend in velocity has been sharply upward. One might also recall previous episodes when shifts from demand to time deposits were induced by banks on a large scale. In the 1927–29 "bull" stock market, banks encouraged their customers to make this shift. Brokers' loans by banks "on accounts of others" at that time had a similar stimulating effect on velocity.[6]

It should be emphasized that the upsurge in time deposits is the handiwork of the Fed. If shifts into time deposits aggravate the regulatory problems of the central bank, then it can revise the ceiling downward! On others grounds, too, one might argue against the present high ceilings. First, the growth in time deposits has serious implications for bank liquidity. Second, as has been alleged by one economist, decisions toward monetary ease may be made in part to compensate for the high costs of time deposits.[7] For Gaines, lowering the interest rate ceiling would be catastrophic, but from the standpoint of both monetary policy and long-run banker interest it may be the wisest policy.[8]

Smith's paper, "Is the Growth of Private Debt a Cause for Concern?" concentrates on household debt. This is appropriate because of its likeness to the public debt which originally stirred up questions of debt burden. The author believes that the greatest danger of consumer debt lies in a possible fall in income. A line of logical inquiry would be the likelihood of such a fall and how it would be converted into financial distress for individual households and into financial crisis—and the consequences of financial crisis for the economy.

---

hypothesis, but Tobin offers no empirical support for it. It would seem difficult to demonstrate in an era of high yields, not only on customer loans, but on open market investments.

[6]Fritz Machlup, *The Stock Market, Credit and Capital Formation* (New York, 1940), p. 138.

[7]See Leland J. Pritchard, "Profit or Loss from Time Deposit Banking," in *Banking and Monetary Studies,* op. cit., pp. 369 ff.

Pritchard argues for the abolition of commercial bank time deposits not only because their profit needs force the Federal Reserve into expansionary policies but for a second reason which is much harder to follow. Time deposits, since they are financed by reductions in demand deposits, cause a drying up of monetary savings which are thereby lost forever to investment. This disastrous effect can only be offset by increasing the money supply (*ibid.,* pp. 375, 385). One can only interpret this to mean that as compared with financial flows into nonbank intermediaries, total credit flows will be reduced. For, given the reserve requirement structure, and other things remaining the same, total bank credit will increase with a shift into time deposits. What is also ambiguous in Pritchard is his view that compensating increases in the money supply are inflationary and that they "dilute" the money supply. If such dosages offset the adverse effects of time deposits, why are they so deplored?

[8]Lowering the interest rate ceiling may precipitate some serious short-run problems for banks with large amounts of C.D.s outstanding, but freer access to the discount window and open market operations could ease the transitional period.

If this is the tack that analysis should take, then much of Smith's emphasis in his paper is misplaced. The heart of his analysis is a Domarlike demonstration that given constancy in the underlying parameters such as the percentage of consumer expenditures financed by debt, the relation of durable expenditures to income, and the maturity structure of the debt, ultimately a stable ratio will be established between debt and income even though at any given time the percentage increase in debt exceeds the percentage increase in income. Thus Smith seems to fall into the familiar trap of seeking a magic touchstone for determining financial capacity. What is so magical about a stable ratio, setting aside the unrealism of the assumptions? Any ratio, no matter how high it is, could be a stable one using his algebraic formulations. If the chief danger of a debt is the difficulty of maintaining payments when income falls, the height of the ratio rather than its stability would seem to be the important criterion.

The possibilities of financial distress depend on the financial situation of individual financial units. The current findings of the Survey Research Center quoted by Smith indicate that the growth in installment debt is due to the increasing number of spending units using credit rather than because individual spending units are increasing the ratio of their debts to income. Such microanalysis would have been a fruitful line of inquiry worth pushing much further. We should like to know more about the liquid asset holdings of debtors and their income status. Additional criteria, too, are necessary if we are to assess the burden of consumer debt. Are debt payments on capital goods made in the place of payments for their services? If so, the burden of debt payments is illusory. The time dimension is another factor. How long will a fixed debt payment have to be maintained, given a decline in income? If one introduces the theory of consumer choice, the question of burden becomes even more complex. Given economic rationality and correct forecasting by the consumer, how can his preference for goods bought on time over other goods bought for cash be deemed a burden on the purchaser?[9]

While he recognizes the limitations of working with aggregative data, Minsky has perhaps gone further than any other contemporary scholar in exploring the possibilities of financial crisis.[10] His (desperate) efforts to simulate a severe recession using different econometric models of the economy are most reassuring. From his book-length study he concludes that "with the present structure of the economy and the present rate of

---

[9]Questions of this kind are raised in Board of Governors of the Federal Reserve System, "The Burden of Consumer Installment Debt," *Consumer Installment Credit,* Part 1, Vol. 1, chap. 10 (Washington, D.C., 1957), pp. 189 ff.

[10]See, for example, H. P. Minsky, "Financial Crisis, Financial Systems, and the Performance of the Economy," in *Private Capital Markets* (Commission on Money and Credit), (Englewood Cliffs, N.J.: Prentice-Hall, Inc., 1964), pp. 374 ff.

government spending, even as sharp a fall in private investment as took place in 1929–31 should not result in severe financial distress."[11] Nonetheless he does point out that the growing illiquidity of the economy increases the likelihood of a financial crisis being triggered by a routine downturn of income. He illustrates the problem in terms of savings and loan associations. They can be thrown into financial distress if beset by cash withdrawals at the same time that households are defaulting on mortgages. The speculations of Minsky are what is needed in working out the possible consequences of income declines.

In discussing policy implications, Smith emphasizes the importance of a growing debt for maintaining employment and output. We would heartily agree, but would object when he suggests that public debt be substituted for private debt if there is concern over private debt. Apparently he is not quite convinced that private debt poses no real danger, even if the level of economic activity is maintained and the central bank functions effectively as a lender of last resort. The optimum mix of public and private debt should depend on fiscal policy and cost-benefit considerations and not on the doubtful notion of private debt burden.

Some conclusions can be drawn applicable to both papers. The growing illiquidity of the economy underscores the importance of the central bank as the ultimate source of liquidity. We think, too, that the role of the central bank as a regulator of the economy will continue to be as important as ever, despite Gaines's contentions. In an economy with a positive growth rate, financial flows must grow faster than the ex ante flow of financial saving. It is up to the central bank to make the needed adjustments in the reserve base so that the optimal increases in finance will be forthcoming.

[11]*Ibid.*, p. 180.

DISCUSSION

Monetary Policy or Credit Policy?

Roland I. Robinson

The excursion Gaines makes into the errors of money and banking teachers is almost pure catnip for anyone who has ever struggled with students through the process of monetary expansion and contraction. We have doubtless been guilty in moments of pedagogical frustration of implying unidirectional causation along with admitted oversimplifications and other doctrinal flaws. But there are two sides to this matter of error. Gaines's avowal that the Federal Reserve is only a passive agent in the deposit expansion process seems equally indefensible. The money and banking textbooks on my bookshelf contain neither error. Monetary expansion and contraction are correctly described as dynamic equilibrium processes in which forces of adjustment come from the demand-for-money side as well as from the supply side. It is possible that in some periods one side may be more active than in other times, but neither side can be neglected. Furthermore, while Gaines was right in noting the role of interest rates in the demand for money, this has long been incorporated into textbooks even at the most elementary level. The leading money and banking texts on my shelves say quite clearly that the demand for money is positively elastic with respect to income and negatively elastic with respect to price level *expectations* and interest rates.

Another tempting bit of bait for dispute is Gaines's glowing picture of the recent burst of financial innovation. Such a story cannot help but stir the recollection of anyone who has been even mildly interested in economic history. Against the long perspective of time, just how remarkable are the current innovations in financial and banking practice?

The first goldsmith who wrote a warehouse receipt for gold he did not hold should be given a high mark for inventiveness if not for financial integrity. The whole development of bank notes out of earlier negotiable instruments was a drastic change from whole-bodied or commodity money to credit money. The promoters who located note-issuing banks in inaccessible places so as to discourage or slow down the rate of note redemption were innovators, even if slippery ones. Certainly the state bankers who, when shorn of their note issues by the prohibitive tax of the National Banking Act, promoted deposit banking deserve high and honorable marks for innovation.

What is more, innovation on the asset side of the balance sheet has a very long history. The tradition of short-term commercial lending was shattered long before bankers were willing to admit that they were innovating—although from the vantage point of the present we can say that this was a useful innovation. The change in lending forms from lump-sum maturities to serial or installment maturities was an innovation initiated by savings and loan associations, and one that was adopted rather belatedly by commercial banks. The term loan was an innovation born of the lack of loan demand during the years of deep depression.

While financial innovation apparently does not follow a steady course, it is a very old story. Some extra spur to innovation has undoubtedly been experienced in recent years, but we should not let our perspective become foreshortened unreasonably.

Further, we can say that monetary innovation not only has a long history, it has always tended to reduce the power and effectiveness of the instruments of monetary policy then in use. In the nineteenth century monetary policy was concerned primarily with a definition of money and related questions such as whether to have a monometallic or a bimetallic standard. Bank notes, which were doubtless first viewed as money substitutes rather than money, reduced the significance of the legal-tender definition of money and came to be regulated. The emergence of deposit banking seemed to provide a money substitute and an escape from prevailing monetary regulation—but deposits were, in turn, subjected to regulation. In most cases, regulation came after some cataclysmic exercise and often with considerable lag after the innovation that had rendered the prior monetary policy ineffective.

While these matters are interesting diversions, I feel they might draw attention away from far more important issues. The first one is raised inferentially by Gaines but never directly: What is the proper focus of monetary policy: bank credit (in the sense of loans and investments) or money? Gaines assumes throughout his paper that the centerpiece of monetary policy is bank credit. This is not a settled issue. We may ask: Should the monetary authorities look at the asset side or the liability side of the balance sheet? This question was not as important when money market banks were largely demand deposit institutions, but as Gaines shows so graphically this is no longer true.

This point is closely related to the unsettled debate as to how to define money. I suspect that each economist's definition of money is congruent with the area of financial claims that he believes should be controlled.

If my informal count of noses is right, most monetary economists still would put the focus of monetary policy mainly on currency and demand deposits. If the total of debt behaves with considerable regularity and does not generate instability, as Smith rather convincingly argues, then the case for regulatory or economic intervention with respect to bank credit as such is weak. And if the volume of private debt has equilibrium limits, as Smith's models suggest, then private bank credit should not be the primary focus of monetary policy.

By innovation or choice the public may reduce the amount of money it keeps for transaction purposes and the monetary authorities must be sensitive to such changes. Although new financial instruments do appear to have substituted for money, the stability of the proportion between money and money substitutes in the short-run is the critical point. Flow-of-funds estimates suggest short-run stability. If so, monetary policy is not as thwarted as first appears. In any event the Treasury Department is still the major generator of a money substituting financial instrument and thus great power to influence liquidity as well as money still resides in the federal government. If the process of "layering" by financial institutions is not itself disruptive of stability, then the total of financial debts and claims can be considered the result of a transfer process. Claims to real economic capital are being transferred from savers to those who promote the real investment process. The relationship between money and financial claims need not be constant. If the technology of money use changes, then the monetary authorities should change money supply accordingly. And in spite of Gaines's words about this process, I see no hindrance to their doing so with dexterity and success. In simple terms, the Federal Reserve should be concerned with monetary policy and not with credit policy.

It must be admitted that the Federal Reserve itself has not helped to clarify this confusion about the real focus of their aims. For the first half of the System's life, it talked a great deal about credit and almost never about money. The phrase "money supply" was sternly edited out of all drafts of System documents until the mid-1940s. Even in recent years there has been no clear statement on this point. The answers of the System to the CMC questions were a kind of ritual dance around the semantics of the issue.

However, if the System's words have been cloudy, their recent actions have been, at least to my mind, far clearer. For the last several years money supply has grown at a far more regular and systematic rate than during any similar interval in the past. Variations from the average growth rate have been far smaller than in the past. I find it hard to believe that this has been accidental.

Gaines may be right in interpreting monetary policy since 1960 as one of passive adaptation to the demand for money and credit—a policy born of frustration because of money buying by commercial banks. This is not my interpretation of policy. Gaines's argument, if I understand him, is that the Federal Reserve has been made quantitatively impotent because (1) it cannot force monetary expansion in any appreciable degree without pushing interest rates so low as to expose us to loss of foreign short-term balance; (2) the Federal Reserve cannot halt monetary expansion—if there be a private demand for it—without forcing interest rates to levels so high as to risk uncontrolled contraction.

It is certainly true that international imperatives have limited expansive monetary policy, but the surprisingly regular growth of money supply since 1961 (until 1965) shows it can be done. Furthermore, since 1961 money supply as conventionally defined has increased twice as fast as it did in the preceding five years. And recent weeks suggest that a gentle tightening of money markets can be managed without explosive violence.

As a secular matter, power of the monetary authority has been eroded by increased and improved money substitutes, but I see no watershed around 1961. The fact that commercial banks got into the act of merchandising a new money substitute appears only to have transferred and not increased the generation of total financial claims.

Gaines's thesis seems to boil down to this: the reduced slack in money holdings has made the monetary system almost hypersensitive to Federal Reserve actions. He finds little or no elasticity in the demand for money between rates of interest from zero to 8 percent. The Fed is powerless because its powers are too great!

This is an old and false line of argument. Perhaps the best rebuttal of it might be made on the basis of the de Leeuw paper presented at this same conference. De Leeuw's test of responses to monetary actions showed a considerable time lag. This finding, of course, is entirely consistent with other studies of lags and with common sense. With such lags in monetary responses, the Federal Reserve need have no fear of explosive responses. It may suffer from uncertain vision if lags are irregular in length (not suggested by the de Leeuw evidence) but it can act rather vigorously without fear of excessive response. Probably the interest rate effects of Federal Reserve action are rather prompter than the secondary effects either of interest rates themselves (the only channel Gaines recognizes) or of other spending effects. Since we have seen almost a decade and a half of Federal Reserve actions without explosive effects, why should we expect such a great change in responses in the future?

Smith may have given us the clue for interpreting recent public economic policy. What Gaines construes to be a rather passive monetary policy during the past several years may be viewed as a happy combination of monetary and fiscal policy. During much of the postwar period, monetary policy bore a large part of the burden of compensatory or countercyclical economic policy. While the intellectual tools of fiscal policy had been developed a full generation ago, the political conditions for implementing them were not favorable. In the meantime, we were learning more about the lags in compensatory monetary policy.

Starting with the tax cut proposed by the late President Kennedy and brought to fruition by President Johnson we have started to have a much more active and even aggressive fiscal policy. This has allowed the monetary authorities to concentrate on the international scene and at the same time to keep the money supply growing at a fairly respectable rate. The excellent level of economic activity kept demand high enough to sustain interest rates at a level that did not encourage the exit of short-term money market funds.

Gaines takes a fairly dim view of the Federal Reserve's future. Reduced in power by financial innovation, he expects them to survive primarily as service agents for the commercial banks, supplying them with reserves when they need and demand them. He seems to contemplate that the System would have some function as interest rate regulators, but whether this is for domestic or international purposes is not made clear.

Gaines made a contribution in pointing out that the new negotiable certificates of deposit have changed the impact of monetary policy. Before the negotiable C.D. it could have been said that the initial impacts of monetary policy tended to be concentrated on the central money markets. The remoter portions of the banking system were less and later influenced by what the Fed did in the market. This fact was combined with another circumstance—that New York City money market banks were suffering a secular attrition of deposits. As a result, New York City would often show all of the technical signs of monetary tightness when other parts of the banking system were suffering no such strains.

Now, by aggressive use of the new C.D.s large banks can command money and shift some of the influences of monetary actions to other parts of the financial structure. However, a wholly even and equal impact of monetary actions has never prevailed and indeed the very concept of impact equality would be hard to specify and measure. In a dynamic financial system competitive pressures constantly change the balance of power among institutions. Monetary action can never hope to have a wholly even impact. The monetary authorities must keep their eyes glued on the economic aggregates; individual financial institutions must work and innovate to preserve or improve their competitive positions. And if innovation starts to weaken general monetary powers, then the monetary authority itself must innovate to restore its power to such a degree of effectiveness as circumstances require.

The future role of the Federal Reserve does not have to be limited. As history shows, Federal Reserve authority could be expanded so as to regulate money substitutes, if there is a good case for doing so. But if I interpret Smith's evidence correctly, such a case for extension does not exist. Does this mean, then, that the future of the Federal Reserve is mainly in price (that is, interest rate) support and not in quantitative monetary regulation? My own guess would be quite the opposite. Just as preaccord experience showed that there is no future in central banking when its function was limited to holding interest rates down, I see no future to central banks if they are primarily concerned with propping up the level of short-term interest rates.

I *do* see a serious constraint on future Federal Reserve effectiveness, but from quite a different source. The informal system of central banking cooperation assumes that each central bank, subject to its domestic political imperatives, "plays the game" by accepted central banking rules. The accepted central banking rules of the Western European countries may be rules that we should not impose on ourselves. Many of these countries prefer monetary policy to fiscal policy and have boosted interest rates rather than use fiscal brakes.

Gaines's views may explain why money market developments have been so variously interpreted in the past few years. Money market professionals have viewed it as an "easy" money market. This view may have prevailed because commercial banks and all credit-worthy borrowers could borrow money readily. We certainly did not have a tight money market, but my construction would be that we had a very natural money market: saving was quite adequate, real investment demand used the funds at about the rate they became available, and the money supply grew at a very natural rate.

Before I close my comments on Gaines, I would like to pose a question to him; one prompted by his assertion that he expects the monetary authorities never again to play a major role. Can we be as confident as Gaines that low interest rates are a thing of the past? Recent policies aimed at keeping short-term interest rates high for balance of payments reasons have been necessary because such rates were rather high in other countries. But will this always continue to be the case? If history has any relevance it suggests that we *will* have future periods of quite low rates for reasons that originate in the balance between saving and investment and because continuation of a healthy rate of growth in the money supply may lead to very ample supplies of bank reserves. The international constraint may disappear sooner than we now expect.

* * * *

Smith's paper is a useful exercise in two respects: first, it shows that with a constant growth rate, relative expansion of debt probably will continue for some time into the future. Second, he shows that the growth of debt has been based more on a broadening of the base rather than a deepening debt burden for a constant and limited part of the population.

Debt clearly serves an important social purpose: it aids in the transfer of property claims from those who have excess savings to those who undertake more real investment than can be financed by saving. It seems intuitively right that as a nation grows richer, the proportion of debt to income would continue to mount. In this informal way it is possible to question whether Smith's upper limits may not be breached by important structural changes.

Smith's computations of equilibria levels for various types of debt assume a constancy of institutional arrangements. For example, mortgage debt on single family homes has been increasing far more than can be accounted for by new house construction. This increase in mortgage debt on existing housing has been explained in a variety of ways, but it can be viewed as a form of consumer debt more like intermediate-term consumer debt than ordinary mortgage debt. Can it be that at the more reasonable interest rates that prevail on mortgages, there is a large untapped market for consumer borrowing? Has this brought a new group into the market for such borrowing or does this represent a deepening of debt for those already in debt? I don't pretend to have a notion about the effects of this on the quality of credit but it certainly could have an important effect on the quantity.

Corporate debt (not covered by Smith) may be expanded by a similar route. The nonborrowing corporation is a familiar figure: one that has elected to forego debt financing even though its financial condition could have supported quite a bit of it. Recently these ordinances of self-denial have been weakening. Some corporations that formerly never borrowed have started to do so. Some who hesitate to make a direct and open change have resorted to the use of captive finance subsidiaries to do about the same thing. (Parenthetically I might add that I fail to understand why banks encourage this practice by giving such captives better credit terms than they give the parent corporations.)

In the same vein, the trade news of state and local government financing report quite frequently these days of the offering of new issues by governmental units that had not approached the capital markets for many years.

All of these circumstances add up to the same general possibility: that along with the innovations of banks, borrowers are innovating in the use of credit—or at least experimenting—and thus the computation of equilibria levels of debt may require new parameters.

All of these comments, however, deal with what might be termed the microanalytical elements of debt quality: the internal financial ability of these economic units to service debt. Very possibly, however, the biggest change in the quality of debt lies outside these debt units and at a macroanalytical level. The much greater stability of income and cash flow during the past generation has removed the most frequent source of debt default.

The quality of credit may have deteriorated a bit recently but this backsliding is modest compared with the advance since the 1920s. The reasons for improvement are numerous; two important ones are: (1) a better tailoring of debt terms to the ability of borrowers to pay and (2) more precise instruments for measuring borrowers' ability to pay. The first point is mainly the conversion of most debts to serial or installment form, already mentioned as an innovation of the 1930s. The measurement of ability to pay is associated with more precise use of cash flow analysis. A comparison of the security analysis textbooks used in the 1920s with those now in use illustrate this latter point better than I could in limited time.

There are offsets, of course. Mortgage debt used to be in lump sum maturities but the debt-to-value ratio limits would seldom be higher than two-thirds and often as low as one-half. Now conventional mortgage loans are in installment form but often for four-fifths and sometimes even more.

It would have been helpful if Smith had emphasized rather more forcefully the extent to which his optimistic picture depended on that assumption that future monetary and fiscal policy will be effective in reducing cyclical instability. We all hope this is a correct assumption and recent favorable experience would seem to support this view.

Nevertheless, one part of our financial structure has not changed: its dependence on a high degree of confidence in the financial community—an intangible that does not fit easily into models or equations. For example, Gaines's paper referred several times to the fact that the negotiable certificate of deposit could be used as a planned source of funds by only a few big banks. That is not only true, but even more true in 1965 than it was in 1964. A relatively few bank failures in 1964 involving solicitation of money by the route of negotiable certificates of deposit through money brokers and involving some much-publicized losses to a few investors was so widely noted that the number of banks that had access to this source of funds was reduced.

The financial structure can be considered a kind of unstable equilibrium: in equilibrium under ordinary circumstances, but sensitive to external shocks. Relatively modest and often quite accidental events can upset the system. If an initial shock does not have repercussions, then the system can survive this one shock, but if it starts to have secondary effects then the system can be upset. Small shocks such as the crisis of confidence in the dollar in the fall of 1960, a sharp deflation of savings and loan holding company stocks, and some increase in bank failures have so far failed to have aftereffects. We can hope that this continues to be the case—but can we be completely confident that it will always be so?

EFFECTS OF MONETARY POLICY, I: THE IMPACT OF FEDERAL RESERVE ACTIONS ON FINANCIAL VARIABLES

A MODEL OF FEDERAL RESERVE BEHAVIOR*

John H. Wood

I. INTRODUCTION: PURPOSE AND APPROACH OF THE STUDY

One of the most prevalent features of macroeconomic models has been their treatment of government policy variables as exogenous. While variables such as income, employment, and prices are considered to be influenced by actions of the fiscal and monetary authorities, policy instruments such as tax rates and the Federal Reserve System's portfolio of securities are treated as free from the influence of income, employment, and prices. But if the causal relation is not in fact one way, this procedure results in inconsistent estimates of the parameters in equations describing the behavior of the private sector of the economy. If government policy makers do not behave randomly with respect to economic events, then we must treat their policy instruments as jointly dependent variables and introduce behavioral equations explaining movements in those instruments.

There has been some movement in recent years, at least with respect to the monetary sector, in the direction of an endogenous treatment of government policies. For example, whereas the stock of money formerly was universally treated as exogenous, de Leeuw and Teigen[1] have estimated models in which the money stock is determined jointly by supply

*This paper was prepared while the author was employed by the Board of Governors of the Federal Reserve System, but it should be emphasized that the results contained herein do not necessarily reflect the views of the Board of Governors or its staff. I wish to acknowledge helpful discussions with Frank de Leeuw, Patric H. Hendershott, Stephen P. Taylor, Dale K. Osborne, James Bennett, and Neva Van Peski and also the extensive computational assistance of Mrs. Ann R. Walka and Louis Zeller.

[1]Frank de Leeuw, "A Model of Financial Behavior," in J. S. Duesenberry *et al.* (eds.), *The Brookings Quarterly Econometric Model of the United States* (Chicago: Rand McNally, 1965), pp. 465–530; and Ronald L. Teigen, "Demand and Supply Functions for Money in the U.S.: Some Structural Estimates," *Econometrica*, Vol. 32 (October, 1964), pp. 476–509.

and demand forces, and the exogenous policy-controlled variables are total bank reserves less member bank borrowing from the Federal Reserve (unborrowed reserves), required reserve ratios against bank deposits, the maximum rate payable on time deposits, and the discount rate.[2] These efforts represent substantial steps in the right direction, but are sufficient only if the Federal Reserve both exercises absolute control over, for example, unborrowed reserves and behaves randomly with respect to events in the private and other government sectors.

Further, treatment of the behavior of government policy makers as endogenous is desirable not only because such treatment may improve our estimates of the private sector but also because the behavior of policy makers is in itself interesting.

The approach that will be followed in the present study may be summarized as follows: We will suppose the Federal Reserve to possess a utility function relating its conception of the public's welfare to income, employment, price levels, and the balance of payments. We will then assume that the Federal Reserve manages its portfolio of government securities in such a way as to maximize utility subject to the constraints imposed by its view of the structure of the economy, including its forecasts of the exogenous variables entering the system. This is analogous to the conditional maximization approach that traditionally has been applied in economic theory to the behavior of consumers and firms. This application of the conditional maximization approach to the formulation of macroeconomic policy owes its development to H. Theil and other Netherlands economists.[3]

The excellent discussions by Theil, Holt,[4] and others regarding the systematic approach to the formulation of macroeconomic policy referred to above have been confined to the realm of *normative* economics, that is, to how economic policy *ought to be* formulated. The major hypothesis to be presented and tested in this paper is that the Federal Reserve System has in fact been behaving more or less in the sophisticated manner recommended by these writers.[5] This hypothesis results in

---

[2]De Leeuw utilizes all four of these policy variables, while only the first two enter Teigen's model.

[3]Cf. H. Theil, *Optimal Decision Rules for Government and Industry* (Amsterdam: North Holland, 1965), and the bibliography contained therein.

[4]C. C. Holt, "Linear Decision Rules for Economic Stabilization and Growth," *Quarterly Journal of Economics,* Vol. LXXVI (February, 1962), pp. 20–45.

[5]This is not the same as asserting that decisions of the Federal Open Market Committee are the results of exercises in marginal analysis and the differential calculus. But the model is based upon the assumption that the manner in which the FOMC approaches its responsibilities, well known to be rough and highly subjective, results in policies very similar to those which would have been produced by the maximization of a well-defined utility function subject to the constraints of a complete and logically consistent model of the economy. I have nothing to add along these lines to the arguments advanced by F. Machlup in his "Marginal Analysis and Empirical Research," *American Economic Review,* Vol. XXXVI (September, 1946), pp. 519–54.

a behavioral equation for the Federal Reserve System which will be estimated within the framework of a model of the financial markets developed by de Leeuw.[6] If monetary policy actions do in fact affect the behavior of private institutions and individuals, it is necessary to treat the Federal Reserve behavioral equations as part of a larger model in order to obtain consistent estimates of the parameters of those equations.

The objective of this study is to develop and test a model that describes quantitatively the reaction of the monetary authorities to variations in their targets and in nonpolicy controlled forces influencing those targets. It is hoped that our results will move us toward the position of being able to discard such abstruse and confusing terms as "easy," "tight," "less ease," and "leaning against the wind," normally used in descriptions of monetary policy actions, and permit us to substitute in their place parameters measuring the response of Federal Reserve instruments to movements in targets and exogenous forces.

II. THE MODEL AND ITS ESTIMATION

A. The Model

We will introduce in this section (1) alternative statements of what seem to be plausible preference or utility functions of the Federal Reserve System and (2) a simple and rather naïve system of equations that is assumed to describe the Federal Reserve's view of the structure of the economy. We will assume that the Federal Reserve conducts open market operations such that (1) is maximized subject to the constraints imposed by (2). This process produces an equation explaining one aspect of Federal Reserve behavior which is then estimated by ordinary least squares and two-stage least squares on the basis of quarterly data during the period 1952–63.

Speeches and policy statements of Federal Reserve officials are commonly focused upon problems and policies involved in the attainment of goals relating to output (or real income), unemployment, the balance of payments, and price levels.[7] It must therefore be supposed that any statement that pretends to approximate the preferences or utilities of the Federal Reserve will contain variables relating to each of these four categories. If the dimensions of each of these categories can be summarized to the Federal Reserve's satisfaction by a single "target" variable[8] (for example, output summarized by deflated gross national prod-

[6] F. de Leeuw, "A Condensed Model of Financial Behavior" (Mimeographed paper) (Federal Reserve Board, July, 1964).

[7] See, for example, the "Record of Policy Actions of the Federal Open Market Committee" contained in any recent *Annual Report of the Board of Governors of the Federal Reserve System.*

[8] Defined below in Section B.

uct) and if the Federal Reserve possesses a static quadratic disutility function containing specific desires with respect to each of these target variables for a given time period, the Federal Reserve's disutility function for period t may be written

$$d_t = w_1(Y_t - \overset{*}{Y}_t)^2 + w_2(U_t - \overset{*}{U}_t)^2 + w_3(BP_t - \overset{*}{BP}_t)^2 + w_4(P_t - \overset{*}{P}_t)^2 \quad (1)$$

where Y is gross national product in constant dollars, U is the unemployment rate, BP is the current surplus in the balance of payments, and P is an index of prices. The starred variables denote values of the targets that the Federal Reserve desires to attain in period t. Disutility, d, is the weighted sum of squared deviations of realized from desired values of the target variables. The weights, w_i, signify the importance attached by the Federal Reserve to the attainment of its desires. If all of the desired target values are in fact realized, then disutility is zero.

It is useful at this point to discuss in what sense, if any, equation (1) is static. It is obvious upon examination that this disutility function contains some arguments that have implications for the utilities of the electorate (and therefore of the policy makers) mainly in future periods. Certainly the price level and the balance of payments during period t are not directly related to the utilities of the public during that same period. These variables are important only insofar as they affect variables, such as real income and employment, that enter directly into the utilities of individuals during the present and future periods. Given current real income, movements in the price level are important for reasons associated with the distribution of income in the current and in future periods and for their effect upon expectations concerning future price changes and therefore upon current and future spending decisions. Thus, a price level index enters the preference function because it is useful as a proxy variable for income distribution and because it is related to future levels of income and employment. Similarly, the balance of payments is included in our static preference function because of the apparent conviction that, if our receipts and expenditures vis-à-vis foreigners are not eventually brought into balance, all kinds of catastrophic events will at some future time descend not only upon our own economy but upon that of the entire free world.

In brief, the inclusion of price level and balance of payments variables in our preference function may be rationalized as follows. The "true" utility function is dynamic and includes only present and future values of variables related to employment and to the level and distribution of real income. But the policy makers, rightly or wrongly, do not feel that they have a dynamic model that adequately relates current policies to future levels of income and employment. As a result, they rely upon the simple models available to them and upon the belief that price level instability and continuing imbalances in international receipts and payments bode ill for future levels of income and employment.[9]

The Federal Reserve System also accepts as a short-term objective the "maintenance of orderly conditions in the government security market."[10] The goal is stated in short-run terms, although the "maintenance of orderly conditions. . . . ." during some current period is important presumably because such conditions are conducive to favorable developments with respect to longer run objectives (future levels of real income and employment). It will be assumed here that by "disorderly conditions in the government security market" the Federal Reserve means large movements in interest rates arising from seasonality and from those aspects of speculation, Treasury financing, and other factors not directly related to longer run trend or even cyclical developments. It is of course impossible, without the aid of a highly sophisticated model, to distinguish between those interest rate movements which are "disorderly" and those that are due to trend or cyclical developments. But it is possible to identify some of the sources of these "disorderly" interest rate movements. Two such sources are seasonal shifts in the demand for money and large issues of government securities. The latter is related to the size of the Federal deficit and therefore to the business cycle, but the Federal Reserve may nevertheless wish to dampen the immediate interest rate effect of a large Treasury financing operation and to spread the effects over a fairly long period. These considerations suggest an additional term for the disutility function, namely, $w_5 r^2_{st}$, where r_{st} denotes that change during period t in "the" interest rate which is due to disorderly conditions (that is, seasonal factors and Treasury financing operations) and w_5 is the weight attached to the square of disorderly interest rate movements. "The" interest rate is that rate or index of rates to which the monetary authorities refer when they speak of disorderly conditions. A precise definition will not be required for the purposes of our model. Our disutility function may now be written

$$d_t = w_1(Y_t - \overset{*}{Y}_t)^2 + w_2(U_t - \overset{*}{U}_t)^2 + w_3(BP_t - \overset{*}{BP}_t)^2 + w_4(P_t - \overset{*}{P}_t)^2 + w_5 r^2_{st} \qquad (2)$$

This preference function is subject to the criticism that society's desires with respect to certain target variables are not in fact symmetric. Equation (2) implies that if the income goal is, say, $700 billion during

[9]Thus, discussions of trade-offs between, for example, current levels of income and prices are in reality based largely upon views concerning trade-offs between current and future levels of income.

[10]See, for example, "Record of Policy Actions of the Federal Open Market Committee" for March 4–5, 1953, in the *Fortieth Annual Report of the Board of Governors of the Federal Reserve System,* pp. 86–92.

some time period, the policy makers will be precisely as unhappy if an income of $720 billion is achieved as if income attains a level of only $680 billion. The marginal utility of income in equation (2) is negative for $Y_t > Y_t^*$, suggesting policies to prevent the growth of income above Y_t^* even when this target is not in conflict with other objectives.[11] If society's desires with respect to income, unemployment, and the balance of payments are insatiable, our preference function should be written as follows:

$$\phi_t = g_1 Y_t - g_2 U_t + g_3 BP_t - g_4 (P_t - P_t^*)^2 - g_5 r_{st}^2 \qquad (3)$$

This preference function implies that there exists no upper limit to the level of income or to the surplus in the balance of payments desired and also that there is no lower limit to the desired rate of unemployment.[12]

We assume that the Federal Reserve seeks to minimize (2) or maximize (3) (or to optimize some function containing the most appropriate aspects of [2] and [3]) subject to the constraints imposed by its view of the structure of the economy. This structure takes the form of a system of equations relating each of the five target variables to (1) an intermediate financial variable through which the Federal Reserve thinks it affects economic conditions, (2) the federal government surplus, (3) the balance of trade (primarily for balance of payments reasons), and (4) recent changes in the target variables. The intermediate financial variable which is most important (in the view of the Federal Reserve) in the causal chain between its instrument, open market operations, and real economic activity may be the money stock (narrowly or broadly defined), total bank reserves, unborrowed reserves, free reserves, or some other variable. Lagged movements in the target variables are included as determinants of current movements in these same variables because the Federal Reserve does not possess a complete reliable model of the economic structure and must, as a result, make use of rather naïve projections. A rationalization for the inclusion of recent changes in, for example, income as a determinant of the change in income during period *t* is as follows: We do not know all of the predetermined variables and their coefficients which affect income, but, whatever they are, they have been causing income to, say, rise in recent periods. Hence, given the government surplus, the balance of trade, and the appropriate intermediate financial variable, our best guess is that the unspecified predeter-

---

[11]For a discussion of this and related points, see J. H. Wood, "Linear Decision Rules for Economic Stabilization and Growth: Comment," *Quarterly Journal of Economics*, Vol. LXXIX (May, 1965), pp. 310–16.

[12]This formulation is more likely to be inappropriate for the balance of payments than for income and unemployment. A continuing large surplus in the balance of payments carries with it as many problems and difficulties for the United States as does a deficit.

mined variables will continue to exert an upward influence on income during the current period.

The Federal Reserve's view of the structure of the economy, the "policy model," may be written as follows, where all the coefficients are positive:

$$Y_t = a_1F_t - b_{11}S_t + b_{12}BT_t + b_{13}L_Y - b_{14}L_U - b_{15}L_{BP} + b_{16}L_P + v_1 \quad (4.1)$$

$$U_t = -a_2F_t + b_{21}S_t - b_{22}BT_t - b_{23}L_Y + b_{24}L_U + b_{25}L_{BP} - b_{26}L_P + v_2 \quad (4.2)$$

$$BP_t = -a_3F_t + b_{31}S_t + b_{32}BT_t - b_{33}L_Y + b_{34}L_U + b_{35}L_{BP} - b_{36}L_P + v_3 \quad (4.3)$$

$$P_t = a_4F_t - b_{41}S_t + b_{42}BT_t + b_{43}L_Y - b_{44}L_U - b_{45}L_{BP} + b_{46}L_P + v_4 \quad (4.4)$$

$$r_{st} = -a_5F_t + cT_t + J_t + v_5 \quad (4.5)$$

All variables are expressed in terms of first differences and are defined as follows:[13]

Y_t = change in real gross national product between periods $t-1$ and t.

U_t = change in average unemployment rate between periods $t-1$ and t.

BP_t = change in the balance of payments surplus between periods $t-1$ and t.

P_t = change in index of prices between periods $t-1$ and t.

F_t = change in the intermediate financial variable through which the Federal Reserve strives to influence the target variables.

r_{st} = the interest rate movement due strictly to the change in the intermediate financial variable, F_t, seasonal influences, J_t, and the change during period t in the quantity of federal government securities outstanding outside the Treasury, T_t.

S_t = change in the federal government surplus in constant dollars.

BT_t = change in the balance of trade.[14]

L_Y, L_U, L_{BP}, L_P = lagged changes in Y, U, BP, and P, respectively.

v_i = stochastic disturbance term in equation (4.i).

Increases in most intermediate financial variables through which the Federal Reserve is likely to operate exert upward influences on Y and P (hence positive signs precede a_1 and a_4) and downward influences on U and BP (hence negative signs precede a_2 and a_3). Increases in S lead to upward movements in U and BP and downward movements in Y and P. Increases in BT cause Y, BP, and P to rise and U to fall. Examining

[13]The variables entering the final form of the model will be defined more precisely in Section B below.

[14]Exports and the exogenous portions of federal expenditures, such as, perhaps, defense spending, would seem superior to BT and S as predetermined variables in the policy model. But equations containing the narrower variables explain less of the variation in Federal Reserve purchases and sales of securities than do equations containing BT and S, suggesting that open market operations are in fact executed subject to forecasts of BT and S.

equation (4.1), it is a reasonable guess that those unspecified forces causing Y to increase in recent past periods will continue to exert an upward influence on Y in period t. Hence a positive sign precedes b_{13}. For analogous reasons, the parallel coefficients in the remaining equations, b_{24}, b_{35}, and b_{46} are preceded by positive signs. Returning to (4.1), it also seems reasonable to suppose that the forces that have caused recent increases in P will continue to induce increases in Y (thus b_{16} is preceded by a positive sign) and that past increases in U and BP result from forces that will exert depressing influences on Y (so that b_{14} and b_{15} are preceded by negative signs). However, one must be less certain of the signs preceding b_{14}, b_{15}, and b_{16} (and b_{23}, b_{25}, b_{26}, b_{33}, b_{34}, b_{36}, b_{43}, b_{44}, and b_{45}) than of those preceding b_{13}, b_{24}, b_{35}, and b_{46}.

It remains to introduce the instrument of monetary policy which we hope to explain in the present paper—the change in the quantity of government securities held by the Federal Reserve, G_t.[15] This is done in equation (5), which relates F_t to G_t:

$$F_t = \rho_t G_t + Z_t. \tag{5}$$

Equation (5) is a definitional statement in which Z_t includes all factors other than $\rho_t G_t$ which determine F_t. These factors include the U.S. monetary gold stock, currency in circulation, Federal Reserve float, and Treasury, nonmember, and foreign accounts at Federal Reserve banks. The coefficient of G_t, ρ_t, has a time subscript attached because the effect of G_t on F_t, given Z_t, varies over time. ρ_t will usually depend upon reserve requirement ratios. The precise definitions of ρ_t and Z_t depend upon our specification of F_t.

The leading candidate for F_t is free reserves or some variant thereof.

---

[15]H. G. Johnson and W. G. Dewald ("Analysis of the Objectives of Monetary Policy," in Dean Carson (ed.), *Banking and Monetary Studies* [Homewood, Illinois: Richard D. Irwin, Inc., 1963], pp. 171–89) fall short of an analysis of Federal Reserve behavior when they consider as instruments of monetary policy the stock of money, free reserves, the Treasury bill rate, and the Treasury long-term bond rate. These variables are influenced by Federal Reserve actions but also by many other forces. Such an approach casts light on Federal Reserve behavior only if the intermediate financial variable studied is completely (or almost so) controlled by the Federal Reserve and manipulated as an instrument of policy. And even in such a case, estimates of the coefficients will be inconsistent if the Federal Reserve succeeds in influencing without a lag longer than the period of observation (a quarter in the Johnson and Dewald study) the variables to which it responds.

The same criticisms may be made of G. L. Reuber, "The Objectives of Canadian Monetary Policy, 1949–61: Empirical "Trade-Offs" and the Reaction Function of the Authorities," *Journal of Political Economy*, Vol. LXXII (April, 1964), pp. 109–32.

G. Kaufman ("The Supply of Money: A Supply Function Explaining Federal Reserve Behavior" [Mimeographed paper, Federal Reserve Bank of Chicago, January, 1964]) considers as instruments of monetary policy the same variables as those employed by Johnson and Dewald. Kaufman's paper constitutes an advance, however, in that he explicitly brings into his analysis desired values of the target variables.

Free reserves are widely regarded by students of the Federal Reserve System as the most reliable indicator of monetary policy.[16] It is clear that, although Federal Reserve publications emphasize the limitations of free reserves as an indicator of policy, the monetary authorities regard free reserves as an important element in the monetary policy process:

> One of the things that the credit market observes in gauging the emphasis of current monetary policy—that is, whether it is tending to be stimulative, neutral, or restraining in its effects upon the volume of credit and money—is the trend of changes in the net reserve position of member banks. The net reserve position is defined as the difference between the excess reserves of member banks and member bank borrowing . . . .
>
> While monetary policy necessarily influences the net reserve position of banks, this position is also much affected by bank responses to the many cross currents that stem from the interplay of diverse market forces and by unforeseen developments. Considering the complexity of the forces affecting the net reserve position in the short run—a fact reflected in the many sizable and irregular fluctuations in this measure from week to week—little or no significance can be attached to the shift during a single week. However, [a] downward trend in net free reserves over a period of several months preceding [a] particular week [confirms] that Federal Reserve policy [has] been tending to become somewhat less stimulative with regard to the growth of credit and money than it had been earlier.
>
> In general, the net reserve position of member banks is an important gauge of pressures on bank reserves. When net free reserves rise, the result is an increased marginal availability of reserves, which the banking system can readily use to expand credit. But when member bank borrowings grow relative to excess reserves, credit expansion comes under restraint. In this process individual banks find extra reserves more difficult and expensive to obtain, and they come under increasing pressure to repay advances from the Federal Reserve. As this continues over time, a net borrowed reserve position emerges for the banking system as a whole.
>
> Of course, the net reserve position of banks is only one index of credit and monetary tendencies and of the direction of reserve banking policy, and in this respect it has to be considered in relation to banks' desires to hold free reserves and to other fundamental indicators of credit conditions. The central task of monetary policy is to regulate expansion in bank reserves, bank credit, and money so that growth in real output is accomplished with a minimum of either inflationary or deflationary pressures. Changes in bank credit and money, along with other changes in credit, the flow of savings, and interest

---

[16]See K. Brunner and A. H. Meltzer, "The Federal Reserve's Attachment to the Free Reserve Concept" (Subcommittee on Domestic Finance, House Committee on Banking and Currency) (Washington, D.C.: U.S. Government Printing Office, May 7, 1964); W. G. Dewald, "Free Reserves, Total Reserves, and Monetary Control," *Journal of Political Economy*, Vol. LXXI (April, 1963), pp. 141–53; and A. J. Meigs, *Free Reserves and the Money Supply* (Chicago: University of Chicago Press, 1962).

rates, are among key indices of the credit situation in the short as well as in the longer run.[17]

A complete model of Federal Reserve behavior would encompass several or all of the indices of "credit and monetary tendencies" mentioned in the above quotation. But, for reasons of manageability and emphasis, the present study will focus upon free reserves as that variable which appears to be foremost in the minds of the formulators of monetary policy. The particular variant of free reserves that will be used in the present study is free reserves adjusted for required reserve ratios. The amount by which commercial banks are able to expand credit as the result of an increase in free reserves (due, say, to increased excess reserves because of security purchases by the Federal Reserve) is inversely related to reserve requirement ratios. Hence, it seems reasonable to assume that the change in average free reserves divided by the average reserve requirement ratio on member bank deposits, $\Delta\left(\frac{R_f}{k}\right)_t \equiv F_t$, is "the" intermediate financial variable through which the Federal Reserve conceives itself as influencing the economy.

We have, from the "bank reserve equation,"[18]

$$R_{f_t} = G_{L_t} + A_t - R_{r_t} \tag{6}$$

where the variables are defined in terms of average levels over the period of observation and

R_{f_t} = average level of free reserves in member banks of the Federal Reserve System during period t.

G_{L_t} = average quantity of U.S. government securities held by the Federal Reserve during period t.

A_t = average level during period t of the U.S. monetary gold stock plus Treasury currency outstanding plus Federal Reserve float less currency in circulation less Treasury cash accounts less nonmember bank, foreign, and other accounts at the Federal Reserve.[19]

R_{r_t} = average level of reserves required against all deposits (demand and time) at member banks during period t.

Dividing both sides of (6) by k, the average reserve requirement

[17] *The Federal Reserve System: Purposes and Functions* (5th ed.; Washington, D.C.: Board of Governors of the Federal Reserve System, 1963), pp. 222–24.

Analyses of statements and publications issuing from the Federal Reserve cannot provide "proof" that the monetary authorities act in any specified manner. Nor, in my view, do such materials even constitute useful evidence to be applied toward hypotheses of Federal Reserve behavior. But these statements and publications can be useful insofar as they are "suggestive" of hypotheses which might then be tested in more systematic ways, that is, by analyses of the behavior, as opposed to the statements, of policy makers.

[18] For the bank reserve equation, see the first table, entitled "Member Bank Reserves, Federal Reserve Bank Credit, and Related Items" in the section of any *Federal Reserve Bulletin* entitled "Financial and Business Statistics."

[19] For discussions of each of these factors "supplying and absorbing reserve funds," see *The Federal Reserve System: Purposes and Functions, op. cit.*, chap. xii.

on all member bank deposits, taking the first-difference of both sides, and rearranging gives

$$\Delta\left(\frac{R_f}{k}\right)_t = \left(\frac{R_{f_t}}{k_t}\right) - \left(\frac{R_{f_{t-1}}}{k_{t-1}}\right) = \frac{1}{k_t} G_t + \frac{1}{k_t} (\Delta A_t - \Delta R_{r_t}) \tag{7}$$

$$- \left(\frac{\Delta k_t}{k_t k_{t-1}}\right) R_{f_{t-1}} = \rho_t G_t + Z_t$$

where

$$\rho_t = \frac{1}{k_t}$$

$$G_t = \Delta G_{L_t}$$

$$Z_t = \frac{1}{k_t} (\Delta A_t - \Delta R_{r_t}) \quad \left(\frac{\Delta k_t}{k_t k_{t-1}}\right) R_{f_{t-1}}$$

We may obtain a behavioral equation explaining the Federal Reserve's conduct of open market operations by substituting equation (5), the variables being defined as shown following equation (7), into equations (4). The result is then substituted into the appropriate preference function, which will be similar to equations (2) and (3). The preference function thus constrained is then optimized by differentiating with respect to G_t, equating the result to zero, and solving for G_t. This yields an equation for the Federal Reserve's "optimal policy" or "maximizing strategy" with respect to open market operations, the parameters of which may be estimated from observed data by least squares regression. Before presenting these estimates, we shall discuss the data to be utilized.

B. The Data

The first major problem one confronts in explaining Federal Reserve actions is that of seasonality. Open market operations are to a large extent directed at offsetting the effects on member bank reserves of seasonal movements in such variables as currency in circulation, Treasury cash holdings, and float. To remove seasonal variation from Federal Reserve purchases and sales of securities, G_t, and other factors influencing the various measures of bank reserves, Z_t, would not only suppress large amounts of interesting information concerning the Federal Reserve's (seasonal) behavior, but would cause the information not so suppressed to be distorted.[20] The same applies to the Federal Reserve's

[20]For discussions of the bias caused in estimates of parameters in linear models, the data of which have been seasonally adjusted by the multiplicative methods now available, see M. C. Lovell, "Seasonal Adjustment of Economic Time Series and Multiple Regression Analysis," *Journal of the American Statistical Association*, Vol. 58 (December, 1963), pp. 993–1010; and G. W. Ladd, "Regression Analysis of Seasonal Data," *Journal of the American Statistical Association*, Vol. 59 (June, 1964), pp. 402–21.

efforts to cause or permit seasonal variation in some possible definitions of F_t (such as total member bank reserves or the money stock) in order to promote stability in the financial markets. Thus, it was decided not to seasonally adjust any of the components of equations (5) and (7). It was also decided not to seasonally adjust the components of equation (4.5), the observed variables of which include T_t and J_t in addition to F_t, because that equation and those variables are designed partly to explain the Federal Reserve's seasonal behavior with respect to interest rate movements.

But in other areas affecting the conduct of open market operations, the Federal Reserve gives ample indication of responding to data which have been adjusted for seasonal variation—gross national product, balance of trade, balance of payments, and unemployment. (There is so little systematic seasonal variation in aggregate price indices that seasonal adjustment of prices is not necessary.) For example, when GNP falls, as it customarily does in the first quarter of the year, the Federal Reserve does not respond with an antirecession policy, as it might if GNP fell during the fourth quarter. Only if the decline is greater than usual for the first quarter will the Federal Reserve behave as if a recession is at hand. Consequently, we have seasonally adjusted those target variables which contain substantial seasonal variation—Y, U, and BP.

These considerations do not suggest that the Federal Reserve has a lower target for GNP in the first than in the fourth quarter. The use of a seasonally adjusted series for GNP is a simple way of taking account of dynamic factors in what appears on the surface to be a static preference function. Institutional and behavioral characteristics of the U.S. economy are such that, if an increase in real GNP over the fourth quarter of the preceding year is to be achieved, expansive policies of an enormous magnitude would be required on the part of the monetary authorities during the first quarter of the year (and during preceding quarters, given a lag in the impact of monetary policy). And expansive actions of the magnitude required might produce undesirable results for other target variables, such as prices and the balance of payments, and in this and other ways inhibit future increases in GNP.

The Federal Reserve, it is assumed in the present paper, maximizes utility subject to the constraints imposed by (1) the equations describing its view of the economic structure, (2) forecasts of the exogenous variables in the system, and (3) estimates of the lagged variables in the model. While the period of observation utilized in the empirical portions of this paper is three months, the decision period of the Federal Reserve is much shorter. In fact, forecasts of future values of some variables and estimates of past or present values of other variables and their use in decisions goes on weekly, daily, and even hourly. Thus, quarterly observations are able to capture only the average Federal Reserve response to average Federal

Reserve forecasts and estimates. If we assume that the Federal Reserve *forecasts perfectly* for very short periods in advance and *estimates perfectly* the values of target variables which have occurred in the very recent past, we can enter current (quarterly) values of the forecast variables and, in case of the lagged target variables, use changes between the current period and some earlier period or periods.[21]

The variables appearing in equations (4) are defined for purposes of our empirical investigations below. All variables are in terms of changes between periods $t - 1$ and t (the variables appearing in equation [7] have been defined above and are daily averages measured in millions of dollars):[22]

The balance of payments surplus (BP) and the surplus in the balance of trade in goods and services (BT) are seasonally adjusted Department of Commerce estimates in millions of current dollars.

Gross national product (Y) is seasonally adjusted and is in billions of 1954 dollars. The effects of steel strikes have been removed from Y on the assumption that the Federal Reserve feels incapable of offsetting decreases in GNP in the face of such events. In particular, we have let Y for 3/53 equal that for 2/52 and Y for 3/59 and 4/59 equal that for 2/59. In other words, we are supposing the monetary authorities to ignore the declines in GNP due to the steel strikes that occurred in 3/52, 3/59, and 4/59.

The price index used (P) is the component of the Wholesale Price Index termed Industrial Materials. Industrial Materials comprise 44.3 percent of the Wholesale Price Index and form the most sensitive part of the overall index. Articles appearing in the *Federal Reserve Bulletin*[23] that are devoted to discussions of price movements emphasize the Industrial Materials Index and its subcomponent, Sensitive Industrial Materials, much more than the aggregate Wholesale and Consumer Price Indices. The Federal Reserve evidently feels that movements in prices of industrial materials signal later movements in consumer prices.

The seasonally adjusted unemployment rate (U) is the ratio of unemployment to the civilian labor force as defined by the Bureau of Labor Statistics.

Federal Reserve purchases and sales of securities (G) and the quantity of U.S. marketable securities outside the Treasury and U.S. government agencies and trust funds (T) are in millions of current dollars.

Forecasts of the federal surplus may be made with somewhat more

---

[21]Aggregation over time will, in circumstances such as those described above, introduce bias into our estimates of the parameters of the final model, the bias increasing directly with the length of the lags involved in the actual decision process.

[22]These and other data used to obtain the ordinary least squares estimates presented in Part II-C below are listed in Appendix B.

[23]Cf. the January issues for 1951, 1954, 1956, 1958, 1962, and 1965.

confidence than can, say, the balance of trade, and it is the total federal surplus for any year (fiscal or calendar) rather than just the surplus for each quarter that holds implications for income, unemployment, prices, and the balance of payments. Thus, the definition of the federal surplus used is the annual cash surplus in billions of dollars deflated by the Wholesale Price Index. This series is smoothed and first differences are taken of the smoothed data.[24]

The targets entering the preference functions are defined as follows. The variables on the left-hand side of each equation are in terms of first differences and those on the right-hand side are levels:

Y^*_t $= 348.6\ (1.009)^{t-1} - GNP_{t-1}$, where $t = 1$ in the first quarter of 1952 and GNP is seasonally adjusted gross national product at annual rates in 1954 dollars. The term 348.6 is the value of GNP, so defined, for the first quarter of 1952. This is similar to the "potential GNP" advanced by the Council of Economic Advisers. The Council assumes a rate of increase in potential GNP of 3.5 percent per annum. We use a quarterly rate of increase of 0.9 percent.[25]

BP^*_t $= -BP_{t-1}$ on the assumption that what is desired is a "balanced" balance of payments.

U^*_t $= .04 - U_{t-1}$ if the Federal Reserve aims at a particular rate of unemployment. The precise constant chosen (.04 here) makes little difference in the empirical results.

P^*_t $= 0$. We assume that the Federal Reserve desires neither inflation nor deflation.

It was found, after extensive experimentation in some instances, that the distributed lags of the target variables which appear best to describe Federal Reserve open market operations take very simple forms. These lagged variables are defined as follows, where the variables on the right side of each equation again denote levels and the period of observation is one quarter:

$$L_Y = Y_t - Y_{t-1}$$

$$L_U = U_t - U_{t-1}$$

$$L_P = P_t - P_{t-8}$$

L_{BP} is omitted because none of the various distributed lags of *BP* introduced into the empirical analysis made any contribution to the explanation of G_t. These definitions of the lagged variables suggest that the Federal Reserve reacts to short-run changes in income and employment, but only to longer run changes in the industrial materials price index.

[24]The smoothing is accomplished by a technique first used to interpolate quarterly from annual data and approximates the freehand smooth curve. The statistical technique, developed by Maurice Liebenberg and Hyman Kaitz, has the advantage over the graphical method of always yielding correct yearly totals. Cf. "Chain Formula to Obtain Quarterly Estimates from Annual Data," Technical Note No. 1 (Office of Business Economics, U.S. Department of Commerce).

[25]See, for example, *The Economic Report of the President,* January, 1965, pp. 81–83.

C. Estimation of the Model

1. ***Ordinary Least Squares.*** Preliminary investigation indicated that the following disutility function was most consistent with Federal Reserve behavior and the constraint equations (4) and (7) during the period 1952–63:

$$d_t = w_1(Y_t - \overset{*}{Y}_t)^2 + w_2U_t + w_3(BP_t - \overset{*}{BP}_t)^2 + w_4P_t^2 + w_5r_{st}^2 + w_6(\rho_tG_t)^2 \qquad (8)$$

Equation (8) suggests that the Federal Reserve has specific values in mind for all of the target variables ($P^* = r^*_{st} = [\rho_tG_t]^* = 0$) except U_t which it wants as low as possible. The variable $\rho_tG_t = \left(\frac{1}{k_t}\right) G_t$ appears as a target if the Federal Reserve attaches a cost to its actions, G_t, and the effects of those actions, ρ_tG_t. The ordinary bureaucratic preference for doing nothing, rather than risking a wrong action, is sufficient to explain a positive value for w_6.

We substitute equation (7) into (4) and the result into (8). Then, upon minimizing d_t, with respect to G_t and solving for G_t, omitting the stochastic terms v_i, we obtain:[26]

$$\begin{aligned} G_t = &- \frac{(a_1^2w_1 + a_3^2w_3 + a_4^2w_4 + a_5^2w_5)}{D}\frac{Z_t}{\rho_t} \\ &+ \frac{(a_1w_1b_{11} + a_3w_3b_{32} + a_4w_4b_{41})}{D}\frac{S_t}{\rho_t} \\ &+ \frac{(-a_1w_1b_{12} + a_3w_3b_{32} + a_4w_4b_{42})}{D}\frac{BT_t}{\rho_t} \\ &- \frac{(a_1w_1b_{13} + a_3w_3b_{33} + a_4w_4b_{43})}{D}\frac{L_Y}{\rho_t} \\ &+ \frac{(a_1w_1b_{14} + a_3w_3b_{34} + a_4w_4b_{44})}{D}\frac{L_U}{\rho_t} \\ &- \frac{(a_1w_1b_{16} + a_3w_3b_{36} + a_4w_4b_{46})}{D}\frac{L_P}{\rho_t} \\ &+ \frac{a_1w_1}{D}\frac{\overset{*}{Y}_t}{\rho_t} - \frac{a_3w_3}{D}\frac{\overset{*}{BP}_t}{\rho_t} + \frac{a_5w_5c}{D}\frac{T_t}{\rho_t} + \frac{a_2w_2}{2D}\frac{1}{\rho_t} \end{aligned} \qquad (9)$$

where $D = a_1^2w_1 + a_3^2w_3 + a_4^2w_4 + a_5^2w_5 + w_6$.

[26]When we have a quadratic preference function whose expected value is to be maximized subject to linear constraints, the solution is precisely the same as that decision which would have been obtained if all uncertainty had been disregarded at the beginning by replacing the disturbance terms by their expectations. This prop-

(Continued on next page)

Equation (9) may be written more briefly as

$$G = \Pi_1\left(\frac{Z_t}{\rho_t}\right) + \Pi_2\left(\frac{S_t}{\rho_t}\right) + \Pi_3\left(\frac{BT_t}{\rho_t}\right) + \Pi_4\left(\frac{L_Y}{\rho_t}\right) + \Pi_5\left(\frac{L_U}{\rho_t}\right) \tag{10}$$
$$+ \Pi_6\left(\frac{L_P}{\rho_t}\right) + \Pi_7\left(\frac{Y_t^*}{\rho_t}\right) + \Pi_8\left(\frac{BP_t^*}{\rho_t}\right) + \Pi_9\left(\frac{T_t}{\rho_t}\right) + \Pi_{10}\left(\frac{1}{\rho_t}\right).$$

A more thorough examination of Federal Reserve behavior would require the construction of a policy model in which, for example, the discount rate, legal reserve requirement ratios, and the minimum rate payable on time deposits would enter as instruments of monetary policy. Disutility, d_t, would then be minimized with respect to each of these instruments as well as open market operations. But we have, for purposes of the present paper, taken instruments of monetary policy other than the quantity of government securities held by the Federal Reserve as given. This does not mean that these other instruments are unimportant in the present model. Changes in the discount rate will influence excess reserves, and the maximum rate payable on time deposits will affect, among other things, the distribution between time and demand deposits and therefore k, the average reserve requirement ratio against all member bank deposits. Excess reserves and k both affect R_f/k and are therefore included among the factors taken into account in the minimization process described above.

All of the variables entering the disutility and constraint functions (7), (8), and (4) have been transformed in the minimization procedure by being divided by ρ_t (that is, multiplied by k_t). This reflects the condition that the greater is the average reserve requirement against member bank deposits, the more securities will the Federal Reserve be required to purchase or sell (that is, the greater must G_t be in absolute value) in order to achieve desired effects with respect to the target variables.

Given positive values for all of the weights, w_i, and for the coefficients a_i, b_{ij}, and c in equations (4) and (8), the signs expected for the coefficients in equations (9) and (10) are unambiguous except for that of BT_t/ρ_t, Π_3. The sign of Π_3 depends on the relative magnitudes of the weights and coefficients entering equations (4) and (8).

erty is known as "certainty equivalence." For the proof see H. Theil, *Economic Forecasts and Policy* (2d ed.; Amsterdam: North Holland, 1961), pp. 414–17, and C. C. Holt, F. Modigliani, J. F. Muth, and H. A. Simon, *Planning Production, Inventories, and Work Force* (Englewood Cliffs, N.J.: Prentice-Hall, Inc., 1960), pp. 123–30.

Note also that the seasonal factor, J_t, which was introduced into the analysis via equation (4.5), will not appear in equation (9) (below). It proved statistically insignificant in preliminary work. However, the omission of J_t here does not mean that seasonal influences are unimportant in the Federal Reserve's policy actions, because Z_t, which the Federal Reserve wishes to offset, other things equal, contains a great deal of seasonal variation.

The value of Π_1 should be minus unity if w_6, the weight attached to $(\rho_t G_t)^2$, is zero. Otherwise, $-1 < \Pi_1 < 0$ for $w_6 > 0$. The response of G_t to Z_t/ρ_t is closely akin to what Roosa has called the "defensive" responsibility of the Federal Reserve System:

> . . . the dual nature of the Federal Reserve System's responsibilities . . . [are] the *defensive,* avoiding mechanical disturbances that could interfere with the smooth functioning of the monetary system, and the *dynamic,* using the potentialities of control over the reserve base of a fractional reserve banking system to help promote economic growth within a pattern of sustained stability. It should be clear . . . at least with respect to open market operations, that there has in fact been a fusion of both types of responsibility. The uppermost concern at the Trading Desk every day is that the prevailing degree of pressure intended by the Federal Open Market Committee's policy (the *dynamic* aspect of the System's responsibilities) shall emerge from the day's confusion as a dominating force. Yet the specific action taken, more often than not, is directed toward offsetting or cushioning the effect of some mechanical by-product of the physical flow of payments (a *defensive* operation).[27]

Before estimating the complete equation (10), it might be interesting to see how much of the variation in the Federal Reserve's holdings of securities is in fact attributable to "defensive" operations—that is, consists of responses to variations in Z_t/ρ_t. The ordinary least squares regression of G_t on Z_t/ρ_t (constraining the usual constant to zero since we are using first differences), using quarterly data from the period, second quarter of 1952 through the fourth quarter of 1963, is

$$G_t = -\underset{(.048)}{.862}\left(\frac{Z_t}{\rho_t}\right) + e_t \tag{11}$$

The standard error of the estimated regression coefficient is shown under the estimate, e_t is the regression residual, and the R^2 adjusted for degrees of freedom is .875.[28] We thus see, as indicated by Roosa, that open market operations are predominately devoted to defensive operations, that is, to cushioning the impact of movements in the components of Z_t/ρ_t on F_t.

---

[27]Robert V. Roosa, *Federal Reserve Operations in the Money and Government Securities Markets* (New York: Federal Reserve Bank of New York, 1956), pp. 104–5. Italics are Roosa's.

[28]The Durbin-Watson statistic is .85, so that we must reject the hypothesis of independence of successive disturbances. One of the causes of autocorrelated disturbances is the omission of explanatory variables when the omitted variables are autocorrelated. It will be seen below that the addition of the other variables shown in equations (9) and (10) eliminates the autocorrelation present in the two-variable case shown in equation (11).

But the purpose of this study is to determine the response, if any, of the Federal Reserve System to such target variables as income, unemployment, prices, and the balance of payments. That is, does the introduction of such target variables and the predetermined variables influencing them add to our understanding of Federal Reserve behavior? An examination of movements in $e_t = G_t + .862\ Z_t/\rho_t$, shown in Chart I, suggests an important countercyclical element in open market operations over and above what is implicit in offsetting Z_t/ρ_t. Chart I indicates that G_t (positive for net open market purchases and negative for net

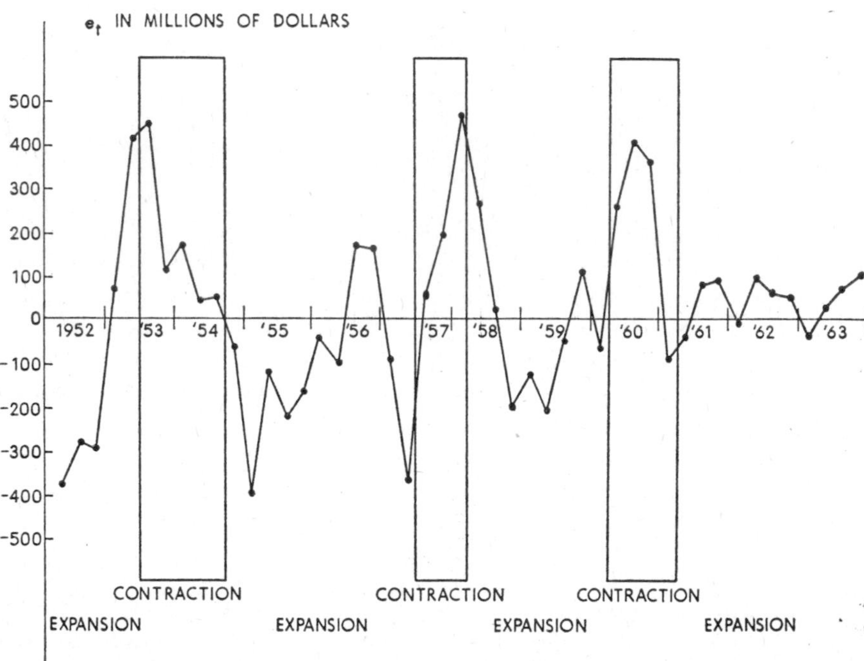

sales) has tended to be positive during contractions and negative during expansions, once we have taken account of the "defensive" component of open market operations. The only exception to this is the expansion period 1961–63, during which open market operations were conducted in such a way as to cause or permit increases in adjusted free reserves, R_f/k. While the balance of payments was worsening during this period, suggesting net open market sales of securities after accounting for defensive operations, conditions were such with regard to other targets that the Federal Reserve pursued expansionist policies: unemployment was at a higher level than during previous postwar expansions, the rate of growth in GNP was lower than in earlier expansions, and price level increases were absent or extremely small.

Estimation of the parameters of the complete model shown in equations (9) and (10) produced the following results:

$$\hat{G}_t = -\ .812\left(\frac{Z_t}{\rho_t}\right) + 26.2\left(\frac{S_t}{\rho_t}\right) + .154\left(\frac{BT_t}{\rho_t}\right) - 57.6\left(\frac{L_Y}{\rho_t}\right) + 50.2\left(\frac{L_U}{\rho_t}\right)$$

$$(.044) \qquad (21.1) \qquad (.071) \qquad (13.9) \qquad (34.6) \quad (12)$$

$$-\ 14.88\left(\frac{L_P}{\rho_t}\right) + 9.9\left(\frac{Y_t^*}{\rho_t}\right) - .013\left(\frac{BP_t^*}{\rho_t}\right) + .019\left(\frac{T_t}{\rho_t}\right) + 38.39\left(\frac{1}{\rho_t}\right)$$

$$(4.71) \qquad (5.0) \qquad (.052) \qquad (.007) \qquad (38.30)$$

where $\hat{G}_t$ is calculated from the regression equation. The adjusted R^2 for the equation is .943, and the Durbin-Watson statistic is 2.16, so that we do not reject the hypothesis of first-order independence of disturbances at either the 1 or 5 percent levels of significance. G, Z/ρ, BT/ρ, BP^*/ρ and T/ρ are measured in millions of dollars; S/ρ, L_Y/ρ, and Y^*/ρ in billions of dollars; and L_U/ρ and L_P/ρ in percentage points. The coefficient of L_Y/ρ, for example, indicates that a decrease in GNP/ρ of $1 billion (that is, a decrease in GNP of $8 billion when $k - 1/\rho = .125$) will induce an increase in the Federal Reserve's average holdings of government securities of $57.6 million during the same quarter.

The evidence is strong that the Federal Reserve reacts to recent GNP and price level changes, to Treasury debt management operations[29], to changes in the balance of trade and, of course, to Z/ρ. The coefficients of S/ρ, L_U/ρ, BP^*/ρ, Y^*/ρ, and $1/\rho$, while mostly promising and with the a priori expected signs, are not significantly different from zero at the 5 percent level.

The coefficient of Z/ρ is significantly different from minus unity at the 5 percent level, suggesting a nonzero value for w_6, the weight associated with $(\rho G)^2$. (See equation [8] and the discussion following that equation.)

An interesting question is whether our estimates of the parameters in the Federal Reserve's behavioral equation enable us to estimate the weights in the preference function (8). The answer is that the estimates of the Π_i in equation (10) imply estimates of those $a_i w_i / a_j w_j$ for which

---

[29]Specifically, an increase of T dollars in federal securities outside the Treasury in a given quarter may be expected to bring about an increase of $.152T$ dollars in Federal Reserve holdings during the same quarter when $k = .125$.

The reader may find it convenient to refer to the definitions of symbols contained in Part II–B above or in Appendix B below.

the targets are not constant over time.[30] But we are unable, without independent knowledge of the *a*s, to estimate the relative weights, w_i/w_j.[31] This result, or rather lack thereof, is intuitively clear: If, say, the income target Y^* is very high, the Federal Reserve may, other things equal, buy large quantities of securities in order to bring about a large increase in R_f/k because either (1) the weight attached to income in the Federal Reserve's preference function is very high relative to the weights attached to other target variables and/or (2) the effect of R_f/k on income, indicated by a_1 in equation (4.1), is very small.[32]

2. ***Two-stage Least Squares.*** Since several of the explanatory variables in equation (12) are determined jointly with the explained variable, G_t, the method of two-stage least squares was utilized in order to obtain consistent estimates of the parameters in this equation. For this purpose, de Leeuw's seven-equation "Condensed Model of Financial Behavior" was modified to include our Federal Reserve behavioral equation and one additional jointly dependent variable, G_t.[33] De Leeuw's model may be treated as one sector in the model of the U.S. economy developed under the auspices of the Social Science Research Council and the Brookings Institution. The predetermined variables used in the first stage of the two-stage least squares procedure were taken from those sectors of the SSRC–Brookings model which explain those jointly dependent variables entering the right side of (12).[34] All of the explanatory variables in (12)

---

[30]Since P^* is constant at zero, it does not enter equations (9), (10), or (12) and we are unable to estimate the ratios a_4w_4/a_jw_j, where P enters equation (4.4) of the Federal Reserve's policy model and is the fourth target variable in the preference function (8). The same holds for the target variable U, for which the Federal Reserve entertains no finite desires, U^*. This leaves us with a_1w_1/a_3w_3, which is easily derived from the first two terms in the last row of equation (9).

[31]This and related points are elaborated for several kinds of preference functions in Appendix A.

[32]This is a point not sufficiently appreciated by Johnson and Dewald, *op. cit.*, who at several points treat the ratios a_iw_i/a_jw_j as equivalent to w_i/w_j.

An example of a source of independent information concerning the parameters of a government policy model is the 1961 model of the Netherlands economy contained in the *Central Economic Plan, 1961* (The Hague: Central Planning Bureau, August, 1961), pp. 113–27.

[33]The original seven equations in de Leeuw's model are (1) an identity relating the bank reserve equation to the balance sheet of commercial banks, (2) an equation explaining the differential between the U.S. long-term and bill rates, (3) an equation explaining the rate on time deposits at commercial banks, and demands for (4) demand deposits, (5) time deposits at commercial banks, (6) free reserves, and (7) currency in the hands of the public. The jointly dependent variables are the four quantities explained in the demand equations and the three interest rates mentioned.

[34]The nonfinancial predetermined variables entering the first stage of the two-stage least squares procedure include levels and/or changes, all lagged one period, of the balance of trade, the federal surplus, the Treasury balance, Treasury security issues, the industrial materials price index, GNP, new orders, unemployment, the capital utilization rate, and the stock of capital goods, and also current changes in exports and defense expenditures, as well as seasonal dummies, Y^*, and BP^*. Twenty-five predetermined variables, financial and nonfinancial, were used.

except Y^*/ρ, BP^*/ρ, and $1/\rho$ are, when observations are quarterly, jointly dependent.[35] The predetermined variables from the financial sector of the model include $1/\rho = k$, the Federal Reserve discount rate, and Z'/ρ, where

$$\frac{Z_t}{\rho_t} = -\Delta C_{c_t} - k_t \Delta D_t + \frac{Z'_t}{\rho_t}$$

$$\frac{Z'_t}{\rho_t} = \Delta A'_t - \Delta k_t D_{t-1} - \left(\frac{\Delta k_t}{k_{t-1}}\right) R_{f_{t-1}}$$

C_{c_t} = currency in circulation.

D_t = total member bank deposits subject to reserve requirements.

$A'_t = A_t + C_{c_t}$, so that the currency-in-circulation component of A_t is removed in order to obtain A'_t, which is assumed to contain only predetermined factors (cf. definition of A_t following equation [6]).

Z'/ρ includes the predetermined components of Z/ρ, but excludes currency in circulation and total member bank deposits subject to reserve requirements, which are jointly dependent variables. The two-stage least squares method produced the following estimates of the parameters of the equation explaining Federal Reserve purchases and sales of securities:

$$\hat{G}_t = \underset{(.067)}{-.789}\left(\frac{Z_t}{\rho_t}\right) + \underset{(27.0)}{29.5}\left(\frac{S_t}{\rho_t}\right) + \underset{(.108)}{.212}\left(\frac{BT_t}{\rho_t}\right) \tag{13}$$

$$- \underset{(21.3)}{50.9}\left(\frac{L_Y}{\rho_t}\right) + \underset{(49.9)}{69.2}\left(\frac{L_U}{\rho_t}\right) - \underset{(7.37)}{16.33}\left(\frac{L_P}{\rho_t}\right)$$

$$+ \underset{(7.4)}{10.1}\left(\frac{Y^*_t}{\rho_t}\right) - \underset{(.078)}{.013}\left(\frac{BP^*_t}{\rho_t}\right) + \underset{(.010)}{.021}\left(\frac{T_t}{\rho_t}\right) + \underset{(58.05)}{33.34}\left(\frac{1}{\rho_t}\right)$$

The adjusted R^2 is .880 and the Durbin-Watson statistic is 1.55. The two-stage least squares estimates all have a lower value of Student's t than do the ordinary least squares estimates, but the only parameter

[35] While preliminary investigation suggested that the Federal Reserve has treated BT and S, the balance of trade and the federal surplus, as predetermined variables in its policy model explaining Y, U, BP, and P, this does not leave us free to treat BT and S as predetermined in our estimation of the parameters of equation (10). These variables depend at least partly in an unlagged fashion upon Y, U, BP, P and/or G.

significant at the 5 percent level in equation (12) that is not so in (13) is the coefficient of BT/ρ. The coefficient of Z/ρ remains significantly above minus unity (but below zero) at the 5 percent level.[36]

III. CONCLUDING REMARKS

The results presented above suggest strongly that the Federal Reserve, in its conduct of open market operations, responds in a systematic fashion to recent movements in such target variables as GNP, the balance of payments, unemployment, and prices, and to changes in GNP and balance of payments targets. While the preponderance of Federal Reserve actions is aimed at smoothing variations in "other factors affecting reserves," a small but statistically significant part of its behavior is in direct response to the targets and target variables specified in the Employment Act of 1946. The Federal Reserve's demand function for securities, from which these results were obtained, was founded upon a hypothesis of constrained utility maximization analogous to that traditionally applied to the study of the behavior of consumers and firms. Such a demand equation would be a useful component in a model that wished to avoid the oversimplifications and inconsistent parameter estimates involved in an exogenous treatment of the Federal Reserve.

But an estimated model of Federal Reserve behavior of the type presented here, while necessary, is not a sufficient basis upon which to develop an assessment of the correctness of Federal Reserve policies. This can be accomplished only in connection with a larger model which explains variations in all of the jointly dependent variables contained in our Federal Reserve behavioral equation. That is, what is needed if we are to evaluate the effects of monetary policies is not the Federal Reserve's view of the structure of the economy but rather the true structure, though the two might be related.[37] The evidence presented indicates that the Federal Reserve possesses a welfare function that may not be unreasonable in light of the provisions of the 1946 Employment Act and other manifestations of the desires of the electorate. The data suggest also that the response of monetary policies to variations in targets and predetermined variables has been fairly rapid, at least when viewed in terms of quarterly data. However, the optimality of monetary policies also depends crucially upon the correctness of the Federal Reserve's view of the structure of the economy (unless, fortuitously, the Federal Reserve pursues the correct policies for the wrong reasons).[38]

---

[36]The two-stage least squares estimate of the coefficient when G is regressed only on Z/ρ is $-.857$, with a standard error of .055 and an adjusted R^2 of .836.

[37]We must, in order to obtain consistent parameter estimates for the non-Federal Reserve equations of the model, treat Federal Reserve behavior as endogenous by introducing an equation (or equations) of the type developed in Part II above.

[38]An example of a framework for evaluating monetary policy actions which includes a behavioral equation for the monetary authority within a larger structural model is contained in A. A. Walters and N. J. Kavanagh, "Demand for Money in the U.K., 1877–1962" (Discussion Paper A-48) (University of Birmingham, 1964).

APPENDIX A

On the Estimation of Policy Models and Preferences of Policy Makers

1. ***Quadratic Preferences.*** Assume that the preferences of policy makers may be described by a static quadratic welfare function of the following form:

$$d(y) = \sum_{i=1}^{N} w_i (y_{it} - y^*_{it})^2 \tag{A.1}$$

The y_{it} are noncontrolled *target variables* which the policy maker wishes to influence, but does not control; y^*_{it} is the most desirable value that may be attained by y_{it}; and w_i is the weight attached to the squared deviation of y_{it} from y^*_{it}, signifying the importance of attaining y^*_{it}. The policy maker wishes to minimize disutility, d, which is the weighted sum of squared deviations of actual from desired values of the targets, subject to the constraints imposed by the structure of the economy. These constraints consist of a set of reduced-form equations, each of which expresses one of the target variables, y_{it}, as a linear function of all of the predetermined variables in the structure from which the reduced form is derived, including those predetermined variables over which the policy maker exercises complete control—the policy *instruments.* These reduced-form equations, referred to hereafter as the policy model,[39] may be written, ignoring uncertainty,[40] as follows:

$$y_t = ax_t + bz_t \tag{A.2}$$

where y_t is an $N \times 1$ vector of target variables, x_t is a $K \times 1$ vector of policy instruments, z_t is a $\Lambda \times 1$ vector of noncontrolled predetermined variables (including lagged values of the instruments), a is an $N \times K$ matrix of coefficients of the instruments, and b is an $N \times \Lambda$ matrix of coefficients of the noncontrolled predetermined variables. We have N targets, K instruments, and Λ noncontrolled predetermined variables:

$$y_t = \begin{bmatrix} y_{1t} \\ y_{2t} \\ \cdot \\ \cdot \\ \cdot \\ y_{Nt} \end{bmatrix}; \quad x_t = \begin{bmatrix} x_{1t} \\ x_{2t} \\ \cdot \\ \cdot \\ \cdot \\ x_{Kt} \end{bmatrix}; \quad z_t = \begin{bmatrix} z_{1t} \\ z_{2t} \\ \cdot \\ \cdot \\ \cdot \\ z_{\Lambda t} \end{bmatrix}$$

Expanding, the disutility function (A.1) may be written

$$d = \sum_{i=1}^{N} w_i y_i^2 - 2\sum_{i=1}^{N} w_i y_i y_i^* + \sum_{i=1}^{N} w_i y_i^{*2},$$

[39]The policy model will usually contain fewer equations than the complete reduced form since some jointly dependent variables will not be targets.

[40]Cf. footnote 26 above.

or, in matrix notation,

$$d = y_t'Wy_t - 2y_t'Wy_t^* + y_t^{*\prime}Wy_t^*, \tag{A.3}$$

where W is an $N \times N$ diagonal matrix of weights and y^*_t is an $N \times 1$ vector of desired target values:

$$W = \begin{bmatrix} w_1 & & & & 0 \\ & w_2 & & & \\ & & \cdot & & \\ & & & \cdot & \\ 0 & & & & w_N \end{bmatrix}; \quad y_t^* = \begin{bmatrix} y_{1t}^* \\ y_{2t}^* \\ \cdot \\ \cdot \\ \cdot \\ y_{Nt}^* \end{bmatrix}$$

Substitution of the constraints (A.2) into the welfare function (A.3) gives

$$\begin{aligned} d &= (ax_t + bz_t)'W(ax_t + bz_t) - 2(ax_t + bz_t)'Wy_t^* + y_t^{*\prime}Wy_t^* \\ &= x_t'a'Wax_t + x_t'a'Wbz_t + z_t'b'Wax_t + z_t'b'Wbz_t - 2x_t'a'Wy_t^* \\ &\quad - 2z_t'b'Wy_t^* + y_t^{*\prime}Wy_t^* \end{aligned} \tag{A.4}$$

Minimizing d with respect to the instruments, x_t, we have

$$\frac{\partial d}{\partial x_t} = 2a'Wax_t + 2a'Wbz_t - 2a'Wy_t^* = 0 \tag{A.5}$$

Solving for the optimal strategy, x_t^o, gives

$$x_t^o = -(a'Wa)^{-1}a'Wbz_t + (a'Wa)^{-1}a'Wy_t^* \tag{A.6}$$

We see that, in order for the solution of x^0_t to exist, the $K \times K$ matrix $a'Wa$ must be nonsingular. Since a is $N \times K$ and W is $N \times N$ and the rank of a product cannot exceed the smaller of the ranks of the matrices being multiplied, we may state the following necessary condition for the nonsingularity of $a'Wa$:

Condition 1: If K is the number of instruments and N is the number of targets, then the existence of a solution of equation (A.6) for the optimal strategy x^0_t requires that $K \leq N$.

This condition will never in practice be a serious problem because, if $K > N$, we may attach arbitrary values to $K - N$ of the instruments, put those instruments into the z_t vector, and use only N instruments in the minimization procedure.

Equation (A.6) may be written

$$x_t^o = Pz_t + Ry_t^*, \tag{A.7}$$

where

$$P = -(a'Wa)^{-1}a'Wb \tag{A.8.1}$$

$$R = (a'Wa)^{-1}a'W, \tag{A.8.2}$$

where P and R are coefficients estimated by regressing each of the instruments on all of the noncontrolled predetermined variables and on desired values of the target variables (which are assumed known).

Now the problem is, can we solve for estimates of the elements of a, W, and b from estimates of P and R? Substitution of (A.8.2) into (A.8.1) gives

$$P = -Rb. \tag{A.9}$$

Premultiplying both sides of (A.9) by R' gives

$$R'P = -R'Rb. \tag{A.10}$$

Premultiplying both sides of (A.10) by $-(R'R)^{-1}$ gives

$$b = -(R'R)^{-1}R'P \tag{A.11}$$

Since $R'R$ is an $N \times N$ product of $N \times K$ and $K \times N$ matrices, we state the following necessary condition for the existence of the inverse of $R'R$, and therefore the solution of b:

Condition 2: If P and R are, respectively, the matrices of estimated coefficients of the noncontrolled predetermined variables and the desired values of the target variables in the equation for the optimal strategy, $x^o{}_t$, then the existence of a solution for b, the matrix of coefficients of the noncontrolled predetermined variables in the policy model, requires that $N \leq K$.

Conditions 1 and 2, taken together, imply the condition $N = K$. That is, if we hope to be able to solve for b (and, as it turns out, a), the number of instruments must be equal to the number of targets. Given $N = K$, the solution for b can be simplified to $b = -R^{-1}P$.

If $N = K$, R, a, and W are all square and of order $N \times N$, equation (A.8.2) may be written

$$R = (a'Wa)^{-1}a'W = a^{-1}W^{-1}a'^{-1}a'W = a^{-1}W^{-1}W = a^{-1} \tag{A.12}$$

and

$$a = R^{-1} \qquad \text{when } K = N \tag{A.13}$$

That is, when $K = N$, the matrix of coefficients of the instruments in the policy model is equal to the inverse of the coefficients of the targets in the policy solution.

We now have, when $K = N$, estimates of a and b, the coefficients of the policy model. Is it possible now to solve for the weights, W? The answer is no, because if $(a'Wa)^{-1}a'W = a^{-1}$, as shown above, and we substitute this result into (A.6), the policy solution, we get

$$x_t = -a^{-1}bz_t + a^{-1}y_t^* \tag{A.14}$$

which is independent of the weights. This is so because when we let the number of instruments be equal to the number of targets, we are able to achieve all targets simultaneously, in which case the weights attached to the separate targets have no significance.

If we approach the policy decision in the same manner as Tinbergen,[41] that is, by replacing y_t in (A.2) by y^*_t to get (where $N = K$)

$$\overset{*}{y}_t = ax_t + bz_t \tag{A.15}$$

and solving for x_t to get that combination of instruments that satisfies all targets simultaneously—in the expected value sense (and subject to forecasts of the zs)—we have

$$ax_t = -bz_t + \overset{*}{y}_t$$

and finally,

$$x_t = -a^{-1}bz_t + a^{-1}\overset{*}{y}_t = a^{-1}(-bz_t + \overset{*}{y}_t) \tag{A.16}$$

which is identical to that solution given by the quadratic welfare function approach in equation (A.14). We may see that this solution leads to zero disutility by substituting (A.16) into (A.4)—remembering that $N = K$—to get

$$\begin{aligned} d &= [aa^{-1}(-bz_t + \overset{*}{y}_t) + bz_t]'W[aa^{-1}(-bz_t + \overset{*}{y}_t) + bz_t] \\ &\quad -2[aa^{-1}(-bz_t + \overset{*}{y}_t) + bz_t]'W\overset{*}{y}_t + \overset{*}{y}_t{}'W\overset{*}{y}_t \\ &= \overset{*}{y}_t{}'W\overset{*}{y}_t - 2\overset{*}{y}_t{}'W\overset{*}{y}_t + \overset{*}{y}_t{}'W\overset{*}{y}_t = 0 \end{aligned} \tag{A.17}$$

If there is only one instrument, so that $K = 1$, and assuming $N > 1$, the $K \times K$ matrix $a'Wa$ is a scalar and so is its inverse. If we denote the scalar $(a'Wa)^{-1}$ by k, equation (A.8.2) may be written as follows:

$$[R_1R_2 \cdot \cdot \cdot R_N] = k[a_1w_1 \; a_2w_2 \cdot \cdot \cdot a_Nw_N] \tag{A.18}$$

so that

$$R_i = ka_iw_i \qquad i = 1, 2, \ldots, N$$

and

$$\frac{R_i}{R_j} = \frac{a_iw_i}{a_jw_j} = \frac{\left(\dfrac{\partial y_{it}}{\partial x_t}\right)}{\left(\dfrac{\partial y_{jt}}{\partial x_t}\right)}\left(\frac{w_i}{w_j}\right) \tag{A.19}$$

where x_t is a scalar when $K = 1$.

2. *Some Targets Enter the Welfare Function Linearly.* Now assume that the policy maker sets no limits on his desires with respect to some of the targets—income, for example—so that the welfare function may be written

$$U = -\sum_{i=1}^{M} w_i(y_{it} - \overset{*}{y}_{it})^2 + \sum_{i=M+1}^{N} g_iy_{it} \tag{A.20}$$

[41]Cf. J. Tinbergen, *On the Theory of Economic Policy* (2d ed.; Amsterdam: North Holland, 1955).

where we still have N jointly dependent variables as targets and K instruments. The policy maker wants the y_{it} for $i = M + 1, \ldots, N$ to be as high as possible. High values of the $g_i y_i$ add to utility and high values of the $w_i(y_{it} - y^*_{it})^2$ detract from utility.

It is now convenient to separate the policy model (A.2) into two parts:

$$\begin{aligned} \overline{y}_{1t} &= a_1 x_t + b_1 z_t \\ \overline{y}_{2t} &= a_2 x_t + b_2 z_t \end{aligned} \tag{A.21}$$

where y_{1t} is an $M \times 1$ vector of those target variables with respect to which the policy maker entertains symmetric preferences and y_{2t} is an $N - M \times 1$ vector of targets entering the utility function in a linear fashion. Of the matrices of coefficients in (A.21), a_1 is $M \times K$, a_2 is $N - M \times K$, b_1 is $M \times \Lambda$, and b_2 is $N - M \times \Lambda$.

The utility function (A.20) may be written in matrix notation as follows:

$$U = - y'_{1t} W y_{1t} + 2 y'_{1t} W y^*_{1t} - y^{*\prime}_{1t} W y^*_{1t} + g y_{2t} \tag{A.22}$$

where W is an $M \times M$ diagonal matrix of weights, y^*_{1t} is an $M \times 1$ vector of desired target values, and g is a $1 \times N - M$ vector of weights.

Substituting (A.21) into (A.22), maximizing U with respect to x_t, and solving for x_t gives

$$x_t = - (a'_1 W a_1)^{-1} a'_1 W b_1 z_t + (a'_1 W a_1)^{-1} a'_1 W y^*_{1t} + \tfrac{1}{2} (a'_1 W a_1)^{-1} a'_2 g', \tag{A.23}$$

provided that $K \leq M$; that is, the number of instruments is no greater than the number of targets entering U in a quadratic fashion.

Equation (A.23) may be written

$$x_t = P z_t + R y^*_{1t} + S \tag{A.24}$$

where

$$P = - (a'_1 W a_1)^{-1} a'_1 W b_1 \tag{A.25.1}$$

$$R = (a'_1 W a_1)^{-1} a'_1 W \tag{A.25.2}$$

$$S = \tfrac{1}{2} (a'_1 W a_1)^{-1} a'_2 g' \tag{A.25.3}$$

We have, substituting (A.25.2) into (A.25.1), if $K = M$,

$$b_1 = R^{-1} P \tag{A.26}$$

and

$$a_1 = R^{-1} \tag{A.27}$$

But, as in the preceding section, we are not able, without additional information, to solve for the weights—the elements of W and g. This can be seen in the simplest case to which it is possible to apply utility function (A.20), namely, where $K = M = \Lambda = 1$ and $N = 2$, so that all the terms in (A.21), and therefore (A.23) and (A.24), are scalars. The solution for x_t in this situation may be written

$$x_t = -\frac{b_1}{a_1} z_t + \frac{1}{a_1} \overset{*}{y}_{1t} + \frac{a_2 g}{2a_1^2 W} \tag{A.28}$$

$$= P z_t + R \overset{*}{y}_{1t} + S$$

from which we obtain the following results:

$$a_1 = \frac{1}{R}$$

$$b_1 = \frac{P}{R} \tag{A.29}$$

$$\frac{a_2 g}{2W} = \frac{S}{R^2}$$

We are unable to estimate the ratio g/W without independent knowledge of a_2.

3. ***Instruments as Targets.*** Now add to the utility function (A.20) elements containing the instruments as targets, some symmetric and some linear. This function may be written

$$U = -\sum_{i=1}^{M} w_i(y_{it} - \overset{*}{y}_{it})^2 + \sum_{i=M+1}^{N} g_i y_{it} \tag{A.30}$$

$$- \sum_{i=1}^{H} \mu_i(x_{it} - \overset{*}{x}_{it})^2 + \sum_{i=H+i}^{K} h_i x_{it}$$

where we continue to have N jointly dependent variables as targets and K instruments. The x^*_{it} for $i = 1, \ldots, H$ are desired values of H of the instruments and the μ_i are weights attached to deviations from those desires. The policy maker derives ever increasing satisfaction from higher and higher values of the x_{it} *for* $i = H + 1, \ldots, K$ as well as from the y_{it} for $i = M + 1, \ldots, N$. Some of the μ_i and/or h_i will be zero if some of the instruments do not also serve as targets. Equation (A.30) may be expressed in matrices as follows:

$$U = - y'_{1t} W y_{1t} + 2y'_{1t} W \overset{*}{y}_{1t} - \overset{*\prime}{y}_{1t} W \overset{*}{y}_{1t} + g y_{2t} \tag{A.31}$$

$$- x'_t \mu x_t + 2x'_t \mu \overset{*}{x}_t - \overset{*\prime}{x}_t \mu \overset{*}{x}_t + h x_t$$

where the first four terms on the right-hand side of (A.31) are identical to the right-hand side of (A.22), μ is a $K \times K$ diagonal matrix with the $H + 1, \ldots, K$ diagonal elements being zero, and h is a $1 \times K$ vector with the first H elements being zero.

Substituting the policy model (A.21) into (A.31), maximizing U with respect to x_t, and solving for x_t gives

$$\begin{aligned} x_t = & -(a_1'Wa_1 + \mu)^{-1}a_1'Wb_1z_t + (a_1'Wa_1 + \mu)^{-1}a_1'Wy_{1t}^* \\ & + (a_1'Wa_1 + \mu)^{-1}\mu x_t^* + (a_1'Wa_1 + \mu)^{-1}(a_2'g' + h') \end{aligned} \quad (A.32)$$

or

$$x_t = Pz_t + Ry_{1t}^* + Qx_t^* + S \quad (A.33)$$

The solution for b_1 is

$$b_1 = -(R'R)^{-1}R'P \quad (A.34)$$

subject to the condition $M \leq K$ so that the inverse of $(R'R)^{-1}$ exists. But we will be unable in any case to disentangle the ratios of any of the weights from the elements of the matrix of coefficients relating the instruments to the target variables.

APPENDIX B

The Data

Definitions and sources of the data entering the empirical portions of the paper are given below. More detailed definitions are contained in Part II–B above. Most of the data are defined in level form, although they were utilized in the estimation procedure primarily in terms of changes. The period of observation is one quarter.

R_f = average level of free reserves in member banks of the Federal Reserve System. Source: *Federal Reserve Bulletin.*

G_L = average quantity (in par value dollars) of U.S. government securities held by the Federal Reserve. Source: *Federal Reserve Bulletin.*

A = average level of the U.S. monetary gold stock plus Treasury currency outstanding plus Federal Reserve float less currency in circulation less Treasury cash accounts less nonmember bank, foreign, and other accounts at the Federal Reserve. Source: *Federal Reserve Bulletin.*

R_r = average level of reserves required against all demand and time deposits at member banks. Source: *Federal Reserve Bulletin.*

$\frac{1}{\rho} = k$ = average reserve requirement as a percentage of all deposits at member banks. Source: *Federal Reserve Bulletin.*

Z = all factors affecting R_f other than Federal Reserve security holdings. See equation (7) and discussion following.

S = a smoothed quarterly version of the annual federal cash surplus. See footnote 24 for a reference to the smoothing method used. The federal cash surplus assumed the following values in billions of current dollars in the fiscal years 1951–64: 3.510, −4.017, −9.449, −3.117, −4.180, 1.626, 1.596, −2.819, −12.427, 1.224, −3.856, −6.378, −6.266, −8.226. Source: *Treasury Bulletin.*

BT = seasonally adjusted balance of trade in goods and services. Source: *Survey of Current Business* and *Balance of Payments Statistical Supplement* (rev. ed.; Office of Business Economics, Department of Commerce).

Y = seasonally adjusted gross national product in billions of 1954 dollars. Source: *Survey of Current Business.*

U = seasonally adjusted ratio of unemployment to the civilian labor force as defined by the Bureau of Labor Statistics. Source: *Federal Reserve Bulletin.*

$BP_t = -BP^*_{t+1}$ = seasonally adjusted balance of payments. Source: *Survey of Current Business* and *Balance of Payments Statistical Supplement* (rev. ed.; Office of Business Economics, Department of Commerce).

P = industrial materials price index. Source: internal memoranda which may be obtained from the Business Conditions Section, Division of Research and Statistics, Board of Governors of the Federal Reserve System.

Y^* = desired change in Y. See definition in Part II–B.

T = quantity of U.S. marketable securities outstanding outside the Treasury and government agencies and trust funds.

$L_Y = Y_t - Y_{t-1}$

$L_U = U_t - U_{t-1}$

$L_P = P_t - P_{t-8}$

Observed values of these data (except L_Y, L_U, and L_P, which may be calculated from Y, U, and P) for the sample period (1952–63) are listed below. The seasonally adjusted data listed here vary slightly from those reported in the *Survey of Current Business* and other sources because of the different approach to seasonal adjustment followed for purposes of the present study. Instead of seasonally adjusting GNP for, say, 1952 on the basis of GNP data taken from the entire 1952–63 period, which would be unknown to the monetary authorities in 1952, it was decided to adjust 1952 GNP on the basis of seasonal factors derived from 1947–51 data, to adjust 1953 GNP on the basis of 1948–52 data, and so forth.

The scaling of the data in the following table varies in some instances from that used in the estimation process. The scaling used for purposes of estimating the model is described in the paragraph immediately following equation (12). The scaling of the data listed below is as follows: U and P are percentages, k is a ratio, BT and BP are in millions of dollars, and the remaining variables are in billions of dollars.

Quarter	R_f	G_L	ΔA	R_r	$1/\rho = k$	Z	S
1952 I	.544	22.80	...	19.386	.158	...	−1.449
II	.159	22.46	− .20	19.232	.157	− .274	−2.210
III	−.252	23.10	− .52	19.773	.158	−6.722	−2.496
IV	−.715	23.90	− .87	20.169	.157	−8.076	−2.536
1953 I	−.642	24.00	− .21	19.987	.156	− .205	−2.371
II	−.206	24.19	− .30	19.426	.155	1.658	−2.046
III	.203	25.04	−1.01	18.862	.147	− 3.109	−1.523
IV	.280	25.38	− .11	19.015	.146	− 1.795	− .966
1954 I	.559	24.89	.77	19.016	.145	5.317	− .475
II	.634	24.78	− .09	18.752	.143	1.273	− .153
III	.735	24.23	− .23	17.865	.134	5.201	− .439
IV	.582	24.69	− .09	18.381	.133	− 4.519	− .885
1955 I	.254	23.89	.31	18.226	.132	3.562	−1.311
II	.159	23.63	.12	18.174	.132	1.303	−1.545
III	−.127	23.86	− .53	18.168	.131	− 3.992	− .898
IV	−.365	24.18	− .27	18.456	.131	− 4.260	− .005
1956 I	−.309	23.61	.53	18.368	.131	4.718	.910
II	−.410	23.42	.05	18.316	.131	.779	1.619
III	−.230	23.61	− .03	18.302	.130	− .146	1.385
IV	−.129	24.19	− .15	18.627	.130	− 3.654	.804
1957 I	−.109	23.42	.64	18.480	.130	6.054	.062
II	−.486	23.09	− .05	18.476	.129	− .364	− .655
III	−.440	23.28	− .18	18.443	.128	− 1.180	− .713
IV	−.256	23.58	.06	18.621	.128	− .922	− .688
1958 I	.314	23.49	.46	18.418	.125	5.256	− .639
II	.508	24.11	−1.08	17.768	.117	− 3.504	− .749
III	.342	25.23	−1.13	17.918	.116	−10.991	−1.741
IV	.025	25.75	− .63	18.124	.116	− 7.207	−2.841
1959 I	−.082	25.59	.08	18.160	.115	.383	−3.734
II	−.364	25.85	− .56	18.141	.115	− 4.704	−4.111
III	−.529	26.54	− .80	18.198	.115	− 7.452	−2.587
IV	−.438	26.76	− .06	18.263	.115	− 1.087	− .552
1960 I	−.313	25.52	1.00	17.901	.114	11.912	1.457
II	−.062	25.81	− .17	17.765	.114	− .298	2.906
III	.260	26.75	− .41	17.967	.113	− 5.425	1.883
IV	.595	27.39	.00	18.286	.113	− 2.823	.052
1961 I	.563	26.87	.59	18.381	.112	4.464	−2.019
II	.521	26.79	.00	18.334	.111	.468	−3.772
III	.538	27.33	− .23	18.628	.110	− 4.718	−3.380
IV	.460	28.59	− .67	19.305	.111	−12.180	−2.290
1962 I	.457	28.49	.00	19.203	.109	1.009	− .939
II	.424	29.40	− .83	19.322	.108	− 8.750	.231
III	.418	29.86	− .30	19.484	.107	− 4.280	− .146
IV	.386	30.33	− .58	19.400	.104	− 4.654	−1.019
1963 I	.315	30.45	− .34	19.250	.101	− 1.772	−2.079
II	.232	31.19	− .84	19.239	.100	− 8.260	−3.022
III	.129	32.28	− .98	19.441	.099	−11.919	−2.895
IV	.112	33.17	− .52	19.835	.099	− 9.232	−2.409

Quarter		BT	Y	U	$BP_t = - BP^*_{t+1}$	P	Y^*	T
1952	I	1211	...	2.7	397	100.3	...	.....
	II	759	.5	2.7	− 343	99.0	.5	− .450
	III	263	.5	2.8	− 669	99.0	1.4	3.316
	IV	− 7	3.3	2.4	− 431	98.8	1.3	4.775
1953	I	133	2.2	2.5	− 637	98.9	− .3	−2.657
	II	23	1.6	2.5	− 422	99.6	− 1.1	3.143
	III	75	−1.5	2.3	− 616	100.9	− 1.3	5.520
	IV	155	−2.2	3.1	− 477	100.4	.2	1.785
1954	I	270	− .4	5.1	− 413	99.8	2.6	−4.735
	II	432	.4	5.6	− 188	99.6	4.4	.363
	III	463	.7	5.6	− 452	100.1	5.4	3.678
	IV	663	1.5	5.2	− 497	100.5	5.7	3.863
1955	I	703	2.9	4.1	− 6	101.3	4.5	−4.701
	II	400	1.9	3.9	− 431	101.8	2.3	1.835
	III	505	2.3	3.8	− 314	104.0	1.4	4.244
	IV	401	.7	4.2	− 394	105.7	.3	3.287
1956	I	577	−1.1	3.8	− 488	107.1	.3	−4.118
	II	957	.1	3.9	− 208	107.7	1.8	−4.834
	III	1037	1.7	3.7	− 380	108.2	2.7	1.417
	IV	1396	1.4	3.8	141	109.7	3.2	3.889
1957	I	1642	−1.1	3.9	491	110.5	2.9	− .668
	II	1574	1.5	4.2	9	110.4	3.3	−4.486
	III	1376	− .5	4.4	406	111.1	3.6	5.547
	IV	1137	−2.1	4.8	− 386	110.6	4.3	2.093
1958	I	652	−2.8	6.2	− 674	110.2	7.1	−1.486
	II	611	1.0	7.1	− 951	109.5	10.7	3.663
	III	594	1.8	7.6	− 927	110.2	11.2	1.039
	IV	349	2.8	6.5	− 977	110.9	10.3	7.896
1959	I	54	2.7	5.6	− 951	111.5	8.6	.463
	II	− 194	2.7	5.0	−1062	112.3	7.6	1.597
	III	94	2.7	5.4	−1191	112.4	5.5	4.992
	IV	180	2.7	6.1	− 539	112.4	8.2	4.857
1960	I	565	4.0	5.1	− 680	112.7	8.3	−3.134
	II	816	0	5.3	− 775	112.4	7.1	−1.726
	III	954	−1.3	5.6	−1157	111.9	7.7	2.357
	IV	1490	− .5	6.5	−1313	111.3	9.2	2.473
1961	I	1621	− .1	6.8	− 319	111.2	11.0	−2.686
	II	1318	1.4	7.1	176	110.9	12.9	.432
	III	964	2.8	6.9	− 910	110.7	11.6	4.894
	IV	1240	2.9	6.0	−1408	110.7	11.0	3.942
1962	I	1209	.6	5.6	− 585	110.9	8.9	− .095
	II	1521	1.3	5.6	− 452	111.0	8.8	− .305
	III	1008	.3	5.7	− 356	110.5	8.5	1.527
	IV	1077	2.1	5.6	− 793	110.2	9.2	4.765
1963	I	1182	1.5	5.8	− 883	110.0	8.9	− .360
	II	1450	.9	5.9	−1288	110.1	9.1	− .624
	III	1227	1.3	5.6	− 225	110.2	9.2	.680
	IV	1626	.9	5.6	...	110.6	9.0	2.614

THE DEMAND FOR MONEY: SPEED OF ADJUSTMENT, INTEREST RATES, AND WEALTH*

Frank de Leeuw

INTRODUCTION

Recent empirical studies of the demand for money are in agreement as to the importance of an interest rate (or interest rates) and some "scale" variable in accounting for much of the variation over time in the amount of money the public holds.[1] They are not in agreement, however, as to which interest rates are the relevant ones or as to whether the "scale" variable should be an income measure, a transactions measure, or a wealth measure. Nor are they in agreement as to whether or not there exists a substantial lag in the adjustment of money holdings to a stock-equilibrium position. It seems worthwhile, therefore, to examine aggregative quarterly postwar data with these three matters of contention—choice of interest rate, choice of "scale" variable, and speed of adjustment—specifically in mind. The present paper reports the results of such an examination.

Underlying the three empirical issues are different theoretical approaches to the demand for money. The theory of optimal inventory

*Helen Cunney ably managed the computer work. Views expressed are those of the author.

[1]See especially Allan Meltzer, "The Demand for Money: The Evidence from the Time Series," *Journal of Political Economy,* Vol. 71 (June, 1963), pp. 219–46; and Ronald L. Teigen, "Demand and Supply Functions for Money in the U.S.: Some Structural Estimates," *Econometrica,* Vol. 32 (October, 1964), pp. 476–509.

Professor Friedman has argued that the influence of interest rates on money holdings is quite small, most recently (in collaboration with Anna J. Schwartz) in *A Monetary History of the United States 1867–1960* (Princeton, 1963), Chap. 12. For contrary points of view, see reviews of the Friedman-Schwartz volume by James Tobin (*American Economic Review,* Vol. 55 [June, 1965], pp. 464–85) and Karl Brunner (*Journal of Political Economy,* Vol. 73 [April, 1965], pp. 197–218).

policy applied to the demand for money leads to the expectation that the current volume of transactions and current interest rates on risk-free assets should influence the size of money balances.[2] The theory of utility maximization applied to money can easily lead to a relationship between money balances, some general wealth or net worth constraint, and an interest rate representing yields on some broad class of assets.[3] Lags in economic behavior have not been the subject of much formal theory; but if long lags in the adjustment of money balances turn out to be important, useful theories of money demand should be able to account for them. The research reported here is thus relevant to the choice between theories of money demand as well as to problems of short-run analysis.

The presentation below will, for each of the three issues, first discuss the significance of alternative views and then summarize the postwar quarterly evidence. The evidence is presented separately for currency and for demand deposits and also includes results for commercial bank time and savings deposits.

A concluding section (pp. 185–86) summarizes the findings. At this point, however, it may be of interest to summarize the summary and note that (1) long lags in adjustment do show up as important, even after attempts to correct for possible sources of statistical bias; (2) no clear verdict as between various interest rates emerges; and (3) a weighted-average income measure seems to fit better than a nonhuman net worth measure in some relationships and worse in others, while a measure of deviations of current income from a weighted average proves to be an important additional variable in either case. This latter finding seems consistent with an inventory theory of money demand.

A few notes about the relationships tested and data employed may be helpful before proceeding to the body of the report. Besides being restricted to quarterly observations since the end of World War II, the analysis below is restricted in that dollar magnitudes are converted to real per capita form—that is, they are deflated by population and by a measure of the general price level (the GNP deflator). This deflation affects the results, as noted below (page 181), but it seems to be required by the underlying theories. The theories all relate to the determinants of the quantity of money demanded by a single unit—a household or a business firm—so that in general we should not expect a doubling of income or wealth to have the same effect if it is due to a doubling of the number of units as if it is due to a doubling of the average size of each

[2]For an early statement of this approach, see William Baumol, "The Transactions Demand for Cash: An Inventory Theoretic Approach," *Quarterly Journal of Economics*, Vol. 66 (November, 1952), pp. 545–56.

[3]See Milton Friedman, "The Quantity Theory of Money—A Restatement," in *Studies in the Quantity Theory of Money* (Chicago: University of Chicago, 1956).

unit. Deflation by population is a crude attempt to adjust for this source of variability in the aggregative relationships.[4]

Not only do the theories relate to demand by a single unit but they also relate to demand at a given level of prices.[5] Under the utility approach, the services that holders derive from their stocks of money depend not on "the number of things called . . . dollars they hold but the real stock of money they have, the command which those pieces of paper gives them over goods and services."[6] In general we should not expect a doubling of nominal income or wealth to have the same effect on money holdings if it is due to a doubling of the price level as if to a doubling of physical quantities of goods and services. Under the inventory approach, if we assume that the transactions costs—which are the fundamental reason for a positive demand for money—vary in proportion to the general level of prices, a stable relationship between price deflated magnitudes is also implied.[7]

The data consist of quarterly averages of currency in circulation, demand deposits, and time and savings deposits at commercial banks, all seasonally adjusted; yields on long-term U.S. securities, Treasury bills, and time deposits; national income seasonally adjusted at annual rates; and "wealth" defined as stocks of tangible goods (except those owned by the federal government) plus net claims by the public on the rest of the world plus net claims by the public on the Federal Reserve System and the federal government.[8] For the time deposit yield, quarterly

---

[4]The comments on population by Meltzer, *op. cit.*, p. 237, suggest that population growth may have effects on money demand beyond sheer multiplication of numbers; but they do not seem to me to dispose of the need to express the fundamental relationship in terms of a "typical" unit, somehow measured.

[5]A given level of prices, of course, is not the same as a given state of expectations about prices.

[6]Milton Friedman, "Postwar Trends in Monetary Theory and Policy," *National Banking Review*, Vol. 2 (September, 1964), p. 5.

[7]Teigen, for example, *op. cit.*, makes use of the "square-root" formula

$$C = \sqrt{\frac{Ya}{2r}}$$

where C is average (nominal) money holdings, Y is (nominal) income, a is the cost per transaction in or out of money, and r is an interest rate. If a is equal to some constant times the general level of prices, say $\bar{a}\,P$, then the relationship among C, Y, and r changes as P changes. Dividing both sides by P we obtain

$$\frac{C}{P} = \frac{1}{P}\sqrt{\frac{Y\bar{a}P}{2r}} = \sqrt{\frac{(Y/P)\,\bar{a}}{2r}}$$

and the relationship among $\frac{C}{P}$, $\frac{Y}{P}$, and r does not change as P changes.

[8]Meltzer, *op. cit.*, employing this concept, finds a stable demand relationship, except that he apparently includes the debt of state and local governments as well as federal debt in the wealth total (p. 224, footnote 20). Since state and local governments are among the holders of money, it is hard to see why their debt should not be netted out of the wealth total, just as, say, corporate debt is.

levels were interpolated from annual ratios of interest payments to deposit levels. Interpolations were based on regression relationships between annual averages of relevant quarterly series and the annual bench marks. Quarterly interpolations based on regression relationships were also used to convert Goldsmith's wealth estimates into a quarterly series and to extend the wealth series past Goldsmith's most recent published estimates for 1958. The wealth estimates, even more than the other figures, may contain significant measurement errors. An appendix listing and describing all the data is available on request.

A few comments on the general movements of currency, deposits, and interest rates, as plotted on the accompanying chart, may help in the

CHART I

Real per Capita Currency, Demand and Time Deposits, and U.S. Long-Term Bond Yields

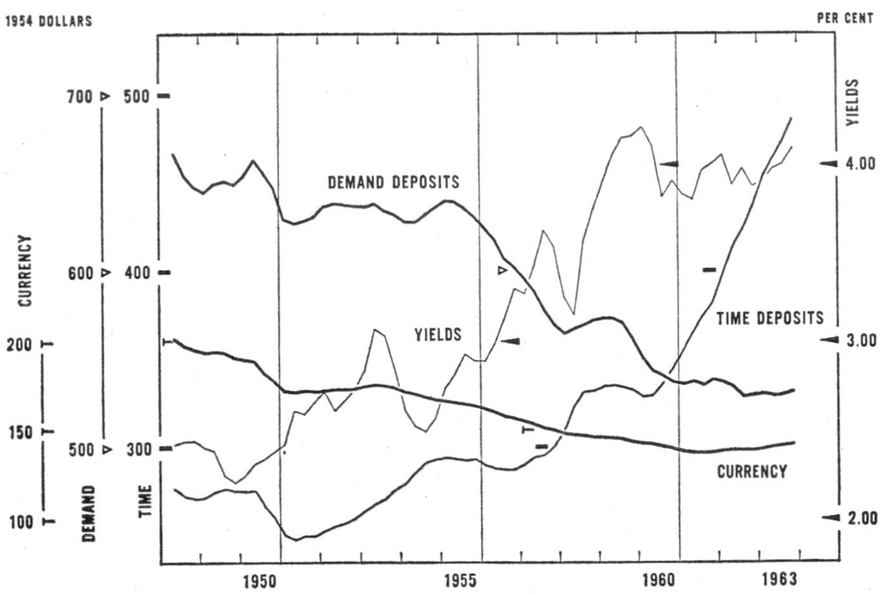

interpretation of some of the evidence below. The chart makes clear that after deflation by population and prices, the 1948–63 trend of currency and demand deposits is downward. These two components of the money supply thus have a negative simple correlation with wealth or income (even on a real per capita basis) which is contrary to the partial relationship we expect to find after allowing for other influences. We expect a negative partial relationship with interest rates and, as the chart illustrates for the U.S. long-term securities rate, the simple relationship is negative also.

In fact, the negative relationship between real per capita demand deposits and the U.S. long-term rate is much more than a negative association of trends. Most of the fluctuations in the long-term rate correspond to inverse fluctuations in real per capita demand deposits, with the latter fluctuations lagging behind and somewhat less sharp than the former. To the naked eye, then, there seems to be some simple evidence of a lagged reaction of money holdings to interest rates.

SPEED OF ADJUSTMENT

It is convenient to begin with the problem of how rapidly the public reacts, as far as its money holdings are concerned, to a change in wealth, income, or interest rates. The investigations reported here narrow this problem somewhat by assuming a relation of the form

$$m_t - m_{t-1} = (1 - k)\,(b'x_t - m_{t-1}) + u_t \qquad (1)$$

where m is real per capita money holdings (actually currency, demand deposits, and time deposits are treated separately), b' is a vector of coefficients, x is a vector of some of the factors influencing money demand (wealth, interest rates, and so on), $1 - k$ is a measure of the speed of adjustment, u is the unexplained residual, and subscripts refer to average values during quarters t and $t - 1$. If $1 - k$, the coefficient of m_{t-1}, equals one, adjustment is complete within one quarter. The relation may also be written

$$m_t = k\,m_{t-1} + (1 - k)b'\,x_t + u_t \qquad (2)$$

by adding m_{t-1} to both sides of (1); and least squares estimates of k and b' will be the same regardless of whether it is (1) or (2) which is estimated.[9] It is quite possible that the actual lag form is more complicated than equation (1) or its equivalent (2), but equation (1) probably provides an adequate first approximation to any plausible lag distribution.

It is important to estimate k as accurately as possible, for the direct effects over time of changes in the quantity of money supplied are quite different if k is approximately equal to zero than if k is close to 1. Suppose, for example, that m had been stationary for some time past. If k equals zero (indicating immediate adjustment), then open market operations which succeed in shifting m to a new level will force one or more

[9]An easy way to convince oneself of this equivalence is to realize that (1) only if the coefficients are the same in the two equations will the estimated residuals be the same; and (2) for either equation the least squares procedure will yield that unique set of estimated residuals with minimum sum of squares. The same equivalence holds, incidentally, for two-stage least squares. But under either estimating procedure the two equations do differ with respect to R^2 and with respect to the significance of the lagged stock.

components of x to shift to new levels also. If k is close to 1, then open market operations which shift m to a new level will produce not a simple shift but a fluctuation in one or more components of x; an initial shift will be followed by a return in the direction of preshift levels. For example, an upward shift in m might cause an initial sharp drop in short-term interest rates followed by a subsequent rise toward old levels. Clearly we should not be indifferent as between these two possible outcomes—as to whether a particular monetary policy causes fluctuations or simple shifts in other economic variables.

Unfortunately, common methods of estimating (1) or (2) may lead to important biases in the value of k. Especially disturbing is the possibility, indicated by Griliches,[10] that even if k is really zero (that is, there is no lag in adjustment), an ordinary least squares estimate may produce an estimated k well above zero and apparently very significant. This result is likely if the unexplained portion of m displays high serial correlation, for the estimate of k under these circumstances reflects the high serial correlation coefficient as well as the speed of adjustment. Two-stage least squares estimates, since they do not deal with this source of bias, would seem to be open to the same criticism.

It is not much help, then, to know that the addition of m_{t-1} to regressions of m_t on interest rates and wealth or income yields highly significant estimates of k closer to 1 than to zero. Both Teigen and the present author have found this to be true using both ordinary least squares and two-stage least squares for equation specifications not too different from those of the present paper. Nor is it helpful, of course, to assume complete adjustment in one time period, without any review of the evidence.

Instead of following either of these procedures it seems useful to experiment with techniques designed to remove the bias in the estimate of k due to serial correlation. One such technique, called "three-pass least squares," has recently been proposed by Taylor and Wilson.[11] The technique assumes that in addition to (2) above, there is a relation between successive residuals of the form

$$u_t = pu_{t-1} + e_t \tag{3}$$

where e_t is not serially correlated. Substituting (3) into (2) gives

$$m_t = k\, m_{t-1} + (1 - k)b'x_t + pu_{t-1} + e_t \tag{4}$$

If values of u_{t-1} were available, then ordinary least squares could be

---

[10] Zvi Griliches, "A Note on Serial Correlation Bias in Estimates of Distributed Lags," *Econometrica*, Vol. 29 (January, 1961), pp. 65–73.

[11] Lester Taylor and Thomas Wilson, "Three-Pass Least Squares: A Method for Estimating Models with a Lagged Dependent Variable," *Review of Economics and Statistics*, Vol. 46 (November, 1964), pp. 329–46.

applied to (4) without introducing a bias into the estimate of k. The method of three-pass least squares consists of developing, by successive approximations, estimated values of u_{t-1} and then applying ordinary least squares to (4). The technique is not designed to deal with simultaneous equation difficulties which may also be present; but its effect on money demand relationships seems of interest nevertheless, especially since ordinary least squares and two-stage least squares often seem to give similar results for these relationships.[12]

Unexpectedly (at least to this investigator) the method of three-pass least squares yielded even slower estimates of average speed of adjustment (that is, estimates of k closer to 1) than ordinary least squares. The estimated speed was not significantly different from zero in a number of cases. Table 1 presents the details for certain choices of interest rates and "scale" variables.

The explantory variables included in Table 1, in addition to lagged stocks, are real per capita wealth, a weighted average of current and lagged values of real per capita national income,[13] the deviations of current real per capita national income from this weighted average, and interest rates. The two income variables add up to current income, so that if current income were the relevant "scale" variable, we would expect the coefficients of interest rates and income to be estimates of $(1 - k)\ b'$; that is, they are single quarter rather than long-run responses. One feature of the regressions which is worth noting at this point is that the lagged stock variables have been divided by current population and prices, not by lagged population and prices. Money holders, that is, are viewed as evaluating their existing stocks at current purchasing power for comparison with "desired" stocks. Since the GNP deflator has, except for two or three quarters, moved very smoothly since 1948, this timing choice probably has very little effect on the regressions. Comments on the results of alternative "scale" variables and presentation of results with alternative interest rates appear later in the paper. For the present, it is sufficient to note that the results of Table 1 provide support for the long lag hypothesis.

However, because of the importance of accurate estimates of the lags involved, it seems worth trying another technique for removing bias in the usual estimates of equation (2). This other technique consists of trying a number of alternative values of k and comparing the results with respect to (a) goodness of fit and (b) plausibility of signs of those coefficients which turn out to be significant.

---

[12]See Teigen, *op. cit.*, p. 503, Tables V and VI; and Frank de Leeuw, "A Model of Financial Behavior," in J. S. Duesenberry et al. (eds.), *The Brookings Quarterly Econometric Model of the United States* (Chicago: Rand McNally, 1965).

[13]The weights employed are quarterly interpolations of the annual weights used by Friedman in constructing a "permanent" income series. See de Leeuw, *op. cit.*

TABLE 1

DEMAND EQUATIONS RELATING REAL PER CAPITA MONEY HOLDINGS TO INTEREST RATES, INCOME, WEALTH, AND LAGGED STOCKS

			Real per Capita Income		*Interest Rates*					
	Lagged Stock	*Real per Capita Wealth*	*Weighted Average*	*Deviations from Average*	*U.S. Long-Term Securities*	*Treasury Bills*	*Time Deposits*	*Constant Term*	R^2	*Durbin-Watson Ratio*
Currency										
Excluding lagged stock	—	−.054	.070	.006	.783	—	—	512.7	.975	.32
		(.004)	(.015)	(.008)	(1.803)					
Including lagged stock										
OLS (1)	.978	—	.002	.012	−.491	—	—	1.0	.999	.94
	(.015)		(.002)	(.002)	(.368)					
(2)	.971	.000	—	.012	−.405	—	—	5.1	.999	.91
	(.025)	(.001)		(.002)	(.400)					
3PLS (1)	1.007	—	.002	.011	−.622	—	—	3.8	.999	1.81
	(.015)		(.002)	(.001)	(.328)					
(2)	.999	−.001	—	.011	−.479	—	—	15.9	.999	1.84
	(.022)	(.001)		(.001)	(.344)					
Demand deposits										
Excluding lagged stock	—	−.104	.230	.118	−27.743	—	—	1189.7	.943	.33
		(.015)	(.054)	(.028)	(6.511)					

Including lagged stock										
OLS (1).......	.887	—	−.003	.033	−8.886	—	—	102.1	.995	.85
	(.027)		(.009)	(.008)	(2.042)					
(2).......	.910	.003	—	.031	−10.253	—	—	57.5	.995	.90
	(.032)	(.003)		(.008)	(2.034)					
3PLS (1).......	.895	—	−.002	.025	−11.289	—	—	128.5	.997	1.94
	(.021)		(.007)	(.006)	(1.712)					
(2).......	.907	.002	—	.024	−11.987	—	—	96.4	.997	1.91
	(.026)	(.003)		(.007)	(1.756)					
Time deposits										
Excluding lagged stock.............	—	−.055	—	.080	−14.297	−1.938	136.705	708.0	.933	.38
		(.015)		(.041)	(13.009)	(5.169)	(9.553)			
Including lagged stock										
OLS (1).......	.959	—	.016	.005	−7.738	−2.676	13.992	−6.5	.999	1.03
	(.017)		(.007)	(.006)	(1.971)	(.751)	(2.270)			
(2).......	.955	.001	—	.004	−7.827	−2.380	15.181	8.8	.999	.95
	(.019)	(.003)		(.006)	(2.069)	(.770)	(2.810)			
3PLS (1).......	1.005	—	.016	.007	−7.211	−2.587	13.154	−8.5	.999	1.89
	(.019)		(.006)	(.005)	(1.766)	(.667)	(2.053)			
(2).......	1.007	.002	—	.007	−7.266	−2.343	13.975	2.5	.999	1.89
	(.020)	(.002)		(.005)	(1.812)	(.665)	(2.439)			

NOTE:

Units of measurement are percentages (that is, 4 percent is 4) for interest rates and constant dollars for other variables. "OLS" refers to ordinary least squares and "3PLS" to three-pass least squares.

Figures in parentheses are standard errors of the coefficients.

More precisely, for any time period j, we can write (2) as

$$m_j = k\, m_{j-1} + (1 - k)b' x_j + u_j \tag{5}$$

and so we can transform (2) as follows:[14]

$$\begin{aligned} m_t &= k[k\, m_{t-2} + (1 - k)b' x_{t-1} + u_{t-1}] + (1 - k)b' x_t + u_t \\ &= k^2[k\, m_{t-3} + (1 - k)b' x_{t-2} + u_{t-2}] + k\,[(1 - k)b' x_{t-1} \\ &\quad + u_{t-1}] + (1 - k)b' x_t + u_t \end{aligned}$$

or

$$m_t = b'\,[(1 - k)\sum_{i=0}^{\infty} k^i x_{t-i}] + \sum_{i=0}^{\infty} k^i u_{t-i} \tag{6}$$

We can then choose alternative values of k between zero and 1, form for each value of k the weighted sums of past xs implied (approximating the infinite sum by a sufficiently long finite one—20 quarters in the present paper), regress m on these alternative weighted sums, and compare the results as to goodness of fit, signs of coefficients, and other criteria. Since the lagged stock has been solved out of this relationship, its statistical peculiarities in relation to the current stock should not distort the regression results. Note also that the simultaneous equations problem is less serious in (6) than in (2), since weighted sums of past xs are, except for very low values of k, largely predetermined.

Results of this experiment for five values of k (k equal to .1, .3, .5, .7, and .9) again supported the long lag hypothesis. A typical result is the equation relating demand deposits to wealth, income deviations, and the long-term rate for k equal to .1, .5, and .9:

	Coefficient of wealth	*Coefficient of income deviations*	*Coefficient of interest rate*	R^2
$k = .1$	−.05 (.01)	.09 (.03)	−33.14 (7.34)	.92
$k = .5$	−.04 (.01)	.06 (.03)	−43.59 (7.49)	.94
$k = .9$	−.02 (.01)	.09 (.05)	−57.20 (9.97)	.96

Coefficients here are estimates of b, not of $(1 - k)\, b$ as in Table 1; that is, they are estimates of long-run responses. As k increases, the significance of the coefficient for wealth, with its "wrong" sign, declines, and the overall goodness of fit improves. However, the differences are not

[14]Actually, there is an approximation involved in this transformation, arising from the fact that the lagged stock is deflated by current population and the price level, not lagged population and prices. Since the product of population and a general price index is very largely a smooth trend, the approximation should cause no distortion as far as estimating equation (6) below is concerned. In the first difference transformation referred to later, the potential distortion seemed great enough to warrant an adjustment in the dependent variable; see note 16 below.

striking; and serial correlation in this group of regressions is very high, as the final term in equation (6) might lead us to expect.

Of greater interest, therefore, is a set of regressions based on first differences of variables in the form specified in equation (6). These regressions, with results shown in Table 2, relate quarterly changes in currency, demand deposits, and time deposits to weighted averages of past changes in interest rates, income, and wealth.[15] Coefficients refer to long-run responses rather than one quarter responses. Constant terms were constrained to equal zero in these regressions, as the first differencing requires (a resultant peculiarity in the measurement of R^2 is noted in the table). Results are shown only for the nonhuman wealth variable and, in the demand deposit and currency relationships, for a single long-term interest rate. However, the pattern of change with changing values of k turns out much the same if average income is used in place of wealth or if (with either "scale" variable) yields on time deposits and Treasury bills appear in place of the long-term rate.

Once more, the results favor a slow speed of adjustment, as Table 2 demonstrates. "Wrong" signs are less frequent for high values of k than for low; and for all three assets, goodness of fit improves significantly as k rises. For the most part, the values of R^2 are low, indicating that much of the variance of quarter-to-quarter changes in currency and deposits is left unexplained; but the R^2s are decidedly lower for low than for high values of k. Serial correlation of residuals persists even after the first difference transformation, perhaps because the form of the underlying lag distribution is more complicated than the one used here, or perhaps for some other reason. In spite of serial correlation and a few other unsatisfactory or unexpected results, the long lag hypothesis emerges from tests against postwar data strongly enough so that future work on the demand for money can ill afford to ignore it.

WEALTH, INCOME, AND TRANSACTIONS

Three measures of income or wealth appear in the work reported here: (1) wealth defined as the domestic public's holdings of capital goods plus "high-powered" money plus U.S. securities plus net claims on the rest of the world, (2) wealth measured by a weighted average of

[15] The dependent variable in the currency equation in Table 2 is $\frac{C_t - C_{t-1}}{N_t P_t}$, not $\frac{C_t}{N_t P_t} - \frac{C_{t-1}}{N_{t-1} P_{t-1}}$ where C, N, and P are currency, population, and the GNP deflator; and similarly for demand deposits and time deposits. The reason for this choice is the approximation referred to in note 14. This approximation slightly distorts the relationships being estimated in any case, but less if the dependent variables appear in the first of two forms just mentioned than if they appear in the second.

TABLE 2

DEMAND EQUATIONS RELATING CHANGES IN REAL PER CAPITA MONEY HOLDINGS TO WEIGHTED AVERAGES OF PAST CHANGES IN INTEREST RATES, INCOME, AND WEALTH

	Real per Capita Wealth	Deviation from Average, Real per Capita Income	Interest Rates			R^2	$\tilde{R}^2$	Durbin-Watson Ratio
			Long-Term U.S. Securities	Treasury Bills	Time Deposits			
Change in currency:								
$k = .1$	.010	−.007	3.651	—	—	.077	.265	.63
	(.004)	(.005)	(1.192)					
$k = .3$	.011	−.009	4.748	—	—	.130	.307	.58
	(.004)	(.006)	(1.405)					
$k = .5$	.011	−.010	5.961	—	—	.157	.329	.51
	(.004)	(.007)	(1.713)					
$k = .7$	.010	−.005	7.143	—	—	.132	.308	.44
	(.005)	(.010)	(2.430)					
$k = .9$	.010	.057	6.504	—	—	.264	.414	.52
	(.006)	(.017)	(4.249)					

Change in demand deposits:								
$k = .1$	.058	.049	4.937	—	—	−.104	.336	1.09
	(.016)	(.024)	(5.276)					
$k = .3$	.073	.057	2.251	—	—	−.047	.370	1.01
	(.017)	(.027)	(6.236)					
$k = .5$	.088	.065	−2.283	—	—	−.012	.392	.89
	(.018)	(.032)	(7.595)					
$k = .7$	.109	.078	−14.074	—	—	.039	.422	.81
	(.020)	(.042)	(10.337)					
$k = .9$	.165	.197	−58.386	—	—	.305	.581	.98
	(.024)	(.066)	(16.726)					
Change in time deposits:								
$k = .1$	.065	−.028	7.787	−4.911	60.845	−.246	.455	.48
	(.026)	(.035)	(9.955)	(3.285)	(14.331)			
$k = .3$	.075	−.027	4.418	−6.513	70.804	−.085	.526	.43
	(.028)	(.038)	(11.607)	(3.762)	(15.315)			
$k = .5$	.074	−.020	−1.737	−8.233	89.052	.126	.618	.42
	(.029)	(.043)	(13.012)	(4.291)	(16.254)			
$k = .7$	.059	−.010	−16.539	−11.667	126.624	.419	.746	.63
	(.028)	(.005)	(14.935)	(5.199)	(16.608)			
$k = .9$	.055	.044	−82.603	−20.513	214.624	.770	.900	1.14
	(.023)	(.056)	(17.904)	(6.823)	(15.977)			

NOTE:

Dependent variables are in the form of quarterly changes in the stock, with the changes divided by population and prices.

Independent variables are in the form

$$\frac{1-k}{1-k^{20}} \sum_{i=0}^{19} k^i \Delta x_{t-i}$$

The column labeled R^2 gives the percentage of the variance of the dependent variables "explained" by the regressions. When the constant term is constrained to equal zero, this figure can be negative; the residuals can exceed the deviations of the dependent variable from its mean. The column labeled $\tilde{R}^2$ gives the percentage of the second moment around the *origin* (rather than around the mean) which is "explained" by the regression. This statistic is not the conventional definition of R^2; but where the constant term is set equal to zero it has the conventional limits of zero and 1.

Units of measurement are percentages for interest rates and constant dollars for other variables.

current and past levels of national income, and (3) current income minus the weighted-average income variable. The sum of the last two is, of course, simply current income, which has been used as an indicator of "transactions" in many studies of the demand for money.[16]

The first of the two wealth variables measures, after eliminating all debts between members of "the public," "nonhuman" net worth—that is, the public's wealth not embodied in the form of health, skills, or general knowledge. It refers to a highly aggregative concept and, as noted earlier, is subject to extremely difficult problems of quarterly measurement. The second wealth variable, weighted-average income, reflects the return on human as well as nonhuman wealth; but it too is a very rough approximation.

The choice between a measure of nonhuman net worth and a measure of average income as a better representation of wealth has important implications for the effect of debt management operations on interest rates. If the demand for money depends significantly on nonhuman net worth, then Treasury borrowing affects interest rates in much the same way (though not to the same degree) as open market operations. That is, if

$$M = F(r, W)$$

where M is money, r an interest rate, and W nonhuman net worth, then changing W through Treasury borrowing while holding M constant must affect interest rates and thereby investment and income (in addition, of course, to the effects generated by the use to which the Treasury puts the proceeds of the borrowing). If, however, average income is a better empirical representation of wealth, then it is difficult to imagine precisely how Treasury borrowing affects the general level of interest rates (it may, of course, affect the structure of rates; and again, the use to which the Treasury puts the proceeds of the borrowing will have effects in many directions). The general level of interest rates is determined by the requirement that money markets clear; and if money demands are not affected significantly by the stock of Treasury securities, then whatever impact that stock has on interest rates must be through its effect on demands for some other assets or for goods and services or on bank behavior affecting the money supply.

The regressions omitting the lagged stock in Table 1 demonstrate that entering these two wealth variables together in a demand equation gives implausible results; and so the discussion below compares results using one of the variables with results using the other.

The third variable, current minus weighted-average income, is a measure of "transitory" income or departures from the trend of income. It might be an important determinant of the demand for money, not only

[16] The Teigen study cited earlier, for example, makes use of income as an indicator of transactions.

because it forms a part of total income, but because money may serve as a buffer stock against temporary fluctuations in receipts. Just as studies of inventory demand often include a variable to represent the unexpected sales which give rise to involuntary inventory fluctuations, an inventory approach to the demand for money in which uncertainty plays a role would seem to require a measure of "unexpected" income. Studies of money demand based on the inventory approach, however, have not made use of such a variable.

Three findings as to the choice of "scale" variables seem to emerge from a review of postwar quarterly data. The first is that expressing currency and deposits on a real per capita basis, rather than as a dollar total, reduces the importance of any wealth or income variable. For example, the following relation between demand deposits, income, and the yield on long term U.S. securities,

$$D_t - .8D_{t-1} = \underset{(.004)}{.038Y_t} - \underset{(.447)}{1.511r} + 13.19 \qquad R^2 = .88$$

with D (demand deposits) and Y (national income) in billions of dollars and r (the interest rate) a percent, and k assumed to be .8, is changed appreciably if money and income are deflated by population and the price level. The deflated relationship is

$$d_t - .8d_{t-1} = \underset{(.007)}{.016y_t} - \underset{(1.397)}{17.219r} + 145.5 \qquad R^2 - .86$$

with d and y real per capita figures. The partial correlation coefficient of the income variable drops from .79 in the first equation to only .28 in the second. Since, as was argued earlier, theories of money demand relate to the demand by a typical economic unit at a given price level, our interest should be in the deflated rather than the undeflated results.

The second finding of interest is that the various regression runs do not indicate any clear choice between the two representations of "wealth." In Table 1 above, neither variant seems to matter when lagged stocks appear among the independent variables; but collinearity between the lagged stocks and the wealth variables makes it difficult to place much confidence in this result. The transformation underlying Table 2, in which lagged stocks are solved out and in which each independent variable appears in the form of weighted averages of past changes, would seem a more promising basis for comparison. It is useful, therefore, to compare the results of Table 2 which refer to the net-worth variable, with results making use of a weighted-income variable.

For currency, the weighted-income variable gives a better fit. For k equal to .9, the regressions are as follows:

$$\Delta c = \underset{(.006)}{.010\Delta w} + \underset{(.017)}{.057\Delta(y - \bar{y})} + \underset{(4.249)}{6.504\Delta r} \qquad R^2 = .26$$

and

$$\Delta c = \underset{(.017)}{.111\Delta\bar{y}} + \underset{(.013)}{.078\Delta(y-\bar{y})} + \underset{(2.887)}{3.881\Delta r} \qquad R^2 = .55$$

in which Δw, $\Delta(y-\bar{y})$, Δr, and $\Delta\bar{y}$ refer to weighted averages of past changes in net worth, deviations from average income, the interest rate on long-term U.S. securities, and weighted-average income (with all variables other than r on a real per capita basis). The interest rate has a sign opposite to expectation, but not far above its standard error in both cases. The difference between the two results is essentially the difference in fit between the two wealth variables. With the weighted-average income variable, in contrast to the nonhuman wealth variable, there is little difference in goodness of fit for different values of k. Values of .7 and .9 are more satisfactory than lower values in one respect, however; namely, that the positive coefficient for the interest rate variable is not significant for these higher values.

For demand deposits the net-worth variant gives a significantly better fit. Here the regressions for k equal to .9, employing the transformations underlying Table 2, are:

$$\Delta d = \underset{(.024)}{.165\Delta w} + \underset{(.066)}{.197\Delta(y-\bar{y})} - \underset{(16.726)}{58.386\Delta r} \qquad R^2 = .31$$

and

$$\Delta d = \underset{(.110)}{.259\Delta\bar{y}} + \underset{(.084)}{.341\Delta(y-\bar{y})} - \underset{(18.806)}{1.781\Delta r} \qquad R^2 = -.16$$ [17]

with Δw, $\Delta(y-\bar{y})$, Δr, and $\Delta\bar{y}$ as defined above. When both wealth variables appear together here, the coefficient of the average-income variant drops to nearly zero, while that of the net worth variant remains positive and several times its standard error.

For time deposits the two wealth variables give nearly identical results in terms of R^2; and both have positive coefficients several times their standard errors.

Wealth elasticities implied by these equations when k is equal to .9 may be of interest. For the currency equations, elasticities at 1948–63 mean levels of the variables are .6 for the net worth variant and 1.3 for the weighted-average income variant. For demand deposits, elasticities are 2.5 for the net-worth variant and .8 for the weighted-average income variant. The comparable time-deposit elasticities are 1.6 and 1.1. These figures refer to long-run rather than single quarter responses of real per capita holdings of currency and deposits to changes in real per capita wealth. Most of them are larger than the results of other studies (or,

[17]The negative value of R^2 is possible because the constant term is constrained to equal zero. See the notes to Table 2.

indeed, other regressions in the present study) would suggest. They are probably more unexpected under an inventory approach than under a utility approach to the demand for money. They are, however, very sensitive to the value of k selected, so that the values just listed are subject to exceptionally large margins of error.

While the high estimated elasticities with respect to "scale" variables are perhaps unexpected under an inventory approach to money demand, the importance of "unexpected" income seems much easier to fit into an inventory than into a utility approach. And both Tables 1 and 2 and the regressions just listed suggest—this is the third finding of interest referred to above—that the income deviation or transitory income variable, $y - \bar{y}$, may be fairly important in accounting for changes in the public's money holdings, although not its time deposit holdings. Because the money stock moves so smoothly from quarter to quarter, it is hard to imagine money serving as a buffer stock against "unexpected" fluctuations in income; but there seems to be evidence that it does serve in this way to some degree, after allowance is made for other influences on demand.

INTEREST RATES

The process by which changes in monetary policy affect incomes and prices clearly depends in part on which interest rate or rates are the ones which serve to clear the money market in the short run. If the rate is some average rate on a wide spectrum of financial and real assets, represented perhaps by a rate on long-term securities,[18] then the transmission of increases in the money supply to markets for capital goods may be fairly direct. However, if rates on specific substitutes for money such as Treasury bills and time deposits are the ones involved, then the term structure of interest rates, the portfolio behavior of banks, and other matters involving the relationship of these rates to other rates of return are all centrally involved in the transmission of money supply changes.

The empirical choice between a long-term interest rate on the one hand and some combination of rates on Treasury bills and time deposits on the other[19] is difficult because of collinearity problems. The coefficient of correlation between the rate on long-term U.S. securities and an unweighted average of the time deposit and Treasury bill rates (based on quarterly averages from 1948 I through 1963 IV) is .96; and for almost any weighted combination of the two rates the correlation with the long-term yield is above .9. This collinearity is probably not a sta-

[18]Meltzer, *op. cit.*, p. 223.

[19]Teigen, *op. cit.*, uses only the commercial paper rate, which moves closely with the Treasury bill rate, in his demand for money relationship; but yields on savings deposits would seem relevant to household money holdings in just the same way that yields on short-term paper and, more recently, on time deposits are to business holdings.

tistical coincidence; regressive interest rate expectations probably contribute to making Treasury bill yields fluctuate more than long-term yields, while banks appear to set time and savings deposit yields in such a way that they fluctuate less than many market yields[20]—at least, until the recent growth of the market for certificates of deposit. An average of the bill rate and savings yields therefore has fluctuations quite similar to those in interest rates on long-term securities.

Postwar evidence thus does not discriminate sharply between different interest rates as influences on money holdings. For currency, Tables 1 and 2 reveal that the existence of a long-term interest rate effect on currency holdings is very difficult to detect; and the same is true if the long-term rate is replaced by the bill rate and the time deposit rate.[21] For demand deposits, the three-pass least squares equation involving a net-worth measure of wealth in Table 1 was

$$\underset{}{d_t} = 96.4 + \underset{(.026)}{.907d_{t-1}} + \underset{(.003)}{.002w} + \underset{(.007)}{.024(y-\bar{y})} - \underset{(1.756)}{11.987r} \quad R^2 = .997, \quad \tilde{R}^2 = .996$$

in which d, w, and $y - \bar{y}$ represent demand deposits, wealth, and deviations from average income, all on a real per capita basis, and r is the rate on long-term U.S. securities. A comparable equation using the two interest rates on "safe" assets is

$$d_t = 46.3 + \underset{(.038)}{.919d_{t-1}} + \underset{(.003)}{.003w} + \underset{(.007)}{.032(y-\bar{y})} - \underset{(.684)}{4.256r'} - \underset{(2.344)}{4.450r''}$$

$$R^2 = .997 \quad \tilde{R}^2 = .996$$

in which r' and r'' represent the three-month Treasury bill yield and the average yield on bank time and savings deposits. Clearly, there is not much basis for choice between the two equations.

The transformation procedure underlying Table 2 does discriminate slightly in favor of rates on the two "safe" assets. The demand deposit equation for k equal to .9 from Table 2 is:

$$\Delta d_t = \underset{(.024)}{.165\Delta w} + \underset{(.066)}{.197\Delta(y-\bar{y})} - \underset{(16.726)}{58.386\Delta r} \quad R^2 = .31 \quad \tilde{R}^2 = .29$$

in which Δw, $\Delta(y - \bar{y})$, and Δr refer to weighted averages of current and past changes. The comparable equation employing interest rates on safe assets is

$$\Delta d_t = \underset{(.027)}{.174\Delta w} + \underset{(.067)}{.256\Delta(y-\bar{y})} - \underset{(6.520)}{30.453\Delta r'} - \underset{(16.897)}{22.444\Delta r''} \quad R^2 = .41 \quad \tilde{R}^2 = .38$$

---

[20]See de Leeuw, *op. cit.*

[21]The currency equations in de Leeuw, *op. cit.*, in which all dollar variables were expressed as a percent of weighted-average GNP, did yield a significant interest rate effect.

in which $\triangle r'$ and $\triangle r''$ also refer to weighted averages of changes. These equations thus provide slight support on the side of an inventory approach as against a general wealth allocation approach to money demand.

For time deposits, all three interest rates show up as important influences on the public's demand, in spite of collinearity problems, as Tables 1 and 2 illustrate.

According to these last two equations, long-run elasticities of demand, with respect to interest rates at 1948–62 means, are .31 with respect to the long-term rate, or alternatively .11 and .07 with respect to the bill rate and the time deposit rate. Long-run elasticities based on the three-pass least squares results are somewhat higher. As in the case of wealth and income elasticities, these estimates are quite sensitive to small changes in the value of k.

SUMMARY OF FINDINGS

Probably the strongest evidence provided by the postwar quarterly data with respect to the three issues raised at the beginning of this paper is on the matter of speeds of adjustment. Here the evidence supports fairly strongly the hypothesis that portfolios adjust with a considerable lag. This finding persists even after attempts to correct for possible statistical biases and seems true for all three of the monetary assets examined in this paper.

With respect to the choice of "scale" variable, the postwar evidence seems to support a nonhuman net worth measure for demand deposits, a weighted-average income measure for currency, and either one for time deposits. Deviations of current from weighted average income seem to influence significantly holdings of both currency and demand deposits.

With respect to interest rates, collinearity among rates makes it difficult to discriminate sharply between a single long-term rate on the one hand and rates on the "safe" assets, Treasury bills and time deposits, on the other. The "safe asset" rates seem to give a slightly better fit in one test and about the same in another. It would be useful to see if the collinearity observed in postwar years has also characterized earlier periods, in order better to evaluate the success of a single long-term interest rate in helping to account for changes in money holdings over long periods.

The importance of an "unexpected" income measure would seem to be evidence in favor of an inventory rather than a more general utility approach to the theory of the demand for money. Evidence on alternative interest rates provides support—but only very weak support—for the same side; while the importance of nonhuman wealth in the demand deposit relationship and the high estimated wealth and income elasticities constitute weak support for the other side.

The implications of long lags in adjustment for the theory of money demand are difficult to deduce. The existence of long lags seems hard to reconcile with an inventory approach if the reason for the lags is costs (in time and effort as well as direct money payments) of adapting to changes in the "desired" stock; for underlying the inventory approach is the notion that money stocks are easier or cheaper to alter than many other balance sheet items. However, if long lags reflect delays in the spread of information, there is no necessary incompatibility with an inventory approach. The inventory and utility approaches are not, of course, mutually exclusive; and it may be that a combination of elements from both theories will turn out more successful than either one alone.

THE MEANING OF MONETARY INDICATORS*

Karl Brunner and Allan H. Meltzer

Among the topics that monetary economists discuss, few have been debated as much or as long as the meaning of a given change or rate of change in the stock of money or the interest rate. Some have stressed the importance of monetary or of interest rate changes as a guide to the future pace of economic activity. Yet it seems reasonable to conclude that the partisans have not succeeded in convincing others that one or the other of these variables is the most reliable measure of the effect of monetary policy. There is not even agreement that the choice is restricted to these two measures. Bank credit, free reserves, liquid assets, and other variables are mentioned frequently. Since it is not unusual to find that quite different—even opposite—conclusions are suggested by the various measures, a comparison of the information provided by some of the variables proposed as indicators is called for.

The problem may be restated as a series of questions. What information about monetary policy is conveyed by the position of, or change in, a particular variable? How do we choose from among the many available time series those that are to be watched more carefully than others? By what criteria do we decide that a particular variable is a good or better indicator of current or recent monetary policy?

Many discussions of monetary policy take a rather different starting point from the one taken here. A particular hypothesis relating monetary policy to prices and output is assumed—usually implicitly—to be well established. Policy implications are obtained from the hypothesis. Attention is then directed toward the problem of forecasting the future, selecting a policy goal, and/or measuring lags of various kinds.[1] Without

*An earlier version of this paper was presented at the Workshop in Money and Banking, University of Chicago, and at a seminar at Purdue University. The authors benefited from the financial support of the National Science Foundation.

[1]L. A. Metzler, "Three Lags in the Circular Flow of Income," *Employment and Public Policy: Essays in Honor of Alvin Hansen* (New York: W. W. Norton, Inc.,

(Continued on next page)

disputing the importance of these problems, an obvious point should be noted, that is, that the policy conclusions depend on the hypothesis selected. Equally important, the measurement of lags depends on two types of hypotheses: (1) relatively crude approximations to an underlying dynamic theory of economic activity or policy-making behavior and (2) hypotheses about the remaining structure of the economy.

In this paper, we acknowledge our ignorance—or relatively incomplete information—about the structure of the economy. Given this state of knowledge, particularly the absence of quantitative estimates of many of the parameters of a general-equilibrium macromodel, of the speeds of adjustment of many of the variables, and of the distribution of the effect of monetary policy through time, a number of questions arise. What information does the policy maker have available to decide on a future course of action, or to judge the present or recent position of the economy? How does he assess the results achieved by past policy or likely to be achieved in the near future? How does he decide whether his policy has resulted in relative restraint or relative ease?

One solution is to decide that additional knowledge is so difficult to obtain, so subject to error, or so hard to interpret that reliance must be placed on simple solutions, for example, monetary rules, very simple qualitative hypotheses,[2] or perhaps on "color, tone, and feel." An alternative is to use the available quantitative and qualitative information, while recognizing the incomplete and uncertain character of the knowledge possessed.

A strategy for combining incomplete information about the structure of the economy with an assumption about the goal of policy is discussed here. The problem is referred to as the "indicator problem," since we are concerned with the relative merits of a number of variables often used to indicate the current direction of monetary policy or the future effect of recent policies. Our tentative results are not presented as a resolution of the problem, only as a means of opening for analysis a topic that is more frequently debated than analyzed. At the outset we acknowledge that many of the questions raised here can be answered more fully if (and only if) more useful knowledge about the structure of the economy is assumed or obtained. Put otherwise, the theorist may choose to ignore this problem by assuming the possession of reliable information

---

1948), pp. 11–32; J. M. Culbertson, "Friedman on the Lag in Effect of Monetary Policy," *Journal of Political Economy*, December, 1960, pp. 617–21; M. Friedman, "The Lag in Effect of Monetary Policy," *Journal of Political Economy*, October, 1961, pp. 447–67; A. Ando, E. C. Brown, R. M. Solow, and J. Kareken, "Lags in Fiscal and Monetary Policy," in *Stabilization Policies* (Commission on Money and Credit) (Englewood Cliffs, N.J.: Prentice-Hall, Inc., 1963), pp. 1–163.

[2]See the recommendations of P. A. Samuelson, "Reflections on Central Banking," *National Banking Review*, September, 1963, pp. 15–28.

currently outside the scope of quantitative economics. The policy maker is not as fortunate.

THE GENERAL PROBLEM

By way of contrast with our present state of knowledge, consider a situation in which there is a fully identified, highly confirmed theory of macroeconomic processes. There is then quantitative information about the structural parameters, or useful knowledge, to use Marschak's apt phrase.[3] Since the policy maker can infer, from the comprehensive model, the expected effect of policy action on any or all variables that are of interest to him, he can determine the amount that policy must contribute to achieve a particular set of social goals. If the structure is known and the goal or social utility function is specified, knowledge of the change in monetary policy permits the policy maker to evaluate the effects of his past actions. The indicator of monetary policy summarizes in an index the relative degree of monetary ease or restraint. Let I be the indicator of monetary policy. Then

$$I = \frac{du}{dy_1}\frac{dy_1}{dx_1}dx_1 + \frac{du}{dy_2}\frac{dy_2}{dx_1}dx_1$$

where u represents the social utility function, y_1 and y_2 are endogenous variables of the system—for example, prices and real output—and dx_1 is the change in variables expressing monetary policy operations.[4]

The derivatives of the endogenous y variables with respect to x_1 describe the responses of the goal variables to policy operations. These derivatives are, of course, total derivatives obtained by differentiating over the whole system of relations, and depend on the derivatives of the structural equations. Since the derivatives of each of the structural equations and of the utility function are assumed to be known, all that is required to measure changes in the degree of ease or restraint is a measure of the change in one or more of the monetary policy variables that has been altered.

Some of the elements in the more general problem have been introduced in the example just considered. First, there is a choice to be made about the nature of the utility function. Second, hypotheses must be

[3] J. Marschak, "Economic Measurements for Policy and Prediction," in Hood and Koopmans (eds.), *Studies in Econometric Methods* (New York: John Wiley & Sons, Inc., 1953), pp. 1–26.

[4] The nature of the index depends, of course, on the goal or utility function. If the latter is unique only up to order-preserving transformations, I must be treated as an ordering. For most practical purposes this would be sufficient. Note that since y_1, y_2, and x_1 are vectors, $\frac{du}{dy_i}$, dx are vectors and the $\frac{dy_i}{dx}$ are matrices.

selected. Economics has not advanced far enough as an empirical science to make the choice obvious. Moreover, very little is known about the values of the parameters of any set of hypotheses that might be used. The example suggests that any change in the structural relations is capable of altering the indicator. Hence, the index value of any particular policy depends on the hypotheses. Third, changes in institutional arrangements alter the channels and effects of monetary policy. With relatively complete knowledge, institutional rearrangements do not create serious problems for the construction of an indicator. However, we will note below that there is a trade-off between complex institutional arrangements and the amount of knowledge about the system that is required. Finally, the example suggests that there is only one relevant strategy, namely, to construct the appropriate indicator for the evaluation of policy. This simple strategy is no longer meaningful when we revert to the position of relatively incomplete knowledge. A choice of strategy must then be made. For example, it may be desirable to choose policies or indicators that minimize the extent to which knowledge is required about the structure of the system; or, the strategy may be one of choosing an indicator that minimizes the chance of serious misinterpretation of the result of policy actions.

The indicators of monetary policy usually mentioned by economists are not even approximately related to the indicator function introduced above. Most of them are endogenous variables. As such, their position or rate of change at any time is the result of the joint interaction of the whole system and reflects more than the effect of current monetary policy. Fiscal policies and noncontrolled exogenous variables also influence the endogenous indicators. Moreover, their current position or rate of change is the result of partial or incomplete adjustment to the long-run position implied by the expected response to changes in policy and other exogenous forces. Information is rarely available on the proportion of the adjustment which has already occurred.[5]

The danger of misinterpreting the current direction of monetary policy exists in principle when any endogenous variable is used as an indicator. Suppose interest rates on financial assets are accepted as the indicator. Relatively high rates are interpreted as a "tighter" policy, and rising rates are taken as an indication of "tightening." Further, assume that interest rates are accepted as the principal financial variable that transmits monetary impulses to the real variables and hence to the pace of economic activity. The bond yield is endogenous. Its behavior is determined by the interaction of the whole system under the impact of changes in the monetary and nonmonetary policy variables and in the noncon-

[5]Even if the length of the lags is assumed to be well established, the time distribution of the adjustment may be known less precisely.

trolled variables. If there is sufficient information available to construct the indicator function I, there is no danger of misinterpretation. A rise in interest rates that results from nonmonetary forces, say an increase in the expected yield on real capital, can be separated from the effect on interest rates of expansive monetary policy. Without the information required for construction of the indicator function, the rise in interest rates will be interpreted as an indication that monetary policy has become tighter and more restrictive when the indicator, if it were available, would reveal the error in this interpretation.

The fact that interest rates are taken as the central element transmitting monetary policy from the financial to the real sector does not establish that they are a better (or worse) indicator of current monetary policy than some other endogenous variable. But the central role assigned to interest rates would suggest that they are influenced greatly by feedbacks from the real to the financial sector, so that their position or direction of change at any time is a result of opposing influences. Similar statements apply to the money supply and other endogenous variables, although the relative size of policy and nonpolicy influences will differ with the endogenous variable selected as an indicator.

It is possible to rank many of the endogenous variables by their quality as indicators, if we are not completely ignorant about the goals of policy and the operation of the economic system. To do so, a class of hypotheses must be selected. In principle, this choice should be made by systematically comparing alternative classes. In practice, we have selected one with which we are familiar, on the grounds that it includes among the endogenous variables many of the indicators that are frequently suggested or used to appraise the direction of monetary policy and is sufficiently rich in detail to bring out clearly the problem of choosing an indicator.[6]

AN OUTLINE OF THE HYPOTHESIS

The indicator function introduced above expressed the connection between monetary policy (x_1) and the indicator I. In the model, changes in policy affect the level of output, prices, and other real variables by changing financial variables and relative prices. Absence of useful knowledge about many structural relations of the transmission process does not alter the need for a framework like the one underlying the indicator func-

[6]The statement in the text should not suggest that no effort has been made to compare alternative theories. The velocity relation plays a key role in the analysis below. It has been compared to a variety of alternatives in our "Predicting Velocity: Implications for Theory and Policy," *Journal of Finance,* May, 1963, pp. 319–54, and in "The Demand for Money: The Evidence from the Time Series," *Journal of Political Economy,* June, 1963, pp. 219–46. See also the references cited in the next footnote.

tion. To appraise the effect of policy operations, we require both a theory and a utility function. Relations summarizing behavior on the financial and output markets must be presented before several of the variables proposed as indicators can be compared. The hypotheses used for this purpose are described briefly in this section. The appendix provides a condensed, formal statement.

The set of relations that determine the partial equilibrium solutions for the money supply, the banks' portfolio of earning assets, and interest rates have been presented in some earlier work.[7] The equations of the monetary system underlying the equilibrium conditions summarize the allocation decisions of the banks and the public and their responses to the decisions of the monetary authority.

The public's behavior is expressed through three relations: (1) the allocation of money between currency and demand deposits, (2) the allocation of bank deposits between demand and time accounts, and (3) the supply function of earning assets to banks. Banks are assumed to allocate assets in response to changes in a number of cost, yield, stock and flow variables. Of particular importance, at present, is the dependence of the money supply and the banks' demand for earning assets on interest rates and real income. This dependence is a consequence of the effect of interest rates on the banks' demand for excess and borrowed reserves, of real income on the currency ratio, and of both interest rates and real income on the ratio of time to demand deposits.[8] Interest rates, real income, and the expected yield on real capital also affect the equilibrium solution for interest rates and bank credit through the public's supply of earning assets to banks (see equation A7).

Six policy variables record the decisions of the monetary authorities. The open market portfolio is one of the sources of the adjusted base—an exogenous variable of the system. The adjusted base is equal to reserves plus currency minus member bank borrowing. The remaining policy variables affect the monetary system by changing the monetary and asset multipliers: equations (A8) and (A9) of the appendix. The rediscount rate and the ceiling rate on time deposits affect the multipliers through the desired free reserve and time deposit ratios, respectively. Changes in the reserve requirement ratios and in the proportion of vault cash included in required reserves change the weighted average of reserve requirement ratios, denoted by r in the appendix.

---

[7]"Some Further Investigations of Demand and Supply Functions for Money," *Journal of Finance*, May, 1964; and "A Credit Market Theory of Money Supply," to be published in the *Essays in Honor of Marco Fanno*.

[8]In the appendix this is expressed by the dependence of the free reserves and time deposit ratios on interest rates. (See equations [A8] and [A10].) Other variables on which f, k, and t are assumed to depend are not discussed, since they do not play an important role in the subsequent analysis. The references in the previous footnote provide more details about the determinants of these ratios.

The solutions for the money supply and interest rates from the financial sector are connected to the real sector by a quantity equation. A demand function for money, akin to the one emphasized in much of our recent work, is expressed as a velocity relation. The aggregate demand for output, $MV + G$, is the sum of government expenditure (G) plus private expenditure (MV). The quantity equation relates aggregate government and private demand with nominal supply. A price-setting function expresses the adjustment of supply prices to variations in current and past output and in capital stock.

Fiscal policy operations affect both financial and real variables. As noted above, the government's income-generating expenditure has been introduced as a component of total spending. In addition, equation (A5) relates the government's cash deficit to the volume of government expenditures and to the means by which the deficit is financed. A surplus or deficit in the cash budget raises or lowers the sum of interest- and noninterest-bearing government debt. Changes in both types of debt affect real output and the equilibrium position of the financial sector. If the deficit is financed by noninterest-bearing debt, the adjusted base is increased.

The relations just described do not constitute a specific hypothesis of the type required for construction of the indicator function introduced above, since little is known about the speeds of adjustment or other parameter values in the equations. Rather, the system remains quite general and is representative of a large class of hypotheses. This is particularly true of the relations describing the real sector.

Nevertheless, preliminary investigations suggest that sufficient information is available about the class of hypotheses to reach tentative conclusions about some of the indicators frequently used by economists. The reason is that the comparative merit of various indicators is not greatly affected by the particular relations used to describe the real system. The analysis presented in a later section furnishes a firmer foundation for this conclusion.

This is not the place to discuss the implications of the model in detail. However, a few of the implications bear directly on the indicator problem since they describe some of the effects of monetary policy on output and prices, the requirements of an effective monetary policy, and some determinants of the length of the lag between policy action and its effect.

First, the elasticity of real output with respect to the coordinates of the monetary policy vector, x_1, is taken as the measure of the effectiveness of monetary policy operations of given size. The necessary and sufficient conditions for an effective monetary policy depend on the interest elasticities of velocity, of the public's supply of assets to banks, and of the monetary and asset multipliers.

Second, the larger the interest elasticity of velocity and/or of the monetary multiplier, the smaller the response of output to monetary policy (and the larger the response to fiscal policy). A large interest elasticity of the public's asset supply and of the banks' earning asset multiplier raises the size of the response to monetary policy.

Third, constant growth of monetary magnitudes affects the *level* of output and the rate of change of prices. Constant growth generates no fluctuations, although fluctuations may occur for other reasons—for example, through the delayed adjustment of supply prices. The variability of monetary magnitudes is more important than their level in explaining their contribution to large fluctuations in output. (Similar statements apply to fiscal policies.)

Fourth, a "Friedman lag" emerges whenever acceleration or deceleration of monetary magnitudes (that is, second differences in the stocks) becomes pronounced and persistent. The length of the lag is dependent on the length and magnitude of the acceleration or deceleration of the monetary variables.

Fifth, the delayed adjustment of output prices in response to past output and capital stock means that the short-term effects of monetary policy are on real output. Over the longer term, the price level absorbs the effects of policy.

THE TRUE OR IDEAL INDICATOR

The relations in the previous section do not provide all the information required for the derivation of the true indicator. A social utility function must be introduced and a policy goal must be selected. Since this paper is concerned primarily with the comparison of several suggested indicators and with the general problem, a rather simple utility function is used. Utility is treated as a monotonic, increasing function of real income which has the form $u(\log \frac{y}{c})$, where y is real income and c is the capacity level of output. The only goal of monetary policy is to increase real income.[9]

Once the goal is selected, the theory outlined in the appendix can be combined with the goal in an index that permits monetary policy to be ordered and compared. If there is enough information to compute the index, vague terms such as "easing" and "tightening," often used to characterize policy, can be replaced by statements about the movement

[9]The choice of per capita real income as the argument of the utility function would not alter the discussion in the text, if population is introduced as an exogenous variable. More complex utility functions containing the rate of change of prices and of real income could be used also. The method used to derive the results would not be affected by the increased complexity of the utility function. But judgments about the trade-off between policy goals—for example, inflation and employment—would be required.

of the indicator. A rising index denotes an easier policy; reductions in the index show that policy is tighter.

The movements of the "true" indicator are given by I, where

$$I = \epsilon(y,B^a)\frac{dQ}{Q}$$

A multiplicative factor consisting of the marginal utility with respect to log y has been omitted. The first component, $\epsilon(y,B^a)$, is the elasticity of real income (the goal) with respect to open market operations and other changes in the adjusted base B^a. Since this component enters the indicator function as a scalar, it can be neglected in the subsequent discussion. The second component, $\frac{dQ}{Q}$, provides all of the information required to order monetary policy under the given hypothesis and a simple goal. It contains three terms:

$$\frac{dQ}{Q} = \frac{dB^a}{B^a} + \frac{dq}{q}\left[\frac{h_1 - h_2\alpha}{h_1 - h_2}\right] \tag{1}$$

The first two ratios contain all of the monetary policy variables—the monetary base, the reserve requirement ratios, the rediscount rate, and so forth. Policy variables other than B^a operate through the monetary multiplier and are expressed in $\frac{dq}{q}$ as weighted relative rates of change.[10] The third (bracketed) term in equation (1) is a combination of interest elasticities on the credit market (h_1) and on the output market (h_2) and a parameter (α) equal to the ratio of the money supply plus time deposits to bank earning assets. These expressions are more fully defined in section C of the appendix, where it is noted that α is greater than unity and that the bracketed expression on the right is positive, but less than unity, under the hypothesis.

Reliable information is available about some, but not all, of the components. The percentage rate of change of the base and of other policy variables can be measured exactly. Some of the weights used to combine the policy variables in $\frac{dq}{q}$ have been computed; others can be placed within a narrow range. Much less is known about several of the elasticities in h_1 and h_2. Without such information, the indicator cannot be computed reliably.

The problem of inadequate information vanishes if policy action is

---

[10] $$\frac{dq}{q} = \epsilon(m,r^d)\frac{dr^d}{r^d} + \epsilon(m,r^t)\frac{dr^t}{r^t} + \ldots$$

plus similar terms for the rediscount rate, the vault cash counted as required reserves, and the ceiling rate on time deposits. The expressions $\epsilon(m,x)$ are elasticities of the monetary multiplier (m) with respect to a particular policy variable. For a description of the variables see the symbol dictionary in the appendix. The definition of m is given as part of equation (A9).

restricted to open market operations. The base and the true indicator then coincide. Construction of the indicator is reduced to measurement of changes in an exogenous variable, and the policy position is completely and accurately described by the growth rate of the base.[11]

It is apparent from the above that prevailing monetary arrangements increase the amount of information required by the policy maker. In short, there is a trade-off between knowledge and the complexity of policy arrangements. The unknown benefits of having a variety of policy instruments seem a high price to pay for the substantial increase in the amount of information required to measure the quantitative impact of policy. Until the requisite knowledge becomes available, it would be useful to restrict policy operations to changes in the adjusted base.

Much of the time, policy operations are dominated by open market operations, so that the true indicator and the percentage rate of change in the base coincide. Unfortunately, this happy coincidence occurs least frequently when the desire for correct information is most pressing. At or near the peak of an expansion, bill rates generally rise above the prevailing discount rate, and the discount rate is raised while the growth rate of the base is compressed. Our estimate of the response in q to a 1 percent change in the discount rate is relatively small, but percentage changes in the discount rate are generally quite large and therefore capable of dominating the movement of the indicator at or near the upper turning point in real income.

A COMPARISON OF SOME PROPOSED ENDOGENOUS INDICATORS

Since construction of the true indicator requires information that is not available, it is useful to consider the merits of variables often accepted as indicators. Movements of interest rates, free reserves, the money supply, and other entities have been used to measure the effect of monetary policy. All of these variables have the advantage of being observable. But each is an endogenous variable in the hypothesis introduced earlier, so that current movements are in part the result of feedback from the financial or output markets. The fact that the endogenous indicators can be measured need not, therefore, be an advantage. Separation of the influence of monetary policy from other influences often requires more information than the construction of the true indicator.

---

[11]The effect on the indicator of redistributions of deposits between classes of banks with different requirement ratios is ignored. Otherwise, the statement in the text must be changed to eliminate the minor effect on the indicator caused by the slight difference in the average reserve requirement ratio resulting from deposit redistribution.

The conclusion that the relative change in the base is equivalent to the ideal indicator when q is unchanged does not hold for every utility function. It holds in the present case because increased real income is chosen as the only goal of policy.

In this section, several endogenous indicators are discussed. Solutions for the rates of change are derived from the hypothesis, and the problems caused by the presence of structural parameters of unknown value are considered. Several of the indicators are expressed in terms of the true indicator, so that differences between them can be compared. The discussion of alternative strategies for choosing an appropriate, observable indicator is deferred, however, to a later section.

The Money Supply

A small but vociferous group of economists takes the rate of change of the money supply as a simple and straightforward indicator of monetary policy. Increases in the money supply are interpreted as expansive and decreases as contractive. Leaving aside, momentarily, differences of opinion about the suitable definition of the money supply, we will define the money supply as currency and demand deposits. The percentage rate of change of the money supply so defined is given by equation (2), where $\epsilon(m,i)$ and $\epsilon(m,y)$ are the interest and real income elasticities of the monetary multiplier, m:

$$\frac{dM}{M} = \frac{dB^a}{B^a} + \frac{dq}{q} + \epsilon(m, i)\frac{di}{i} + \epsilon(m, y)\frac{dy}{y} \tag{2}$$

The money supply is by no means an ideal indicator. It misstates the magnitude of changes in the policy variables and records the effects of changes in other exogenous variables. The solution for $\frac{dM}{M}$ incorporates the influence of monetary policy variables, feedback effects, and the influences of fiscal and noncontrolled exogenous variables. The latter are merged with the feedback effects and summarized by the variations in two endogenous variables, interest rates (i) and real income (y).

Changes in the adjusted base appear to have the same effect on the money supply as on the ideal indicator. But policies that expand the money supply lower interest rates on financial assets, so that a given percentage change in the base induces a smaller percentage change in the money supply. The size of the difference depends on the size of the interest elasticity of the monetary multiplier, $\epsilon(m,i)$. Our estimates suggest that this elasticity is in the neighborhood of .1 or .2.[12] If these

[12] See "Some Further Investigations . . ." *op. cit.* Additional estimates have since been computed using both quarterly and annual data. While such estimates are tentative, $\epsilon(m,i)$ is generally small and positive. It is, of course, possible that $\epsilon(m,i)\frac{di}{i} = \epsilon(m,y)\frac{dy}{y}$, so that the error in using $\frac{dM}{M}$ in place of the true indicator would be quite small. Our analysis gives no reason to believe that this fortunate result should be expected. Nor can the similar terms appearing below in the equations for free reserves and interest rates be expected to cancel.

estimates are correct, the effect of changes in interest rates on the money supply is attenuated. Nevertheless, the money supply slightly understates the effect of changes in B^a relative to the true indicator.

On the other hand, a money supply indicator overstates the direct effect of changes in the reserve requirement ratios, the rediscount rate, and other policy variables in q. The reason is that $\frac{dq}{q}$ appears in the solution for the ideal indicator, weighted by a ratio of elasticities with a value less than 1. Changes in interest rates (induced by the changes in q) lower the amount by which $\frac{dM}{M}$ overstates the effect on the ideal indicator of policies operating through q. But it is unlikely that the induced change in interest rates offsets the error caused by the absence of the ratio $\frac{h_1 - h_2\alpha}{h_1 - h_2}$ in equation (2).

Finally, $\frac{dM}{M}$ is affected by the exogenous, noncontrolled, and fiscal policy variables which affect i and y but which do not appear in the solution for the ideal indicator. Since $\epsilon(m,i)$ is quite small, variations in interest rates induced by changes in interest-bearing government debt, capital stock, and so forth do not greatly reduce the usefulness of $\frac{dM}{M}$ as an indicator. However, the combined effects of the many changes summarized by $\frac{dy}{y}$ have not been carefully estimated. Although the evidence which has been collected strongly suggests that monetary policy operations and changes in the currency ratio are the dominant influences on the money supply, the problem of separating the effects of monetary policy from other influences remains if the money supply is used as an indicator.

Other Monetary Variables

The rates of change of commercial bank credit (E) and the money supply plus time deposits ($M + T$) are also used as indicators of monetary policy. The solutions for these variables contain terms very similar to the solution for the money supply. Relative to the true indicator, they, too, overstate the effect of policy variables combined in q, and understate the effects of policies operating through the adjusted base. Moreover, $M + T$ and E are more responsive than the money supply to relative changes in interest rates and in the variables operating through the relative change in real income. The reason is that the elasticities of the multipliers of $M + T$ and E with respect to interest rates and real income are larger than the similar elasticities for the money supply.

Our analysis suggests that because the elasticities are largest for E and smallest for M, the difference, relative to the ideal indicator, is also largest for E and smallest for M. This is particularly true for open market operations and other changes in the base. In addition, nonmonetary policy changes are more fully reflected in E and $M + T$ than in M. The money supply is likely to be a better indicator of current or recent monetary policy than the other monetary variables. However, it bears repeating that the money supply is not equivalent to the ideal indicator.

Interest Rates

Market rates of interest are perhaps the most popular indicators of monetary policy among academic economists. One reason may be that the transmission of monetary policy is generally described as operating through a number of interest rates before reaching the components of aggregate expenditure. The theory underlying the discussion of indicators is not incompatible with general statements about the importance of interest rates in the transmission mechanism. But it does not follow from such statements that interest rates are (or are not) closely related to the ideal indicator. The quality of interest rates as an indicator is given by the comparison of the information they convey with the information conveyed by the ideal indicator.

Equation (3) states the solution for the relative change in i in terms of the ideal indicator, where z is a vector of fiscal and noncontrolled variables including the capital stock, the stock of outstanding government debt, and other variables treated as exogenous under the hypothesis; g_1 and g_2 are combinations of elasticities with respect to real income on the output and credit markets, defined in section C of the appendix; and $\epsilon(i,B^a)$ and $\epsilon(y,B^a)$ are the elasticities of interest rates and output with respect to the extended base:[13]

$$\frac{di}{i} = \epsilon(i, B^a)\left[\frac{dQ}{Q} + \frac{dq}{q}\,\frac{(\alpha - 1)}{(g_1 - g_2)\,\epsilon(y, B^a)}\right] + \epsilon(i, z)\,\frac{dz}{z} \qquad (3)$$

The bracketed expression contains all of the monetary policy variables. Since $\epsilon(i,B^a)$ is negative, and the ratio modifying the effect of $\frac{dq}{q}$ is positive, expansive policies (rising B^a or q) lower interest rates on financial assets. Lower interest rates are interpreted, therefore, as an indication of expansive policies.

---

[13] To obtain the solution for $\frac{di}{i}$ in terms of Q, we make use of the solution for $\epsilon(y,B^a)$ derived from the hypothesis:

$$\epsilon(y,B^a) = \frac{h_1 - h_2 a}{g_1 h_1 - g_2 h_2}$$

Two important consequences follow from this interpretation of interest rate movements. First, the bracketed expression containing the monetary policy variables exceeds the true indicator whenever policy operates through q. Thus the effects of changes in the reserve requirement ratios, the rediscount rate, vault cash policy, or the ceiling rate on time deposits are subject to misinterpretation. This difficulty can be removed by restricting monetary policy to open market operations. The relative change in interest rates is then proportional to the relative change in the indicator. But there would then be no reason to use interest rates or any other endogenous variable as an indicator. Monetary policy would be measured correctly by the relative change in the adjusted base.

The second consequence is the result of a more fundamental problem. The choice of i as an indicator attributes the effects of changes in the fiscal and noncontrolled variables, represented by dz, to monetary policy. Changes in the outstanding stocks of interest-bearing government debt or of real capital are important influences on $\frac{di}{i}$. A large government deficit financed by new debt issues imparts substantial momentum to rising interest rates. Even if an increasing portion of the new issues is absorbed through expansion of the monetary base so that Q rises, $\frac{di}{i}$ may increase. Reliance on interest rates would lead to the conclusion that monetary policy is restrictive, despite the rise in $\frac{dQ}{Q}$ indicative of an acceleration of expansive policy action.

With the exception of the thirties, interest rates generally move procyclically. The influence of $\frac{dQ}{Q}$ is usually overwhelmed by the effects of variables combined in $\frac{dz}{z}$. Interpretations of monetary policy based on interest rate movements neglect the powerful influence on interest rates of new issues of interest-bearing debt or of changes in the capital stock. Policies are judged to be restrictive whenever the effect of $\frac{dQ}{Q}$ is dominated by the effect of $\frac{dz}{z}$, despite the possible large value of $\frac{dQ}{Q}$ and the true effect of monetary policy on output and economic activity. Similarly, monetary policy is judged to be easy early in the downswing because of the delayed effects of a slower growth rate of Q. The slower growth rate of Q gradually reduces the growth rate of income and prices and thus lowers $\frac{dz}{z}$. The effect of falling $\frac{dz}{z}$ more than offsets the fall in $\frac{dQ}{Q}$, generating falling interest rates or falling $\frac{di}{i}$. The interpretation of policy as easy when the true indicator decelerates convinces the monetary authority that a policy of expansion has been initiated, when their actual policies are in the opposite direction.[14]

Free Reserves

Few indicators of monetary policy have been used more consistently than the level of free reserves. Nearly every week, the financial press describes Federal Reserve policy in terms of the movement of free reserves, and evidence of the Federal Reserve's attachment to free reserves has been presented elsewhere.[15] Increases in free reserves are interpreted as expansive or indicative of easier policy; reductions are presumed to reflect less ease or greater restraint.

The solution for the volume of free reserves, F^*, implied by our theory,

$$F^* = \phi B^a$$

makes free reserves depend on all of the monetary policy variables. Open market operations affect free reserves through the base, B^a, and other monetary policies affect F^* through ϕ, where ϕ is a rational function of the free reserve ratio and of the time deposit, currency, and weighted average reserve requirement ratios.[16] In short, ϕ depends on the monetary policy variables summarized in q, on the components of the monetary and asset multipliers, and thus indirectly on output and interest rates as well. The joint determination of these central endogenous variables in terms of the policy and noncontrolled exogenous variables makes ϕ dependent on all of the exogenous variables—fiscal, monetary, and noncontrolled. Equation (4) is a compact statement of the result for nonzero F^*[17]

$$\frac{dF^*}{F^*} = \frac{dB^a}{B^a} + \frac{dq}{q} + \epsilon(f, \rho)\frac{d\rho}{\rho} + \epsilon(\phi, i)\frac{di}{i} + \epsilon(\phi, y)\frac{dy}{y} \tag{4}$$

[14]It may appear that the problem just discussed arises if $\frac{dM}{M}$ is used as an indicator. Since $\frac{dM}{M}$ depends on $\frac{di}{i}$ and, in addition, on the components of $\frac{dz}{z}$, the relative change in the money supply can lead to a misinterpretation of monetary policy. However, the data suggest that the behavior of the money supply is generally dominated by the currency ratio and the monetary policy variables, as noted earlier, so that the problem is much less serious for M than for i.

[15]See our *The Federal Reserve's Attachment to the Free Reserves Concept* (Washington, D.C.: House Banking and Currency Committee, 1964).

[16]
$$\phi = \frac{f(1+t)}{(r+f)(1+t)+k}$$

[17]A coefficient of the third term has been assumed to be unity and hence omitted. The coefficient is $1 - \epsilon(m,f)$, where $\epsilon(m,f)$ is the elasticity of the monetary multiplier with respect to the free reserve ratio. The omitted term is almost always between .99 and 1.01.

The first three terms contain the monetary policy variables. The direct effect of changes in B^a are recorded correctly by the free reserves indicator. But changes in the base modify interest rates on financial assets so that the full effect of open market operations and other changes in B^a on $\frac{dF^*}{F^*}$ includes the response represented by $\epsilon(\phi,i)\,\frac{di}{i}$. While the effect of i on the money supply is small, its effect on free reserves is quite large. Moreover, the sign of $\epsilon(\phi,i)$ is opposite to the sign of F^*. When free reserves are negative, the free reserves indicator exaggerates the magnitude of expansive policy actions and understates the size of contractive policies. Positive free reserves have precisely the opposite effect. They cause the free reserves indicator to overstate the size of reductions in the base and understate the size of increases.

Additional problems arise when monetary policy operates through q. Since $\frac{dq}{q}$ is not multiplied by the ratio of interest elasticities that appears in the true indicator, the direct effects of variations in the reserve requirement ratios, the rediscount rate, and other policies are misstated. Moreover, the rediscount rate, ρ, appears as a separate term in addition to its effect on $\frac{dF^*}{F^*}$ through dq. This term is another source of differences between the free reserves indicator and the true indicator when the discount rate is changed. Furthermore, changes in any of the terms in q induce changes in interest rates and hence lead to either overestimates or underestimates of the magnitude of policy operations, depending on the sign of F^*. Those who rely on free reserves as an indicator are likely to be misled by their interpretation of the size of policy actions.

Toward the end of a period of economic expansion, free reserves are generally negative and monetary policy is frequently moving in a deflationary direction. The use of free reserves as an indicator underrates the size of the deflationary impulse. A drastic application of policies designed to "prevent inflation" might seem called for because of the attenuated response in free reserves. During a downswing, free reserves are generally positive. Expansions in the base or in the variables denoted by q are understated by the free reserves indicator. If the F^* indicator is used by policy makers as a guide to desired policy, it is likely to produce abrupt changes in the direction and magnitude of the size of policy action.

Variations in interest rates and in free reserves induced by monetary policies cannot be separated from the influence of fiscal and noncontrolled forces without reliable information about the structure of the process. Major changes in free reserves are often a response to changes in real variables. For example, a decline in the expected yield on real capital induces an increase in free reserves. This typically happens toward the end of an expansion phase and is one of the forces contributing to the termination of the expansion. Influenced by the expansion in free reserves, the monetary authority becomes convinced that policy is "aggressively easy." This error in interpretation is superimposed on the underestimation of deflationary policies associated with the sign of F^*, discussed above. Attributing the movements in free reserves to monetary policy misconstrues the effect of actual policy operations.

THE CHOICE OF STRATEGY AND INDICATOR

None of the endogenous variables we have considered indicates the exact effect of monetary policy on real income. Each is potentially or actually misleading. But the imperfections are not the same and vary substantially with the choice of endogenous indicators. In the absence of knowledge about the structure, some choice must be made among imperfect alternatives.

One solution is to confine policy operations to changes in the base, so that relative changes in the base become the ideal indicator. Another is to choose a strategy or criterion under which the performance of the various endogenous indicators can be compared. A third alternative is to search for measurable indicators that bracket the ideal indicator between an overestimate and an underestimate. In this section, some alternative solutions are discussed.

The choice of a strategy depends on the utility function of the policy maker. He may wish to minimize the expected loss of utility or minimize some function of the mean and variance of the deviations between measured and ideal indicators. Most choices of strategy require substantially greater additions to knowledge than is required to compute the ideal indicator.

The strategy we have selected for illustrative purposes is a minimax strategy.[18] Given the hypothesis and the simple goal, we minimize the worst possible outcome (misinterpretation) attributable to incomplete knowledge about the effect of a specific set of policy changes occurring through changes in B^a and q. In the particular case, this means that the maximum deviations between the various endogenous indicators and the ideal indicator are computed, using our limited knowledge of the structural parameters. The endogenous variable that has the smallest maximum deviation is then chosen as the optimal indicator.[19]

[18]Theories of search provide another means of investigating the problem of choosing an optimal indicator. Optimal search procedures can generally be stated as a minimax problem. See D. J. Wilde, *Optimum Seeking Methods* (Englewood Cliffs, N.J.: Prentice-Hall, Inc., 1964). We are indebted to M. Kamien for this reference.

[19]Appendix D presents the formal outline of the procedure. The appendix was added in the last draft of the paper.

The material for the solution has been provided. The ideal indicator, $\frac{dQ}{Q}$, is given in equation (1) above. The difference between the value of $\frac{dQ}{Q}$ and the solution for each of the endogenous variables can be computed easily. When the computations are performed, the money supply (currency and demand deposits) emerges as the optimal indicator.

Investigation of five frequently used financial variables thus establishes that, relative to the goal function, hypothesis, and strategy, the money stock is the best approximation to the true indicator. It is not ideal and has been quite misleading on occasion in the postwar period. Nevertheless, it is the least misleading and least dangerous single guide to the position of monetary policy.

A solution of quite a different kind is to combine two indicators, one more responsive and one less responsive than the ideal indicator. Fortunately, a prolonged search for measures with these properties is not required if the particular hypothesis and goal are maintained. Let one approximate indicator be

$$\frac{dQ^*}{Q^*} = \frac{dB^a}{B^a} + \frac{dq}{q}$$

It is clear from inspection of the ideal indicator that $\frac{dQ^*}{Q^*}$ is identical to the ideal indicator whenever q is unchanged. Otherwise, this approximation misstates the influence of q on the ideal indicator. When $\frac{dq}{q}$ is positive, $\frac{dQ^*}{Q^*}$ exceeds $\frac{dQ}{Q}$ by an amount $\left[\frac{h_2(\alpha-1)}{h_1-h_2}\right]\frac{dq}{q}$; reductions in q are understated by the same amount. We will refer to the bracketed expression as the "error of overstatement," since it exaggerates the influence of q relative to the ideal indicator.

For the "error of understatement," a measure is required that always is less than $\frac{dQ}{Q}$ when $\frac{dq}{q}$ is positive and always is greater than the ideal indicator when $\frac{dq}{q}$ is negative. Relative changes in the base have this property. The error of understatement is the bracketed term in

$$\frac{dQ}{Q} - \frac{dB^a}{B^a} = \left[\frac{h_1 - h_2\alpha}{h_1 - h_2}\right]\frac{dq}{q}$$

Since the hypothesis implies that the error of understatement is numerically larger than the error of overstatement, the true indicator is nearer to $\frac{dQ^*}{Q^*}$ than to $\frac{dB^a}{B^a}$ whenever q changes. The sum of the two errors is always unity. Unless the change in q is extremely large, a reasonable approximation to the ideal indicator is given by

$$\frac{1}{2}\left(\frac{dQ^*}{Q^*} + \frac{dB^a}{B^a}\right) = \frac{dB^a}{B^a} + \frac{dq}{2q}$$

The difference between the ideal indicator and this approximation has the same sign as $\frac{dq}{q}$ and hence is known. The approximate indicator is greater than the ideal when $\frac{dq}{q}$ is negative and less than the ideal indicator for positive $\frac{dq}{q}$.

Thus the approximate indicator has three distinct advantages. First, it is easily computed, since $\frac{dB^a}{B^a}$ can be measured exactly and most of the components of $\frac{dq}{q}$ can be approximated quite closely. Second, the direction of error is known—an advantage that is not generally obtained with the use of endogenous indicators. Third, for small changes in $\frac{dq}{q}$, the error is quite small.[20]

LIMITATIONS

Computation of the approximate indicator would not reveal the magnitude of the change in real income induced by monetary policy. At best, the indicator would correctly scale the size of the impulse that policy is directing toward the final goal. Measurement of the magnitude of the change in real income induced by monetary policy requires information about the structure, and particularly about the elasticity of output with respect to the base, $\epsilon(y,B^a)$, as noted earlier.

Successive computations of the indicator would not furnish information useful for the computation of the correct lags or of $\epsilon(y,B^a)$. The length of the lags depends, in part, on the acceleration and deceleration of monetary policy, while the computation of the "true" value of $\epsilon(y,B^a)$ depends on knowledge of the structure. More importantly, changes in income depend on the fiscal and noncontrolled exogenous variables. The indicator, therefore, does not provide a forecast of future output, but only a scale on which the relative magnitudes of the monetary impulse can be measured.

Moreover, the scale is not unique. It depends on the particular class of hypotheses and goal selected. Some of the more complicated goal

[20] Using the hypothesis, goal, and strategy above, the proposed indicator is better than any of the endogenous indicators considered.

functions require substantially more information about structural properties than is required in the case discussed here. Although we have not investigated the problem thoroughly, this is likely to be true of alternative hypotheses as well. The analysis underlying our effort has the advantage of reducing, perhaps to a minimum, the required amount of knowledge about structural details.

Random elements have been ignored. The structural equations have been treated as if they held exactly. Errors in these equations will appear in the partially reduced forms used to compare the endogenous indicators and in the equation for the ideal indicator. However, it should be noted that the problem of errors in the equation is likely to be at least as serious for the endogenous indicators that are in common use as for the approximate indicator we have developed.[21]

CONCLUSION

One means of obtaining information about the direction and effect of monetary policy has been illustrated in this paper. While our solution is neither exact nor ideal, it is likely to be less misleading than many of the variables used to describe the content of monetary policy.

Policy makers must continuously interpret the effects of their past decisions. Their future actions depend on these interpretations. If the indicators they select are misleading, their policy decisions will be inappropriate or misinterpreted and will introduce fluctuations in output, prices, and other goal variables. One need only look at 1962–63 to recognize that when the Federal Reserve described its action as a shift to "slightly less ease," our suggested indicator began growing at the fastest rate in the postaccord period.

Numerous other years reveal the same pattern. When the Federal Reserve describes its action as a move toward restraint, the indicator accelerates. Description of policies as "increased ease" is frequently followed by deceleration of the indicator summarizing the effect of monetary policy on real output. Clearly, the problem is worthy of more attention than it has received from government or academic economists.

APPENDIX A

Alphabetical List of Symbols

a the banks' earning asset multiplier

B^a the adjusted monetary base: the monetary base minus member bank borrowing

[21]The introduction of errors in the equations would not alter the comparative merits of the indicators considered here. Under the hypothesis and goal we have discussed, the ordering of indicators would remain identical.

APPENDIX A—*Continued*

- E commercial banks' earning assets net of Treasury deposits and the banks' net worth
- E_b banks' demand for earning assets
- E_p public's supply of earning assets to banks
- f the ratio of free reserves to total deposits
- G government expenditures (national income accounting definition)
- I the ideal indicator
- i an index of interest rates on financial assets
- i_e expected rate of interest
- i^t interest rate paid on commercial bank time deposits
- k the ratio of currency to demand deposits
- K the stock of real private capital
- m the monetary multiplier
- M the money supply: currency and demand deposits of the public
- n the real yield on real capital
- p the income deflator
- P_a the deflator for wealth
- q the component of the indicator incorporating monetary policy variables not included in B^a
- Q the "true" indicator
- r a weighted average of reserve requirement ratios including the vault cash ratio
- S the stock of interest bearing government debt
- t the ratio of time to demand deposits
- T the stock of time deposits
- V circuit velocity of private expenditures
- W the nominal stock of wealth held by the public
- Y nominal income or output
- y real income or output
- y_p expected real income
- α the ratio of money plus time deposits to bank earning assets
- β the ratio of money supply to bank earning assets
- γ money expenditures of the government sector
- ϵ an elasticity
- θ money receipts of the government sector
- ρ the rediscount rate

APPENDIX B

A Compact Statement of the Underlying Model

A. *The Macromodel*		*Description*
(A 1)	$Y = MV + G$ M = currency and demand deposits	A quantity equation.
(A 2)	$V = V(i_e, i, y/y_p, W/P_a, P_a/p, n)$	The velocity relation.
(A 3)	$M_s = \beta(i)E_b$ where $\beta = \dfrac{1+k}{(1+t)(1-r-f)}$	The money supply generated by the banks' desired portfolio position.

APPENDIX B—*Continued*

(A 4)	$p = p(y, K, w)$ $p_1 > 0 > p_2$	The price level. The parameter w formalizes the revision of supply prices on the basis of changing market conditions. w depends on past y and K.
(A 5)	$\Delta S + \Delta F = \gamma(G) - \Theta$	The change in interest-bearing and noninterest-bearing debt equals the government's cash flow deficit.

B. *The Condensed Monetary System*

(A 6)	$E_b = E_p = E$	Equilibrium on the bank credit market.
(A 7)	$E_p = s(i_e, y/y_p, W/P_a, p, n)$ $s_1 < 0 < s_2;\ s_3 > 0 < s_4;\ s_5 > 0$	The supply of financial assets to banks.
(A 8)	$E_b = a(i, \rho, i^t)\ B^a$ where $a = \dfrac{(1+t)(1-r-f)}{(1+t)(r+f)+k}$	The banks' demand for earning assets. The earning asset multiplier is dependent on interest and rediscount rates through the components of a.
(A 9)	$M_s = M(i, \rho, i^t)\ B^a$	The money supply function.
	where $m = \dfrac{1+k}{(1+t)(r+f)+k}$	The monetary multiplier depends on the same parameters as the earning asset multiplier, but with different derivatives.
(A 10)	$f = f(i, \rho, \pi)$	The ratio of free reserves to total deposits.
(A 11)	$M + T = \alpha\ (i)\ E_b$	The ratio of money supply plus time deposits to bank earning assets. The ratio is greater than one by definition.

APPENDIX B—*Continued*

Other behavior relations of the monetary system and discussion of the adjusted base may be found in several of our papers. See especially "Some Further Investigations of Demand and Supply Functions for Money," *Journal of Finance*, May, 1964, and "Liquidity Traps for Money, Bank Credit and Interest Rates," forthcoming.

C. *The Reduced System*

A condensed statement of the reduced forms is given by substituting equations (A7) and (A8) into equation (A6) and substituting (A4), (A9), and (A2) into equation (A1) to obtain

(A 12) $$a(\ )B^a = s(\ )$$

(A 13) $$yp(\ ) = [m(\ )B^a]\,V(\ ) + G$$

The monetary policy variables enter either directly as B^a or through the monetary and asset multipliers.

Differentiating the system and stating the results as elasticities yields the following expressions, where $\epsilon(j,k)$ is the elasticity of j with respect to k. For example, $\epsilon(y, B^a) = \dfrac{h_1 - h_2\alpha}{g_1 h_1 - g_2 h_2}$, where

$$h_1 = \epsilon(a, i) - \epsilon(s, i_e)\,\epsilon(i_e, i) - \epsilon\left(s, \frac{W}{P_a}\right)\epsilon\left(\frac{W}{P_a}, i\right)$$

$$h_2 = \epsilon(m, i) + \epsilon(V, i_e)\,\epsilon(i_e, i) + \epsilon(V, i) + \epsilon\left(V, \frac{W}{P_a}\right)\epsilon\left(\frac{W}{P_a}, i\right)$$

The class of hypotheses implies that h_1 and h_2 are positive and that $h_1 > h_2\alpha$, where α is the ratio of the money supply plus time deposits to bank credit. The ratio in the text, $\dfrac{h_1 - h_2\alpha}{h_1 - h_2}$, is a proper fraction.

g and g_2 summarize the elasticities on the output market:

$$g_1 = 1 - \epsilon\left(V, \frac{y}{y_p}\right)[1 - \epsilon(y_p, y)] - \epsilon\left(V, \frac{W}{P_a}\right)\epsilon\left(\frac{W}{P_a}, y\right) -$$
$$\epsilon(V, n)\,\epsilon(n, y) + \epsilon(p, y) - \epsilon(m, t)\,\epsilon\left(t, \frac{W}{P_a}\right)\epsilon\left(\frac{W}{P_a}, y\right)$$

$$g_2 = \epsilon\left(s, \frac{y}{y_p}\right)[1 - \epsilon(y_p, y)] - \epsilon\left(s, \frac{W}{P_a}\right)\epsilon\left(\frac{W}{P_a}, y\right) - \epsilon(s, n)\,\epsilon(n, y) -$$
$$\epsilon(s, p)\,\epsilon(p, y) + \epsilon(a, t)\,\epsilon\left(t, \frac{W}{P_a}\right)\epsilon\left(\frac{W}{P_a}, y\right)$$

APPENDIX B—*Continued*

Under the class of hypotheses, $g_1 > g_2$, hence

$$\frac{\alpha g_1 - g_2}{g_1 - g_2} > 1$$

D: An Outline of the Formal Procedure

Let H denote a class of hypotheses, h any member of the class and u the goal or social utility function. The general form of the index function is expressed by the relation

$$I = f(dx; h; H, u)$$

This formulation reveals three important properties of the index function: (1) the general format of the function depends on the class of hypotheses H and the goal function u; (2) given H and u, the computation of I associated with the policy vector dx requires knowledge of h; (3) the value of f associated with any dx—and the derivative of f with respect to dx—depend on the particular h and the class H.

If we knew which h in the class H is the true hypothesis, we could construct the appropriate index function. Until we have that information, an alternative is to choose an observable indicator that approximates the true indicator as closely as possible. Let A denote a set of approximations, and let S be a member of the set A. In the text, A contains the money supply, the money supply plus time deposits, bank earning assets, interest rates and free reserves; the class H is given in appendix A; and the utility function has been specified.

The formula for selecting an optimal approximation is:

$$\min_{S} \quad \max_{dx} \quad \max_{h} \quad \left| f(dx; h; H, u) - S(dx; h) \right|$$

The function $S(dx; h)$ expresses the dependence of each of the observable indicators on the policy vector, dx, and on the particular hypothesis, h.

Our procedure involves the following steps:

1. Compute the absolute value of the difference between the true indicator function and the approximation, $|f - S|$.
2. Maximize this difference over the class of hypotheses, H. We thus obtain a function expressing the maximum deviation of S from I, for given dx, attributable to our uncertainty about the structure of the world.
3. Maximize the function obtained in step 2 for the feasible (closed) set of policy actions. For every value of S, we obtain a function of S which expresses the maximum deviation of S from I due to our uncertain knowledge *and* the range of feasible policy actions.
4. Minimize the function obtained in step 3 with respect to S and obtain

APPENDIX B—*Continued*

the S which has the smallest maximum deviation. This is the optimal approximation.

The analysis can be extended to cover alternative classes of hypotheses H_1 and H_2 and alternative utility functions. A comparison of the ranking of the elements S achieved under H_1 and H_2 or u_1 and u_2 may yield a compromise candidate usefully guiding our interpretations even if we are more uncertain than in the case described here.

E: *An Illustration of the Macrosystem's Characteristics*[22]

The money and bank credit subsystem and the output subsystem express, in a formal way, the response in financial and nonfinancial markets to changes in relative prices, output, and policy operations. In this section, we discuss some properties of the two subsystems, using a diagram to illustrate the effect of a change in the adjusted base and to clarify the meaning of the four parameters denoted h_i and g_i. The discussion will make clear why the use of a quantity equation as an equilibrium condition has no bearing on the comparison of endogenous indicators of monetary policy. The reason, stated briefly, is that the transmission of policy changes depends on the interest rate and relative price mechanisms and not on the equilibrium conditions.

There are two subsystems, financial and nonfinancial. The nonfinancial sector contains a description of aggregate demand and supply on the output markets. Interest rates, output, wealth, government expenditure, and asset and output prices affect aggregate demand directly or through their effects on velocity and the supply of money; aggregate supply is expressed by means of price-setting and price adjustment equations for the prices of output and nonfinancial assets. The financial subsystem describes the allocation of financial assets by the banks and the public. This interaction on the credit market generates the money stock and hence feeds into the aggregate demand function, $MV + G$.

Each subsystem can be reduced to a single equation, shown in section C, so that the two reduced equations express the interaction between the output and the credit markets and the proximate determination of interest rates and output. Since the reduced system contains the policy variables, it can be used to derive the response of output and interest rates to monetary and fiscal policy changes or to other exogenous changes. By differentiating over the reduced system and expressing the results as elasticities, four combinations of elasticities—h_1, h_2, g_1 and g_2—are obtained. These combinations are formally stated in section C of this appendix. The h_i are combinations of elasticities with respect to interest rates; the g_i

[22]This section was added just prior to publication at the request of the editor. It was not available at the conference or to the discussant.

APPENDIX B—*Continued*

are combinations with respect to output. Changes in monetary or fiscal policies change output and interest rates by amounts that depend on the h_i and g_i.

As an illustration, consider the effect of a change in the adjusted base, B^a. The elasticity of output, y, with respect to the base is denoted $\epsilon(y,B^a)$ where

$$\epsilon(y, B^a) = \frac{h_1 - h_2\alpha}{g_1h_1 - g_2h_2}$$

It is apparent from the formula that the interest elasticities combined in h_1 and h_2 have a dominant role in determining the size of the response of output. The combinations of output elasticities, g_1 and g_2, play a similar role in determining the response of interest rates. Moreover, the class of hypotheses implies that the combinations h_1, h_2, and g_1 are positive while the combination g_2 is negative. It follows that a sufficient (but not a necessary) condition for an open market operation to affect output in the expected direction is that the combined response to changes in interest rates on the credit market (h_1) is large relative to the response of aggregate demand to changes in interest rates (h_2).

A diagram further clarifies the meaning of each combination of elasticities. In Figure 1, the slopes of the curves depend upon the elasticities, and all variables are measured positively starting at the common origin. We will, first, explain the relation of the curves in each quadrant to the equations in the appendix above, using an increase in the base to illustrate the adjustment but concentrating on the determinants of the slopes and positions of each curve. We will then discuss the adjustment from one equilibrium to another. A discussion of a reduction in the reserve requirement ratios or in the rediscount rate or an increase in the percentage of vault cash counted as part of required reserves would be similar, apart from minor details. Illustration of the effects of an increase in the government's interest-bearing debt or of a larger government deficit will not be attempted here.

In the upper left quadrant, we have drawn the public's supply of earning assets to banks (E_p) and the banks' demand for earning assets (E_b). The quantities demanded and supplied depend on interest rates (i), and the positions of each curve depend on the other arguments of the E_p and E_b functions given in the formal statement of the system above. An increase in B^a moves the E_b curve to the left from the solid line E_{b1} to the broken line E_{b2}, lowering interest rates. The percentage change in interest rates depends on h_1, since the reciprocal of h_1 is the relative change in interest rates—holding output constant—resulting from a shift of the E_b curve by 1 percent.

APPENDIX B—*Continued*

The reduction in interest rates is shown also by the credit market (CM) curve in the upper right hand quadrant. The slope of this curve is $\frac{-1}{h_1}$, so it shows the responsiveness of the bank credit market to interest rate changes, holding output constant but acknowledging the interaction within the financial system. The larger h_1, the flatter is the CM curve and the smaller is the response of interest rates to changes in the base. But a large h_1 and "flat" CM curve imply a large value for $\epsilon(y,B^a)$ in the formula above and hence a large increase in output in response to a given change in the base.

FIGURE 1

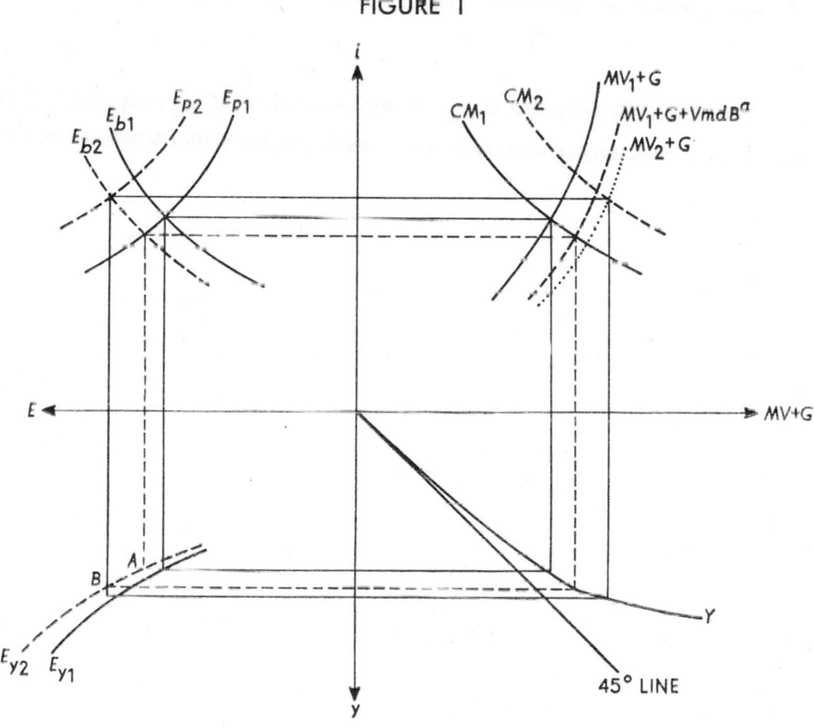

The effect of the increase in B^a on aggregate demand is shown in the upper right quadrant also. Since the money supply (M) can be expressed as the product mB^a, the increase in the base (dB^a) increases aggregate demand ($MV_1 + G$) by $VmdB^a$, as shown by the position of the broken curve in the diagram. The position of the aggregate demand curve also depends on the volume of government expenditures and, to a minor extent, on the level of output. The slope of the aggregate demand curve shows the response of aggregate excess demand to changes in interest

APPENDIX B—*Continued*

rates, holding output constant but incorporating the interaction over the nonfinancial subsystem, that is, the combination summarized by h_2. More precisely, the slope of $MV + G$ is $\frac{1}{h_2}$.

The broken line drawn between the upper quadrants connects the new, partial equilibrium positions. The percentage increase in aggregate demand (given by the movement from the solid to the broken aggregate demand curve along the curve labeled CM_1) is attenuated by the reduction in interest rates. However, the hypothesis implies that the increase in the base generates aggregate excess demand that spills over to the output markets. The broken line, therefore, continues into the lower right quadrant.

The curve in the lower right panel shows aggregate supply (at current prices) as a function of output and thus expresses the combined response of output and prices. The slope of the curve, relative to the output or y axis, is given by the dominant component of $[1 + \epsilon(p,y)]$ in g_1[23] At very low levels of output, the curve has a slope equal (or very close) to unity. Since $\epsilon(p,y)$ increases with y, the curve turns away from the 45° line at higher levels of output. Given the effect of an increase in the base on aggregate demand, the effect on output is larger the steeper the relevant portion of the curve and the smaller is g_1. The size of the response in prices also depends on the slope of the curve. The flatter the curve, the greater is the inflationary impact of an increase in the base.

However, the position of the curve depends on current and prior changes in the capital stock, on the level of output in the recent past, and upon information about the adjustment of supply prices. Increases in the stock of real capital, for example, rotate the curve toward the 45° line and thus enlarge the response of output and diminish the change in prices resulting from a given increase in aggregate demand.

Increases in output induce additional changes in aggregate demand and in the public's supply of assets to banks and thus change the positions of the aggregate demand and of the E_p curve. The new position of the former is shown by the dotted line, $MV_2 + G$, in the upper right quadrant. The increase from the broken to the dotted line reflects the response of V to changes in output and real wealth, that is, to components of g_1. The shift from E_{p1} to E_{p2} in the upper left quadrant shows the effect of increased income and wealth on the public's supply of assets to banks (including an increased volume of borrowing). The elasticities that determine the size of this response in E_p are the principal components of g_2.

---

[23]The other components of g_1 shift the curve $MV + G$ in the quadrant above. There is a feedback from this quadrant to the quadrant above that will be considered below.

APPENDIX B—*Continued*

These changes in aggregate demand and in E_p induce further changes in interest rates. The increase in E_p raises interest rates and shifts the *CM* curve to the right; the increase in aggregate demand lowers interest rates. We will discuss these interactions and their further effects more fully below.

The effect of a change in output on E_p is also shown in the lower left quadrant. The slope of the curve in that quadrant shows the effect of output on E_p and thus a principal component of g_2, as just noted. However, the elasticity of E_p with respect to output appears in g_2 with a negative sign, so the slope in the lower right quadrant is a main component of $-g_2$.[24]

We may summarize the discussion of the four combinations of elasticities by noting that each of the slopes is represented in the diagram. The *CM* curve depends on the interest elasticities of the financial sector and has slope $\frac{-1}{h_1}$. The slope of the aggregate demand curve is $\frac{1}{h_2}$. The principal component of g_1 determines the slope of the curve in the lower right quadrant, and the other components of g_1 shift the aggregate demand curve. The percentage change of the horizontal distance between the E_p and E_b curves at each level of interest rates is a measure of the components of g_2, one component of which is shown also by the slope of the curve in the lower left quadrant.

The response of output to monetary (or fiscal) policy depends on the four combinations. Policy actions have a larger effect on output if the curves in the two upper quadrants are flat. Moreover, a flat E_p curve means that there is a large feedback from the upper left to the lower left quadrant and a correspondingly larger effect on output. A flat curve in the lower left quadrant suggests that relatively small increases in output (or prices) generate relatively large increases in the supply of assets to the banking system and a relatively large induced shift in the *CM* curve. Similarly a relatively large feedback from output and prices to aggregate demand raises the response of aggregate demand and the further response of output and prices. Thus the size of the "multiplier" effect resulting from a change in monetary or fiscal policy depends on the slopes of the output and credit market curves.

It is a by-product of the class of hypotheses that the size of the response of output to monetary policy is *not* positively related to the size of the response of interest rates. On the contrary, if the combinations of elasticities magnify the response of interest rates to monetary or fiscal policy, they attenuate the response of output. Although interest rates

[24]It is implicit in the discussion just above that the combination g_2 can be interpreted, using the curves in the upper left quadrant, as the relative change in the horizontal distance between the two curves, at each level of interest rates, induced by a 1 percent change in output.

APPENDIX B—*Continued*

have an important role in transmitting changes in policy between the two sectors, the size of the response in the nonfinancial sector decreases with the magnitude of the change in interest rates.

We can now trace the effect of an increase in the base on interest rates, output, and bank credit using the diagram shown in Figure 1. Initially the system is in an equilibrium shown by the solid line connecting the four quadrants and passing through the intersection of E_{b1} with E_{p1} and of $MV_1 + G$ with CM_1. Suppose this equilibrium is disturbed by a gold inflow, at constant exchange rates, that raises the base. A new, partial equilibrium is reached in the bank credit market by an increase in the banks' demand for credit, shown by the movement from E_{b1} to E_{b2} along the existing E_{p1} curve. The increased demand for bank credit reduces interest rates and increases the money supply. Both changes carry over to the upper right quadrant. The reduction in interest rates is shown by the movement down the CM_1 curve; the increase in the money supply by the shift to the right of the aggregate demand curve. The broken line connecting the two upper quadrants connects the new partial equilibrium points and continues into the lower right quadrant to show the increase in output (and prices) resulting from the increase in the base. The initial increase in the base also increases the horizontal distance between the E_p and E_b curves at each level of interest rates. This shifts the E_y curve in the lower left quadrant to the left; the new position is shown by the E_{y2} curve.

The increase in output induces an increase in the public's supply of earning assets to banks. The broken line connecting the lower right and lower left quadrants intersects the E_{y2} curve at *B*. The distance from E_{y1} to E_{y2} at point *A* shows the increase in the quantity of bank credit supplied by the public as a result of the fall in interest rates. The horizontal distance between *A* and *B* is, therefore, the amount by which the supply of bank credit must increase to maintain the existing levels of output, prices, and interest rates.

However, an increase in the public's supply of earning assets to banks (shown by the shift from E_{p1} to E_{p2}) moves the *CM* curve to the right raising interest rates, as shown by the intersection of E_{b2} and E_{p2} or by the position of the CM_2 curve. The feedback from the output market to aggregate demand (resulting from the initial increase in aggregate demand) shifts the aggregate demand curve to the position shown by the dotted $MV_2 + G$ curve and partially offsets the effect on interest rates of an increased supply of earning assets to banks.

Interaction between the financial and nonfinancial sector continues until a new equilibrium is established. The solid line connecting the intersection of E_{b2} with E_{p2} and CM_2 with $MV_2 + G$ is used to represent

APPENDIX B—*Continued*

the new equilibrium positions.[25] As the curves are drawn, the new equilibrium "box" lies outside the old "box." Output and interest rates are higher than before the gold inflow.

[25]In the lower left quadrant, this line intersects the E_{y3} curve (not shown) that lies slightly to the left of E_{y1}.

DISCUSSION

Comments

Samuel B. Chase, Jr.

I

Limitations of time prevent me from doing justice to all three papers. I have the least to say about Wood's ingenious contribution. It is, of course, disappointing that his analysis of Federal Reserve behavior does not permit disentangling the Fed's preferences from its notions about the parameters of the structural equations which constrain it. But Wood's findings do indicate that the Fed follows a systematic approach to policy, is at least broadly consistent in its pursuit of multiple goals, and apparently understands the nature of the trade-offs involved, despite occasional official statements that seem to deny the necessity of making choices among competing objectives.

Wood's chart (p. 152) showing "nondefensive" transactions of the open market account reflects favorably on the timing of ups and downs of the Fed's portfolio over postwar cycles. This chart seems hard to reconcile with the contentions of Brunner and Meltzer[1] that open market operations have been so ill-timed as to foster cyclical fluctuations.

II

De Leeuw's report on his further research into the demand for money is a welcome contribution. His results dispel some of the optimism that might have been generated by his earlier work for the Brookings-SSRC model and by Teigen's model.[2] Publication of negative results is in this case very worthwhile. Perhaps the most important conclusion drawn by de Leeuw is that future work on the demand for money can ill afford to neglect the long-lag hypothesis.

---

[1] "An Alternative Approach to the Monetary Mechanism" (House Committee on Banking and Currency, Subcommittee on Domestic Finance, 88th Cong. 2d sess.) (1964).

[2] R. L. Teigen, "Demand and Supply Functions for Money in the U.S.," *Econometrica*, Vol. 32 (October, 1964), pp. 476–509.

This conclusion was, of course, suggested by earlier work. But, as he has made clear in this paper, the use of lagged values of the money stock to explain current money holdings provides very questionable evidence about the lag in adjustment. But now we are told that less objectionable techniques—three-pass least squares (whose properties in this context are somewhat obscure) and use of Koyck transformations of the independent variables—strengthen the case for a long lag. I share de Leeuw's surprise at this finding.

It is somewhat disappointing that de Leeuw did not admit a trend variable into the explanation of the changes in the demand for money. His final approach, using distributed lags, explains one-fourth to one-half of the change in money demand by changes in interest rates and the scale variables. Friedman and Schwartz have argued that interest rates explain only a small part of the postwar rise in velocity.[3] Inclusion of a trend variable in de Leeuw's equations might help to assess this contention.

Although de Leeuw's work should make it difficult for future studies to *ignore* the long-lag hypothesis, it does not compel us to *accept* the hypothesis. The nature of the distributed lag tested by de Leeuw is, of course, an arbitrary one that is used, more because it is convenient than because it has real merit on a priori grounds. Why should we expect money holders to close, in each quarter, some constant fraction of the difference between "desired" and "actual" holdings of money? Delays in adjustment are due, presumably, to the short-run costs of adjustment. Only by considering carefully the nature of these costs, which doubtless are different for different classes of transactions, can intelligent a priori guesses as to the nature of the lag be formed. For example, it could be that the adjustment of time deposits, which are held primarily by individuals, takes place in a framework of gross flows into and out of various banks and competing intermediaries that are given, to a first approximation. The magnitudes of these flows may thus set constraints on the magnitudes of the adjustment that can take place. In such a case, we would expect the percentage of the difference between long-run "desired" and actual holdings of money made up in any period to be larger the smaller is the size of the discrepancy relative to the size of the flows.

De Leeuw does not consider the implications of a long lag in the adjustment of money holdings for monetary policy. It seems worthwhile to mention, however, that a long lag makes policy more, not less, potent. If the short-run elasticity of demand for money is low, a small change in the money stock will necessitate a large change in the variables that

[3]Milton Friedman and Anna J. Schwartz, *A Monetary History of the United States, 1867–1960* (Princeton, N.J.: Princeton University Press, 1963), pp. 655–57.

influence the demand for money. If, for example, the link between money and real activity is interest rates, interest rates will have to move substantially to accommodate a small change in money. The effect on expenditures, via the interest rate movement, may therefore be substantial in relation to the size of the change in the money stock, even if the demand for investment also exhibits a lagged response to interest rate changes. (This observation holds for any lagged adjustment model, including Friedman's permanent income demand function.)

Moving on to de Leeuw's investigation of alternative scale variables, it should be noted that the income variable used is national income. The wealth variable, however, is private wealth, defined as the stock of privately owned real assets plus net private claims of government. De Leeuw notes that changes in the national debt reflecting Treasury surpluses and deficits have no direct impact on interest rates, using $M = f(Y,r)$, whereas they do if $M = f(W,r)$, since W is affected directly by these operations. However, if the income and wealth measures were made coordinate by using private disposable income, defined as total private income less net transfers to government, current changes in government debt would have "direct" effects on interest rates, although the oustanding stock would not.

De Leeuw contends that his use of transitory income as an argument in the demand function provides a test of the "shock absorber" version of the inventory approach to the demand for money. As spending rises above trend, cash inventories are run down, and vice versa. But surely such a test calls for use of current transitory income, not a weighted average of current and past values. It does not seem that de Leeuw has provided the test at all.

III

In the introduction to their paper, Professors Brunner and Meltzer say that their work on indicators of monetary policy is exploratory and is not intended to yield reliable guides to policy makers. But later the authors draw some fairly strong policy conclusions. My discussion therefore treats the paper as more than an exercise.

The idea of developing a quantitative gauge of monetary policy is appealing. One has only to attend a conference such as this one to realize that there is distressing conflict among the experts on whether policy is, or was during some past period, "tight" or "easy," to say nothing of "appropriate." Much of the dispute arises out of conflicting interpretations of the monetary process. Brunner and Meltzer, if I understand them, believe that their paper not only focuses attention on the issues, but offers an approach that bypasses many of the complexities that beset a complete analysis of the monetary process.

The first equation (on page 189) posits that

$$\text{(A)} \quad I = \frac{du}{dy_1}\frac{dy_1}{dx_1}dx_1 + \frac{du}{dy_2}\frac{dy_2}{dx_1}dx_1$$

where I is the indicator of monetary policy, u is social utility, the ys (in principle limitless in number) are objective states of affairs which enter into the utility function, and dx_1 represents the change in variables that express monetary policy operations.[4] In this example, I is the total differential of social utility. It is instructive to consider the case in which all the elements of equation (A) are known, since in this case one can judge the appropriateness of trade-offs between competing goals. Given the sign of dx_1, I can be either positive or negative, and its sign may depend on the levels of y_1 and y_2. Suppose, for example, that there is only one policy instrument—open market operations in a single class of security—and that open market purchases always raise both real income (y_1) and prices (y_2). For simplicity, suppose also that $\frac{du}{dy_1}$ is positive and constant and $\frac{du}{dy_2}$ is negative and constant. Then I may be either positive or negative when dx_1 is positive. Furthermore, if $\epsilon(y_1, x_1)$, the elasticity of real income with respect to open market purchases, decreases, and $\epsilon(y_2, x_1)$ increases, as x_1 increases (the case represented by a conventional Phillips curve), I declines as x_1 rises and may be positive over lower ranges of x_1 and negative over higher ranges. "Good" policy presumably entails $I > 0$, "bad" policy entails $I < 0$. Optimal policy requires maximizing u, which entails $I = 0$, and in this case is achieved by setting x_1 where

$$\frac{du}{dy_1}\;\frac{dy_1}{dx_1} = \frac{du}{dy_2}\;\frac{dy_2}{dx_1}$$

Had the authors pointed up these implications, they perhaps would have drawn the moral that terms such as "easing" and "tightening" are inappropriate as descriptions of the relation between policy actions and social utility. Instead, they say that the indicator "summarizes in an index the relative degree of monetary ease or restraint." But it seems strange, for example, to refer to a monetary policy that reduces the rate of price increase during an inflation as "easing" merely because it is desirable in terms of social utility.

---

[4]In preparing these remarks, I interpreted dx_1, dy_1, and dy_2 as scalars. At the time, this seemed consistent with the statement "y_1 and y_2 are endogenous variables of the system—for example, prices and real output—and dx_1 is the change in variables expressing monetary policy operations." In a footnote of the revised draft, however, the authors tell us that y_1, y_2, and x_1 are vectors. If this is so, I do not see why y_1 and y_2 are not combined in one vector. In any event, my example for a two-goal world could be expanded to an n-goal world.

Most of what the authors have to say concerns a one-goal model. In this setting, the "ideal" indicator function (page 195) is

$$(B) \quad I = \epsilon\,(y, B^a)\,\frac{dQ}{Q}$$

Utility is assumed to be a monotonic, increasing function of real income and only real income. The authors tell us (page 195) that since $\epsilon(y,B^a)$, which is, apparently, always greater than or equal to zero, "enters the indicator function as a scalar, it can be neglected in the subsequent discussion." $\frac{dQ}{Q}$ is a complicated term which takes into account both the percentage change in the adjusted base and the influence of other policy variables such as reserve requirements and discount rates. Output always rises when $\frac{dQ}{Q}$ is positive, unless ceiling output has been reached. Furthermore, $\frac{dQ}{Q} = \frac{dB^a}{B^a}$ if policy action is restricted to open market operations. Therefore, the sign of I is always the same as the sign of dB^a (except that I is zero at ceiling output) if only open market operations are employed. The adjusted base provides an unambiguous index of social utility. Subject to the capacity constraint, the monetary authority can always raise real income and social utility if it can raise B^a without limit.[5] Since nothing but real income enters the social utility function, the appropriate policy is always one of expanding the reserve base, at least until capacity is reached. Beyond that point, it really doesn't matter.

Presumably no one believes in such a world—or do they? Brunner and Meltzer draw the conclusion that prevailing monetary arrangements, which permit $\frac{dB^a}{B^a} \neq \frac{dQ}{Q}$, increase the amount of information required by the policy maker, and pass judgment (page 196) that

> . . . the unknown benefits of having a variety of policy instruments seems a high price to pay for the substantial increase in the amount of information required to measure the quantitative impact of policy. Until the requisite knowledge becomes available, it would be useful to restrict policy operations to changes in the adjusted base.

The statement and its context indicate that the authors are talking about the United States in the present day.

But the validity of the judgment seems to depend on the assumption of a one-goal world that has nothing to do, as far as I can tell, with

[5] I had earlier interpreted Brunner and Meltzer to be saying that social utility changed proportionately with B^a. Thanks to their insistence that I misinterpreted them, and a change in their notation, I have amended my original remarks, but not my main conclusion.

equation (A), which embraces multiple goals, and may thereby justify the use of more than one policy instrument. Use of the indicator in a multiple-goal system requires that we know not only the responsiveness of the goal variables to policy but the values (not just the signs) of the partial derivatives of the social utility function with respect to the goal variables. It seems that limited knowledge about the process through which monetary policy exerts its effects, and an almost inevitable incompatibility of multiple goals, still provide stumbling blocks to the discovery of a single indicator by which to measure and assess policy.

The comparison of proposed endogenous indicators loses most of its impact when it is recognized that the performance of the endogenous variables as indicators is judged primarily in terms of their conformity with movements in $\frac{dQ}{Q}$, whose value as a proxy for the ideal indicator of equation (A) has simply not been established.

Nonetheless, the authors are correct on at least one important point. Naïve use of money supply, free reserves, or interest rates as indicators of policy is pernicious. It is essential to recognize that these variables change for reasons other than direct policy action. During a recession, the central bank should not take comfort from the mere fact that interest rates are falling, or the money supply is rising, for example. The authors have possibly provided impetus to needed discussion of an important issue, but development of an unambiguous indicator of monetary policy in terms of social utility seems as far away as ever.

INTERNATIONAL CONSTRAINTS

HARMONIZATION OF NATIONAL MONETARY POLICIES

S. Posthuma

INTRODUCTION

When I was asked to speak about harmonization of national monetary policies before an audience of economists and bankers, I had a feeling that I had been invited to ride two horses at the same time. Perhaps it would have been possible for me to perform this feat if I had had more time at my disposal. Anticipating that I would not succeed, I have decided to proceed on a different line. I have chosen the course often taken by publishers when publishing books about foreign countries, giving in the first part a general characterization of the country to be visited, and in the second the illustrations. I have not at each illustration referred to the exact page and line of the first part relating thereto, and it may well be that the peculiarities of some illustrations have not been elucidated sufficiently. I am prepared to admit also that this is due to my being pressed for time, and I have consoled myself with the thought that this could be remedied during the discussions.

I hope that my general observations have not become too dry and that my illustrations every now and then will give a fresh view of a landscape which, generally speaking, will be known to you but which remains, all the same, fascinating.

PART I

Implications of the Subject

When speaking of harmonization of national monetary policies we assume by implication that monetary measures are of significance:

a. for the attainment of important national economic purposes, which means that these measures are an instrument of welfare policy, and

b. that these measures affect not only the monetary situation at home, but also abroad.

When money is understood to mean any generally accepted purchasing power in a country which is available for the holder at call, and when monetary policy is understood to be every central influencing of this quantity, monetary policy not only affects the demand for commodities and services at home but—in a free exchange market—also monetary conditions in other countries. At a fixed rate of exchange, a balance of payments surplus will lead to an increase in the quantity of money at home and to a decrease in purchasing power in some other country. A balance of payments deficit will have the reverse effects. Depending on the circumstances, either the one or the other may suit the needs or be experienced as disturbing at home or abroad.

Disequilibrated Balances of Payments

A balance of payments surplus suits the needs if the monetary reserves are considered too small. This may result from a loss of reserves in the past or from a marked increase of production, or both.

A balance of payments disequilibrium is rightly not experienced as disturbing if the deficit does not lead to a considerable decrease of the gross reserves of the deficit country and if the surplus countries are prepared to consider liabilities of the deficit country as a lasting part of their foreign reserves.

If both circumstances coincide, balance of payments deficits and surpluses are indispensable components in a satisfactory international development. The question as to whether such coincidence is not to be considered "abnormal" evokes the counterquestion: what is regarded as normal? Is it not so that when stigmatizing every balance of payments disequilibrium as "abnormal," one becomes entangled in the illusion that an academic working hypothesis of a stationary balance has a normative value? Or is "abnormal" intended to mean "improbable"? Anticipating the second part of my lecture, I would observe here and now that this "improbable" situation has been exactly the one which has characterized the relations between the United States and Western Europe during all the years after the war up to about 1957.

The Need for a Well-equilibrated Balance of Payments

If, contrary to the constellation just referred to, both countries—or one country and a group of other countries—are in about the same monetary economic situation at home, and the national monetary policies are directed at roughly identical aims, a well-equilibrated balance of payments will be the more or less natural result of a development wanted by all parties—the more so if not only the phase of the economic cycle in the countries concerned is more or less the same but also if there is not too much difference in size and general structure. Disturbances in the balance of payments in that case will be due mainly to difference in dosage and tempo of national monetary measures. The climate for entering into mutual consultations in order to remove these differences as much as possible will then be favorable.

Such consultations are desirable in the first place, insofar as uncertainty as to each other's views and intentions may, out of fear of a disturbance to the balance, lead each country independently, and so all together, to exercising restraint which otherwise one would have rightly avoided. Such has been the situation repeatedly in the past in case of universal deflationary developments. It may very well happen again.

These consultations, however, will lead to nothing if, apart from the pronounced intention to prevent *deflation*, there is no consensus as to the necessity to prevent *inflation*.

The Need for Effective Monetary Instruments

Of at least equal importance is a mutual trust that the intentions pronounced can be realized. In this connection I am thinking not only of possible doubts as to the firmness of each other's intentions, or of internal political obstacles affecting the execution, but also of a possible lack of instruments. When in general there is agreement to keep monetary expansion within certain limits, differences in the efficiency of the technical apparatus should not hamper achievement of the goals. I shall refer to this again later. Within the more far-reaching problem of monetary harmonization, it is only a relatively limited issue, but for that reason it is not unimportant. It is a preliminary duty not to lag behind one's partners with respect to available instruments. In a situation in which it is intended to attain certain identical purposes, obsolete traditions or provisions of the law should not present insurmountable obstacles.

Fixed Rates of Exchange Can Go Hand-in-hand with Deflationary and Inflationary Trends

The supposition that in a certain constellation a well-equilibrated balance of payments is the result of a development wanted by all parties does not in the least imply that—contrariwise—a well-equilibrated balance of payments indicates that a development aimed at by all parties has been realized. I have already referred to the universal deflationary developments which in the past have repeatedly occurred when fixed rates of exchange were maintained. There have also been periods with fixed rates of exchange and inflationary trends.

When at any time the balance of payments equilibrium between the most important Western countries or groups of countries (United States, United Kingdom, continental Western Europe) may in some way or other be restored, one may once again have to face a situation in which there is a threat of a universal undesirable development. This may be either inflationary or deflationary.

Apart from the reinforcement, nationally, of the available monetary instruments, joint measures aimed at expanding or restraining the increase in international purchasing power may also be desirable. But it is also true here that the creation of monetary instruments does not in itself guarantee that the aims are actually pursued.

Conflicting Aims

The fundamental conflicts with regard to the monetary policy to be pursued will come to the fore in situations in which maintenance of fixed rates of exchange requires measures which reciprocally produce effects at home clashing with what is deemed desirable from the national point of view.

Efforts to meet requirements at home with monetary measures will in such cases be made at the expense of the equilibrium in other countries and vice versa. If, nonetheless, parties stick to maintenance of stable rates of exchange, one or the other will have to relinquish the realization of one or more of its ambitions or will have to try to attain them with means other than those of monetary policy. If, through circumstances which may be of the most varying nature, one of the two parties does not come to a certain position of power, the cry for a harmonization of sorts will be heard, but the possibility of attaining a satisfactory solution in that case declines progressively in proportion to the number of independent variables. As neither the relative value of the aims nor that of the media can be brought to a common denominator, that which is strived for as harmonization can only turn out to be the outcome of the respective positions of power. Actually this situation is typical for American-European relations since 1957.

Two ways Out

When seeking a solution without breaking through the system of fixed rates of exchange, one must tackle the problem from two sides. On the one hand, concessions will have to be made with regard to aims; on the other, one will have to bring the whole arsenal of welfare-political measures into the issue. Monetary measures alone will never do the trick.

Restriction of Aims

It is customary, internationally, to present the purposes of monetary policy, namely, fixed rates of exchange, stable prices, and full employment, as a trinity. In many cases this trinity is even enlarged by the addition of more aims, such as a certain rate of growth or a certain distribution of income, so that the magical triangle becomes a magical polygon.

An equal valuation of certain categories of aims, however, does not imply any indication of the extent to which one will be prepared to subordinate the partial realization of one end to that of another, when actually the optimal demands strived for do not appear to be realizable at the same time and the limitation of the means compels a choice. Presenting three or more categories of aims as being of equal importance when dealing with an economic problem is no more than a cheap trick to divert attention from the impossibility of formulating schemes of preference. Even if every government can be supposed to have certain schemes of preference, these schemes will not be similar in each country.

Moreover, such preference schemes lend themselves to scientific approach only to a very limited degree; they are predominantly determined politically.

Inadequacy of Instruments in General

As for the media of execution, in principle it may be assumed that the effects of certain measures do lend themselves to scientific analyses, although ascertaining the intensity and timing will often be very difficult.

If more aims are being pursued, one must have more media at one's disposal. Now the essence of "money" is that the owner can dispose of it indiscriminately. Monetary policy does not alter this. Monetary policy is understood to be the total of measures which may bring about an increase or decrease of the available quantity of money. It is true that one hopes therewith to influence the volume of *spending*, but this effect is often indirect. As for the *direction of spending*—again generally speaking—the influence of monetary policy does not reach further than creating differences in interest at home and abroad, thereby determining the direction of movement of capital from one country to another. However, therewith one influences not only the balance of payments but at the same time the demand for credit at home, as a result of which the effect of the differences in interest at home and abroad are wholly or partially leveled off. Because of this interdependence, monetary policy by its nature is too undifferentiated in its effect to attain, within the framework of fixed rates of exchange, a stable level of prices and full employment at the same time. Disturbances ensuing from the balance of payments may present an impediment to the realization of even one of these internal objectives through monetary policy alone.

The reverse is equally true: pursuing one of the internal desiderata may disturb the balance of payments equilibrium.

What applies to the pursuit of three aims through a medium which, by its nature, cannot or can hardly be differentiated progressively prevails at each further addition to the number of aims.

The concept of harmonizing gains substance only when the number of media is equal to the number of objects pursued. In order to achieve this, one has to limit the number of objects to be attained to the most essential ones, while measures of monetary policy must be supplemented by specifically directed government measures beyond the monetary field. The effects of changes in the quantity of purchasing power are nonspecific by nature; however, in order to attain a series of specific aims, one needs specifically directed instruments.

Inadequacy of Monetary Instruments

As for monetary policy itself, it would even be going too far to assume that it has sufficient instruments at its disposal to attain a control of total spending via control of the quantity of money. I have already referred to this, but now I would like to go into it a little further.

When the concept of quantity of money is understood to mean all purchasing power available for spending in the hands of nonmoney-creating institutions, this not only comprises ready money and deposits (the so-called primary liquidity) but also all claims which, pursuant to laws and traditions, can be converted by the holder into primary liquidity with a minimum of costs at short notice (so-called secondary liquidity). The banks preeminently are creators of primary liquidity, the public authorities of secondary liquidity.

In this context the concept of monetary policy not only comprises the policy of the central bank insofar as it can influence the total credit of the commercial banking system, but also the policy of the public authorities insofar as it leads to an expansion or contraction of their immediately claimable debts. This prevails when the government (central and local authorities as well as government institutions) does not cover its spending out of taxes and other revenues, but by loans which, by law or tradition, can at any time be converted into money at the holder's discretion. Insofar as the banking system thereby mediates, either by law or custom, without being responsible for the size of the obligations, the concept of monetary policy comprises not only the policy of the central bank but also government policy (fiscal and budgetary).

Insofar as monetary policy involves control of the credit policy of the banking system, it goes without saying that in the first place the central bank is obliged to examine the extent to which its instruments must be adapted to the development of the commercial banking system. Examples of such adaptation may be found in almost every country, but there is no lack of examples of insufficient adaptation either. Examples of the first can be found particularly in cases in which the commercial banking system disposed of such a large portfolio of treasury paper obtained during the war that the discount policy of the central bank lost a great deal of its effectiveness and had to be supplemented by more direct methods of credit restriction. Examples of the second are mainly found in cases in which, within or outside the traditional circle of commercial banks, forms of credit have developed which, through lack of adaptation of the central bank's traditional facilities, can offset its policy or escape its control.

For political as well as technical reasons the central bank cannot counteract government policy except to a very limited extent. It cannot itself prevent the government from creating or withdrawing money. In case of inflationary government policy, the central bank can go no further than trying to mitigate the effects thereof by measures to the contrary. In case of deflationary government policy, whether an increase in available credit will lead to a proportional increase of spending will depend on the circumstances.

The Need for Complementary Government Measures Beyond the Field of Monetary Policy

The most important aspect of government budget policy, however, is that it can also influence the *direction* of spending and thereby can introduce the additional media which are indispensable when the government is pursuing more than one object at the same time. In budget policy, after all, are concentrated the instruments which, apart from a rough influencing of the quantity of money, can influence not only the direct transition from "quantity" to "spending" but, above all, through specific measures, the direction of spending and thereby, in particular, the level of employment.

These specific measures, however, are not confined to budget policy. There is no clear borderline between budget policy and social laws, as far as effects on employment are concerned. Both wage subsidies and provisions as to minimum wages affect—in a positive or negative way—the structure of the labor market.

A general increase in demand leads to a marked absorption of more manpower only in case of great elasticity of labor supply. This will not be the case if there are minimum wages (pursuant to law or in fact) which are substantially higher than the productivity of the unemployed to be absorbed. Breaking through this inelasticity by abolishing these wage minima or by introducing wage subsidies may have a much greater effect on the demand for labor than a general increase in spending.

Also in case of a strong local concentration of unemployment, a directed increase in demand can be much more effective than a general monetary expansion which makes itself felt marginally in the whole country. Without contributing much to a solution of the more or less local unemployment problem, it may easily lead to a general increase in wages and prices and therewith to a deficit in the balance of payments. If the capital accounts of the balance of payments show a surplus of national savings, the possibility presents itself of solving the unemployment problem through directed government spending, financed out of the proceeds either of increased taxes or of long-term loans, without affecting the overall balance.

Similar considerations apply to a conflict of balance of payments equilibrium and price stability. When price stability is endangered by a faster increase in wages than in labor productivity, it may be necessary to proceed to specific measures in order to control the rise in wages. This amounts to the introduction of a wage policy.

If, furthermore, the impulse to an excessive wage increase is of a highly localized nature, the soundest solution is to influence the demand and supply in that particular sector through specific measures within the limits of a monetary policy aimed at either price stability or balance of payments equilibrium.

In a constellation in which the national preferences to be attained in various countries are different, one will be able to maintain fixed rates of exchange only if one can realize these preferences with nonmonetary media or if the effects of the monetary media on the balance of payments happen to fit into the scheme of preferences. This means that the country which builds up a balance of payments surplus wants an increase in its monetary reserves, and the country which gets a balance of payments deficit has sufficent reserves at its disposal.

The Specific Character of Balance of Payments Surpluses

The inflationary impulses of balance of payments surpluses have a character entirely of their own insofar as they are not directly caused by the policy of the national authorities, as in the case of money creation by a fiscal deficit. Nor are they subject to the sanction of the central bank, as in the case of credit extension by the commercial banks. The money-creating effect of balance of payments surpluses follows directly from the freedom of international trade and payments. Under a system of fixed exchange rates and free convertibility, possession of a surplus of foreign currency gives the holders collectively the right to claim the creation of national currency. Insofar as the balance of payments surplus is due to a surplus on current account or to direct foreign investments, the monetary authorities cannot do anything, except to take ex post measures designed to offset undesired inflationary (or deflationary) effects. The same applies, although perhaps to a lesser extent, to long-term capital movements and sales of shares.

The government, as monetary authority, can offset the effects only by creating budget surpluses out of taxes or long-term loans, applying the proceeds to the prepayment of foreign debt or the amortization of debt owed to the central bank, or to building up a balance with the central bank. These devices, however, can seldom be reverted to.

The central bank in general is in a position to restrict credit facilities of commercial banks, but in this instance its actions would amount to repressing investment in those sectors of the economy which do not obtain their money from abroad. The activities, however, of those who can borrow foreign capital and who get their funds from abroad by selling to foreign countries would not be directly affected, particularly if the restrictive policy leads to a downward pressure on the national wage level. The least affected by a policy of restraint, therefore, are companies who (*a*) have access to foreign capital, (*b*) are exporting a large part of their output, and (*c*) are benefiting from a low level of wages. Among these companies are a long number of affiliates of foreign firms. The greater this group, the less will be the net effect on the balance of payments and the heavier the burden on home companies.

Insofar as the restrictive policy is accompanied by, and depends on, a rise in the rate of interest at home, it will lead to more import of foreign capital and repatriation of balances held abroad. Therefore, with regard to direct investment as well as to the movement of fixed interest, capital restrictive policy will have a limited effect only.

Finally, the effect of the restrictive measures will from the outset lag behind the effect of the expansion. Surpluses on current account, direct foreign investment, and capital borrowed from abroad will as a rule be used for spending and will set the income multiplier at once into motion. Restrictive measures to offset ex post the inflationary effects of these elements of the balance of payments surplus will thus have to be more stringent than ex ante restrictions anticipating possible internal inflationary impulses.

The possibility of a directly neutralizing effect is limited in principle to short-term credit movements. This can be effected by inviting commercial banks to increase balances held abroad, through short-term interest manipulating and forward exchange transaction. These actions must, however, be accompanied by measures that deprive foreign balances of their ability to serve as a basis for internal credit. This may necessitate the introduction of credit ceilings which, however, have the effect of curbing competitiveness among banks, since credit ceilings are inevitably based on a situation which happens to prevail at a given date in the past.

Therefore, monetary instruments specifically designed for coping with a balance of payments surplus can in most cases also have nonmonetary effects.

Insofar as a policy of restraint ultimately does have the effect of curbing the inflation and leads to an (unwanted) increase of reserves, it will not contribute to a restoration of international equilibrium, and the basic problem will remain unsolved.

Summary and Conclusion

When one keeps the above clearly in mind, the call for harmonization of monetary policy gets a tenor quite different from that conceived initially. It then boils down to a rather unspecified appeal to take into consideration in a most general way the effects on other countries when pursuing national objectives. This appeal implies that for the sake of other countries one should be prepared to:

1. abandon part of one's ambitions, insofar as the same would have to be realized with instruments of monetary policy, and
2. call upon and introduce instruments not only of a monetary and fiscal but even of a general economic and social character. This may

have many undesired consequences for objectives which were not included in the original triangle or polygon of desiderata but which are perhaps just as urgent. In the last instance the initial distinction between aims and means becomes fictitious. Aims and means merge into one another.

More than one objective cannot be simultaneously attained if there is only one medium at one's disposal. One has either to choose or to subordinate one object to another depending on the actual circumstances, or one must, besides taking measures of general monetary and fiscal policy, be prepared from the outset to take measures of a quite different nature as well—measures which are specifically directed and which, for that reason, as a matter of principle do not belong to the field of monetary policy.

These may be measures combating unemployment by government action, which in essence amounts to transfer of income and not to creation of money; these may be measures of wage policy; these may be measures absorbing the effects of a balance of payments deficit or surplus so as to do the least harm to both parties, particularly where this surplus is of a temporary or receding character.

If, however, one aims at overcoming general international cost and price differences, specific measures can never be adequate. On the international plane we must in that case choose among acceptance of deflation, on the one hand, and inflation on the other, a combination of both, or an adaptation of the rate of exchange. The concept of harmonization fits in with none of these cases; at the most we can expect a rather haphazard development resulting from the real or fancied interests of each separate country and based on actual positions of power.

PART II

The Relationship between the U.S. and Western Europe Since the War

In the postwar relationship between the U.S. and Western Europe two periods are to be distinguished, the transition of the first into the second taking place around 1957. The first era is that of the so-called dollar scarcity, the second one, still current, is of the oversupply of dollars; or as it is experienced in most of the continental European countries, an era of dollar inflation.

The First Period

The main characteristic of the first period is a great need for dollar goods that could only be met by the Marshall aid funds and, afterward, by other financial assistance. The period coincides with the physical reconstruction of Europe and the replenishment of European monetary reserves. The stimulus of American aid had such a strong and multiple income effect that the growth of production and exports also enabled an increase in reserves to such an extent that ultimately the latter approximately increased with the amount of Marshall aid. About half of the increase was held in dollars, so that the balance of payments deficit of the U.S. in this period, amounting to some $1.2 billion per year, was *pro tanto* offset. The other half of the increase in reserves was obtained by buying practically all of the newly mined gold that became available. Ultimately this caused the U.S. hardly any loss of gold. The entire process was supported by the devaluation of practically all Western European currencies in 1949.

During this period the phenomenon of a balance of payments deficit did not have an ominous meaning for the U.S. For Europe the surplus, although smaller than most countries would have wished for, was a godsend. Deficits and surpluses only reflected some aspects of the reconstruction under way; the same applies to the different rates of growth of the national products in the two parts of the world. Reconstruction of the productive equipment apparatus and the replenishment of the European monetary reserves, of either gold or foreign exchange, were both part of the restoration of the overall equilibrium. The concept of "dollar scarcity" expressed in general terms the desire to accelerate the reconstruction beyond the possibilities offered by the phenomenal willingness of the American government to grant aid and assistance. It gave no indication of the possible tensions that were bound to present themselves in either one or the other direction after the completion of the reconstruction. From the monetary point of view, one might say that the concept of "dollar scarcity" boiled down to the need felt in Europe to reinforce the monetary reserves at the expense of a certain delay in the actual reconstruction.

The Second Period

In hindsight one can see that the transition to the second period begins in 1956–57, when the American export of private capital gathered momentum. As governmental aid and military expenditure were maintained at an invariably high level, the flow of dollars to the rest of the world increased. The circumstance that in this context the dollar flow originating from aid and military expenditure was directed more toward countries other than those of Western Europe, and that the American export of private capital was mainly attracted by Western Europe, was of less importance than the fact that the increase in the *aggregate* flow of dollars coincided with the relative growth of the competitiveness of Western Europe and the diminishing need for a further increase in monetary reserves.

In addition to this was the fact that the increase of the American export of private capital was sparked not only by a "normal" restoration of confidence in the economic viability of Europe but additionally by the prospective establishment of the European Economic Community. The anticipated protectionistic effect of the European common tariff invited American manufacturers to make direct investments in Europe. The prevailing fiscal structure was favorable for such a development both in the United States and in the various European countries.

In the report of the Brookings Institution in Washington (*The United States Balance of Payments in 1968*) attention is rightly drawn to the fact that the common EEC tariff, based, by virtue of the Rome treaty, on the unweighted averages of the tariffs in four areas (Benelux, France, Germany, and Italy), has an unmistakable protectionistic effect. The low-cost prices of the great producers will be decisive for the competitiveness of the EEC as a whole. The common tariff will be protectionistic insofar as it protects the low-cost producers. A tariff that is high enough to protect German producers in Germany will also be high enough to protect producers in other member countries. This is the essence of the European integration. It implies, further, according to the report, that 75 percent of all producers will obtain greater protection against the outside world than previously. Of the 61 most important products that were further analyzed, 22 are of major interest to the U.S. For eight of them, a drop in the common tariff should be 50 percent or more, in order to reduce protection to the original level; and for nine, the decrease should range from 25 to 50 percent.

This incentive for American investment in Europe coincided with a persistent high level of unemployment in the U.S., inducing the monetary authorities to compensate the restraining effect of the outflow of capital by creation of internal liquidity.

In spite of the price-increasing effect resulting from balance of payments surpluses in most of the European countries and the relatively stable prices in the U.S., the *overall* American balance of payments deficit increased from the average of $1.2 billion in the previous period to $3.9 billion in 1960. In the following years the overall deficit fluctuated around $2.5 billion.

Although, after a minor deficit in 1959, the American *current account* ran ever increasing surpluses (1959: −$0.7 billion; 1960: +$3.1 billion; 1961: +$4.9 billion; 1962: +$4.4 billion; 1963: +$4.9 billion; 1964: +$7.4 billion), the persistent deficit of the overall balance of payments created a rapidly spreading atmosphere of uneasiness all over the world. The fact that the counterpart of these deficits was an increase of American investment abroad did not do away with the fact that the U.S. as a nation ran short of international monetary reserves.

Two Different Reasons for Concern

The concern over the American balance of payments originated from two basically different views of the situation. The first reaction was one of doubt about the stability of the dollar; the second reaction, which, as far as the EEC countries were concerned, was especially pronounced in the Netherlands and Germany, and, outside the EEC, in Switzerland, was brought about by the inflationary impact of the American balance of payments deficit on the economy of Europe in general and on the economies of the said countries in particular.

The first reaction I should like to characterize as a "bankers' reaction"; the second one as a reaction of "economists."

The "Bankers' Concern"

The bankers' reaction led to the conversion of dollars into gold, involving a drain on the gold reserves of the U.S. and giving rise to growing misgivings about the stability of the dollar.

On the part of the U.S., attempts were made to restrain this reaction by using various techniques, in essence amounting to granting exchange rate guarantees for the increasing dollar claims held outside the U.S. In this respect I think of the U.S. drawings on the International Monetary Fund, as well as the special gold/dollars transactions of the IMF, in principle ending in gold-guaranteed dollar claims. I think also of the issues of American Treasury bills denominated in the creditor country's currency—the so-called Roosa bonds. I also include among these techniques all swap transactions and comparable bilateral credit arrangements between the Federal Reserve and various other central banks. Through these techniques American dollar liabilities are converted into liabilities denominated either in gold or in the creditor countries' currencies.

On the part of Europe, *ad hoc* measures were taken to use the growing flow of dollar claims for prepayment of military aid and advance amortization of long-term debts incurred during the period of Europe's recovery. The strain on the liquidity position of the U.S. was accordingly eased.

In order to curb possible speculative transactions on the part of the private sector, a series of mutual credit arrangements came into being: the so-called General Arrangements to Borrow.

In connection with the latter, one has to bear in mind that once speculation has burst out one has not only to reckon with the conversion in gold of already existing dollar balances at the central banks, but also with the withdrawal of dollar balances held at commercial banks outside the U.S.

Moreover, one has to take into consideration the possibilities of capital flight from the U.S. The imminent threat to the dollar's par value is not susceptible to quantitative measurement, since the possibility of such conversion of dollars into other currencies depends on the surplus liquid resources which U.S. citizens can dispose of. This surplus finds its limitations only in the need for liquid resources required to maintain the internal economic process and is liable to be expanded by the prevailing possibilities for turning capital assets into money and obtaining credit.

The "Economists' Concern"

The economists' concern, which at first was restricted to a small group but in the meantime has met with a growing response, has been prompted by the general inflationary effect that a persistent balance of payments surplus exerts, *irrespective of the resulting exchange risks.* According to simple arithmetic, the balance of payments deficit of one country involves a balance of payments surplus of another. The conversion of the surplus of foreign purchasing power in the surplus country's own money leads to an increase of national purchasing power. The concern about the inflationary effect of a persistent international disequilibrium holds true irrespective of the existence or absence of eventual exchange guarantees. It holds true even more if exchange guarantees increase the chance of perpetuating the disequilibria, *a risk that in principle will always exist.*

Every country considers the world initially from its own point of view. It is therefore natural that the concern about possible inflationary effects of balance of payments disequilibria is firstly and most deeply felt in the countries whose balances of payments run the greatest surplus in relation to their national product, and whose full employment of their economic capacity already brings them on the verge of an inflationary situation. However, their concern has a universal bearing, insofar as inflationary impulses have a tendency to spread worldwide.

Their concern will, however, meet with a minor response of the deficit countries, when—as is the case in the relationship of the U.S. to Western Europe—the deficit country does not run a deficit because of a creation of money that is harmful to its internal economy, but deliberately aims at neutralizing an imminent deflationary effect of a lucrative private capital export. This will be the more so when domestic prices and wages remain rather stable, unemployment remains at a level that is still considered higher than justified for reasons of social policy, and the rate of growth—though not unsatisfactory—lags behind the same rate in the surplus countries. Besides, conditions during 30 years had been such that the authorities had been able to carry on a monetary policy aimed entirely at the compliance of internal desiderata without having to consider the balance of payments issue. Furthermore, the U.S. can point out that practically all European countries, Germany excepted, followed a monetary policy that, except for some incidental and temporary interruptions, led to an internal creation of money that was excessive relative to the physical decrease of their national product. In putting it this way, Americans may well argue that these countries can at most complain that the external inflationary impulses have *aggravated,* but not created, a problem they evidently could not control themselves. In this respect the figures derived from the *Annual Report of the Netherlands Bank, 1964,* pages 62 and 63, are revealing (see *Appendix*).

This reasoning, however, jumps at conclusions, since nothing has been said about the *causes* of the internal inflationary tendencies in Europe. Notably the figures say nothing about the question whether and to what extent the impulses originating from abroad have in fact been *additional* or *causally primary*.

Fundamental Changes

Finally, there remains the question whether, despite the tangle of effects of incidental measures, some conclusions can be drawn with respect to the possible future trend of the "overall" movement.

The current account of the balance of payments of the U.S. since 1959 runs a rather steadily increasing surplus. On the other hand, we see an equally regular decrease of the surplus on current account of the EEC countries. Only last year was there an interruption in this trend.

As I have pointed out earlier, in the period 1959 to 1963, the American surplus on current account increased from minus $0.7 billion to plus $4.9 billion. The surplus of EEC countries in the corresponding period decreased from $3.7 billion to $0.8 billion, at the same time that labor costs, per man-hour as well as per unit, rose more steeply in Western Europe than in the U.S. As far as we are concerned with a long-term movement, the trend within a foreseeable future will lead to the restoration of equilibrium in the overall balance of payments of both. To a certain extent, the year 1964 seems to confirm this trend.

The American surplus on current account in 1964 increased by no less than $2.5 billion. It is true that in the past year the European surplus on current account increased as well, but the rise was considerably smaller. The relative rise of labor cost, however, was higher in Europe. The prospects of 1965 point in the same direction.

The only thing that does not fit into this picture is the increase in 1964 of the deficit in the overall balance of payments of the U.S. from $2.5 billion to $2.8 billion and a renewed increase of nearly $0.5 billion in the overall surplus of continental Europe.

In this context some additional observations may be made. In the first place, the improvement of the Italian balance of payments needs some comment: noteworthy is the vigorous reaction to the drastic internal measures to eliminate the enormous deficit incurred in the previous year. Furthermore, the balance of payments of the United Kingdom in 1964 ran an intolerable deficit. It is hardly conceivable that—whatever measures England may take to remedy the deficit—the resulting effect on the balance of payments of most of the continental European countries will not soon be felt.

As to the U.S. deficit on the overall balance of payments in 1964, mention has to be made of the remarkable shift in the components of the deficit. No less than $2.5 billion out of the total of $2.8 billion comes under the item "other transactions," against a mere $0.4 billion in 1963.

Is this due to an expansion of credits directly related to the increase in exports, and should it therefore be considered as an integral part of the total deficit that is only to be eliminated if and when the rise in exports comes to a standstill? Is it a kind of one-time capital flight invited under the threat of restrictive measures to be applied to international capital movements? Or is it—at least partially—a conversion by foreign holders of American securities into American Treasury bills; a conversion that statistically comes within the definition of "balance of payments deficit" without, however, having a fundamental meaning?

I am inclined to assume that the somewhat confusing picture of 1964 will, in hindsight, prove to be a fluctuation rather than a deviation from the aforementioned trend toward restoration of equilibrium in the balance of payments between America and Europe.

It may even occur that we will reach the equilibrium point sooner than we expect and that we will go beyond it. As the restoration of equilibrium will mainly involve the items on current account, while the initial disturbance affected the capital movements, it is highly probable that at a given moment the capital accounts will show a drastic reversal. If the increases in costs in Europe no longer invite the American manufacturer to make direct investments in Europe, the one-sided capital flow from the U.S. will dry up and may be reversed—even without government measures to curb international movements. The reversed position may be brought about by a withdrawal of dollar balances from Europe, as well as by selling shares in European enterprises and a tendency to increase the European holdings of American shares. For the time being the prevailing differences in interest levels will continue to have contrary effects, but differences in interest levels have in the course of the years become of less importance for international capital movements than differences in expectations with respect to capital returns.

Only if the United States should not succeed in checking the rise in wage costs, now also imminent in the U.S., and if Germany—contrary to expectations—should be able to keep the increase in wage costs below the increase in production costs, will the problem of excessive dollar holdings not be solved.

In this context a major factor seems to be the political evolution that might induce the U.S. to a further overspending with regard to military and nuclear expenditure.

Problems Ahead

However, transition to a period of equilibrium and, even more, to a period of American surplus will give rise to new problems.

Aid to Developing Countries

In their relation to the developing countries the industrial countries will have to perform together an export of capital in order to fulfill the duties they have undertaken on behalf of the developing countries. Such export of capital (irrespective of whether it is in the nature of credits, loans, or grants) should have a counterpart in a surplus on current account. It necessitates the creation of a surplus of real savings in excess of total internal investment, but it easily induces governments to resort to money creation and banks to credit expansion beyond the limits afforded by the labor market and the exigencies of price stability.

Restoration of the balance between the U.S. and Western Europe confronts the whole Western world with the problem of a balanced, non-inflationary growth within the limits of a common net export of capital and goods.

Growth of Monetary Reserves

A second problem that presents itself at the restoration of balanced American payments is the slowing down in the growth of monetary reserves. When the flow of dollars stops and the increase of the gold component of monetary reserves lags considerably behind the real growth of production and trade, authorities must provide, in concerted action, for a replenishment of reserves.

Several solutions to the problem present themselves. I myself advanced a solution that makes allowance for a further elaboration in various directions according to whether one wants to assign more importance to one or the other aspect of the problem involved. This, however, is a problem in itself, upon which I do not want to dwell, since it is beyond the scope of my subject. I only want to stress that one has to bear in mind that the problem of the growth of monetary reserves is closely linked to the necessity for each of the participating countries to refrain from inflationary policies internally.

A restored balance in American and European payments means for Europe that at least one of the major inflationary impulses would cease to exist. On the other hand, the duty of both parties to finance net capital export out of real savings, together with the necessity to create in concerted action a new foreign reserves medium, offers a temptation towards an oversupply of purchasing power. For this reason it is inadmissible to identify rashly an eventual restoration of equilibrium in the relationship between America and Europe with a solution to the problem of inflation, even if that restoration of equilibrium will temporarily amount to a general shortage of capital funds in Europe and a possible slowing down in the rate of growth.

THE INTERNATIONAL MONETARY SYSTEM AND THE RECONCILIATION OF POLICY GOALS*

J. Marcus Fleming

I. INTRODUCTION

In speaking of the "international monetary system" I shall be concerned not merely with exchange rates, external reserves, the financing of balance of payments deficits, and so forth but rather with the whole complex of arrangements and practices, whether resting on law or custom, that condition the behavior of national authorities with respect to the balance of payments. In other words, I shall have in mind the real as well as the monetary side of the international economic mechanism. And I shall inquire into the extent to which this system hinders or permits a simultaneous realization of "domestic" policy objectives, like full employment, price stability, and economic growth, on the one hand, and "international" policy objectives, like freedom of trade and freedom of capital movements, on the other.

The possibility of conflict between domestic and international objectives arises mainly because of the inflexible or otherwise noncompetitive behavior of the prices of goods and services, and notably of labor, within each country. When Keynes first discussed this problem, the point he stressed was the downward inflexibility of wages, as a result of which any attempt at a domestic adjustment of the price level in a deficit country might lead to unemployment. Since then, the situation has been complicated by the appearance, or emergence to consciousness, of various "cost-push" mechanisms which sometimes carry prices farther from, instead of nearer to, equilibrium. These price rigidities and perverse

*This paper expresses the author's personal opinions and does not necessarily reflect the views of the International Monetary Fund.

spontaneities create difficulties in bringing about even long-term adjustments in relative national price levels and render impossible those short-term adjustments to temporary balance of payments factors which would occur in an ideal price system and which, in turn, would tend to evoke equilibrating capital flows.

II. THE SYSTEM AS ORIGINALLY ENVISAGED

The system of adjustment set up during and immediately after World War II in the Articles of Agreement of the International Monetary Fund and in the General Agreement on Tariffs and Trade contained various features designed to resolve any tension between domestic and international economic objectives—on the whole, in favor of the former.

Thus, one of the principal objects of the par value system of the Fund was to permit countries, through exchange rate adjustments, to correct long-term disequilibria in international price levels when these had accumulated to the point of being serious. (The other principal object was to prevent competitive devaluations.)

To cope with more temporary disturbances to the balance of payments a number of different expedients were envisaged:

In the first place, there would be facilities for financing payments deficits through movements in national reserves, supplemented by recourse to international credit facilities, notably those provided by drawing rights in the IMF itself.

Secondly, countries would be *allowed* to control outward and inward capital movements, and indeed, in certain circumstances, *expected* to control the former.

Thirdly, though this was the least preferred alternative, countries in balance of payments difficulties would be permitted, as a temporary measure, to apply quantitative restrictions to imports and, with the Fund's permission, to current account payments.

It will be seen that this system protected national autonomy with respect to domestic economic policies and objectives at the expense of at least temporary departures from international norms. This was particularly true wtih respect to capital movements, which seemed to be held in rather low esteem by the Founding Fathers of the system. But it is true to some extent also of current transactions. For example, the provisions of the GATT designed to insure the temporary character of quantitative restrictions on trade were decidedly weak.

What I have been describing is, of course, not the regime under which countries were expected to live in the immediate postwar period. That was governed by the very permissive arrangements of which almost all countries were allowed to avail themselves under Article XIV of the Fund Agreement. It represents, rather, the goal that countries were expected to reach after they had grown strong enough to throw away the crutch of these transitional arrangements. In practice it was not until 1961 that most industrial countries felt able finally to accept the full obligations of the Articles of Agreement of the Fund, though for a good many years they had been gradually dropping first the bilateral and later the regional discriminatory practices which had been allowed them under Article XIV. As for the less developed countries, most of them are still "living in sin" with Article XIV, though in a world in which the main currencies are interconvertible, they have little incentive to discriminate over the greater part of their trade.

III. SUBSEQUENT DEVELOPMENT OF THE SYSTEM

As the industrial countries approached convertibility and full acceptance of the obligations of Article VIII, the international system on which they converged was one that differed in spirit and in practice, though not in law, from what had been envisaged at Bretton Woods.

In the first place, there was, and continues to be, a tendency, so far as industrial countries are concerned, to interpret the exchange stability envisaged in the par value system in the sense of fixity of exchange rates. Since the general readjustment of initial par values in 1949, there have been rather few adjustments of exchange rates on the part of industrial countries. The main exceptions are the French devaluations of 1957 and 1958, and the revaluations of the deutsche mark and the guilder in 1961. Canada, which conducted an experiment in fluctuating rates from 1950, returned to the fixed rate fold in 1962.

Secondly, there was, until recently, a tendency to consider that the architects of the Fund and the GATT had set their sights too low, from the standpoint of liberal internationalism, in allowing such easy, even if temporary, access to trade restrictions and such unhampered access to capital restrictions in defense of the balance of payments. As the industrial countries, under the impetus of the liberalization program of the OEEC, gradually discarded their import restrictions—with certain exceptions in the agricultural sphere—they tended to abjure their use for good and all, even in the event of payments difficulties. As such countries adopted the obligations of Article VIII, it was the intention that they should not, save in dire emergencies, be allowed by the Fund to have recourse to exchange restrictions on current account. A similar change in attitude, though less strong and less universal, occurred with respect to capital restrictions. For a time, at least, it became fashionable to advocate what was called "Swiss convertibility," namely the notion that countries should be deemed to have fallen short of their duty in the matter of restoring convertibility if they stopped short at converting balances of their currencies acquired by nonresidents and did not extend the privilege to domestic residents who wanted to exchange domestic for foreign currency for the purpose of acquiring assets abroad.

The third departure, at least in emphasis, from the Bretton Woods system was with respect to the role of national financial policy and, in particular, monetary policy. The implication of the IMF Articles—and this was made fairly clear by an interpretation elicited by the United Kingdom in 1946—was that domestic monetary policy should, or at least could, be directed exclusively toward domestic goals—full employment, growth, or what not—while the responsibility for preserving external equilibrium was left to other instruments of policy. By the time most industrial countries became legally convertible, however, the orthodox view was that monetary policy should, to a considerable extent, be directed toward the objective of preserving or restoring balance of payments equilibrium. This was particularly true so far as deficit countries were concerned. Surplus countries were inclined to feel, with some justice, that in the generally buoyant state of world demand it was up to the others to restore balance by abstaining from inflation for a while.

IV. REASONS FOR THESE DEVELOPMENTS

There were a number of reasons for this somewhat surprising reversion to the gold standard ideal of a liberal international system with fixed exchange rates. Trade and exchange restrictions were found in practice to be extremely irksome and hampering to enterprise, and their removal correspondingly favorable to expansion. Moreover, the experience that neither import restrictions nor currency devaluations afforded more than a temporary fillip to the balance of payments, unless accompanied by a contraction of monetary demand, encouraged countries to rely primarily on the latter instrument. Again, the fact that it proved so difficult to control capital movements and that such movements could be very disruptive if motivated by exchange anticipations made countries reluctant to contemplate, and even more reluctant to admit that they contemplated, alterations of exchange rates. On the other hand, the belief that with fixed rates, and suitable monetary policies, capital movements could play a useful equilibrating role was an argument for removing capital controls.

Perhaps the most important reason why countries felt able to do without restrictions or exchange rate adjustments, however, was that they found it possible to defend their balances of payments by means of demand policies alone, with effects on employment and economic growth that were slight and, in most cases, temporary. This—from a Keynesian standpoint—unexpected outcome can, however, be largely accounted for by the special circumstances of the time.

In the first place, the rapid reconstruction and modernization of the economy in Europe and Japan, in conjunction with the substantial and widespread adjustment of exchange rates which took place in 1949 (with subsequent devaluations in France), brought about a state of general balance of payments ease in which the countries that entered on the postwar period with low reserves and payments restrictions enjoyed payments surpluses, while the corresponding deficits were largely confined to the United States, which not only had enormous reserves to start with, but also was able to finance the major portion of its deficit through an accumulation of short-term liabilities.[1] In such an environment, widespread abandonment of restrictions and discriminations was relatively easy, though the European countries deserve credit for the cooperative effort by which this liberalization was speeded up.[2]

The second, and even more important, factor was the generally high pressure of monetary demand which prevailed and, with slight interruption, persisted in most industrial countries. This was attributable partly to such "autonomous" factors as the reconstruction needs, the increase in population growth, and the capital-intensive technological developments of the postwar period; partly to full-employment policies and national planning efforts that checked any flagging of demand, and partly to the situation of high international liquidity and balance of payments ease which has just been described. In such a situation it seemed possible for such fundamental disequilibria as might develop, either owing to differential rates of inflation or to differential rates of productivity growth, to be corrected by a relatively mild and short period of disinflation on the part of the deficit country. This was true largely, though not completely, even for the United Kingdom, where the trends of competitiveness were least favorable.

Even in the halcyon period of fixed exchange rates and financial corrective techniques, however, exceptions to the rule occurred. For example, France had to devalue. Germany and Holland preferred to revalue rather than endure the price increases that would otherwise have been the necessary result of, and remedy for, their payments surpluses. And Canada preferred, for about a decade, to maintain a fluctuating rate rather than to absorb in price movements the disturbing effects of variations in the massive influx of U.S. capital.

It might be said with some justification that in the 1950s and early 1960s international liquidity was excessive and that had there been less of it, there would have been less inflationary pressure. From the standpoint of real income, or even of income distribution, however, this bias, in the degree to which it applied, was probably an error on the right side.

---

[1]The United Kingdom, whose reserves fluctuated round a low average level, was a special case.

[2]Cf. Anne Romanis, "Balance of Payments Adjustment among Developed Countries," IMF *Staff Papers*, Vol. XII, No. 1, March, 1965.

V. DIFFICULTIES OF RECENT YEARS

In the last few years, a number of developments have occurred, largely growing out of the situation just described, which have tended to complicate the task of reconciling domestic and international objectives.

In the first place, the adoption of convertibility and the abandonment of various restrictions in Europe and Japan have greatly enhanced the international mobility of capital and thereby increased the potentialities for disequilibrium in international payments. In particular, it has become attractive and profitable for short- and long-term funds to flow on a large scale from America to other industrial countries, in many of which output has been growing faster than in the United States and in some of which new opportunities for large-scale industry have been opening up owing to the widening of the market. This has naturally tended to raise the equilibrium level of prices in other industrial countries relative to the United States. Owing to the very high level of demand pressure and employment that has prevailed until very recently in Europe, relative price levels have in fact been moving somewhat in the required direction. Nevertheless, the United States has not been able to avoid considerable strain in its balance of payments.

In the second place, the problem of cost inflation has in recent years become more pressing, or at least more prominent in people's minds. In many countries—though this is perhaps not true of the United States—money wages have in recent years tended to rise faster for any given level of employment and productivity growth than in the 1950s. How far this is a delayed consequence of long-continued demand pressure is difficult to say. In several of the continental countries, for example, the Netherlands and Germany, this is less a matter of wage-push than of the dwindling of wage-restraint—not so much an intensification of the overpricing as a diminution of the underpricing of labor. However that may be, the result is to make it more difficult than formerly to reconcile the domestic objectives of price stability and full employment. These cost-inflationary factors are sometimes active causes of balance of payments disequilibria. In addition, they make it very difficult for governments in surplus countries to give weight to balance of payments considerations in determining their domestic demand policies, and in this way probably have a systematic tendency to impede the process of adjustment to disequilibria that arise from other causes. As was pointed out in the Fund's *Annual Report* for 1964,

> Countries that are tending to fall into persistent payments deficits should be willing to pursue less expansionary policies than they would otherwise prefer, though they should not be expected to endure situations of high or prolonged unemployment of resources or economic stagnation. Again, countries that are tending to run into persistent surpluses should be willing to pursue, within

limits, a more expansionary policy than they would have been inclined to adopt for purely domestic reasons.

But in the last year or so, important surplus countries have felt that, with costs in any case tending to rise faster than desired, they could not be expected to maintain demand at a higher level than purely domestic considerations made inevitable.

It might be thought that the growing attention being paid to incomes policies in many countries is an item favorable to the adjustment process. To some extent this is no doubt true. Countries in payments difficulty have a greater incentive than those in payments surplus to take the political risks involved in measures tending to hold back increases in wages and prices. On the other hand, the instruments available for the purpose are so extremely feeble at the moment in most countries that little assistance in the cause of international equilibrium is to be looked for from this source in the foreseeable future. Moreover, governments often think it more convenient, in the present embryonic stage of incomes policies, to aim at a very simple target, namely, price stability, than to adapt their targets to the state of the balance of payments.[3]

The third important development casting a pall over the balance of payments situation has, of course, been the growing precariousness of the structure of international liquidity and, since 1964, the decline in the rate of growth of national reserves. Both of the countries whose currencies are held as reserves by the monetary authorities of other countries have in recent years encountered balance of payments difficulties. The United Kingdom has for most of the postwar period struggled on with low reserves and a low rate of productivity growth. Any attempt to force the pace of growth has tended to evoke a payments deficit. The U.S. deficit, which has been much larger in amount has, until recent years, been an engine of world prosperity and growth. After about 1958, however, it gradually began to undermine the strength of the United States' own reserve position and to impair confidence in the dollar. As a result, many countries have become increasingly uneasy about their holdings of reserve currencies, and anxious, if not to reduce their holdings of foreign exchange, at least to increase, where decently possible, the ratio of gold to currency in their reserves.

If the situation just described spelled growing illiquidity and balance of payments difficulty for the reserve centers themselves, the measures which these centers, and particularly the United States, have taken to put a stop to their deficits are likely to give rise sooner or later to liquidity shortage in the rest of the world. As has been shown by many

[3]This attitude is not necessarily a wise one. The attempt to maintain too much stability in costs at a time when balance of payments circumstances dictated a rise in the domestic price level probably contributed to the recent disintegration of the wage control system in the Netherlands.

writers and in the *Annual Report* of the Fund for 1964, the rate of growth of monetary gold stocks, even in the absence of gold hoarding, is unlikely to keep pace with the rising world need for reserves unless it is supplemented by a more than proportionate increase in the currency holdings of monetary authorities. Such an increase is, of course, very unlikely to occur, save in the unusual circumstances that prevailed in the 1950s, namely, a combination of substantial payments deficit in the main reserve country with the maintenance of full confidence in the gold value of its currency.

In the first half of this year, world reserves, other than those created by the IMF, declined substantially for the first time since before the war.[4] This is probably a temporary and transitional situation. Though the payments deficits of the principal reserve centers have been checked, they have not yet been eliminated and confidence has not yet been fully restored, gold hoarding has been very severe, and the proportion of currencies to gold in national reserves has fallen. But even when confidence is restored, the growth of reserves will probably be slow. Such a slowing down would not be likely to have any significant effect on the stock of reserves, or on the ratio of reserves to international transactions, for some years to come. It might nevertheless have a very speedy effect on the demand for, and hence the scarcity of, reserves. Countries whose reserves are declining anticipate to a greater or lesser extent the continuance of this decline, and a given stock of reserves will seem to them much less adequate than if their reserves were increasing. Any sharp deterioration in the rate of growth of reserves is, therefore, likely to stimulate the same kind of defensive actions with respect to the balance of payments as would a sharp once-for-all drop in the stock of reserves.

VI. POLICY REACTIONS TO RECENT DIFFICULTIES

How have countries reacted to the intensified balance of payments strains that have resulted from, or been aggravated by, the various factors I have mentioned? To put the answer in a nutshell, countries have neither been willing nor, as yet, compelled to sacrifice internal financial stability to balance of payments adjustment. Nor have they been shaken in their adherence to fixed exchange rates. Deficit countries have sought to expand their access to balance of payments financing, but have been forced increasingly to restrict external expenditures both on capital and on current account.

---

[4]The decline in world reserves, other than reserve positions in the Fund and gold sold by the Fund, amounted to some $2 billion, or 3 percent. This was offset in part by a rise in reserve positions in the Fund and a sale of gold by the Fund, together totaling some $1.5 billion. These were largely accounted for by a U.K. drawing of $1.4 billion in the second quarter.

I have already indicated that, owing to cost-inflationary tendencies, countries in surplus have become increasingly reluctant in the last year or two to pay much regard to balance of payments considerations in their overall demand policies, though within the framework of these policies they have made some efforts to keep interest rates down in order to avoid attracting foreign funds. More surprisingly, most deficit countries too have managed to avoid adopting financial policies significantly more restrictive than might reasonably have been adopted for purely domestic purposes—that is, to relieve undue pressure of demand on resources. This has been true, thus far, even of the measures adopted in 1965 by the United Kingdom, though perhaps less so of those adopted in 1963–64 by Italy, which in the end turned out to be more severe than was strictly necessary, even for balance of payments reasons. In the United States, it seemed several years ago that the government was willing, partly for balance of payments reasons, to tolerate the perpetuation of a level of employment and use of capacity which, by international standards, was decidedly low. In recent years, however, the degree of utilization of resources has risen steadily, though more slowly than in neighboring Canada.

The payments strains of recent years have not led to any weakening in the tendency of the main industrial countries to interpret the par value system in terms of fixity of exchange rates. The last exchange rate devaluation by an industrial country, that of Canada in 1962, was accompanied by a return from a flexible rate to a fixed exchange rate system. No doubt the refusal to contemplate exchange rate adjustments is partly due to the fact that the principal countries that have been in payments difficulties have been reserve centers where the case against devaluation is particularly strong, and partly, also, to a belief on the part of members of the European Economic Community that an exchange rate adjustment by any of their members would create difficulties for their agricultural price maintenance system and other measures of economic integration within the Community. However, there has also been a widespread realization, especially since the revaluations of 1961, that the system under which exchange rates are regarded as movable, but only by substantial amounts at lengthy intervals, is one that requires very large amounts of balance of payments financing to offset the speculative capital movements to which anticipation of exchange rate alteration gives rise. The desire to avoid speculative capital movements is a primary reason why the par value system tends to be interpreted as a rigidly fixed exchange rate system.

In view of the reduced responsiveness of relative national price levels and exchange rates, it was predictable that increased reliance would have to be put either on international official financing or on interference with the liberty of private international transactions. In fact, both tendencies have been in evidence.

VII. FINANCING VERSUS ADJUSTMENT

Naturally enough, it has been the countries in deficit, notably the reserve center countries, that have been keenest on increasing their access to balance of payments financing in order to maintain domestic prosperity without interfering with international transactions. The surplus countries, notably on the continent of Europe, have in general gone along with the provision of such financing, but have been increasingly anxious that its form should be such as to provide the creditors with safeguards against exchange risk and to give them more collective control over the amount provided. Their main object in seeking such control has been to insure that the deficit countries paid due regard to the need for adjustment processes that would limit their requirements for official financing, both in amount and in time.

These features can be seen in the various measures that have been adopted to provide balance of payments financing in recent years. The General Arrangements to Borrow of 1962 were principally designed to insure that the International Monetary Fund had sufficient access to borrowed resources to enable the reserve center countries, if necessary, to exercise to the full their drawing rights with that institution. Since, however, voting arrangements in the Fund give a very considerable influence to reserve center countries, because of their large quotas—whether or not they are in credit with the Fund—the GAB provided for the exercise, by participants, of a substantial degree of control over the use made of the arrangements and hence over any drawing which might require that use.

The network of bilateral swap arrangements which the United States began to build up in 1962 and which has now reached a total magnitude of nearly $2,500 million, was designed to facilitate short-term interventions on the exchange markets that might obviate unnecessary conversions of official dollar holdings into gold. Like the placing of Roosa bonds[5] with monetary authorities, which also began in 1962, they were a practical answer to the increasing restiveness of some continental central banks about holding on to the dollar balances which, as a result of U.S. deficits, came into their hands. The creditor claims arising out of the use of these arrangements, like those arising out of the more *ad hoc* operations undertaken by various monetary authorities in support of

[5]Medium-term obligations of the United States, denominated in the currency of the holding country, nonnegotiable, but, in most cases, convertible at short notice, into dollars.

sterling in 1961, 1963, 1964, and 1965, enjoy an exchange guarantee. They do not, however, provide for any collective supervision or control by the creditors, and dissatisfaction with this feature was largely responsible for the decision of the Group of Ten in 1964 to set up a system of "multilateral surveillance" over the financing of payments disequilibria among their own members. This system comprises both provision through the Bank for International Settlements of statistical information relating to official and private financing and discussion in a working party of the OECD of the steps being taken to finance and to correct payments disequilibria.

There are much firmer convictions among surplus countries about the desirability of speeding up adjustment processes than about the methods that deficit countries should use to attain this end. And yet this is the vital question, since some methods of adjustment produce economic distortion or misallocation of resources, and others, relatively speaking, do not. Indeed, to an economist, the important distinction is not between the financing and the correction of payments disequilibria, but between balance of payments policies, including excessive financing, that do and those that do not induce distortion.

VIII. MEASURES AFFECTING CAPITAL FLOWS

Few responsible officials in surplus countries would advocate the adoption by deficit countries of demand policies that would create substantial unemployment or would increase unemployment, where that is already substantial. Nor would the surplus countries in general welcome measures like devaluation or import restriction that act directly on the current balance of payments. Indeed, they are apt to think that their own current balance is not favorable enough. What they generally mean by adjustment measures are measures that will damp down the capital flow from deficit to surplus countries. And, of course, such measures have in fact been adopted in the last few years on a substantial scale. The United Kingdom has progressively tightened its exchange controls over capital movements to the nonsterling area. The United States introduced in 1963 and extended in 1965 a tax on the acquisition of long-term securities or indebtedness in developed countries, and on the second occasion introduced in addition a voluntary program for financial institutions and industrial firms operating abroad calculated to check or reverse the outflow of short-term funds, as well as to encourage foreign subsidiaries of U.S. firms to secure foreign financing. At the same time, not only have several continental countries made advance repayments of external public debt but the same or other countries have taken steps to discourage the inflow of short-term, and occasionally even long-term, private funds. Nothing in the field of balance of payments ideology has been more striking in recent years than the retreat from liberalism on the capital front.

Now, if one accepts the current account balance as a datum—as is not unreasonable if the relative levels of activity and the relative price levels of surplus and deficit countries are assumed to be unresponsive to the balance of payments—then the objections of surplus countries to financing the net private capital exports of deficit countries—I am speaking here of industrial countries—make a good deal of sense. Such capital movements are largely functionless,[6] and involve the surplus countries in a net payment of interest or profits and make it technically more difficult for them to resist what they regard as inflationary pressures.

However, this argument is based on premises which an economist must be reluctant to accept. From the standpoint of any satisfactory long-term adjustment, if the choice lies between maintaining a flow of official balance of payments financing from surplus to deficit countries, or restricting private capital flows from deficit to surplus countries, there is a presumption that the net flow of real capital from deficit to surplus countries is being unduly restricted. In other words, the current account balance of the deficit countries should be more positive, that of the surplus countries more negative.

This presumption, of course, is not infallible. First, the market system provides less reliable signals for capital transactions than for current transactions. Second, international fiscal discrepancies can lead to capital movements from a more productive to a less productive use. Third, exchange speculation can lead to capital movements that are similarly perverse. Finally, capital movements, even if not perverse, may be too erratic to be transferred smoothly from country to country, save perhaps under a system of floating exchange rates.

Admitting all this, I nevertheless feel we are swinging too far back toward the Bretton Woods fallacy that the capital items ought always to be adapted to other items in the balance of payments, and that capital restrictions don't matter. Perhaps the fact that such restrictions are notoriously difficult to enforce over long periods of time is not altogether to be regretted.

This seems as good a point as any to refer to a particular prescription for restoring external equilibrium without disturbing domestic equilibrium which is much in favor at the present time, namely, the idea of so combining banking and budgetary policies that capital is encouraged, in the case of surplus countries, to move out, or, in the case of deficit countries, to move in, while domestic expenditure remains in the aggregate unchanged. As I see it, this policy mix has one great advantage over measures of exchange control or taxation affecting domestic acqui-

---

[6]Not entirely so, however, since enterprise and "know-how" move with certain types of capital, and a cross-flow of different types of funds may improve the capital structure.

sition or holding of property abroad, in that it affects not only domestic but also foreign capital flows. Operating as it does through familiar domestic procedures, it is also less irksome than the alternative policies I have just mentioned. On the other hand, it may lead in some respects to even greater distortions than the alternative methods, especially if, as is usually the case, the budgetary element in the policy mix is designed to act primarily on consumption. Suppose, for example, that for balance of payments reasons it is desired to cut down the export of domestic capital by a given amount. The cleanest way of doing this would be by taxing exports of domestic capital and subsidizing imports of foreign capital. If the method adopted is that of contracting credit to raise interest rates while reducing taxes on consumption or even on income to maintain national expenditure, the effect will be not merely to curtail capital exports but also to force the community to save less and to invest less, than it would prefer to do.[7] Moreover, as I have pointed out in a previous paper,[8] if interest rates in each country were fixed solely with regard to balance of payments considerations, the general level of world rates of interest would become indeterminate and need not correspond to the requirements of cyclical policy in the world as a whole. Finally, if deficit countries gear interest rates to balance of payments considerations, and surplus countries to domestic considerations, the stage is set for the sort of general increase in rates that has occurred in 1964–65.

In addition to the various restrictions on capital transfers that I have mentioned, there have been a number of cases in recent years in which balance of payments difficulties have induced industrial countries to raise barriers to trade and other current transactions. Both Canada and the United Kingdom have recently had resort to temporary surcharges on imports; these, though greatly preferable in their economic effects to the quantitative restrictions on imports which the deficit countries in question would have been entitled to impose under GATT regulations, have aroused a degree of hostility that makes it doubtful whether they can be employed by major countries in the future. Again, the United States has introduced considerable distortions into its current account transactions, both public and private, by measures such as the application of substantial margins of preference for home suppliers in government contracts, the tying of aid and government expenditures abroad to U.S. export products, and possibly the curtailment of economic and military aid expenditures below what would otherwise have been desired.

It is a general principle of "the welfare economics of the second best"

---

[7]This disadvantage could be avoided if any rise in interest rates, undertaken in order to restrain capital export, were offset by budgetary subsidization of new *investment* outlay, financed by borrowing.

[8]"Developments in the International Payments System," IMF *Staff Papers,* November, 1963.

that if some departures from the criteria of optimization are inevitable, it is better that they be widely, though not evenly, spread. So the fact that there are distortions in international capital flows creates a presumption in favor of interfering with the current account items also. From a less academic standpoint, however, it is a pity to find a recrudescence of restrictions and interventions for balance of payments reasons in a field where such action is apt to provoke ill will and even retaliation.

IX. TWO PATHS OF ADVANCE

To get out of a situation in which the expansion of the world economy is increasingly threatened by restrictions on trade and capital movements and possibly even though this has not yet emerged to any serious extent—by deflationary measures in deficit countries, there are, in my opinion, two routes which deserve to be explored. The first route is that of increasing the supply of international liquidity or—what is much the same thing—increasing the availability of balance of payments financing. The second route is that of restoring a higher degree of flexibility to exchange rates.

I do not agree entirely with the school of thought represented by Walter Salant and his associates in the Brookings Institution,[9] whose preferred solution would be to fix exchange parities permanently and cover by balance of payment financing the rather prolonged deficits that would tend to occur while industrial countries were correcting their structural disequilibria through slow adaptation of price levels. This view, it seems to me, overlooks several important considerations. First, these prolonged deficits themselves may involve an undesirable distortion of capital flows. Capital is forced, as it were, to run uphill, in the form of reserve movements or other official financing. Again, if, as this view would require, a substantial proportion of the financing in question were available on tap, it might lead deficit countries to prolong their deficits indefinitely. And if financing were available in amounts sufficient to remove all anxieties from the minds of deficit countries, especially if it took a form involving the creation of reserves, the result might be to encourage unduly inflationary policies in the world as a whole. But in fact the surplus countries, whose cooperation in such a scheme would be indispensable, would never agree to a system which would force them to supply exports in exchange for inflationary pressure.

All the same, I think there are good reasons why international liquidity should be expanded in the not too distant future. The Fund, in its recently issued *Annual Report,* while emphasizing the importance of further prog-

[9]Walter S. Salant *et al., The United States Balance of Payments in 1968* (Washington, D.C.: Brookings Institution, August, 1963).

ress toward a consensus on possible new methods of supplementing reserves if required, takes the view that there is at present no urgent need for such supplementation. I would certainly agree that discussions as to the best methods of reserve creation can, and should, be carried on deliberately and free from any stress of urgency. However, just as one judges the need for additional domestic money supply in terms of indices like unemployment and price movements, so one has to judge the need for international reserves primarily in terms of such indices as the prevalence, or otherwise, of restrictions on international transactions imposed on balance of payments grounds, and the general situation in the world with respect to demand pressure. Now at the present time we have a situation in which both main reserve centers can only maintain equilibrium by imposing restrictions on capital movements and current transactions. There is still substantial unemployment in North America, the prices of primary products are sagging, and in the principal surplus countries of Europe there is no marked excess of demand. I therefore incline to the view that even now the world as a whole would be better off if there were more rather than less international liquidity. The only qualification would be that once the disequilibrium between reserve centers and other industrial countries is resolved, it might then turn out that too much liquidity had been created to suit the new situation. For reasons I explained earlier, I think this is unlikely to be the case. Once the reserve centers have eliminated their deficits, the other industrial countries will have to compete for a much smaller aggregate surplus than they have enjoyed in the past. This will make them take a new look at the adequacy of their reserves, which incidentally are, if anything, lower relative to trade than they were ten years ago.[10]

Ideally, the best way of taking care of the world's need for international liquidity would be to expand the supply of "conditional liquidity," that is, balance of payments financing that is available to deficit countries on condition that they adopt suitable adjustment policies, such as the avoidance of inflation and of restrictions on international transactions or the adjustment of overvalued exchange rates. This is the kind of liquidity that is provided by an expansion of Fund quotas. Now a 30 percent expansion of Fund quotas, the first in six years, has just been agreed.[11] But this, though sufficient to insure that Fund facilities do not diminish in proportion to other forms of international liquidity, such as gold and

[10]From end-1959 to end-1964 the aggregate reserves of developed countries other than the United States and the United Kingdom rose by 60 percent. From 1959 to 1964, however, the imports of the same countries rose even more—by 71 percent. End-1964 reserves were in fact equivalent to only a little over five months' imports, at the 1964 rate.

[11]25 percent in the form of a general increase, the remaining 5 percent in the form of additional individual increases.

foreign exchange holdings, is far from sufficient to bridge the prospective gap in the supply of international liquidity as a whole. Even the countries that are keenest on multilateral surveillance are anxious to have the major proportion of their international liquidity under their own hands in the form of freely disposable reserves.

Over the last year there has been intensive official examination, under the auspices of the Ten and of the IMF, of various possible ways of creating new fiduciary reserves, if these should be required. While there has been a good deal of clarification on technical issues, there is as yet no agreement on such questions as whether the reserves would be created within the Fund or outside, how reserve creation would be controlled, how wide the group would be for which reserves would initially be created, whether there would be any connection between reserve creation and development finance, and so on.

Whatever be the procedure for deciding when and in what amounts reserve assets are to be created, a considerable influence over the decision must always be exercised by the countries which at the time are expected to be in payments surplus, since it is these countries that must give reserve quality to the assets by accepting them in settlement. Since these are the countries least likely to be feeling the pinch of any reserve shortage, I am driven to the conclusion that so long as reserves have to be created by deliberate collective action, there will be a systematic tendency for their supply to fall short of world needs, as an economist from Mars might estimate them.

Since the liquidity route will certainly not take us all the way to our destination of optimal balance of payments behavior, what of the other route I mentioned earlier, namely, the enhancement of exchange rate flexibility? Even if the supply of international reserves and credit facilities were ideal, this would not dispense with the need for occasional par value adjustments. These are required to permit of a speedier adaptation of relative international price levels than can be achieved by financial policies without sacrificing domestic economic goals. The prospect of an external liquidity shortage, however, strengthens the case for making exchange rate adjustments more frequently and in a manner more difficult to anticipate and hence less apt to give rise to disequilibrating capital flows than under the present system.

I am not, however, advocating the abolition of the par value system and a return to complete national autonomy over exchange rates. This might be abused to secure competitive advantage. Nor am I advocating a system in which monetary authorities would refrain from intervening in exchange markets and would allow exchange rates to fluctuate freely. Such a solution is not only unlikely to be acceptable to governments in this interventionistic age but is liable to have undesirable cost-push repercussions on wages and prices. Nor, finally, am I supporting the new scheme of Professor Meade[12] under which deficit countries would be allowed—though not compelled—to adjust their exchange rates at a maximum rate of, say, 2 percent per annum. This is an ingenious attempt to permit a gradual adjustment of relative international price levels while so limiting the rate of possible adjustment that exchange speculation could be fairly easily offset, say, by a banking-cum-budgetary policy mix. The trouble with this to my mind is that monetary authorities would be reluctant to alter the exchange rates for the sake of so small a gain as would be permissible from year to year. At the same time they would probably be reluctant to give up altogether the possibility of substantial devaluation in case of emergency. Hence we might be back in practice with something like the present system, except the speculation would have rather more to feed on.

I see more attraction in ideas of the "wider spread" or "movable band" variety, under which par values in terms of gold would be alterable only, as at present, with consent of the Fund, but exchange rates between currencies would be allowed to diverge from their relative parities by substantially more than at present. This might be accomplished, for example, by allowing countries, at their choice, either to buy and sell gold freely, vis-à-vis monetary authorities, within 5 percent of their par values, or to peg their exchange rates within 5 percent of par vis-à-vis the currencies of countries that buy and sell gold freely in the manner described.[13] Schemes of this general type have had some distinguished advocates, from Keynes onward.[14] The main advantages which I see in the system would be threefold:[15]

1. Countries in temporary surplus or deficit could evoke equilibrating capital movements by letting their spot exchange rates approach the limits while keeping forward rates, through official intervention, near the center of the range.

---

[12] J. E. Meade, "The International Monetary Mechanism," *Three Banks Review*, September, 1964.

[13] This system could theoretically result in a spread of 20 percent between the most appreciated and the most depreciated currency if the former were attached to a reserve currency with a low gold price and the latter to a reserve currency with a high gold price. In practice, however, the great majority of currencies would probably remain within 5 percent of parity vis-à-vis the dollar, and 10 percent of parity vis-à-vis each other.

[14] For a description of a number of historical proposals for a wider spread of exchange rates round par values see G. N. Halm, *The 'Band' Proposal: the Limits of Permissible Exchange Rate Variations* (Special Papers in International Economics, No. 6) (Princeton, N.J.: Princeton University Press, January, 1965). The latest variant, not mentioned by Halm, is contained in R. A. Mundell, *The International Monetary System: Conflict and Reform* (Montreal: Canadian Trade Committee, Private Planning Association of Canada, 1965).

[15] Another advantage which is often claimed for the wider spread is that by discouraging the taking of exchange risks it would diminish the flow of interest-motivated short-term capital movements and so enable countries to maintain divergent levels of interest rates. While no doubt useful in many cases, this does not seem to me to work uniformly in the direction of balance of payments equilibrium.

2. Countries in temporary surplus or deficit could also promote an equilibrating adjustment in their current trade balance, which is less distorting, because it is more widely spread, than an adjustment achieved by restrictions or other special measures.

3. Countries moving into long-run deficit could forestall disequilibrating speculation by depreciating at an early stage to a rate closer to the new par value to which they might later devalue. An analogous argument would hold for countries moving into long-run surplus.

On the other hand, there are a number of difficulties and disadvantages. In the first place, with limits as wide as those suggested above, there might be some danger of countries forcing down their rates by aggressive intervention on exchange markets to secure a competitive advantage. To prevent this it would be necessary to introduce supplementary rules or conventions restricting official intervention to a defensive role. Again, there is a danger that monetary authorities would be reluctant to allow rates to vary to the extent that the system would permit. If they intervened too soon the advantages of evoking equilibrating capital movements would be lost, and, indeed, the thought that the authorities might later take fuller advantage of the spread might evoke disequilibrating flows. This suggests it would be unsafe to introduce such a system before there was clear understanding among monetary authorities as to how it would be worked.

Still further difficulties arise with respect to reserve centers. To the extent that countries continued to peg to the dollar, the advantages of exchange flexibility would be denied to the United States, save insofar as other countries chose to apply it from their side. However, there would be some compensation for the United States in that countries pegging on the dollar might be reluctant to hold in their reserves a metal whose value would now be rather loosely related to the dollar. On the other hand, to the extent that countries pegged to gold, the incentive to hold dollars either from motives of convenience or as a store of value would be reduced.

It is clear that a great many technical problems would have to be solved before such a proposal could enter the realm of practical politics, and I should emphasize that in the Fund and in the monetary authorities of most countries there would be, to put it mildly, strong doubts as to the usefulness of wider spreads. If, however, one takes the view, as I do, that exchange rates will have to be limbered up somehow or other if we are to avoid a multiplication of barriers to trade and to the movement of capital, it would seem that the device of wider spreads is at any rate worthy of further study.

EFFECTS OF MONETARY POLICY, II: THE IMPACT OF FINANCIAL VARIABLES ON AGGREGATE DEMAND

MONEY, OTHER FINANCIAL VARIABLES, AND AGGREGATE DEMAND IN THE SHORT RUN*

Hyman P. Minsky

I. INTRODUCTION

I will assume that the topic set for this session is to be taken seriously; that is, we are to discuss impact effects. As impact implies immediacy, our interest is in the short run and in the paths that connect financial changes and various components of demand. Our concern is not with whether the way a financial change occurs is relevant to whether it washes out in the long run. Almost all of equilibrium monetary theory is irrelevant to this session.

From the logic of the program (this session is entitled "The Effects of Monetary Policy II") it seems as if we are to assume that the direction of influence is from Federal Reserve actions to financial variables to aggregate demand. As I have just edited a set of studies on California banking,[1] I am not at all sure that the assumption is valid. Within a state such as California, it seems as if demand is an "independent" factor and the financial variables, particularly narrowly defined money, adjust to demand. That is, instead of "the" influence running from money to income, a major influence seems to run from aggregate demand to money.

In particular, a path running from demand, to finance, to income,

*I want to thank Tom Mayer, Mike DePrano, Jack Michaelson, Peter Diamond, and David Laidler, as well as the student participants in the Continuing Seminar on Monetary Economics at the University of California, Berkeley, for useful and serious discussions of these issues. Needless to say, the shortcomings in what follows are all my responsibility.

[1] H. P. Minsky (ed.), *California Banking in a Growing Economy: 1946–1975* (Berkeley: Institution of Business and Economic Research, University of California, 1965).

to the money supply seems to be very significant in determining what happens. The reserve base of the commercial banks in a state must be earned in the large national economy. It cannot be assumed that the amount and the rate of change of reserve money is either exogenously determined or the result of a policy decision based upon a sophisticated interpretation of the 'state' interest.

The inherited set of financial variables, the financial connections among various economic units, as well as the reactions to financial changes are conditioned by the institutional setting. An economy with a central bank that behaves in a particular manner, with specified directives, powers, and known preferences is different, with respect to its financial behavior, than a world without this particular central bank. For example, it can be argued that an erroneous belief that the Federal Reserve System would protect financial institutions, especially commercial banks, against financial instability contributed to the evolution, during the 1920s, of financial positions which, in the early 1930s, amplified a downturn into the Great Depression.

Monetary theory, perhaps more than other parts of economics, is a mongrel. To be of value it must incorporate propositions which describe in an abstract form how institutions behave. Almost always a relevant question in monetary analysis is "How does this particular set of institutions—with its own peculiar reactions—affect the behavior of the system?" In any discussion of impact effects the institutional aspect weighs particularly heavy, for while the effects of institutional arrangements may wash out in the long run, in the short run they almost certainly can affect system behavior.

Four topics will be taken up. Two deal with definitions and concepts and two with behavior. In the next section (Section II) the appropriate definition of money and financial variables is discussed, in the following section (Section III) the meaning to be attached to "impact" is examined. In Section IV the question is: "Under what circumstances can monetary changes quickly return the system to equilibrium?" In Section V one aspect of the state of the system, the demand and supply of accommodations, is examined.

The analysis reinforces the contention that once the open market path from monetary change to demand is taken, the relationship between money and demand is not well articulated and precise. It is also pointed out that the reaction to a change in the money supply depends upon whether it is inside or outside money. Because the more meaningful money concept seems to be outside money, the empirical observation that money—defined as the means of payment and as a liability of the commercial banking system—affects the behavior of the economy needs explaining.

II. THE DEFINITION OF MONEY AND FINANCIAL VARIABLES

In the econometric money game much ado is made about the proper definition of money. Distinguished economists mean quite different things when they say money. Perhaps "money" is really like "corn," so that its definition must depend upon local custom as well as the problem at hand.

Two apparently sharp and clear definitions of money, as the means of payment (demand deposits and currency) and as the outside asset (gold stock plus government debt) exist.[2] However, the sharpness and clarity of these concepts is more apparent than real. Nevertheless these concepts are more precise and really more meaningful than those definitions which emphasize the moneyness of the liabilities of financial intermediaries[3] and those which consider time deposits at commercial banks as money.[4]

If portfolio transformations are the mechanism by which an initial change affecting financial variables works its way to the arena where it affects demand, then the appropriate definition of money is as a means of payment. Although the emphasis in such discussions may be on the way in which an increase in money increases demand,[5] it is clear that money as a means of payment may be most important as a determinant of system behavior during or following a financial crisis.[6]

However, defining money as a means of payment does not lead to an unambiguous concept. Bankers do not use the same means of payments as households and ordinary business firms. Each type of money has a specified set of economic units for which it is the means of payment. Only gold coins, when they circulated, were simultaneously inter-

---

[2]The two definitions would be identical with a strict gold coin monetary system with no banking and no government liabilities.

[3]J. G. Gurley, "Financial Aspects of Postwar Economic Developments in the United States," in *Study of Employment, Growth, and Price Levels* (Joint Economic Committee, Study Paper #14, U.S. Congress. [Washington, D.C.: U.S. Government Printing Office, 1959]).

[4]M. Friedman, "The Demand for Money: Some Theoretical and Empirical Results," *Journal of Political Economy,* Vol. LXVII (August, 1959), pp. 327–51.

[5]Phillip Cagan has defined the effect of open market operations as lowering ". . . rates of return across the board. The decline in rates thus spreads to all financial and physical assets, so that an increase in the money stock may eventually stimulate investment spending in many dimensions." Phillip Cagan, "A Commentary on Some Current Issues in the Theory of Monetary Policy," in M. H. Brennan (ed.), *Patterns of Market Behavior, Essays in Honor of Philip Taft* (Providence, R.I.: Brown University Press, 1965), p. 135.

[6]H. P. Minsky, "Financial Crisis, Financial Systems, and the Performance of the Economy," in *Private Capital Markets* (Commission on Money and Credit) (Englewood Cliffs, N.J.: Prentice-Hall, Inc., 1964).

national, bankers', and public money; today these are three slightly overlapping types of narrow money. Changes from one to another type of money can affect system behavior. In particular, the classical bank crisis occurred when holders of one type of money demanded another type.

If the concern is with the effect of money in determining demand, then the relevant factor is not so much the size of the means of payment, relative to income, as the riskiness of portfolios. Whether a monetary change ultimately will affect demand depends upon the initial and the resultant riskiness of portfolios, which is conveniently measured by the relative size of inside and outside money.

The full significance of the dichotomy between inside and outside money has been lost in the emphasis upon real balance effects.[7] In addition to whatever effects these two types of money have upon the public's wealth when the price level changes, inside and outside money differ in the commitments to make payments to the banking system which result from how the money was created. For inside money, some private economic units[8] are operating under a constraint to meet payments that were agreed upon at the time the money was brought into being. With outside money no such private payment commitments exist—money is an asset that is not anyone's liability.

Contractual payment commitments constrain debtor units. The vulnerability of a unit to either a local or general decline in demand increases as the relative size of its contractual obligations increases. As business investment always implies the taking on of new financial commitments, the investment demand schedule is affected by existing financial commitments.[9] If all other circumstances are exactly the same, a community with a high ratio of outside money can be expected to invest more than one with a low ratio. That is, a determinant of realized investment is the portfolio make-up of the investing and financing units. With a larger relative supply of outside money, the typical business liability structure is cleaner than if inside money dominates.[10] As a result,

---

[7]J. G. Gurley and E. S. Shaw, *Money in a Theory of Finance* (Washington, D.C.: Brookings Institution, 1960); F. Modigliani, "The Monetary Mechanism and its Interaction with Real Phenomena," *Review of Economics and Statistics,* Supplement, Vol. XLL (February, 1963), pp. 79–107.

[8]State and local governments are best considered as private economic units.

[9]Investment financed by retaining earnings involves a financial commitment by the investing firm. However, this commitment, being contingent, is much less restrictive than the contractural payment commitments of other financing instruments.

[10]This is an empirical generalization based upon the structure of sectoral surpluses and deficits in the United States. Outside money increases rapidly whenever the federal government runs a deficit. At such times the corporate nonfinancial business sectors are either balanced or running a small surplus. Federal government surpluses or balanced positions are associated with large deficits by the nonfinancial corporate sector.

entrepreneurs, feeling safer, are more willing to take on additional "uncertainties." In addition, asset holders, having a larger proportion of safe assets, are willing to take on the risks inherent in financing business investments at relatively favorable terms for the investing unit.

A federal deficit leaves behind default-free assets whose market value is independent of the behavior of any component part of the economy.[11] These "independent" and "freedom from default" attributes do not depend upon the terms of the securities and whether the securities were introduced into the economy in such a way that an equal amount of "private spending" did not occur. A rise in the government debt is expansionary, for by making households and business firms more secure it increases the willingness to invest. The net expansionary effect of portfolio changes over a period will depend upon the rates of growth of the government deficit relative to private "capital."

One condition for steady growth is that the stock of outside money grow fast enough. This implies a growing deficit. Whether outside money must grow more rapidly or can grow less rapidly than productive capacity and inside assets depends upon the evolving portfolio preferences of private economic units as wealth increases and as usages change. There is no reason to believe that these preferences will necessarily remain constant over time and institutions.[12]

Institutional arrangements blur the line between inside and outside money. An inside money supply with government deposit insurance is at least in a contingent sense outside money. However, even though the asset, "demand deposits," is protected, debts constrain those units whose liabilities are owned by the banks. Although the nominal value of inside money guaranteed by a government agency is independent of the behavior of the system, it still is not fully equivalent to outside money, because "borrowers' risk" and the associated constraints exist.

Even in the absence of government guarantees, banks and other financial institutions absorb and attenuate risk. Presumably the empirical significance of liquid assets and the currency plus commercial bank liabilities definitions of money are due to the "outsidedness" that results from the way in which these financial variables are created.

In an enterprise economy the distinction between financial and real variables is not at all precise. The meaningful distinction between the two is whether their production is a part of income. Real tangible assets in a closed economy can be increased only at a rate determined by

[11] J. Tobin, "An Essay in Principles of Debt Management," in *Fiscal and Debt Management Policies* (Commission on Money and Credit), (Englewood Cliffs, N.J.: Prentice-Hall, Inc., 1964).

[12] If we combine 100 percent money, a required rate of growth of the money stock, and an aversion to gold, we get a target federal deficit which is equal to the required rate of growth times the existing money stock.

saving decisions; the rate of increase of financial variables is limited only by ingenuity and acceptability. In a world with layering, the rate of change of financial variables really has no bounds. The ability of financial layering to increase the burden on the payments mechanism is one way in which the conditions necessary for financial instability can be generated.[13]

Of course, the transmission process between an initiating financial change and an induced change in aggregate demand depends upon tangible and financial assets being substitutes with respect to price and complements with respect to scale.

Financial variables include all sorts of lease and contingent contracts. Some of the impact that financial variables have upon system behavior depends upon the circumstances which make contingent contracts current. Perhaps one reason for the great crash was that the private and banking communities believed that there was an implicit contingent liability of the Federal Reserve System in member bank liabilities, whereas the Federal Reserve System, being narrowly legalistic, operated as if no such commitment existed. Institutions such as the Federal Deposit Insurance Corporation were invented in order to remove this element of discretion from central banking.

III. IMPACT EFFECTS

Impact connotes a forceful impingement, a collision that communicates force. It therefore carries overtones of immediacy, of short period reactions. To study impact problems the how, where, and when of financial changes must be specified, as well as the components of aggregate demand that are to feel the impact.

An initial financial change may set off a time-consuming sequence of financial adjustments which depend not only on financial market interrelations but also on feedbacks from nonfinancial markets. Each element of the sequence will have its own particular effect upon demand: the working out of an initial change leads to a time series of impacts upon demand. The time between an initial financial change and a change in financial variables that are immediately relevant to decisions in a particular market will depend upon the location of the initial financial change. As initiating financial changes are always taking place, the long-run equilibrium implicit in any current situation really is of no interest.

The financial "past" of the economy can be considered as determining a set of initial conditions for "today." As the initial conditions are almost always not equilibrium conditions, even in the absence of any new financial changes during the period, the end-of-period financial relations

[13]H. P. Minsky, "Can 'It' Happen Again?" in Dean Carson (ed.), *Banking and Monetary Studies* (Homewood, Illinois: Richard D. Irwin, Inc., 1963).

will differ from the initial conditions. The end-of-period set of financial variables are also affected by independent, largely—but not solely—policy determined financial changes and the financial residue from the generation of current income.

There is no need to consider "independent" changes in financial variables in detail. These are largely due to central bank action or legislation; however, something like a major gold discovery is also an independent financial change. In addition, the effect that the evolution of financial usages has upon the availability of various types of financial instruments can be interpreted as an independent financial change.

The income-generating process leaves behind a financial residue. Ex post sectoral deficits (as stated in the flow of funds data) result in a set of financial liabilities that, with modifications due to layering, reflect how the deficit units were financed. For example, if, over a time period, the major deficit sector is the federal government, then the primary financial residue will be a rise in "outside" money. If the major deficit sector is private business, then, over a time period, the assets acquired by surplus units—directly or by way of financial intermediaries—will reflect private liabilities. That is, just as a period's "income" leaves to subsequent periods a set of capital goods, some of which reflects the investment carried on during the period, so the period's "income" leaves behind a set of financial variables, some of which reflect how last period's investment was financed.[14]

Ofttimes the short-period rate of growth of a particular dimension of either real or financial variables is not sustainable. As the basic financial changes over a period are the result of the effective income-generating process, the relative saturation of particular "financial" markets that can develop will feed back upon and affect the generation of future income.

Let us make the above a bit more precise by drawing upon the California banking studies I mentioned earlier. One factor associated with the rapid growth of the state has been a house-building boom. Some 40 percent of the funds in California real estate mortgages come from out of state. These funds are not only a major source of financing for the home-building industry but they are also the source of a major flow of reserves to the California banking system.

One constituent of this flow of funds into California real estate mortgages has been investments by Eastern mutual savings banks. Between 1951 and 1960 the amount the mutual savings banks committed to California real estate grew at the rate of 55 percent per year. This is obviously a nonsustainable rate of growth: it implies that the invest-

[14]Refinancing possibilities make it possible to have marked changes in the stock of outstanding financial instruments, whereas the stock of existing real capital can change but relatively slowly. (A financial crisis generates a massive, forced refinancing.)

ment by these institutions in California soon would be greater than their total assets.

The stock of "foreign-owned" mortgages outstanding generates payments from the California economy to the rest of the country. Since the stock of such liabilities has been growing about twice as fast as the California economy, the payment burden due to this debt has increased relative to income. Only the continued accelerated flow of out-of-state investment funds to the state has made the burden feasible: California has been playing a "Ponzi" game[15] with the rest of the country.[16]

The accumulation of residues that are left behind by the financial processes associated with the way in which income is generated over a period of time feed back upon and affect the income-generating process in two ways. Either the effect is steady and mild, affecting decisions but not generating any rapid, self-stimulating financial changes, or an epidemic, which sharply affects asset values, takes place. (There is a discontinuity between financial stability and instability.)

A third aspect of the accumulation of financial residues is that for a growth process to be an equilibrium process, the "stocks" and "values" of financial variables must grow along with income, so that at the end of each "period" all actors are willing to take another, appropriately larger, balanced step. However, if the value of current financial variables reflects subjective uncertainties about the stability of income, a long period of sustained growth will lead to a rise in the value of real and financial assets relative to income by inducing a reduction in these uncertainties. This will tend to induce a larger than equilibrium step in income, or the desire to increase the size of the step must be offset by some constraining change in income or financial variables. If the animal spirits released by a successful run lead to growth that unbalances the outside-inside money ratio, the potential for financial instability is increased.[17]

The accumulation of financial variables from past incomes can be subsumed under the initial conditions. However, as in the California case, the evolution of some of these initial conditions may be such as to indicate that the income-generating process ruling over this period is not in the longer run sustainable.

We therefore have *three* financial impacts during any period. One flows from the initial disequilibrium inherited from the past. Inherited

---

[15]A "Ponzi" game takes place when a financial intermediary uses "deposits" to pay "dividends."

[16]H. P. Minsky, "Commercial Banking and Rapid Economic Growth in California," and A. H. Schaaf, "The Savings Function and Mortgages Investment by California Banks and Financial Institutions," in Minsky, *California Banking in a Growing Economy, op. cit.*

[17]I have dealt at some length with these ideas in Minsky, "Financial Crisis, Financial Systems and the Performance of the Economy," *op. cit.*

balance sheets are not "desired" and units operate to adjust their balance sheets. The second is the result of the current income generating process. Its initial impact can be considered as the ex ante desire of various units to emit certain financial liabilities and the ex ante desire of units that run financial surpluses to acquire particular financial assets. The third is due to exogenous changes—the realm of monetary and financial policy. All three can affect variables that are relevant for income decisions.

Fortunately the time series of financial changes that would result if an initial situation is allowed to work itself out can be ignored if the dynamic process is "linear." All of the past—the entire past set of exogenous changes, as well as the residues left behind—can be summed up into the "initial" conditions. The effects of whatever "new shock" takes place can be added onto the time sequence that would have resulted in the absence of the shock.

IV. THE DYNAMICS OF ADJUSTMENT TO AN INITIAL DISPLACEMENT

In one of his characteristic "en passant" flashes of genius, Professor Harry G. Johnson remarked that the *General Theory* ". . . attempts to bring markets with widely different speeds of adjustment—the goods market, the money market, and the labor market—into one short-period equilibrium analysis; . . ."[18] As far as I know he nowhere spells out what this means. As I see it the Keynesian dynamic specifications are that the goods and labor markets react slowly—in particular they tend to be quantity rather than price reactors—and the money market(s) reacts quickly, and tends to be a price reactor.

The quickly reacting money market(s) may or may not induce changes in aggregate demand which effectively eliminate the excess supply. When Keynes wrote that there were ". . . several slips between the cup and the lip . . .,"[19] with reference to the effectiveness of money in calling the tune for system behavior, the allusion obviously was to the conditional nature of the effect of a monetary change. How the reaction depends upon the state of the economy and the nature of the monetary change needs to be spelled out. In particular it should be noted under what circumstances the complex financial system can work to attenuate or intensify an initial monetary impulse.

In terms of the controversy between quantity theorists and Keynesians,

---

[18]H. G. Johnson, "The 'General Theory' After Twenty-five Years," *Money Trade and Economic Growth* (Cambridge, Mass., 1962), chap. vi, p. 130. Reprinted from *American Economic Review,* Vol. LI (May, 1961), pp. 3–4.

[19]"If however we are tempted to assert that money is the drink that stimulates the system to activity, we must remind ourselves that there may be several slips between the cup and the lip." J. M. Keynes, *The General Theory of Employment, Interest and Money* (New York, 1936), p. 173.

the point of departure for this section is that the relevant question is not which view to accept, but ". . . the circumstances under which the one or the other view is likely to be more fruitful."[20] That Friedman and Meiselman found a naïve income expenditure model better than their quantity theory for the Great Depression period indicates that allowing for switching in the mode of system operation improves our understanding. Keynesian economics, correctly interpreted, incorporates "switching" among operation modes; hence its claim to generality.

The conditional view of system response to a monetary change indicates that the length of the lag between a monetary and an income change will be variable.

What follows is based upon particular specifications of relative speeds of adjustment and impact points. Ultimately this is an empirical, rather than theoretical, problem. In a world with evolving institutions, there is no reason to expect that relative reaction times within markets, and contacts between markets, will always remain the same.

In addition, as the growth and development of market institutions and usages depend upon profit opportunities, the very adjustment path taken by the economy can affect the "how" and the "rate" of future adjustments. Finance affects system behavior in a much more complicated fashion than a simple reading of existence theorems and econometric equations leads one to believe.

1. Aggregate Demand

Consider aggregate demand and supply schedules, D_1 and S, which yield an equilibrium at A_0 (Diagram 1). The schedules can be for either labor or commodities, as it is assumed that in these markets prices move slowly. In the first instance, any adjustment to a change (schedule shift) in these markets will be with constant prices.

A decline of demand to D_2 will lead to a quantity change. Excess supply of ξs at p_0 will appear, and no significant change in p will occur while this is taking place: The market will not in the first instance move toward A_1, its new "equilibrium."[21] In the labor market, where short-period transitory unemployment is common, a fall in labor demand will not lead to an immediate decline in wages. This is particularly true if

[20] M. Friedman and D. Meiselman, "Relative Stability of Monetary Velocity and the Investment Multiplier in the United States, 1897–1958," in *Stabilization Policies* (Commission on Money and Credit) (Englewood Cliffs, N.J.: Prentice-Hall, Inc., 1963), p. 170.

[21] The Phillips curve 'closes' the Keynesian system as it describes how wages and prices in fact react to market demand situations. See A. W. Phillips, "The Relation Between Unemployment and the Rate of Change in Money Wage Rates in the United Kingdom, 1862–1957," *Economica* (November, 1958), pp. 283–99.

unemployment first increases by a decrease in the hiring rate, and employment decreases as a result of attrition.

Assume that this shift in demand (aggregate or for labor) occurs in an enterprise economy with a mixed (inside and outside) money supply, a banking system with an unimpaired—perhaps even augmented—capacity to acquire earning assets, and a demand schedule for bank accommodation that is related to output. The shift in the aggregate demand schedule and the decline in output will be associated with a fall in the demand schedule for bank accommodations.

DIAGRAM 1

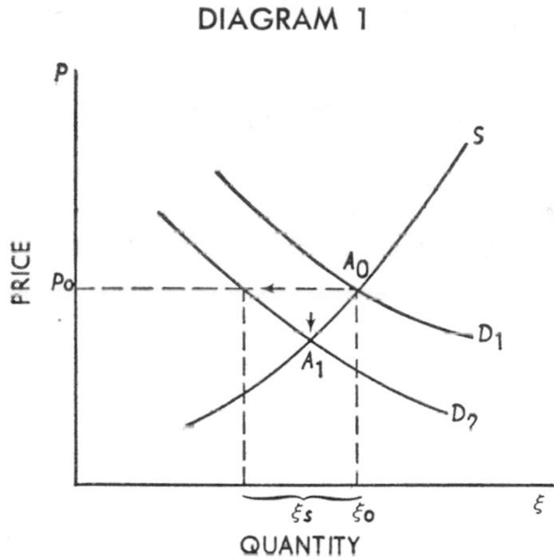

The shift in the demand schedule for bank accommodations may be an initiating factor or a consequence of the shift in aggregate demand. On the basis of constrained, intertemporal income-generating systems, a downward shift of those demands sensitive to the overall rate of growth of the economy is not difficult to explain.[22] Under these conditions, the initial downward shift of the aggregate demand function is based upon an assumed constancy of interest rates. It may very well be a "virtual" shift, as the other things assumed to be constant will not in fact remain unchanged. Nevertheless, if, for any reason whatsoever, aggregate demand decreases, the associated fall in the value of goods in process of being produced leads to a decline in the demand for bank accommodations.

Assume that market processes operate so that wages and prices remain constant (move slowly) in the face of excess supply, while interest rates fall (move rapidly). The rapidly falling interest rates and the associated increased availability of "credit" tend to shift the aggregate de-

[22] H. P. Minsky, "A Linear Model of Cyclical Growth," *Review of Economics and Statistics*, Vol. XLI (May, 1959), pp. 133–45.

mand curve upward. How great an original shift in demand can be offset by financial market changes in a given time period? The answer depends upon the nature of the underlying demand relations and how the financial market reactions occur.

In the Hicksian *IS-LM* diagram (Diagram 2), the reaction of r and Y to a shift in *IS* depends upon the elasticity of the *LM* curve. If *LM* infinitely elastic, r does not change; if *LM* has zero elasticity, Y does not change; and if *LM* is as conventionally drawn, both r and Y change. The nature of the *LM* curve depends upon institutional arrangements.

DIAGRAM 2

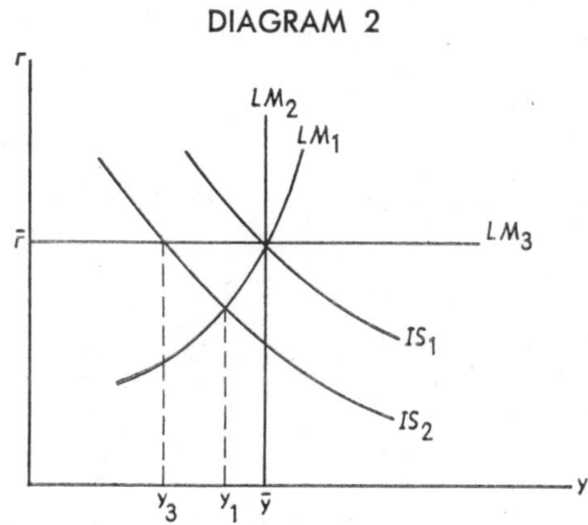

We can posit that with a given monetary system—including how money is fed into the economy as part of the monetary system—there is a maximum to the decline in demand that can be overcome by purely monetary means within a period in which wages and prices remain essentially fixed. A special Keynesian view—modified by real balance effect arguments—is that wage and price level flexibility is an inefficient way to raise aggregate demand. But our domain of concern stops short of the effect of wage and price flexibility. We are concerned only with whether the return to equilibrium in the labor and commodity markets can be achieved by monetary means that operate more quickly than price flexibility.

Note that the "Keynesian" policy position with regard to government spending is designed to shift the aggregate demand curve to a position where a permissive monetary mechanism can return the system to equilibrium. Keynesian fiscal policy is not a substitute for monetary policy—it can, if you wish, be considered as a way of making money effective when the direct link between money and demand has been attenuated.

2. Bank Behavior

In the face of a decline in demand for their output, banks will try to remain fully invested. To do this they "sweeten" accommodation terms and purchase inherited eligible paper from the open market. Both reactions are subsumed into a fall in the interest rate. For the time horizon being considered, bankers are quantity maintainers and price adjusters, whereas both labor and commodity sellers adjust quantity and maintain price.

Two modes of operation of the banking system, one labeled "commercial loan" and the other "open market," can be distinguished. Both terms as used here are not identical with their common usage. Commercial banks can engage in open market operations, as when they purchase Treasury bills from the market during a period of slack loan demand. Central banks can engage in commercial loan operations as when they rediscount, purchase bankers' acceptances, or purchase newly issued government debt from the Treasury. The distinction between the two is between their impact; whether the monetary change initially modifies portfolios or finances demand. Open market operations, in the first instance, modify portfolios; commercial loan operations, in the first instance, finance operations.[23]

One way of distinguishing between the two is by the past of the financial asset acquired by the banking system. If the asset existed prior to the banks' purchase, then it is an open market operation. If it is created *de novo* in the process of the banks' operations, then it is a commercial loan operation.

The line between open market and commercial loan operations may be even fuzzier in fact than in principle. The use of the proceeds of a sale of preexisting assets to finance operations transforms what looks like an open market operation into a commercial loan operation. In a world with a complex financial structure, portfolio adjustments often are the way in which idle cash is activated. In particular, bank and financial institution sale of seasoned (and endorsed) earning assets is a way to mobilize funds to finance new expenditures.[24] Once the scope of open market operations is expanded to include commercial bank activities, the traditional expansionary operation (purchases) may be associated with contractions and the traditional contractionary operation (sales) may be associated with expansions.

In addition to bank creation of money, money may be "mined," earned by the foreign balance, or printed by the government. A government deficit, independently of whether it is financed by "new money"

[23]I have dealt with these concepts in my "Comment" on M. Friedman and A. Schwartz, "Money and Business Cycles," *Review of Economics and Statistics*, Supplement, Vol. XLL, No. 1, Part 2 (February, 1963), pp. 64–72. See also J. Tobin, "Monetary Interpretation of History (A Review Article)," *American Economic Review*, Vol. LV (June, 1965), pp. 464–85.

[24]If we assume banks and financial institutions only sell endorsed paper, then it becomes clear that this open market sale is really part of a commercial loan operation—the total of bank liabilities, primary and contingent, increases as a result of these paired transactions.

or by "activating" idle money, has the same impact as a "commercial loan." Of course, if the debt emitted is fully competitive with private debt, so that the public deficit in full or in part is offset by a reduction in private deficits, then it would not have a net impact equal to the size of the deficit. The impact of a government deficit depends in part upon the way the debt is managed.

An increase of the money supply that is due to the mining of gold and an export surplus is also a "commercial loan" increase in money.

Government deficit and produced money are outside money. The repercussions of the mix of outside and inside money upon system behavior are considered later.

Note that "commercial loan" banking as used here has nothing to do with any rule for the determination of the "correct" amount of money.

3. Commercial Loan Banking

If banks remain fully invested by maintaining their demand-related accommodations, the effect upon bank earning assets of a shift in demand for private accommodations from A_1 to A_2 (Diagram 3) will be offset by a decline in interest rates to r_2.

DIAGRAM 3

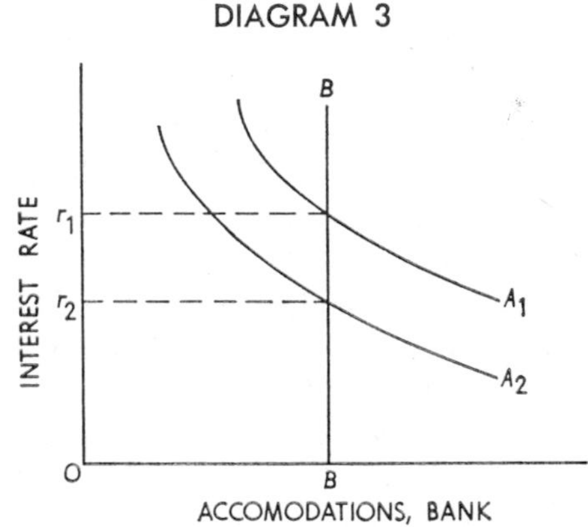

If interest rates fall fast enough and far enough, the movement along A_2 (Diagram 3) will shift D_2 back to D_1 (Diagram 1). Of course, for this always to be true, all interest rates (including, if need be, negative interest rates) must be possible and, in addition, with low enough interest rates, the level of accommodations will exceed any preassigned amount.

The above is a commercial loan view of banking. The proceeds of bank loans are spent on output and a rise in bank loans are associated with a net increase in financial paper. In such a world—no portfolio alternatives and borrowers who spend—the only price that needs to adjust is the interest rate and the only quantity that is relevant is the amount of bank accommodations available. The transmission line is that the creation of money makes "demand" effective—its impact is that it finances planned expenditures.

In the commercial loan view of banking, the relation between the money supply and the financing of operations is very close. If at the "beginning" of a period *OB* of money is created to finance operations (Diagram 3), then at the "end" of the period *OB* of money is destroyed as the borrowers repay bank debt. To undertake the same level of operations in the next period the process has to be repeated. In this view a net decline in the quantity of money means a reduction, and a net rise means an increase, of spending—and this change takes place immediately and without any further intermediation. A shift in *OB* will lead either to a rise or a decline in operations.

Diagram 3 can be interpreted in a static or a dynamic context: *OB* may be the amount of investment in excess of ex ante saving (saving based upon "last period's income") that is needed if the economy is to grow at the desired rate. To achieve this growth, all that is necessary in the way of economic policy is to have the money supply grow at the "proper rate." If portfolio money is a simple known relation to transactions money, then once again growth at a proper rate of money balances will do the job; but in this case "idle" money may have to be fed into the system by open market operations.

The A_1 and A_2 schedules can be interpreted as relating to the productivity—implicitly we are assuming that thrift is independent of interest rates—of the "productivity and thrift" pair that "determines" interest rates. If money is fed into the system to finance investment plans, then, under the assumption made above, a shift in the productivity of investment with no change in thrift or the supply of money will, in the first instance, affect only interest rates.

In the above, a decline of interest rates is associated with the impact of money upon demand. Earlier, gold mining and an export surplus were identified as being similar to a "commercial loan" increase in money. However, a decline in interest rates is not part of the mechanism by which mining and exports affect demand. The very process of mining gold or producing for export generates income. What happens to interest rates depends upon how the increased money supply and the rise in income due to the production of money interact in generating demand and supply of finance. The income due to the production of the money commodity is a particularly high-powered type of investment as far as the Keynesian model is concerned.

Not all of external finance is by way of bank credit; many units emit liabilities which are not bank eligible. Whether monetary changes, operating through a banking system that remains fully invested, but not necessarily fully loaned up, will impinge upon such financing depends upon the path from "fully invested" banks to these other financial markets.

4. Open Market Banking

A banking system that remains fully invested in the face of a decline in the demand for accommodations may do so by purchasing existing earning assets from the market. For this to take place, a sufficiently large stock of bank eligible earning assets must exist. (The definition of what is bank eligible need not remain unchanged over time.) The seller of the asset to banks exchanges an earning asset for money; his portfolio is altered. There is no direct link between money creation and spending.

Normally there are households and business firms who are seeking to get out of nonmonetary temporary abodes of purchasing power into money in order to effect some purchase or fulfill some commitment. At the same time other units are trying to place cash into such temporary abodes. Much of the action that characterizes the markets for nonmonetary liquid assets is due to the association of these markets with payments related to financial rather than income transactions. When banks move into—or out of—these markets, either to be fully loaned up or to acquire funds to satisfy customer loan demand, they affect the price of these assets; that is, interest rates are either raised or lowered.

The supply of some financial instruments which usually serve as nonmonetary temporary abodes of purchasing power is not, in the short period, responsive to demand. In fact their behavior may be "perverse"; the supply of near-money marketable assets may decrease as a result of the same income conditions which led to a decline in the demand for bank accommodation. As a result some units will have to choose between holding money and holding assets that are not conventionally accepted as temporary abodes of purchasing power.

The maintenance of the money supply by means of open market operations can mean no more than the substitution of money for the closest of substitutes for money in some household and business firm portfolios. The open market path may lead to no appreciable short-term impact upon demand. However, under the assumed conditions, as the money supply is maintained or increased by open market operations, the price of bank eligible securities rises. As the preferred money substitutes are short term, even a large decline in interest rates will not yield any substantial capital gains. However, once short-term interest rates to "preferred" borrowers fall below the running yield on longer term securities, the possibility of "making on the carry" will induce position taking in longer term securities. A decline in interest rates throughout the economy may follow, even though such position taking on the basis of short-long rate differentials is in part dependent upon the existence of adequate refinancing arrangements. The easing of longer term market rates can lead to a rise in the value of paper which reflects some tangible sources of income or services, particularly if the nominal returns or the price of the services do not change.

The rise of the market value of existing tangible assets, with unchanging labor and commodity prices, favors a substitution of "newly produced" for "secondhand" capital goods. Such increase in demand for investment at a particular price and wage level will shift both the demand for accommodations and the aggregate demand schedule upward. A process which can lead to the return of D_2 to D_1 (Diagram 1) may be set into motion by open market operations.

DIAGRAM 4

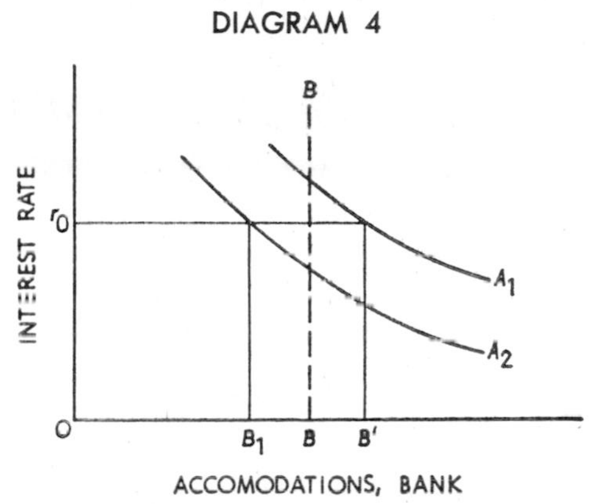

This rise in the market value of secondhand tangible assets relative to their production costs depends upon a pervasive oozing of the money generated by open market operations to other markets. For demand to respond as indicated, in the case where money is substituted for temporary repositories of purchasing power, an appreciable proportion of portfolio managers will have to reach for yield with funds that, as risk averters, they held in short-term assets under previous relative yields. It is problematical whether yield differentials can be increased enough to generate a significant shift to longer term securities. At best this is a highly tenuous process; a large part of the money created by such open market actions will gravitate to idle balances.

Even if expansionary open market operations have little impact upon demand in the short run, they can affect aggregate demand with a lag—in a longer run. In Diagram 4, *OB* of earning assets can be acquired by the banking system during a period. If the banking system can acquire an unlimited amount of preexisting, eligible paper from the market at r_0, then with accommodations demand A_2, OB_1 of accommodations and

B_1B of open market asset acquisition will take place. An autonomous shift of the demand-for-accommodations schedule from A_2 to A_1 will enable the banking system to acquire OB' ($OB' = OB+BB'$) of earning assets during the "period." The assets acquired in open market operations when demand is slack are sold to the public, where they function as "temporary" abodes of purchasing power.

The overshooting possibility inherent in such portfolio changes is evident. The existence of a complex financial structure enhances both the attenuation and the overshoot possibilities. It also indicates that the effect of bank operations during any short period depends upon portfolio changes as well as the net change in liabilities. A steady increase in the money supply, combined with a large stock of eligible open market paper and a shifting demand-for-private-accommodations schedule, can lead to short-run variability in the impact of the money-generating process upon the system.

Open market operations, broadly conceived, need not be restricted to short-term securities. The issue is broader than the "bills only" doctrine of the Federal Reserve System, once the term open market operations is extended to include all banking system dealings in existing securities.

Commercial banks are conglomerate financial institutions which not only have the payment means, demand deposits, as their liability but also various savings or time deposit liabilities. As a result of their savings intermediary role, banks hold longer term securities, especially mortgages. In the mortgage market, "action" centers not only around the financing of new construction but in the refinancing of existing houses. Commercial banks' activity in the mortgage market is therefore a mixture of "commercial loan" and "open market" operations. Whenever a decline in business loan demand (or other aspects of an easing of credit) leads to an increase in commercial bank activity in mortgage markets, a direct impact upon longer term interest rates will occur—the oozing from short to longs by way of many markets will not need to carry all of the burden.

Banks compete actively with other investors in home mortgages. To the extent that the commitments by banks to mortgages increases when other demand for bank accommodation decreases, nonbank intermediary funds, which normally would look to the mortgage market for placement, will, under the new relative rates of return, seek other outlets.

Although the permeation of open market operations to all market rates is not as ephemeral when open market operations in long securities are taken into account, nevertheless the choice between remaining liquid and reaching for yield will always exist. With the lower rate pattern that will emerge under open market maintenance or expansion of the money supply, the impact of the monetary change will almost always be attenuated.

The changing proportion of placements into longs and the pockets of idle cash that accompany a decline in interest rates will make an amplified reaction to any independent demand stimulus possible. The open market path between money and activity is slippery and mucky.

5. Excess Reserves

A third reaction open to banks generates excess reserves. A shift of the demand-for-accommodations schedule downward, and a low yield on eligible paper, will induce some banks not to follow the market but to settle for an easy life. Excess reserves are, in the longer run, a transitory phenomenon, but, in the short period, they constitute another slippage between money and aggregate demand.

The accumulation of excess reserves in the banking system may induce some banks to reach for yield. As money men do not like to realize capital losses, they will reach for yield only if they are in a position to treat a speculation as an investment if the need arises. They will reach for yield only if the volume of excess reserves and short-term assets they hold is so large that, over a period in which the 'longs' will mature into 'shorts,' they can satisfy any 'normal' rise in customers' demand without being forced to sell their 'long' positions. A rise in excess reserves and an accumulation of a large volume of short-term securities is a necessary condition for pure commercial banks to affect directly the interest rate on marketable longer term investments.

It is evident from the above that how money is fed into the system by the banking system is important in determining the effect of a monetary change. If money is introduced to finance expenditure decisions, then the link between money and income is direct. If money enters as a portfolio transformation in which money is substituted for another asset, then the linkage is vague, and the impact upon demand may occur with a considerable lag.

V. THE DEMAND AND SUPPLY OF ACCOMMODATIONS

The demand for accommodations, introduced in the preceding section, requires further analysis. Although the diagram is drawn as if there is only one type of "accommodation," in the discussion it is clear that there are many. It is necessary to disaggregate.

Liabilities are emitted to finance the acquisition of financial and secondhand tangible assets as well as to finance investment. The layering of financial assets through financial intermediaries absorbs and distributes risks. Thus financial intermediation is a determinant of realized investment. Nevertheless, it seems best initially to ignore this. Let us assume that liabilities are emitted solely to acquire goods and services which are part of current income; our concern is with sectoral net financial deficits and surpluses.

Demand and supply schedules for the various types of accommodations yield ex ante sectoral financial surpluses or deficits. The demand schedules are derived from tangible investment opportunities. The supply schedules are based upon portfolio preferences. The demand and supply schedules that rule at any time depend upon institutional limitations and reflect the existing situation as to the existence of markets.

All positions, including those taken by business firms in capital goods, are portfolios. Investment can be interpreted as flowing from a disequilibrium asset and liability structure. Units desire to acquire some tangible assets and "emit" particular financial liabilities in order to move to a "better" position. Technical progress, relative prices, and the past of the economy, as well as financial variables, determine not only each moment's desired position in tangible assets but also the pace at which this position will be approached. Monetary policy actions are undertaken to generate disequilibrium.

An investment decision is based upon a simultaneous analysis of the expected returns from the tangible asset to be acquired and terms upon which it can be financed.[25] Although the two are not really separable we will first look at the investment decision, ignoring financing aspects, and then take up finance. Both sets of decisions are dependent upon how risks are evaluated.

Portfolio preferences of units with "poor" own investment opportunities determine the net supply of accommodations.[26] Their existing portfolio and current cash flow generate supply schedules of accommodations. The terms upon which particular assets will be acquired, in exchange for accumulating cash, depend upon the initial portfolio conditions as well as the expected returns.

Thus the initial portfolio conditions of private deficit and surplus sectors (or units) are proximate determinants of realized ex post investment. In particular, the safety and security of the initial asset structure of surplus units is a determinant of the rate at which the various liabilities emitted by deficit units will be absorbed.

In this section we will first examine the basic determinants of investment demand. This discussion will in part be looking back to the material of Section IV, as we will be asking under what conditions can the open market oozing phenomena work to increase "realized" investment.

---

[25] A. G. Hart, "Capital Appropriations and the Accelerator," *Review of Economics and Statistics,* Vol. XLVII (May, 1965), pp. 123–36; E. Greenberg, "Appropriations Data and the Investment Decision," *Journal of the American Statistical Association,* Vol. 60 (June, 1965), pp. 503–15.

[26] J. Hirshleifer, "On the Theory of the Optimal Investment Decision," *Journal of Political Economy,* Vol. LXVI (August, 1958), pp. 329–52.

This will be followed by a discussion of the effect of the liability structure of investing units. The willingness to absorb private financial assets by surplus units is discussed next. The effect that nonbank financial intermediaries and commercial banks have upon the investment process will be taken up in the final section.

1. Investment Demand

Investment occurs when the capital stock is changed. The "initial" capital stock is not the desired capital stock, and for the continued normal functioning of an enterprise system it is necessary to make sure that the actual capital stock is never equal to or greater than the desired stock. The function of policy is to rig the game, that is, continually to generate an appropriate disequilibrium.

Open market operations initially lower specified interest rates. For this to call the tune for aggregate demand, decreases in the market rates directly affected by traditional open market operations must spill over to raise the value of tangible assets and of the liabilities used to finance their purchase.

For lower market interest rates to raise the aggregate demand schedule, the value of existing capital must be increased. Given the sluggishness of wages, the price of "secondhand" capital must rise relative to the construction costs of new capital. Under these circumstances a lower discount rate will change the ratio of the value of existing capital to the cost of new capital.

The value of existing tangible capital is not determined by discounting the value of future services at default-free interest rates. The discount rate applicable to real capital is much higher, due to various risks which are inherent in inside capital. The applicable risk premium for any particular tangible asset reflects various types of uncertainties. Among the uncertainties that are relevant are those about the economy, the particular market, and the firm. The "expected" behavior of these three classes of uncertainties is not necessarily independent. For a decline in the default-free rate to mean a rise in the present value of capital, the risk premiums cannot be inversely related to the default-free rate.

Those risks that are classified as being due to the behavior of the economy can be imputed to cyclical instability.[27] Postwar trends indicate that the premiums of government securities over higher grade private debt, and of higher grade private debt over lower grade private debt, have decreased. These changes in relative yields reflect the de-

---

[27]In the theory of economic development, "economy" risks can be related to political stability. For a developed economy, we can ignore the risks due to political stability—although firm prospects may often be related to policy decisions.

pendence of market risk premiums upon an extrapolation of the past of the economy.

If private investors assume that no depression will occur, their desired tangible capital-income ratio will be higher than if the contrary assumption is made. Successful contracyclical policy can uncover a large potential for capital deepening—which in turn will sustain investment demand.[28] Successful economic policy generates external benefits such as this capital deepening. The external benefits flowing from successful policy can be considered as a low-cost substitute for insurance policies that risk averters would gladly buy, but which no private organization will supply.[29]

Market risks are due to the behavior of the market in which the output produced by the capital goods will be sold. These may very well be correlated with cyclical risks—although they are in part independent. Risks due to the "competence and capabilities" of the firm's management may be considered independent of the cyclical behavior of the economy, although the past sins of management often come to light during "hard times."

Using a stream of returns in perpetuity for our example, the present value (V) of a constant dollar stream of returns of R per year is $V = \dfrac{R}{r_1+r_2+r_3+r_4}$, where r_1 is the default-free interest rate; r_2, r_3, and r_4 are the discount premiums due to economy, market, and firm risks. If the expected stream of returns is to grow at g percent per year, then, with R as the next return, the present value of this perpetuity is $V_g = \dfrac{R}{r_1+r_2+r_3+r_4 - g}$.

Let us return to our initial situation: the aggregate demand schedule falls from D_1 to D_2, the prices of output and of capital goods do not decline, interest rates on "open market" paper fall as banks and others try to remain fully "invested." Presumably in time, r_1, the rate on a default-free perpetuity declines. Ignoring changes in r_3 and r_4, the decline in r_1 will be certain to raise the present value (V or V_g) if r_2 does not rise and R or g do not fall.

For r_2 not to rise and g not to fall, the decline in demand must have been both anticipated and discounted. That is, the decline in aggregate demand is a normal, fully expected event. For this to be true a cyclical

[28] R. M. Goodwin, in "The Non-Linear Accelerator and the Persistence of Business Cycles," *Econometrica,* Vol. 19 (January, 1951), pp. 1–17, has the accelerator turn down when income is at the ceiling. If anything can be expected to happen at the ceiling it is that the inducement to invest becomes more powerful. Realized investment may decline as a ratio to the change in income, but that is ex post, not ex ante, and depends upon market processes.

[29] K. J., Arrow, "Uncertainty and the Welfare Economics of Medical Care," *American Economic Review,* Vol. LIII (December, 1963), pp. 941–73.

growth pattern must be taken as the norm, and the observed decline is interpreted as of normal size. There is a maximum to the initial decline in demand which will be considered as normal and not induce a further decline in the demand for accommodations by reducing the expected returns.

A decline in income must mean a decline in "profits." Hence the current and near *Rs* must be lower than their expected normal or permanent value. If the combined discount rate $r_1+r_2+r_3+r_4-g$ is large, then the current and near returns weigh heavily in determining present value.

Investment started this period has a gestation period. There is a lag between the start and the capacity coming on-stream. For such investments the near term *Rs* are zero; hence the cyclical stage is no real determinant of the value of these investments.

Open market operations would be effective in raising aggregate demand in a mild recession if the recession is considered to be a usual event, and if investments such as described above are a large part of total capital formation. The demand-for-accommodations schedule which would result from such investments is elastic with respect to market interest rates and stable with respect to normal cyclical variation in income. In addition, as we are dealing with the demand for external financing, the investments must be those which are normally financed by emitting liabilities.

In an economy where income growth is expected, utility and housing investments conform to the specifications discussed above. This is true even though both would be quite sensitive to a more than normal decline in income or a retardation in the growth rate. As the linkage between money and capital market conditions and the financing of mortgages was quite clear in the early post-World War II period, it is not surprising that housing led in the upswings.

On the other hand, if a larger than normal decline in income, or a retardation in the expected growth rate, occurs, the rise in r_2, or the decline in g, will offset declines in r_1. Open market operations will not effectively expand demand—even if the appropriate financing terms are affected—if it is necessary to offset the effect upon risk of a more than normal decline in demand.

Open market operations will not necessarily increase the demand for outputs with short gestation periods, for the decline in the near period *Rs* will offset the decline in r_1. However, if a large enough sector reacts to lower financing terms by increasing its investment activity—the initial shift of the curve will be offset in part by a movement along the curve—then the fall in income is checked. If income is maintained, even investments with short gestation periods and relatively long life might become desirable when the default-free rate falls.

Open market operations may work, and then again they may not. They are a weak reed upon which to base policy, especially as their effectiveness when expansion is desired may be limited to situations in which demand is maintained close to capacity by other than monetary means.

2. Liability Structure

Corporate finance is one starting place for monetary economics. A decision to invest is simultaneously a decision to spend; and the spending can be financed by some combination of cash generated by operations, drawing down of cash balances, sale of assets, or sale of liabilities. A financial plan is as important to a firm as a facilities plan. Each economic unit is limited in the liabilities it can emit. A willingness to pay premium rates of interest often does not serve to broaden the range of liabilities a unit can emit.

For a risk-averting decision maker of a business firm, there exists a hierarchy of liability structures. A liability structure with only equity liabilities is less risky than one with debt instruments—in particular, a firm without debt can survive adverse circumstances that would put a firm with debt into bankruptcy. On the other hand, the gains from leverage can induce risk taking—and the liability structure is a result of the "balancing of forces" and the interpretation of evidence.

The vulnerability of a firm to adverse market developments can be illustrated by means of conventional cost curve diagrams (Diagram 5).

Total cost curve TC_1 is the out-of-pocket costs (including overhead labor), and AC_1 is the associated average cost curve. A_1A_2 is the per period gross payment commitment due to debt financing, AC_2 is the equivalent average cost curve. A_1A_3 is the gross per period returns on the capital invested that are in some sense "normal." AC_3 is the associated average cost curve. The investment in the firm is based upon an expectation of output q_3 being sold at price p_3.

If price is maintained in the face of a fall in demand, then the firm with no debt can, on a cash flow basis, sustain a fall of output to q_1 (on a maintenance-of-capital basis, a fall of output to q_1' can be sustained). For a firm with debt, as illustrated, a fall in output below q_2 would result in a default on financial commitments or forced borrowing. The probability of financial difficulty following a given shortfall in output depends upon the liability structure. As small shortfalls are believed to be much more likely than large ones, any decrease in the maximum price decline that can be withstood leads to a more than proportional increase in the probability of financial difficulties.

The complete investment decision involves estimates of both the profitability of the investment and the likelihood that at some date the cash flow from operations will fall short of the requirements imposed by financial obligations. The willingness to undertake a particular investment-financing combination depends in part upon estimates of the future stability of the economy. In general, units will be more willing to undertake an investment if it can be financed by retaining earnings than if it requires external financing. Nevertheless, the reluctance to use external debt financing depends upon estimates of the future. Expectational relations seem to conform to learning models.

Both the evaluation of the value of an investment and the willingness to undertake external finance are related to the estimate of economy-wide uncertainties. The result is that events that tend to decrease economy-wide uncertainty, such as a prolonged period of steady growth, can lead to an investment boom and an increase in positions that are sensitive to income declines.

DIAGRAM 5

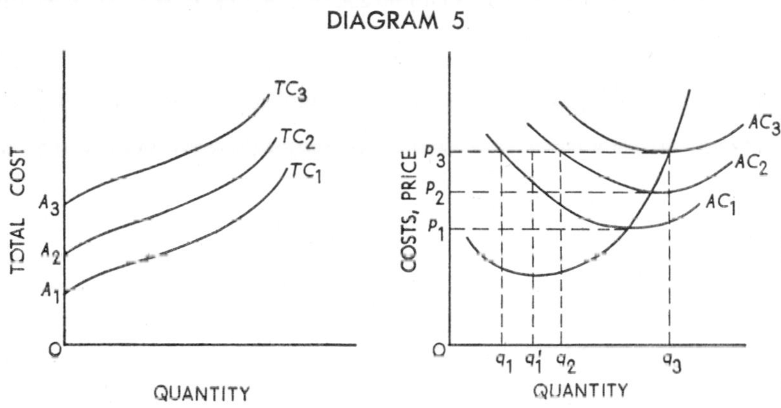

A rise in the value of additional capital to some set of firms will lead to a willingness to emit some particular set of liabilities. However, each firm is a monopsonist in its own liabilities—a rise in the ratio of external financing will lead to higher borrowing rates. In addition to this objective phenomenon, a rise in the ratio of external financing to income will lead to a rise in the subjective probability that financial difficulties will arise. This subjective estimate of the probability of difficulties does not depend solely upon the leverage factor; a run of successful or of unsuccessful periods will change the estimates.

Be that as it may, the liability structure that firms are willing to assume entails the carrying of specified risks. Even if other financing instruments are available at apparently more favorable terms, a management may, of its own will, not accept them. Necessity can lead to an "undesired" liability structure, and such a liability structure can become a dominant factor in determining future behavior.

An example might help make the above more precise. A firm undertakes an investment commitment which has, say, a two-year gestation period. The financing plan includes cash flows from operations and the sale of debentures. During the first year the cash flow from operations falls short of what had been expected and the firm makes up the difference by bank borrowing. The liability structure is now different from the plan. The firm's management has a number of alternatives; nevertheless, one constraint upon their planning will be to develop a program that eliminates the undesired or unplanned bank debt. This constraint will affect the determination of next year's investment.

Financing a long position by short-term liabilities is a very dangerous way to live, unless guaranteed refinancing exists. If all units were guaranteed accommodations at some "discount window," no unit would pay a premium over a short-term rate. In fact such guarantees do not exist. Thus, to constrain "borrower's" risk, payments on acceptable contractual and contingent financial liabilities are related to the expected cash flow from operations.

Constraints upon the willingness to emit particular types of liabilities decreases the likelihood that monetary policy is an efficient way to call the tune. For a fall in interest rates to affect units which can finance investment by emitting only certain specified types of liabilities, it is necessary that the rate on these particular liabilities decrease. The contact between the particular financial market and the money market may be weak.

In addition, the improvement in the terms upon which external financing is available may have to offset the effect upon the desirability of undertaking a specific project of a decline in cash flows—where the decline in cash flows has little or nothing to do with the expected value of the undertaking, but is a constraint upon how it can be financed.

3. The Supply of Accommodations

Let us consider the *IS* and *LM* curves in the light of the above discussion of investment and financing. The *IS* curve combines investment as a function of the rate of interest and savings as a function of the level of income. However, a financing decision is an integral part of any investment. Not wishing to open a discussion of the financial determinants of savings, we will assume that the savings function is independent of the asset that will be acquired by the saving unit.

The liquidity preference relation—or rather its *LM* transform—is a portfolio balance relation. Implicitly it states the willingness of wealth owners to absorb the particular liabilities that will be used to finance investment. Each point on the *LM* curve states that at that particular interest rate, liabilities associated with the financing of the investment underlying that income level will be absorbed into portfolios. In a simple model it can be assumed that private investment results in the emission of a particular type of bond. The *LM* curve states that at each interest rate and income level (each income level means a rise in net worth as given by the savings function), the bonds needed to finance the required investment will be absorbed. In a world with complex liability alternatives, the *LM* curve, as generalized, states how much of each type of financial instrument will be absorbed into portfolios.

The *LM* relation states the willingness to absorb the risks carried by an increment of private financial liabilities. As conventionally drawn, the *LM* curve shifts with the quantity of money. What kind of money—inside or outside—is relevant to the *LM* curve?

On the above interpretation, "money" is outside money.[30]

If the willingness to take risks depends upon the initial position, and if outside money is free of some uncertainty that inside money carries, then the greater the proportion of outside assets in portfolios the "lower" the *LM* curve.

In Diagram 6, LM_2 reflects a larger amount of outside money than LM_1; as a result, financing terms are improved. Terms are so favorable that investing (deficit) units are induced to emit sufficient (and the right kind of) liabilities to finance the larger amount of investment needed to generate Y_2. Both the asset acquiring and emitting units will take on more inside risks with the greater quantity of outside money.

Note that with LM_2, realized saving, investment, and income are greater than with LM_1. This reflects what can be interpreted as a rise in

DIAGRAM 6

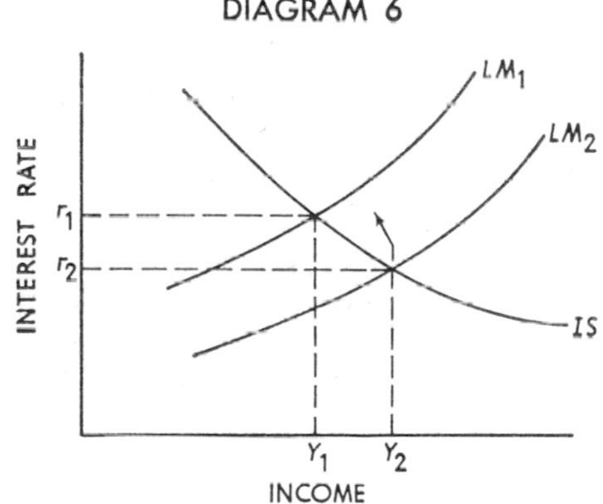

productivity. This has taken place because the rise in security, due to the larger stock of outside money, has lowered the implicit insurance premiums that are contained in the gross returns on investment.

In order to continue to generate the favorable supply conditions for

[30]Even though with central banking there can be some element of outside money in inside money, they are not identical. The inside bank assets do imply cash payments to the banks by some private units. Outside bank assets impose no such constraints upon private units.

private investment, part of the rise in net worth must take the form of a rise in outside assets. If no such increase takes place, over time the *LM* curve can be expected to swing up and to the left as the arrow in Diagram 6 indicates.

4. Bank and Nonbank Financial Intermediaries

In the standard presentation, a change in the conventionally defined money supply shifts the *LM* curve. The assumed process is almost always an open market chain that runs from an initial substitution of money for outstanding assets to an improvement in the terms upon which new investment can be financed. If this oozing chain does not increase the willingness of units to acquire the liabilities that can be emitted by potential investing units, no rise in investment need take place. Thus a rise in conventionally defined money need not shift the *LM* curve.

Banks and other financial intermediaries are risk absorbers. The cause of this risk absorption, whether it is because of their professional skill in portfolio management, the workings of the law of large numbers, or the implicit (explicit) underwriting of their liabilities by government agencies, need not concern us. While banks and other financial intermediaries do not necessarily decrease the risks borne by liability emitters, they decrease the risk carried by the asset holder. Thus with a given net worth and stock of outside money, the greater the amount of risk-absorbing intermediation, the more favorable are the financing terms for new investment. In this way, a rise in the amount of conventionally defined money will increase the willingness of units to absorb new liabilities emitted by investing units. In Diagram 6, LM_2 can be interpreted as reflecting a greater absorption of lenders' risk by financial intermediaries than LM_1. In this interpretation both LM_1 and LM_2 reflect the same amount of outside money and net worth.

Obviously the absorption of uncertainty by banks and other financial intermediaries depends upon the assets acquired. If "open market" operations are carried out in Treasury bills and similar instruments, then very little if any "risks" exists for the banks to absorb—the *LM* curve will shift out very little, if at all, with a rise in conventionally defined money by this path. If private business or household debt is acquired, then a relatively large amount of risk is absorbed and the shift will be greater. This is another "explanation" of the greater relative efficiency of conventional commercial loan operations as against open market operations. This argument is not a substitute for, but rather a complement to, the earlier argument.

Of all existing financial intermediaries, commercial banks historically have had the most powerful risk-absorbing effects. Thus a given increase of nominal money will shift the *LM* curve more than an equal change in the liability of other financial intermediaries. Commercial bank time deposits, even though they are not means of payment, benefit from the risk-absorption properties of commercial banks. This may be why definitions of money which include such time deposits work well in some empirical investigations.

The introduction of a new "type" of financial intermediary, and the making of the implicit government underwriting of financial intermediaries explicit (having the automatic FDIC replace the discretionary Federal Reserve System) swings the *LM* curve down and to the right. Vigorous financial innovation may be a substitute for a rapid growth in outside money in generating favorable supply-of-finance conditions.

VI. CONCLUSION

The impact of money and financial variables upon aggregate demand is conditioned by the nature of the monetary or financial variables that change and by the state of the economy as measured both by the ratio of income to capacity and by its past. Money introduced into the system either to finance, or as a result of, an income-generating operation has a different impact upon system behavior than money that is introduced as a "portfolio change."

Inside and outside money are in part similar because banks and other financial institutions are risk absorbers. Financial institutions and instruments differ in the extent to which they diminish lenders' risk. Banks are somewhat special in that they seem to absorb more of the risk—and hence time deposits at commercial banks can seem to be like money.

Inherent in any subjective evaluation of risks and of the absorptive powers of financial institutions is the possibility of overshoots due to waves of optimism and pessimism. As we tend to learn from the past and as horizons are short, a run of success or failure will feed back quickly into the evaluation of risks.

For example, a run of success will release the animal spirits of entrepreneurs and property owners, will raise capital values and net worth relative to conventional income, and will act to increase investment. When modern capitalism takes off in this fashion, governments run surpluses and the stock of outside money is decreased. Even as the success of the system induces feelings of safety and security, making both borrowers and lenders willing to take greater chances, one of the objective determinants of security and safety is being eroded; the quality of the insurance protection due to the relative size of outside money deteriorates.

A balanced growth path, on which outside money grows at the same rate as the system, can be defined. Nevertheless, as long as investment depends upon the evaluation of risks, and this evaluation, in part, depends upon the past of the system, such a path is unstable. For if success decreases risk premiums, the required quantity of outside money is lowered. Thus a change in the government's tax and spending schedules is needed in order to maintain balance.

The best we can hope for is not a rule but an awareness of how complex is the task of an authority possessing discretion.

EMPIRICAL EVIDENCE ON THE IMPACT OF MONETARY VARIABLES ON AGGREGATE EXPENDITURE

Robert H. Strotz

The plan of this paper is as follows. In Section 1, I shall report on findings regarding the role of monetary variables in *directly* influencing both consumer expenditure and investment expenditure. In Section 2, I shall examine studies of the effects of changes in monetary variables on consumption, investment, and national income as these work themselves out *indirectly* in a simultaneous equation system, especially through the medium of the desire for liquid balances. Finally, in Section 3, I shall report critically on some recent studies relating the quantity of money to aggregate income or to the level of business activity.

My survey will be far from exhaustive as I shall restrict myself to a relatively few select studies that strike me as especially interesting. In particular, I shall ignore single equation studies of the demand for liquidity or of the determinants of the velocity of circulation because expenditure does not enter as a dependent variable. Liquidity preference functions will arise, however, in the context of simultaneous equation models.

1. CONSUMPTION AND INVESTMENT

The impact of monetary variables on consumption and on investment has recently been the object of extensive surveys done for the Commission on Money and Credit, and there seems to be neither adequate purpose nor space to repeat these surveys here. Only a summary of findings will be given.

Relying on the excellent survey of the determinants of consumer expenditure by Daniel Suits,[1] we can identify four main monetary variables that may affect consumer expenditure.

(1) *The price level.* Suits identifies three direct ways in which a change in prices may affect consumer expenditure. (*a*) Rising prices, including rising factor prices, may, if there is a "money illusion," cause people to feel better off and induce greater real expenditure out of the same real income. (*b*) Rising prices may create a positive speculative component in demand. Finally, (*c*) rising prices may alter relative prices and thereby affect household decisions regarding consumption and saving. But, according to Suits, there is no empirical evidence bearing on any of these propositions.

(2) *The rate of interest.* Regarding the rate of interest, Suits says:

> . . . although considerable emphasis on the direct and indirect roles of the interest rate as a determinant of consumer expenditure is found in both classical and Keynesian theory, the preponderance of evidence is that its influence, if any, is negligible in comparison to other factors and any reliance on it as a substantial control weapon is misplaced (p. 41).

(3) *Consumer credit.* Inasmuch as the interest rate is suspect as a measure of credit availability, one may wish to look instead at the empirical evidence regarding the terms of consumer credit as they affect consumer expenditure. Here, unfortunately, the evidence, for aggregate consumer expenditure, also fails to show any important or reliable effect.

(4) *Liquid assets.* On the role of liquid assets in the consumption function, Suits has this to say (p. 43):

> The accumulation of conflicting empirical evidence from cross-section studies added to the highly unstable coefficient found for liquid assets in the time series analysis of the preceding section is convincing evidence that the role of liquid assets in the consumption function has not yet been discovered.

Thus, for one monetary variable after another, it has not been possible to verify empirically any important direct effects of monetary magnitudes on consumer expenditure. I should urge considerable caution, however, in concluding from this that monetary policy has little direct effect on consumer expenditure; our ability to discern the effect statistically from the available data may conceal what, from a common sense and theoretical point of view, we might quite correctly regard as important. Indeed, our experience with statistical investment demand functions suggests the danger of denying that which we simply have had trouble finding.

In a survey of investment demand studies for the Commission on

[1]Daniel B. Suits, "The Determinants of Consumer Expenditure: A Review of Present Knowledge," in *Impacts of Monetary Policy* (The Commission on Money and Credit) (Englewood Cliffs, N.J.: Prentice-Hall, Inc., 1963), pp. 1–57.

Money and Credit, Eisner and I[2] concluded, regarding plant and equipment investment:

Evidence regarding other variables is generally inconclusive. The interest rate has occasionally been found to be negatively related to capital expenditures, but such findings are not general. Coefficients are frequently uncertain, or, more important, so small in relation to the variations of the interest rate which have been allowed to occur as to deny that variable much historical role in influencing the rate of investment. However, procedures for estimating the role of the rate of interest have generally been poor (p. 192).

Since those words were written, there have been several studies that have successfully identified an important and statistically significant role for the interest rate. These are referred to by David Meiselman in his critique of an earlier version of this paper.[3]

Unhappily, it can also be reported that studies of the demand for inventories have failed to show any consistent role for the interest rate. By contrast, however, it is generally conceded that the interest rate does have an important effect on the demand for housing and on investment in the highly capital-intensive utilities.

With these brief passages I set aside a good deal of empirical research on the role of monetary variables in influencing consumption and investment outlays. I should like to turn my attention instead to those studies of the effect of monetary variables on aggregate expenditure that involve entire systems of relationships, that is, to the simultaneous equation models.

2. SIMULTANEOUS EQUATION MODELS

Of the simultaneous equation systems, the first one I wish to review is the only one dealing with a long span of time, 1869 to 1948, and focusing principally on secular rather than short-run relationships. It is a model by Stefan Valavanis-Vail[4] that consists of 12 structural equations, all of which are behavioral relations. Valavanis used overlapping decadal averages to provide observations every five years. The long-term interest rate was introduced in an investment demand function along with the ratio to capital stock of the sum of depreciation, entrepreneurial income,

[2]Robert Eisner and Robert H. Strotz, "Determinants of Business Investment," in *Impacts of Monetary Policy* (The Commission on Money and Credit) (Englewood Cliffs, N.J.: Prentice-Hall, Inc., 1963), pp. 60–337 (with bibliography by George R. Post).

[3]I single out in this connection Frank de Leeuw, "The Demand for Capital Goods by Manufacturers: A Study of Quarterly Time Series," *Econometrica*, Vol. 30, No. 3 (July, 1962), pp. 407–23; Frederick S. Hammer, *The Demand for Physical Capital: Application of a Wealth Model* (Englewood Cliffs, N.J.: Prentice-Hall, Inc., 1964), and Dale W. Jorgenson, "Capital Theory in Investment Behavior," *American Economic Review*, Vol. LIII, No. 2 (May, 1963), pp. 247–59.

[4]Stefan Valavanis-Vail, "An Econometric Model of Growth, U.S.A., 1869–1963," *American Economic Review*, Vol. XLV, No. 2 (May, 1955), pp. 208–21.

rents, and financial income (that is, the ratio to capital stock of nonwage income). The coefficient of the interest rate did not appear to be very reliable statistically, but, as to magnitude, it implied that a one-point rise in the interest rate is associated with a reduction of the *rate* of investment (that is the percentage rate of increase in capital) by one-half of a percentage point. The effect as estimated is therefore of considerable significance economically, even if not significant statistically. Unfortunately, it seems impossible to establish that a change in the interest rate *causes* a change in the rate of capital accumulation (there is no time lag), except for such reassurance as is provided by the fact that the relation is *inverse,* namely, that with a high rate of capital accumulation the interest rate is lower, not higher. But that is a slim reed for a causal inference. The system is not recursive, and it is difficult to understand what the causal interpretation, if any, is intended to be. Both the interest rate and the price level are endogenous and determined implicitly within the model. One relation connecting them is the liquidity preference function, two versions of which are presented.

One version in effect gives income velocity as a function of the rate of profit and the interest rate. Velocity is positively associated with both. A 1 percent rise in the *long-term* interest rate increases income velocity by 0.15, and the estimate is just double its standard error. In the alternative formulation the real value of money balances held by the public is related to the value of capital and land (wealth) and to the interest rate as well. Real balances go up when other assets rise, as if maintaining some portfolio balance, and decline when interest rates rise. The elasticity of real balances with respect to the interest rate at the point of means appears substantial, though the linearity assumed for this relationship disturbs the meaning of this statement considerably for anyone concerned with what happens at very low or very high interest rates.

What should really be of interest about this system is which monetary variable appears as the prime mover. It is not the interest rate but the quantity of money that is an exogenous variable. What we should like to know is the coefficient of the quantity of money in the reduced form equation for income. That would tell us the overall effect of money on income. This coefficient is not presented, and it would be difficult to compute because of the nonlinearities in the system.

We may now inject a methodological note. A model is, of course, a theory, and all we can hope to learn regarding alternative propositions as to whether or not money counts, and how much, must stem from the following. First, monetary variables must either be exogenous so that their effects can be examined, as in the reduced form, or else they must be determined by an *autonomous* relation that explains the behavior of those who make monetary policy, so that by dropping that relation one can ascertain what the effects would have been of policies other than those pursued during the observation period. For this to be done a certain block recursive structure seems necessary, so that the system can be decomposed into the endogenous variables of interest, on the one hand, and those determining the monetary variables on the other.

Secondly, we may come to understand the role of money by comparing the explanatory and forecasting success of different models in which monetary variables enter in different ways. The trouble is that in any two models to be contrasted, there are apt to be many important differences, so that their relative degree of empirical verification cannot be ascribed uniquely to any single monetary feature that distinguishes them. This objection can be overcome when, as in the work of a single author, alternative versions of the role of monetary variables are considered in an otherwise similar system.

Finally, when monetary variables do appear as exogenous, we may compare their importance with that of other exogenous variables, most likely some measure of autonomous expenditure. In the Valavanis model, no alternative exogenous variables appear, except for the percent of wage earners unionized. This variable appears to be importantly related to the wage rate (as cause or effect can be in dispute), but, lacking the reduced form, one cannot trace its importance for real income.

There are two other simultaneous equation systems I should like to consider. One is the most recent in the series of models developed by L. R. Klein (this one in collaboration with Joel Popkin).[5] The other is by Ta-Chung Liu,[6] which is done very much in the spirit of the Klein models. The Klein-Popkin model uses quarterly data for the period 1948–58 and some 29 behavioral equations. The Liu model also uses quarterly data though for a slightly extended period, 1947–59. It consists of 19 behavioral equations. It is more aggregated than the Klein-Popkin model but introduces fiscal as well as monetary variables.

In the Klein-Popkin model there are two prime movers on the monetary front. One is the Federal Reserve discount rate; the other is the percentage of total reserves in excess of required reserves. The discount rate is, of course, a direct and precise instrument determinable by fiat. The percentage of excess reserves is also controllable by the Federal Reserve System, but it is not a precise instrument, the response of banks to changes in total reserves or in required reserves playing an important role in determining the percentage of excess reserves. But both of these monetary variables, the discount rate and the percentage of excess re-

[5]Lawrence R. Klein and Joel Popkin, "An Econometric Analysis of the Postwar Relationship between Inventory Fluctuations and Changes in Aggregate Economic Activity," in *Inventory Fluctuations in Economic Stabilization*, Part III (Joint Economic Committee, 87th Cong., 1st sess.), (Washington, D.C.: U.S. Government Printing Office, 1961), pp. 71–89.

[6]Ta-Chung Liu, "An Exploratory Quarterly Econometric Model of Effective Demand in the Postwar U.S. Economy," *Econometrica*, Vol. 31, No. 3 (July, 1963), pp. 301–48.

serves, enter the system autonomously. Together they have the single role of determining the short-term rate of interest, as measured by the rate on 90-day commercial paper. The estimated relation looks good in that it is both statistically significant and economically plausible.

The short-term rate of interest, i_s, thus determined, does not affect inventory investment or purchases of consumer goods but has the single role of determining the long-term rate of interest, i_L (measured by the yield on corporate bonds). The estimated relation giving the long-term rate is

$$i_L = \underset{(.15)}{.0541} + \underset{(.034)}{.0497}\, i_s + \underset{(.060)}{.959}\, (i_L)_{-1}$$

Standard errors are in parentheses.

If the coefficients in this regression are taken seriously, the long-term rate responds very sluggishly to the short-term rate and to monetary controls. Viewed as a distributed lag function of the short-term rate, the only variable hypothesized to be directly manipulable by central bank policy, the function can be written as

$$i_L = .0022 + .0497 \sum_{n=0}^{\infty} (.959)^n\, (i_s)_{-n}$$

This states that in two years' time there would occur only about one-third of the ultimate adjustment of the long rate to a change in the level of the short rate, a frightful lag in the effect of monetary policy.[7]

We note, however, that the regression coefficient for the short rate is not significant statistically. The estimates are such that little violence would be done to them if this relation were rewritten simply as

$$i_L = (i_L)_{-1} + \text{random disturbance},$$

stating that the dynamic of the long-term interest rate is one of neutral equilibrium, or that this rate enters the model as a predetermined variable. All the concern about the discount rate, the percentage of excess reserves, and the short-term rate would then be beside the point. These variables could be dropped from the system and the long-term rate would be the only prime mover on the monetary side.

The long-term rate, however determined, next has two roles to play. It enters into the determination of nonfarm residential construction (price deflated), but not with great statistical significance. (Neither it nor any other interest rate enters directly as a determinant of any other expenditure component, presumably because of lack of statistical significance.) The other role for the long-term rate is to affect the demand for

---

[7]A permanent change of 1 percent in the short-term rate induces a 1.2 percent change in the long-term rate.

real cash balances (the quantity of money deflated by gross national product).

This demand for real balances is assumed to depend on the change in the price level and on the long-term interest rate, the latter entering in a statistically significant way. One may wonder, however, what the causal relation is in view of the fact that the system provides no very good explanation of the long-term interest rate, which in fact appears virtually as an exogenous variable. Perhaps this interest rate should be regarded as an endogenous variable determined by the liquidity preference function, and the quantity of money (or some other endogenous variable) should be reclassified as exogenous. This could reverse the causal interpretation to be given the liquidity preference function.

In any case, real cash balances next appear in regressions for consumer nondurables and for expenditures on consumer services. They are inconsequential in the case of nondurables, but more important for services. Cash balances do not appear as a regressor in the relation giving consumer durable expenditures, I presume because of wrong sign or lack of significance if included. My expectation, of course, would be that cash balances, exerting an asset effect, should be more important in influencing the expenditure on durables than on nondurable goods or services. In the Klein-Popkin model all three categories of expenditures are functions of disposable real income, the ratio of nonlabor personal income to labor income, and their own lagged values, except that for consumer durables an index of consumer durable buying plans, as an exogenous variable, is included as an additional regressor, and money balances are excluded. It is unfortunate from our point of view that consumer buying plans are included in the consumer durables equation because, although that may improve forecasting, they add no information about structure and may deprive any variable with which they are correlated of significant explanatory power.

The inclusion in all three consumer expenditure equations of the lagged values of the dependent variable also makes it impossible to ascertain the total lagged effect of any one of the other explanatory variables, in particular, the cash balance variable, whether present or absent from the equation. An examination of the reason for this difficulty in interpretation may be worth a digression.

With most economic time series, which are so highly autocorrelated, one will generally obtain a good fit by regressing a variable on itself lagged, for example,

$$y(t) = \alpha + \beta y(t-1),\ 1 > \beta > 0$$

But this provides little information about structure. If a different variable, $x(t)$, is brought in as an explanatory variable, for example,

$$y(t) = \alpha + \beta y(t-1) + \gamma x(t),$$

the contribution of $x(t)$ to the regression is apt to be small. But this relation can be interpreted in a different way. Had we written $y(t)$ as a distributed lag function of $x(t)$, thus

$$y(t) = \alpha' + \gamma \sum_{i=0}^{\infty} \beta^i x(t-i),$$

this could have been transformed into the previous equation with $\alpha' = \alpha(1-\beta)$. Thus the regression

$$y(t) = \alpha + \beta y(t-1) + \gamma x(t)$$

can be thought of as making $y(t)$ depend solely on x, but on the xs at the present and all past dates. It has in recent years become fashionable for economists to use regressions of this form in time series analysis.

But suppose we have *two* independent variables and write, in analogy with the above, $y(t) = \alpha + \beta y(t-1) + \gamma x(t) + \delta z(t)$. Then how can we interpret this upon eliminating $y(t-1)$? The above equation is in fact equivalent to

$$y(t) = \frac{\alpha}{1-\beta} + \gamma \sum_{i=0}^{\infty} \beta^i x(t-i) + \delta \sum_{i=0}^{\infty} \beta^i z(t-i)$$

but this requires that the lagged coefficients of the xs and zs be in constant proportion to each other, and that is a severe constraint to impose.

We could also have obtained

$$y(t) = \alpha + \beta y(t-1) + \gamma x(t) + \delta z(t)$$

by having started with either

$$y(t) = \alpha' + \gamma \sum_{i=0}^{\infty} \beta^i x(t-i) + \delta z(t)$$

or

$$y(t) = \alpha' + \delta \sum_{i=0}^{\infty} \beta^i z(t-i) + \gamma x(t)$$

and having absorbed a term, $-\beta\delta z(t-1)$ in the first case, or $-\beta\gamma x(t-1)$ in the second case, into the residual. Since $\beta\delta$ and $\beta\gamma$ are apt to be small, the dropping of either of these terms may appear reasonable, though complicating a technical problem of autocorrelated residuals. But all this means that when we see a regression such as

$$y(t) = \alpha + \beta y(t-1) + \gamma x(t) + \delta z(t)$$

we cannot know whether $\beta y(t-1)$ really represents the effect of an entire weighted sum of all the past xs or of all the past zs, and in this regard our results become very difficult to interpret.

This is the problem that arises with the Klein-Popkin expenditure equations and, hence, lack of evidence in these equations that cash balances are very important is far from conclusive. But, in any case, as the Klein-Popkin model is defined and estimated, no important role for the Federal Reserve System is in evidence.

In Professor Liu's model monetary variables are introduced in much the same way as by Klein and Popkin. As with Klein-Popkin, the short-term rate of interest is obtained from the rediscount rate and the ratio of excess to required reserves. A very plausible relation is obtained and very close to Klein's, as is to be expected. The long-term interest rate is then made to depend on itself lagged, on the current and lagged short-term rates, and on the rate of change in prices. A very plausible relation results with statistically significant coefficients except for the price change variable. This relation is more gratifying than the one in the Klein-Popkin model. It is, using the Klein-Popkin notation,

$$i_L = \underset{(0.033)}{0.240}\, i_s - \underset{(0.037)}{0.201}\, (i_s)_{-1} + \underset{(0.040)}{0.978}\, (i_L)_{-1} + \underset{(0.015)}{0.017}\, p - 0.27 \qquad R^2 = 0.980$$

To ease interpretation, let us drop the variable p (rate of change of prices), equate the coefficients of i_s and $(i_s)_{-1}$ at 0.22, and change 0.978 to 1.0. We then have

$$\Delta i_L = -0.27 + .22\, \Delta i_s$$

a reasonable and economically interesting relation—and surely still a good fit.

The interest rate on time deposits and savings shares is then presented as a distributed lag function of the long-term rate. The adjustment, however, is very slow. It takes three years for half the effect of a change in the long-term rate to work itself out on the rate on time deposits and savings shares. (Note that in the original article $(r_L)_{-1}$ should be $(r'_L)_{-1}$.)

Again, following Klein, real liquid asset holdings are then made to depend in part on the interest rates. In particular, personal holdings of currency and demand deposits depend on the long-term interest rate, consumption expenditure, and the rate of change of prices measured by the GNP deflator. The coefficient of the long-term interest rate has the right sign and is between two and three times its standard error. A 1 percent rise in the long-term interest rate reduces personal currency and demand deposit holdings by an amount in the neighborhood of $1 billion in the *current* quarter. The long-run effect is hard to assess. The appearance of the lagged value of the dependent variable as one of the regressors implies a distributed lag effect of one or more of the regressor variables, but as stated earlier, we cannot identify the effect because of the presence of more than one explanatory variable. Much the same kind of relationship, quantitatively, is obtained for a function giving personal holdings of time deposits and savings shares as depending on the interest rate on these deposits and shares, on personal disposable income, and on the rate of change of prices. Price change plays a stronger role than it did in explaining currency and demand deposit holdings, as one would expect. A 1 percent rise in the interest paid on time deposits and savings shares increases their holdings by an estimated 1.176 billion of 1954 dollars in the same quarter and with a lagged effect that cannot be separated out.

The real value of the money holdings of nonfarm, nonfinancial businesses also works out in much the same way, with coefficients for changes in transactions (measured by GNP), changes in prices, and the short-term interest rate running roughly twice their standard errors. A 1 percent change in the short-term rate calls forth an increase in money holdings during the same quarter of about 400 million of 1954 dollars and with the longer run effect impossible to isolate.

Various liquid asset holdings and interest rates then enter into various expenditure functions. Business construction seems to depend importantly on the long-term interest rate; so does residential construction, though the coefficient of the interest rate is not convincingly significant statistically. Taking the coefficients seriously, we can say that a 1 percent rise in the long-term interest rate has a direct current effect on construction of reducing the total by about 1.4 billion per year in 1954 dollars.

The short-term interest rate, at the margin of statistical significance, affects nonfarm business inventories directly by a 300 million reduction (in 1954 dollars) for each 1 percent rise. Indirect effects through liquid asset holdings need to be added in. Interest rates do not appear in any other expenditure function, presumably because they were not found to play any important or reliable role.

As for the role of the liquidity variables, we may report the following. Money, including time deposits, held by the business sector, appears with economic significance, but not with statistical significance, in the determination of nonfarm business inventories. For every billion dollar (1954) increase in business money holdings, inventory investment rises by between a quarter and a half a billion dollars (1954), depending on how the equation is estimated, but the coefficient seems subject to considerable error of estimate. Personal holdings of money *and government securities* affect current consumption, but not dramatically. A $1 billion rise in these assets increases consumption by about one-tenth as much with no effect reported for durable goods expenditure. This exclusion seems unsatisfactory unless it is to be explained by the problem of causal direction or the absence of a time lag. Residential construction is slightly responsive to money and government security holdings, rising by 50 million for each billion-dollar increase in personal liquid asset holdings.

Liquid assets do not appear in the functions for business construction or equipment investment.

How does all this work out? Suppose, for example, that a 1 percent decrease in all interest rates could be brought about. The first order effects on expenditure components, both directly and through the effects on liquid asset holdings, would be to raise total expenditure by about $2 billion, not an impressive amount, but then this ignores secondary effects via the multipliers. Liu has performed some simulations with his model. He has found that the effects of interest rate changes are (*a*) importantly delayed, (*b*) during some periods perverse, and (*c*) destabilizing. But these simulation studies are presented as "highly crude and experimental." Nevertheless, they give no comfort to those who would regard interest rate policy as a prompt, gentle, and smooth working tool for economic stabilization.

Before leaving the simultaneous equation models, I should like to point to a severe defect for our purposes in both the Klein and the Liu models. It is that no distinction is drawn between desired money holdings and actual money holdings. These are always treated as the same variable and so equilibrium of spenders' portfolios is always assumed. This allows no scope whatsoever for what would perhaps interest us most. If as a consequence of easy money and bank expansion, interest rates fall and the stock of money increases, desired money holdings will rise because of the decline in interest rates. But the actual stock will also have risen and presumably by at least as much as the desired stock. Will the excess holdings of money then increase expenditures, and at what rate will this portfolio adjustment occur? These several models shed no light on this mechanism, though the relations among the variables do go in the presumed direction.

There is a remaining methodological caution I should like to introduce at this point. It is the danger of excessive disaggregation of either consumer or firms' expenditure functions. I shall make this point in terms of an extreme example. Suppose in fact that money holdings were a very important determinant of total consumer expenditure, but that instead of fitting a single consumption function we fitted an expenditure function for each of a thousand different goods and services. Consider the function for soft drinks. It may be that total money assets would account insignificantly for the variation over time in soft drink expenditure, weather, for example, being much more important. And similarly for each and every commodity, there could be special variables that would account for most of the variation. It could happen that money would be unimportant in each of these individual functions, though important for the aggregate. What determines the size of the annual pie may not very well explain variations in the annual slices.

Of all the other simultaneous equation models for the U.S. that I have reviewed, none deal to even this extent with monetary phenomena. The Brookings-SSRC model, with hundreds of equations, will deal with them but it has not been published at the time of this writing.

3. MONEY AND INCOME

In this section I shall deal essentially with two major empirical findings or contentions of Professor Milton Friedman and associates. They are quite distinct. The first, ignoring many important qualifications, is that money matters, and indeed that changes in the quantity of money serve better to explain changes in aggregate expenditure than do changes in autonomous expenditure. The second proposition is that, despite the first, it is hard to predict the time delay of the effects on the general level of business activity of changes in the quantity of money. These may sound like contradictory propositions. They are not. The first statement regarding the superiority of quantity-of-money theory over an autonomous expenditure theory is a comparative statement. That one theory should be better than the other does not mean that it must be wholly satisfactory. It can still be subject to substantial forecasting error. Moreover, the notion of substantial variability of the time lag of effect is relative to some norm of performance, and for control purposes that norm requires that we measure variability in months or quarters. The first proposition regarding the stability of the relationship rests almost entirely on annual data.

I shall take the first proposition up first. This is based on the work by Friedman and David Meiselman.[8] Divide total expenditure, Y, however defined, into two components, A and U, for autonomous and induced. Let induced expenditure, U, be a stochastic function of Y, $U = f(Y) + u$, where u is a random variable. Then the two equations, $U = f(Y) + u$ and $Y = A + U$ define a relation $U = g(A) + w$, where w is a random variable, being a transformation of u. If A has been properly defined, w and A are statistically independent. Approximate $U = g(A) + w$ by the linear relationship $U = \alpha + \beta A + w$, where β is a multiplier. How much of the variance of U can be explained by variation of A?

Another theory is simply that $U = \gamma + \delta M + v$, where M is the quantity of money, δ is a marginal income velocity of circulation, and v is a random variable. How much of the variance of U can be explained by variation in M? More or less than was explained by variation in A? However variables are to be defined, it is essential that U should be the same in both models.

---

[8]Milton Friedman and David Meiselman, "The Relative Stability of Monetary Velocity and the Investment Multiplier in the United States, 1897–1958," in *Stabilization Policies* (Commission on Money and Credit) (Englewood Cliffs, N.J.: Prentice-Hall, Inc., 1963), pp. 165–268.

Note also that one might compare the relations

$$Y = \alpha' + \beta' A + w'$$

and

$$Y = \gamma' + \delta' M + v'$$

though there is the problem that Y as the dependent variable has the explanatory variable A as one of its components, working to assure some perhaps important correlation for the first of the two relations, though not for the second.

It should be stressed that once we decide to determine whether

$$U = \alpha + \beta A + w$$

or

$$U = \gamma + \delta M + v$$

is the better relationship we do so without reference to any set of structural equations from which one or the other of these relations may be derived. These are both reduced form relationships and imply only that (barring odd cases) the underlying structural relations are linear and that either A or M is the only exogenous variable in the model. In particular, they tell us nothing about what specific income or expenditure components, such as disposable income, might determine other income or expenditure components, such as consumption. We also note that there are no time lags in either relation, that is, no lagged endogenous variables in the system. This means that at best these relations can be derived only from extremely simple static models, and that one regression should give a better fit than another does not mean that the category of models from which it may have been derived is superior to the category from which the other reduced form regression may have come. As alternative categories of structural theories, they are being compared in only very naïve form, and this must never be lost sight of in drawing conclusions from the results. Moreover, especially for the quantity theory model, it is impossible to derive any conclusion about the direction of causation unless either a time lag is introduced or outside evidence is invoked.

Why are such simple models being used? The answer given is that of data limitations coupled with a desire to test these alternative theories not simply from the 1930s on but over a much longer span of American economic history, going back to 1897—thus a period of 62 years, 1897–1958. Each is welcome to his private judgment as to whether it is better to derive knowledge from a simple theory tested over a long period of time and a considerable variety of historical situations or from a more sophisticated theory tested only over more limited but more recent experience.

Then there is the problem of deciding on definitions. Friedman and

Meiselman define M to include currency, demand and time deposits. The main question that can be raised has to do with the inclusion of time deposits, but there is a good case for including them, and in any case it seems to make little difference, so we pass the question by. The other variables, A, U, and Y, are defined in money rather than in real terms. As the authors recognize, it would be especially nice to split income changes into components reflecting change in prices and change in real income, but this would require a much more elaborate model. The decision was made to deal with money values and to experiment with a price index as an additional explanatory variable. Next is the problem of how to define autonomous expenditure. An interesting methodology was used, though it left scope for some exercise of judgment and presented some uncommented upon problems in application that I shall consider later. Suppose that A_1 is clearly a component of A, and that $Y - A_1 - X \equiv U_1$ is clearly a component of U. How should we classify X, the only component that remains unclassified? If X is perfectly substitutable in the theory for A_1, that is, if it is autonomous, then $r^2_{U_1,A_1+X}$ should exceed both $r^2_{U_1,A_1}$ and $r^2_{U_1,X}$ (where $r^2_{i,j}$ is the square of the correlation coefficient of i and j), because if U_1 depends on A_1+X, it should be more highly correlated with the total than with either irregularly varying component part. Similarly, if X is perfectly substitutable for U_1, then $r^2_{A_1,U_1+X}$ should exceed both $r^2_{A_1,U_1}$ and $r^2_{A_1,X}$. It is possible that both or neither of these conditions might be satisfied, in which case the test is ambivalent and judgment must be resorted to. I shall go into no further details regarding the applications of these tests performed by the authors. Suffice it to say that I find no reason to dispute their judgment where they had to exercise it—that is, when the test results are ambivalent. They were thus led to define A as including net private domestic investment plus the government deficit on income and product account plus the net foreign balance. U therefore turned out to be consumption with Y defined as national income. Three problems, however, are very disturbing:

1. To apply this method one must start with some arbitrarily chosen A_1 to be initially classified as autonomous.

The authors started with net private investment. Now, in view of all the work that has been done with some measure of success to relate investment, both inventory and plant and equipment, to sales and sales changes, this seems to be a very unfortunate place to start, though I do not in fact know what the test criteria would have shown had private investment been the variable X to be classified, with A_1 differently defined. Had it led to classifying private investment as autonomous, I would have felt A_1 unsatisfactorily defined or that the test had miscarried. This is not casual empiricism; it is based on many other empirical studies that convincingly show that private investment is far from independent of consumption, though admittedly it is change in consumption rather than its level that is most important, and "sophisticated" equations—involving lags!—are ordinarily used. This criticism, however, is not to prejudge whether the regression $U = \hat{\alpha} + \hat{\beta}A$ would have been better fitted with private net investment included in the dependent rather than the independent variable.

2. A second criticism generalizes the first. To test any component, X, of Y, decisions about how to classify all other components must already have been made, but this seems impossible because each decision to be made correctly requires that every other decision has already been made correctly.

3. A third problem is also not an easy one to do much about. It is that we are trapped by our data categories. Some component X that we need to classify might be divisible into two subcomponents X_1 and X_2, one of which would be classified as autonomous and the other as induced. Our national income accounts may not be broken down in the optimal way. This may be especially important for the aggregations of government receipts and government expenditures.

These three difficulties all leave me wondering whether classification by casual empiricism might not have made more sense, provided that autonomous expenditure categories are not allowed to loom too large in total expenditures.

Before turning to the empirical findings, one very important aspect of the competing theories to be tested must be brought out. It is that neither relation $U = \alpha + \beta A + w$ nor $U = \gamma + \delta M + v$ is claimed to hold for a very long period of time. Structural changes in the parameters are expected from business cycle to business cycle, so that the matter of the relative *stability* of the two relations is not precisely what is involved. The question instead is whether A or M explains more of the variance in U *within* the cycle. Because of structural changes from cycle to cycle, problems of predicting the future effects of changes in M or A are left wide open.

I shall not review the empirical evidence in detail. It indicates overwhelmingly that for the various subperiods of one-cycle duration from 1897 to 1958, U and M are more strongly correlated than U and A. The major exception is for the first few years of the Great Depression. Moreover, even if a single regression is fitted to the annual data for the entire period, the coefficient of correlation between U and M is .985, whereas between U and A it is only .756. Apparently the most adverse test of any interest that can be performed, given the Friedman-Meiselman classification of Y into U and A, is to choose the period starting with the Great Depression and skipping the war years (as seems right and proper).

Albert Ando and Franco Modigliani[9] have found even then that the correlation of U with M is .98, whereas that of U with A is only .92. Different definitions of A can reverse these results for the combined period 1929–1941—1947–1958, though the difference is then not dramatic. One problem remaining for the subjective judgment of the reader is whether results for the combined period 1897–1941 and 1947–58 are more or less pertinent to the future than the combined period 1929–41 and 1947–58. Do we want to include or exclude our experience prior to 1929 in approaching the late 1960s and the 1970s? Nevertheless, if we should exclude all experience prior to World War II and use either annual or quarterly data, we would still be forced to the Friedman-Meiselman conclusion, with their definitions of U and A.

Restricting ourselves to the post-World War II period when quarterly data are available, lagged relations and relations between first differences may be tried. None of this upsets the results, though it does reveal that money fits best if it precedes U by two quarters and autonomous investment fits best if it precedes U not at all. Two interpretations follow from this observation. One is that the view that perhaps changes in U cause the changes in M, rather than the other way around, loses in credibility. Of course, we cannot say that the opposite is proved, namely, that M causes U just because it precedes it. There is always the possibility that both are simply responding to a third variable which lags neither. But this sort of argument can always be made against any causal claim of this sort and could be taken more seriously if the causally governing variable hidden in the background were brought to light and evidence adduced in support of the claim that it is really the common "prime mover." In fact, tribute must be paid to the efforts of Milton Friedman and Anna Schwartz[10] to gather evidence on this causal question by reviewing with great care much further historical evidence relating to what caused changes in the money supply to come about.

Of interest however, from a policy point of view, is the fact that the effect of A, if less than that of M, is quicker.

Prices have also been introduced and the regressions

$$U = \hat{\alpha} + \hat{\beta}A + \hat{\epsilon}P$$

---

[9]Albert Ando and Franco Modigliani, "Velocity in the Investment Multiplier," *American Economic Review*, Vol. LV, No. 4 (September, 1965), pp. 693–728. For another critique see Michael DePrano and Thomas Mayer, "Autonomous Expenditures and Money," *ibid*, pp. 729–52, and the ensuing reply and rejoinders in the same issue. See also Donald D. Hester, "Keynes and the Quantity Theory: A Comment on the Friedman-Meiselman CMC Paper," *Review of Economics and Statistics*, Vol. XLVI, No. 4 (November, 1964), pp. 364–68 and the subsequent exchange by Friedman, Meiselman, and Hester in the same issue.

[10]Milton Friedman and Anna Schwartz, *A Monetary History of the United States, 1867–1960* (National Bureau of Economic Research) (Princeton, N.J.: Princeton University Press, 1963).

and

$$U = \hat{\gamma} + \hat{\delta}M + \hat{\eta}P$$

examined. Again, higher correlations are obtained for the quantity of money equation than for the autonomous expenditure equation, except for the period 1938–53 (including the war years) when both $\hat{\beta}$ and $\hat{\delta}$ are negative (!) and for 1939–48 (including the war years) when $\hat{\alpha}$ is negative (!).

So much for the review of the empirical results. I have a complaint about the underlying concept of this contraposition of theories in terms of what Keynes taught me. My interpretation of the central lesson in the *General Theory* may, of course, differ from that of others and from the textbook writers as well. But here it is: money does matter—unless the economy is in the liquidity trap. Moreover, if the economy is *near* the liquidity trap in that the demand for money is highly interest elastic, it may take an extremely great (and perhaps politically impossible) change in the quantity of money to stimulate investment in the short run by lowering the interest rate. Moreover, even if the Pigou effect is considered under such circumstances, it may operate too slowly. (This I very much doubt.) What must be done under such circumstances to get away from the liquidity trap so that monetary policy may once again become effective? It is necessary to shift the functions that have been defining a less-than-full-employment equilibrium, even for flexible prices. What function to shift? Here the focus is on the investment function and the contention is not that investment is autonomous, but, on the contrary, that the parameters relating it to income and to the interest rate are not very stable and can be altered by policy measures. In particular, under such circumstances, the investment function can be shifted laterally by adding a component of government investment (which really means government expenditure of any sort) that is not offset by a reduction in private expenditure as might be brought about by increased taxes. Once the investment function has been shifted so that we are out of the mire, money can take over once again. If there remains a classical problem of unemployment because of price-cost maladjustments, for example, inflation (more commonly reflation) can work to cure it.

Whatever may be its empirical validity, this was a theory born in the 1930s to deal with a chronic depression the likes of which had not been known before. I have never thought of this theory as one that was supposed to be relevant back to 1897. It was never put to a solid empirical test even for the Great Depression. But as we entered the war in the 1940s, we feared it had been applicable for the 1930s and the chronic stagnationists feared it would be valid for the years beyond the war. It clearly has not been, certainly not with the persistently high level of military expenditure. Perhaps the theory never again will be valid, if it ever was. But should we someday fall into a liquidity trap, perhaps through gross monetary mismanagement in the early phase of a depression, we may want to turn to the episodic control A when the perennial control M has failed us; actually we may not even find A in the national accounts, for what we may want is an autonomous, that is, policy-determined increase in the investments that are induced by the state of the economy. If my meaning is understood correctly, there is a difference between an autonomous shift in an investment function and a shift in autonomous investment. Whatever its merits or effectiveness may have been, the recent investment tax credit is a case in point. An autonomous increase in consumption might also be brought about, for example, by improving expectations of future income or reducing personal income and other consumer taxes. This can be the case even if consumption is an exact function of national income. We can autonomously try to change parameters in any induced expenditure function.

Indeed, for stabilization purposes even under normal circumstances we may prefer to shift the parameters of expenditure relations or other behavioral relations rather than to operate on the amount of money, if we believe the response will be quicker and the policy more quickly reversible. Indeed, some may prefer to leave the quantity of money—or its rate of increase—quite alone. And this brings me to the next topic.

How far does a change in the stock of money lag behind its effect on the level of aggregate expenditure? And how variable is that lag? If it is both long and variable, then even prompt perception of a business cycle turning point by the Federal Reserve System and a prompt implementation of monetary policy may have much too delayed an effect and the delay itself may be subject to considerable forecast error, with the result that when the effect occurs it may in retrospect have been perversely chosen relative to the events then occurring.

Professor Friedman has argued[11] that the lag of the impact on business activity of a change in the rate of change in the money supply is both long and highly variable. Some of Friedman's evidence comes from a comparison of the dates of upper and lower turning points in the rate of change of money series and the corresponding lagged upper and lower turning points of the National Bureau reference cycles, since 1870. The lag from peak to peak averages 17.6 months and from trough to trough, 12 months. The range of variation in these lags is considerable. Since 1870 the peak-to-peak lag had a standard deviation of 6.9 months and the trough-to-trough lag had a standard deviation of 5.7 months.

---

[11]Milton Friedman, "The Lag in Effect of Monetary Policy," *Journal of Political Economy*, Vol. LXIX, No. 5 (October, 1961), pp. 447–66; and Milton Friedman and Anna J. Schwartz, "Money and Business Cycles," *Review of Economics and Statistics*, Vol. XLV, No. 1, Part 2 (Supplement: February, 1963), pp. 32–64.

One of the difficulties with this analysis has to do with the irregularities of the movement in the rate of change of the money supply series. We are not dealing with a beautiful sine function in the first place, and peak-to-peak and trough-to-trough comparisons are far from being "sufficient" statistics. An effort to reduce some of this erratic character was made by approximating the series with a step function and dating so-called step peaks and step troughs where they terminate. This method, by its very nature, tends to reduce the lag somewhat. The averages of 17.6 months and 12 months are, however, reduced to 7.1 months and 4.1 months, a substantial change.

Other evidence consists of correlating the quarter-to-quarter percentage change in the money supply with either consumption or income after removal of trend. This Friedman has done for the period 1948–58. The results indicate a lag of 9 to 12 months.

What has bothered others (J. M. Culbertson[12] and John Kareken and Robert M. Solow[13]) and bothers me is why the leading series should be "the change in the *rate of change* of the money supply" rather than the change in the money supply itself. That is, should business activity, however measured, be related to M or to $d\log M/dt$? Friedman advances three reasons for the latter choice: (1) Business activity, as it might be measured, say by GNP, is a flow, whereas M is a stock and therefore dimensionally different. This concern makes no sense to me at all, and, after explaining the dimensional difference at some length, Friedman himself appears to drop the point. A second argument given is that M is trend dominated and trend removal is crude and arbitrary. With a desire to use the National Bureau reference cycle turning points as the dependent observations, in order to go back to 1870, change in the rate of change was the superior monetary series to use, because this series is not trend dominated. But if this series is in principle the *wrong* one to use, one should not select it because of its statistical convenience!

A more serious argument is that output and the stock of money might both rise at constant percentage rates in the long run. What causes cyclical behavior in the former series may be earlier departures from a constant rate of expansion of the money supply. It would then be the departure from trend in the money supply that would produce a business cycle. Now this departure can be measured in two ways: (1) as a departure in the actual rate of growth of M from the trend rate of growth, which upsets price level expectations, and so on or (2) as the percentage

[12] J. M. Culbertson, "Friedman on the Lag in Effect of Monetary Policy," *Journal of Political Economy,* Vol. LXVIII, No. 6 (December, 1960), pp. 617–21; also see Culbertson's reply to the JPE article by Friedman cited in the previous footnote, which appears in the same issue as that article.

[13] Albert Ando, E. Cary Brown, Robert M. Solow, and John Kareken, "Lags in Fiscal and Monetary Policy," in *Stabilization Policies* (Commission on Money and Credit), (Englewood Cliffs, N.J.: Prentice-Hall, Inc., 1963), pp. 1–96.

difference of M from its trend value. These are in effect different theories of the business cycle. The first makes business activity depend on $d\log M/dt$, relative to a normal value; the second makes it depend on M, relative to a normal value. With the first theory, Friedman's choice of $d\log M/dt$ is the reasonable one; for the second theory one should use M (as a percent of trend). The highly variable lag of business activity behind $d\log M/dt$ suggests that the first theory is a quite unsatisfactory one.

What happens if we look at the other one? How does business activity lag behind M? For a report on this, we turn to Kareken and Solow. What Kareken and Solow have done is to use the monthly Index of Industrial Production averaged into a quarterly series as one variable and the stock of money (including time deposits) as the other. To avoid trend problems they have taken first differences. Data have been used for the period 1919–59 and for subperiods, and with comparable results. GNP has been used instead of industrial production for 1939–59. Unfortunately for any strict confrontation with Friedman's views, the Kareken-Solow industrial production and GNP data are all price-deflated, whereas the National Bureau reference cycle dates reflect turning points in current price series as well. In a footnote, however, the authors indicate that Professor Joel Segall's students obtained with nondeflated series results generally supporting the Kareken-Solow findings. The findings can be simply stated. The correlation between the two series is commonly highest when there is no lag at all, though the correlation coefficients are low (they range from .2 to .6); yet they are statistically significant. Because of the contemporaneity thus found, there is no opportunity to infer anything about the causal direction. The lag between peak and peak and trough and trough in the first-difference series has an average absolute deviation of about one quarter.

We must now comment, as Kareken and Solow have, that not much can be inferred about the effectiveness or the promptness of effect of monetary policy in this way in any case. This is because to make much sense out of the analysis we should need to know what other factors are also at play so that we could contrast the performance of the economy in consequence of a given monetary policy with how it would have performed with a neutral or different monetary policy. For example, an expansionary monetary policy early in a recession may slow down the recession and cause it to bottom out at a higher level of activity than it otherwise would, or might by contrast promptly reverse the decline, depending on what other forces, including what other policies, are at play. Our best hope is to gain an understanding of the structure of the economy, as through simultaneous equation methods.

A very interesting approach to the problem of measuring the lag in monetary policy is that of Thomas Mayer.[14] He has attempted to synthe-

[14] Thomas Mayer, "The Inflexibility of Monetary Policy," *Review of Economics and Statistics*, Vol. XL, No. 3 (November, 1958), pp. 358–74.

size the lag. This is done by considering the delays in expenditure that follow expenditure decisions for such individual categories as residential construction, manufacturers' plant and equipment investment, state and local government construction, nonresidential building, farm equipment and construction, inventory investment, and consumer credit extensions. These components are then weighted by their importance to show the time pattern of response after both a restrictive and an expansionary change in monetary policy, dating the change from the change in credit availability. He estimates that it takes nine months to achieve three-fourths of the effect of a restrictive policy and ten months for three-fourths of the effect of an expansionary policy. His analysis is restricted to what I shall call the *moderate* easing or tightening of monetary controls in a situation of *moderate* recession or boom. If one adds some lag time for the perception by the authorities of a need for a policy change, or their decision to effect a change, and for their actions to affect credit availability, this analysis suggests that monetary policy is a very sluggish control indeed.

Mayer's estimates have, however, been challenged on specific grounds by William H. White.[15] White finds upon modifying Mayer's estimates that even allowing for lags in determining what monetary policy ought to be, it is sufficiently quick to constitute an effective anticyclical tool. Pending further research on the part of the profession, I cannot report any genuine consensus among reasonable men as to the prospective efficacy of future monetary policy in regulating the level of economic activity.

A further and worthwhile effort to estimate the lag of monetary policy was undertaken by Kareken and Solow *(op. cit.)* by fitting distributed lag regressions to the various links in the expansion or contraction process. There is much too much detail in their work for me to report it here. Their general substantive conclusion was that the lag seems very great from a policy point of view. The inside cognizance and decision lag on the part of the authorities can hardly be less than three months. The lag between action and the effect on gross reserves of the member banks is about one month. The delayed effects of changes in gross reserves on business investment are so tenuously estimated that it would be misleading to cite a number, but it appears substantial. A major difficulty is that these lags of investment are most easily computed following a change in interest rates, but investment, especially inventory investment, may respond to other parameters of credit availability, and these may change importantly well before interest rates change. No one knows because there exists no usable index of credit availability.

The authors are therefore very cautious in drawing any firm conclusion, and I shall be, too.

---

[15]William H. White, "The Flexibility of Anticyclical Monetary Policy," *Review of Economics and Statistics*, Vol. XLIII, No. 2 (May, 1961), pp. 142–47.

DISCUSSION

Comments*

Thomas Mayer

Professor Strotz starts out by reviewing the findings of econometric models. These generally show discouraging results for interest rate manipulation, and hence for monetary policy. But it should be noted that these econometric studies are biased against the interest rate in several ways.

One of these biases results from the effect of changes in the profitability of investment on the interest rate. To see this, consider for the moment not a sophisticated model but a very simple one which makes investment a function of only one variable, the interest rate. Such a model could easily give perverse results: during an expansion both investment and the interest rate are rising, and during a contraction both variables are falling. Clearly, what is wrong here is that such a model ignores the profitability of investment.[1] Surely, since Wicksell we know that it is the *difference* between the natural rate and market rate of interest, and not the absolute level of the market rate, that is important.

Now the econometric models discussed by Strotz do avoid this crude error and include in their investment equations some variables which measure the profitability of investment, such as the rate of change of sales. But obviously these models necessarily leave out some factors which influence the profitability of investment, such as innovations, optimism, and so forth. Insofar as these omitted variables are important they bias the results against the interest rate. First, for example, assume that innovations raise the marginal efficiency of investment. The market rate of interest is pulled up by this increase in the natural rate, and we obtain a positive correlation between investment and the interest rate. Conversely, during the Great Depression, widespread pessimism probably reduced investment significantly, and this reluctance to borrow

*I am indebted for helpful comments to Michael DePrano and Hyman Minsky.

[1]Cf. Karl Brunner, "The Report of the Commission on Money and Credit," *Journal of Political Economy*, Vol. LXIX (December, 1961), p. 613.

reduced the market rate, again producing a positive correlation between the interest rate and investment. These instances of positive correlation then reduce, or perhaps even eliminate, an overall negative correlation for the whole period analyzed.

Second, there is the effect of price expectations. Assume that prices are expected to rise: then both the natural rate and the market rate rise, and investment is maintained. Again it looks as though the rise in the market rate has had no effect on investment. And the same thing occurs if prices are expected to fall. When one considers the fact that during much of the period covered by these models there were substantial price trends (down in the early thirties and up in the postwar period), price expectations may account for much of the poor showing of the interest rate.

Third, the interest rate may not be a good proxy for the monetary variable. To start with, as is mentioned by Strotz, the observed market rates do not measure the availability of credit. In fact, availability and interest rates may show divergent movements in the short run. As Tobin has pointed out, the first reaction of banks to tight money might be to raise credit standards and to ration credit, since interest rates are sticky.[2] Then as interest rates catch up rationing may be relaxed.

Then there is the fact that the cost of capital to the firm includes a component to take account of the increase in risk resulting from greater indebtedness. In a recession period, when cash flow is falling, the risk element may be rising enough (at least subjectively) so that the cost of capital is rising in spite of falling interest rates. Thus, the cost of capital may have seemed greater to a firm in 1934 than in 1928 in spite of lower market rates. To be sure, some of the other variables in the investment equation, such as the sales variable, should in principle pick up the effect of a decline in the cash flow and the increase in risk, but insofar as other variables do not do so, some of this effect may be picked up by the interest rate variable.[3]

Some of the models discussed by Strotz use liquid assets as the monetary variable rather than the interest rate. But this too involves biases.

---

[2] J. Tobin, "Monetary Policy and the Management of the Public Debt: The Patman Inquiry," *Review of Economics and Statistics*, Vol. XXXV (May, 1953), p. 123.

[3] In a way, this argument is the counterpart of the previous point about the market rate and the natural rate rising at the same time. There, the impossibility of covering all the determinants of investment creates a bias because the equation ignores some of the rise in the natural rate; here there is a bias because the equation ignores some of the changes in the market rate.

It is worth noting, however, that the fact that the cost of capital substantially exceeds the market rate may explain why the interest rate really does have little effect on investment. Assume that the elasticity of investment with respect to the cost of capital is 0.3, that the noninterest cost of capital is 15 percent and that the interest rate is 5 percent. If the interest rate falls to 4 percent, that is, by about 25 percent, investment increases by only about 1.5 percent.

Consider first the effect of liquid asset holdings on investment. A regression of investment on liquid asset holdings is likely to understate this effect for the following reason: Assume that the marginal efficiency of investment falls at a time when the firm's cash flow is greater than its debt service and dividend requirements. If the firm does not have outstanding debt which it can (and wants to) repay, it has little choice but to accumulate liquid assets, since it does not want to invest. A regression interprets these events as an increase in liquid assets causing a decline in investment, instead of as a decline in investment causing an increase in liquid assets. Such instances of *apparent* negative effects of liquid assets on investment are then combined with instances of positive effects and serve to reduce the size of the positive coefficient, or even to make the coefficient negative.

Admittedly, there is also a bias in the opposite direction. In the prosperity phase of the cycle both the marginal efficiency of investment and cash flows are high, and this tends to result in a spurious positive relation, since some of the cash flow may be used to build up liquid assets. This is likely to happen if only because of the need for tax reserves. The fact that the transactions demand is high during the prosperity phase also results in a spurious correlation. But again, the other variables in the investment equation, rather than liquid asset holdings, should pick up most of these effects.

For the household sectors some of the econometric models discussed by Strotz use liquid asset holdings of households as the only monetary variable. But liquid assets of financial institutions may be relevant for the consumption function too, through their effect on consumer credit extension. I do not know whether the authors of these econometric models experimented with business liquid assets and omitted this variable because it was not significant, or whether they ignored it altogether.

I have no evidence on how strong these biases really are. Small errors in intercorrelated independent variables can cause large errors in estimating the significance of a variable. And since the independent variables used in these models are frequently intercorrelated, these biases may be sufficient to invalidate the results of the "t" tests. I do not wish to argue that the existence of these biases necessarily disconfirms any negative findings for monetary variables shown in these models. But I do want to suggest that the results of these models do not necessarily *foreclose* the possibility that monetary factors are important after all.

I would like to suggest an alternative approach which avoids these troubles. Large firms using modern management techniques presumably prepare written estimates of expected yields on investment projects. By going into the files of a sample of firms, one could compare, via both cross-section and time series, changes in the market rate paid by these firms, the natural rate, and the level of investment.[4] Admittedly, such an approach has its own bias. Since presumably only large firms could provide such information, the sample would have to exclude small firms, and it may well be small firms which are most affected by monetary changes.

Turning to Strotz's discussion of Friedman and Meiselman's study, I am surprised that Strotz criticizes it primarily because they use investment as an exogenous variable. Admittedly, the inventory and residential construction components of private investment probably are endogenous. But for the equipment and nonresidential construction components the problem of two-way correlation is mitigated, though not completely eliminated, by the long lag of investment behind its determinants—there is clearly a recursive element here. Friedman and Meiselman's treatment of net exports and of the government deficit as exogenous seems more subject to criticism. In a recent paper Michael DePrano and I have shown that if one removes the endogenous element from the *A* variable, one removes Friedman and Meiselman's conclusion, too. Money and *A* are then of roughly equal importance.[5]

The final problem discussed by Strotz is the lag in the effect of changes in the money stock. The criticisms of Friedman's use of the rate of change are interesting, but they were answered very neatly by Arthur Okun.[6] Okun uses a strict portfolio balance model in which the public wants to hold a constant proportion of its wealth in money balances. The *stock* of money is then related to the *stock* of capital, and the rate of change of money is then related to the rate of change of capital, that is, to investment, and hence to income. Admittedly, in a less rigid portfolio balance model where the interest rate is allowed to determine the optimal ratio of money to capital, the level of the money stock (per unit of transaction) affects interest rates and, in this way, the level of investment and income. Other (partial) defenses of using the rate of change of money have been given by Phillip Cagan and Richard Selden.[7]

Incidentally, it is worth noting, though it appears to have been overlooked by Friedman's critics, that his result does *not* depend upon the use of the rate of change. Many years ago Clark Warburton analyzed the re-

---

[4]Firms may be willing to make such data available, not for current operations, where they may be afraid of "leaks" to their competitors, but for an earlier period. The responsiveness of firms probably varies among industries.

[5]Michael DePrano and Thomas Mayer, "Tests of the Relative Importance of Autonomous Expenditures and Money," *American Economic Review*, Vol. LV (September, 1965), pp. 729–52.

[6]Arthur Okun, "Comment," *Review of Economics and Statistics, Supplement,* Vol. LXV (February, 1963), p. 76.

[7]Phillip Cagan, "A Commentary on Some Current Issues in the Theory of Monetary Policy," in Michael Brennan (ed.), *Patterns of Market Behavior, Essays in Honor of Philip Taft* (Providence, R.I.: Brown University Press, 1965), p. 140; Richard Selden, "Stable Money Growth," in Leland Yaeger (ed.), *In Search of a Monetary Constitution* (Cambridge, Mass.: Harvard University Press, 1962), p. 351.

lation of turning points in money and business cycles by comparing, just as Friedman did, the turning points of the two series.[8] But instead of using the rate of change of money he eliminated the trend from the money series by fitting a least square trend. And this procedure too yielded a long lag. Moreover, this result of a long lag is quite general. Just recently I looked at the available studies of the lag of monetary policy for various countries. I found five independent and complete studies for the United States, two for Canada, and one each for Chile and Brazil. All of these studies, which are based on a wide variety of methods, found long lags. Friedman's hypothesis of a long lag therefore has considerable outside support. However, as I hope to show elsewhere, his belief that the lag is highly variable is less well founded; his method of estimating the variability substantially exaggerates it.

Turning to Minsky's paper, I by and large agree with him. In recent years there has been a shift from emphasizing flows such as income to emphasizing stocks such as balance sheets. Minsky's paper fits well into this trend.

To me, the most interesting part of the paper is his distinction between commercial loan operations and open market operations of banks. For many years a standard criticism of easy money as a countercyclical tool has been the argument that raising bank reserves does little to raise the stock of money. By pushing on a piece of string you can lead the cliché to the water, but you can't make it drink. In recent years this view has been severely damaged in three ways. First, in the postwar period excess reserves have been relatively low and stable. Second, Friedman and Schwartz have raised very severe doubts about the conventional interpretation of the monetary events in the thirties, and third, Brunner and Meltzer, as well as Teigen, have shown that there is a stable supply function of money.[9] But even if banks stay fully loaned up in the face of aggressive easy money policy, such a policy may still fail if the unwillingness of banks to pile up excess liquidity indirectly causes other sectors to do so. Minsky suggests that this is likely to happen if banks undertake open market operations rather than commercial loan operations.

Hence, the argument about the ineffectiveness of an aggressive easy money policy is shifted from the question of whether it is possible to induce the money stock to grow to the question of the effect of the growth of the money stock on velocity. Recent studies of the demand function

---

[8] Clark Warburton, "The Theory of Turning Points in Business Fluctuations," *Quarterly Journal of Economics* (November, 1950), pp. 525–49.

[9] Milton Friedman and Anna Schwartz, *A Monetary History of the United States, 1867–1960* (Princeton, N.J.: Princeton University Press, 1963); Karl Brunner and Allan Meltzer, "Some Further Investigations of Demand and Supply Functions for Money," *Journal of Finance* (May, 1964), pp. 240–83; Ronald Teigen, "Demand and Supply Functions for Money in the United States," *Econometrica* (October, 1964), pp. 476–509.

for money leave room for optimism here but do not compel it. It should be noted, however, that the problem is more severe than Minsky suggests. Suppose that banks undertake commercial loan operations. This too will have some of the effects of open market operations on velocity. Some of the firms obtaining bank loans are firms which otherwise would have financed their outlays by running down their liquid assets or by borrowing on the open market.

Commercial loan operations and open market operations, therefore, have a different effect on velocity only insofar as the receipt of bank loans does not discourage borrowers from reducing their liquid assets or from borrowing elsewhere. The extent to which commercial loan operations and open market operations do have a different effect on velocity is therefore an empirical matter. My guess is that there is a substantial difference, but this is merely a guess. It would be extremely worthwhile to obtain a thorough empirical investigation of this matter and of the related "oozing chain" problem. This would be relevant not only to the magnitude of the effect of monetary policy but also to the problem of the length of the lag. It should be possible to approach this problem by using the "flow of funds" data.

In conclusion, I have two minor points. I am somewhat uneasy about the emphasis Minsky places on the difference between inside and outside money. Granted that the ratio of inside to outside money affects lenders' willingness to assume risks, many other things do this, too. It is yet to be seen whether the difference between inside and outside money should be singled out for so much attention. Finally, one point on the interpretation of Keynes. Does the money market really adjust rapidly? Surely one of the determinants of L_2 is the public's expectation that interest rates will return to their "normal" level, a point, incidentally, on which Meiselman's work on the determinants of the long term rate neatly supports and supplements Keynes' intuition. What prevents long-term rates from falling enough to restore full employment is, at least in part, the *slow* adaptation of the money market. Though this market quickly reaches an equilibrium, it is only a short-period equilibrium and not a full equilibrium.

DISCUSSION

Strotz and Minsky on Monetary Variables and Aggregate Demand

David Meiselman

I shall devote the major portion of my comments to Strotz's paper. I shall also have several observations on the Minsky paper.

The Strotz survey impresses me as a very professional, well-made effort which has successfully surveyed and summarized much useful material. Although I usually share the justifiably widespread dislike for long papers, in this case I wish Strotz's fine critique were longer, because it seems to me that he would have done well to have covered more of the empirical studies of the past several years, a period of much technical and substantive progress in the empirical investigation of macrophenomena. For example, I regret that Strotz's survey does not encompass several recent and important studies which, in contrast with earlier work, appear to show that the rate of interest "matters" in private investment spending. Among the leading examples concluding that interest rates influence private spending are the works on the determinants of business fixed investment of Frank de Leeuw,[1] Dale Jorgensen,[2] Fred Hammer,[3] and Yehuda Grunfeld,[4] and the work on housing and consumer durables of Dick Muth and others in the Harberger volume, *The Demand for Durable Goods*.[5] Also, I wish Strotz had evaluated the role of monetary variables, or the lack of

[1]Frank de Leeuw, "The Demand for Capital Goods by Manufacturers—Study of Quarterly Time Series," *Econometrica*, XXXI (July, 1962), pp. 407–23.

[2]Dale W. Jorgensen, "Capital Theory and Investment Behavior," *America Economic Review, Papers and Proceedings,* 1963.

[3]Fred Hammer, *Demand for Physical Capital, The Application of a Wealth Model* (Englewood Cliffs, N.J.: Prentice-Hall, Inc., 1964).

[4]Yehuda Grunfeld, "The Determinants of Corporate Investment," in Arnold C. Harberger (ed.), *The Demand for Durable Goods* (Chicago: University of Chicago Press, 1960), pp. 211–66.

[5]Richard F. Muth, "The Demand for Non-Farm Housing," in Harberger (ed.), *op. cit.*, pp. 29–96.

them, in the kinds of models prepared by Suits[6] and others—some of which are essentially concerned with forecasting, rather than with scientific prediction—as well as the work in progress on the SSRC model; or, important single and simultaneous-equations studies of the demand for, and supply of, money, which I shall list later; or, the series of studies under way for some years at Yale.

Regarding the simultaneous-equations literature that Professor Strotz surveys—much of which now is, or ought to be, of greater interest to the historian of doctrine than to the economist more directly concerned with advancing our understanding of substantive problems currently at issue—there seem to be several patterns in the models. The demand for money is a function of income, maybe prices, generally some rate of interest—typically the short-term rate—and the demand for money is often divided between household and business demands. The money stock somehow sneaks in, but it is largely whatever the central bank wishes. Alternatively, the stock of money is exogenous, or sometimes endogenous, but more frequently there is no money supply mechanism or supply function—which may not be a crucial omission, because the quantity of money really doesn't make very much difference anyway.

What may make a difference are several essentially banking variables that many "practical men" slavishly believe important,[7] such as free reserves, or several other variants of the intellectually defunct Riefler free reserve theory. These somehow strongly influence, perhaps even rigidly fix, short-term rates. In turn, short-term rates may, but then they may not, affect long term rates, because of shifting[8] between short- and long-term markets, and long-term rates are asserted to be the important interest rates influencing spending. Short-term rates may, but then they may not, influence some portfolio decisions about liquid assets, and we are all presumed to know what "liquid" means, even though each of us probably has his own favored definition of the vague and ill-defined, but widely used term.[9]

I have serious doubts about most of the equations and the implied hypotheses of the models. Moreover, I fail to see how resorting to more complex models containing additional variables and equations, which themselves contain additional measurement and specification errors, can dependably be counted on to correct the deficiencies of the less complex models. And, because additional variables typically are not added and

---

[6]Daniel B. Suits, "Forecasting and Analysis with an Econometric Model," *American Economic Review,* LII (March, 1962), pp. 104–32.

[7]See J. M. Keynes, *The General Theory of Employment, Interest and Money* (New York: Harcourt, Brace & World, Inc., 1936), pp. 383–84.

[8]Or, as Minsky more picturesquely and viscerally terms it, "oozing."

[9]For a detailed listing and critique of many of the most popular definitions of "liquidity," see Arthur Broida, *Liquidity As a Variable in Monetary Analysis* (Ph. D. dissertation, University of Chicago, 1963).

evaluated systematically, nor are alternative models forced to compete with each other, it is difficult to know whether additional complexity adds more explanatory power by improving predictions of aggregate income and/or by widening the range of substantive implications or merely that further complexity and elaboration obscure matters by blunting Occam's razor. Complexity for its own sake is hardly a virtue.

Regarding specific deficiencies of some elements in the models, I submit that the evidence about the free reserve theory widely used in the models is so overwhelming and so contradictory to it that we ought not to take some of these equations seriously, even though good fits and high correlations for them are reported. In addition, other recent work on the relationship between short- and long-term markets also indicates that these models are deficient here too.[10] Free market short-term rates are an element determining free reserves, or excess legal reserves, not vice versa. Many of these models have the chain of causation completely reversed, as did Riefler, and the models generally seem to go along with a doctrine that is clearly so wrong, where the errors have been so well established by Meigs,[11] Brunner and Meltzer,[12] and others, that it has become somewhat tiresome to keep repeating why this is so.[13]

There are other problems about the rate of interest in these and related models, as well as much of the Minsky paper, where the rate of interest is essentially the "monetary" variable affecting aggregate expenditure. (Incidentally, I wish Strotz had defined the terms in the title of his paper, especially with regard to what a monetary variable is, or had more closely distinguished between monetary and credit variables.) I take very strong exception to the view that the impact of central bank actions is appropriately measured by interest rates, which, in practice, have come to be taken as the nominal market rates of discount on a few varieties of fixed money value *debts*. Money can be exchanged for many items of wealth. Indeed,

---

[10]See D. Meiselman, *The Term Structure of Interest Rates* (Englewood Cliffs, N.J.: Prentice-Hall, Inc., 1962); and R. Kessel, *The Cyclical Behavior of the Term Structure of Interest Rates* (Princeton, N.J.: Princeton University Press, 1965).

[11]See A. James Meigs, *Free Reserves and the Money Supply* (Chicago: University of Chicago Press, 1962).

[12]See K. Brunner and A. Meltzer, "The Federal Reserves' Attachment to the Free Reserve Concept" (A Staff Analysis submitted to the Subcommittee on Domestic Finance of the Committee on Banking and Currency, U.S. House of Representatives, May 7, 1964).

[13]Under the free reserve theory, how is one to interpret the impact of a rise in the discount rate? On the one hand, the rise is typically viewed by all schools of thought as tending to move in the direction of monetary and credit stringency. On the other hand, because the costs of this one source of bank funds have risen, commercial banks will tend to make less use of the discount window. Free reserves are defined as the difference between excess legal reserves and gross member banks' borrowing from the central bank. Thus, the decline in these borrowings and the tightening of money and credit resulting from the fall in total banks' reserves, bank credit, and so forth, *ceteris paribus,* will tend to be associated with a rise in free reserves!

many students of monetary phenomena point to what is essentially the ease with which money can be exchanged for other assets—low transactions costs—as the crucial element distinguishing money from other assets. Yet the view that the intent of monetary policy is indicated by interest rates, which seems to be the prevailing orthodoxy, stems from highly restrictive and special empirical presumptions that money is exchanged only for debt instruments and that, as a matter of descriptive reality, the sequence of events linking money and income leads successively from money to nominal interest rates to investment expenditures and income to induced expenditures on consumer goods and perhaps on capital goods too.

Thus, adjustment of disequilibrium between desired and actual cash balances initially disturbs only the "bond" market, *never* the fact that money buys other items such as goods or services or equities. In other words, money affects the financial sector of the economy—one of many factors doing so—and the financial sector may affect the "real" sector. Moreover, this view, which confuses money and credit, also presumes that price expectations have no role in determining bond yields, which follows if the elasticity of price level expectations is zero, which is to say that people's expectations of future prices *never* change.

Perhaps there is some merit to it, but it still remains to be seen whether it is useful to dichotomize the economy into the "financial" and "nonfinancial" sectors for purposes of investigating monetary phenomena. However, it seems to me that in practice the statistical results of many of these investigations have been strongly biased toward zero because of a wide range of specification errors.

Even if, in fact, the route between money and income depended on the intervening credit market and investment expenditure domains, it is by no means clear that the interest rates and expenditure categories generally specified in these models are the correct ones. There are many rates of discount linking many different varieties of income and service streams to their respective capital sources, not merely the nominal yields on a small range of claims, data for which happen to be conveniently available. In addition, the distinction between business and household capital and between nonhuman and human capital may easily be overdrawn, too. Thus, trying to trace the effects of monetary change through several interest rates and several classes of producer durable expenditures is likely to result in "left-out" interest rate, asset, and expenditure variables, and hence to bias the results toward zero.

Regarding the role of the central bank and the banking system in determining rates on bonds, bills, commercial paper, and the like, it is clear that, when income is constant, these rates can and do change for many reasons independent of what the banking system is concurrently doing. Bankers are important transactors in these markets, but they are by no means the only ones, and all transactors can shift among existing classes of assets, so that rates need not respond to central bank disturbances or income alone.

Of course, some of these rates may respond to central bank actions, but with a more complex dynamic than the usual Keynesian models presume. For example, it seems to me that an open market operation initially lowers some interest rates, especially on money market instruments. But, once we move away from the initial impact, and the additional money and the lower rates generate more spending, we usually set into motion changes that are likely to cause rates to rise above where they started in the first place. More spending tends to raise prices, which will tend to drive up nominal interest rates because of revisions of price level expectations. As more spending increases employment and output in the short run, factor proportions typically change in the direction of making output more labor intensive and capital extensive, therefore raising the productivity of capital, which also tends to drive up real rates too.

If this analysis is correct,[14] and I believe it is, how are we to interpret the interest rate variables in the context of the usual liquidity preference or free reserve theories of interest rates and solve the implied identification problem? Since changes in the stock of money, in effect, influence both the supply of, and demand for, credit instruments, it is quite incorrect to interpret interest rates solely as a reflection of monetary ease or stringency, or the impact of monetary change on aggregate demand.

Interest rates of 30 to 60 percent in Brazil certainly do not indicate a restrictive monetary policy in that inflation-ridden country. Nor can we interpret the fact that interest rates in 1933 were below those of 1929 as indicative of an expansionary monetary policy during that sad period.

After the critique of simultaneous-equation systems, the Strotz survey moves on to a discussion of some of the single equation links between money and business activity. Before commenting on this section, I must again note that some very important studies have been omitted, not the least among them being the two papers of Latané[15] and several of the Brunner-Meltzer[16] papers, written jointly or separately, on velocity, the demand for money, and the supply of money. In the same intellectual

---

[14]For a more detailed analysis of these issues see D. Meiselman, "Bond Yields and the Price Level: The Gibson Paradox Regained," in D. Carson (ed.), *Banking and Monetary Studies* (Homewood, Illinois: Richard D. Irwin, Inc., 1963), and D. Meiselman, "Money, Factor Proportions and the Real Cycle," *Journal of Political Economy* (forthcoming).

[15]Henry A. Latané, "Cash Balances and the Interest Rate—A Pragmatic Approach," *Review of Economics and Statistics,* XXXVI (September, 1954), pp. 456–64, and "Income Velocity and Interest Rates—A Pragmatic Approach," *Review of Economics and Statistics,* XLII (November, 1960), pp. 445–49.

[16]Karl Brunner and Allan H. Meltzer, "Predicting Velocity: Implications for Theory and Policy," *Journal of Finance,* XVIII (May, 1963), pp. 319–54.

tradition are two papers by Teigen[17] and by Zellner:[18] Teigen's on simultaneous-equations estimates of the supply and the demand for money, and Zellner's on liquid assets and the consumption function, which have appeared recently in that journal with the gray cover, printed in Holland, and available in the United States with a long and variable lag.

Models are theories, but it is not always clear that the theories, especially simultaneous-equations models, are being tested in the sense that the substantive assertions have been subject to tests capable of refuting the hypotheses, even though estimates of various sorts have been rammed through the computer and high R^2*s obtained.* In this connection, I think Strotz's caveat about some of the hazards in the use of lagged variables is well taken, especially when there is autocorrelation in the residuals, a situation we are likely to find when, as in much postwar experience, everything seems to be drifting secularly with relatively minor cyclical variability. Also, are computer outputs the only relevant data for testing hypotheses?

Regarding the studies Strotz does survey, first, I wish to agree with much of Strotz's comments on the Friedman-Meiselman paper.[19] In fact, some of these very issues have been pointed up more clearly than in our original paper in our exchange with Donald Hester in the November, 1964, *Review of Economics and Statistics*[20] and in our exchange with Ando and Modigliani and with DePrano and Mayer which appears in the September, 1965, issue of the *American Economic Review.*[21]

However, I disagree with him on his appraisal of the usefulness of the exercise. The way to improve our knowledge is to establish validated hypotheses subject to change as improvements occur. To know whether an improvement has taken place it is necessary to compare competing hypotheses. If we do not compare competing hypotheses and, in effect, run

---

[17]Ronald L. Teigen, "Demand and Supply Functions for Money in the United States: Some Structural Estimates," *Econometrica,* XXXII (October, 1964), pp. 476–509.

[18]A. Zellner, "The Short-Run Consumption Function," *Econometrica,* XXV (October, 1957), pp. 552–66. See also A. Zellner, D. S. Huang, and L. C. Chav, "Further Analysis of the Short-Run Consumption Function with Emphasis on the Rate of Liquid Assets," *Econometrica,* XXXIII (July, 1965), pp. 571–81.

[19]Milton Friedman and David Meiselman, "The Relative Stability of Monetary Velocity and the Investment Multiplier in the United States, 1897–1958," in *Stabilization Policies* (Englewood Cliffs, N.J.: Prentice-Hall, Inc., 1963).

[20]See Donald D. Hester, "Keynes and the Quantity Theory: A Comment on the Friedman-Meiselman CMC Paper"; M. Friedman and D. Meiselman, "Reply to Donald Hester"; and Hester's "Rejoinder," *Review of Economics and Statistics,* November, 1964.

[21]Albert Ando and Franco Modigliani, "The Relative Stability of Monetary Velocity and the Investment Multiplier"; Michael DePrano and Thomas Mayer, "Tests of the Relative Importance of Autonomous Expenditures and Money"; M. Friedman and D. Meiselman, "Reply to Ando and Modigliani and to DePrano and Mayer"; and Rejoinders of Ando and Modigliani and of DePrano and Mayer, *American Economic Review,* September, 1965.

tests of the null hypotheses, where an R^2 rated as greater than zero is taken as a positive finding, we implicitly admit that we start with complete ignorance and have no a priori knowledge. It should be an embarrassment to the economics profession that, as we have seen, the complex empirical macromodels of the sort Strotz has surveyed tell us virtually nothing, even after almost 30 years have passed since the *General Theory*. The tests that Friedman and I ran were admittedly rudimentary, but if this step-by-step job had been started 25 years ago we would have been much further advanced today. As I view it, our work *did* establish something about the substance of simple models, which also happened to be widely used ones, and against which we can evaluate the performance of more complex models. At the very least, we can say something when these simple models are used. More than that, our study pointed up many problems somehow covered up in the mad rush to the computer, or to the navel. From here on out, future work faces the task of improving on the performance of the simple models we used.

Regarding Strotz's discussion of our method for selecting variables such as autonomous expenditures, however, I am troubled by his view that perhaps casual empiricism might have made more sense, given the problems of reaching even a tentative conclusion regarding what are autonomous expenditures for purposes of the original paper. It would seem to be a very strong indictment of the theory itself if this is the best we can do to isolate the expenditures that are supposed to be the driving force for determining the level of income. Indeed, this very problem comes through most clearly in the exchanges with our critics. I note that whereas our critics asserted that our measure of autonomous expenditures was unsatisfactory because our methods were faulty, we concluded that nobody had improved upon our admittedly unsatisfactory methods and that the theory itself is at fault.

So it rests, at least for this round.

Finally, it is interesting to contrast the Kareken-Solow[22] conclusions on the lag of monetary policy with the more recent work of Brunner and Meltzer. Whereas Kareken and Solow report an "inside recognition and decision lag" by the Fed of something like three months, as I read them, Brunner and Meltzer claim that the inside recognition lag is essentially zero, as is the lag between recognition and action, but that the lag between recognition and *effective* action is essentially infinite. Strotz reports that Kareken and Solow are very cautious in drawing any firm conclusion. Of course, Brunner and Meltzer have no such timidity about drawing conclusions.

---

[22]Albert Ando, E. Cary Brown, Robert M. Solow, and John Kareken, "Lags in Fiscal and Monetary Policy," *Stabilization Policies* (Englewood Cliffs, N.J.: Prentice-Hall, Inc., 1963).

I want to repeat that Strotz has written a constructive and interesting, but incomplete, survey. I know you all join me in looking forward to the final product.

Finally, regarding the Minsky paper, he has made generous use of the stock-flow capital stock adjustment model which is rapidly becoming a standard part of our apparatus. I find myself in general agreement with this approach. Within this framework, I wish Minsky had considered human capital and household capital in addition to the housing and business capital he did treat. Perhaps he might then have derived more consumption (personal consumption expenditures) response to monetary change.

Although many of us, perhaps most of us these days, go along with the general outlines of the analysis of the wealth adjustment process, I find it difficult to agree with Minsky's conclusion that "the open market path between money and activity is slippery and mucky." Perhaps it is, but I wish Minsky had cited the evidence for this flaccid conclusion. In addition, Minsky's other substantively empty boxes[23] force me to await more systematic empirical study.

[23]Which he filled with carrots, chickens, eggs, milk, cream, and the like.

EFFECTS OF MONETARY POLICY, III: CRITERIA FOR THE CONDUCT OF MONETARY POLICY—THE IMPLICATIONS OF RECENT RESEARCH

CRITERIA FOR THE CONDUCT OF MONETARY POLICY— THE IMPLICATIONS OF RECENT RESEARCH; FOR THE FEDERAL RESERVE:

Daniel H. Brill

I must begin this paper with the classic meeting gambit of disavowing the title as it appears on the program. It would be unfortunate to view this session as a boxing match, with the Federal Reserve in one corner and academia in the other. We're not *inherently* opposed, you know, and I've spent some years trying to find and further areas of common interest. I hope the final version of the program will present this as a dialogue, not a debate.

But more important, the title of the session is incorrect in billing me as speaking for the Federal Reserve. This is not just the usual disclaimer most institutions require in fear of being discredited by the public utterances of their employees. Unfortunately, I *know* I don't speak for the Federal Reserve on the subject of criteria for the conduct of monetary policy. There are a few empathetic souls who go part of the way with me, but the agreement is partial. I wouldn't want to tar them with all of the views I shall express, and the range of dissent within the System staff extends unto polar positions.[1] So I must be accepted today as just another mone-

[1]In absolving my colleagues and principals from the sins committed herein, I want at the same time to express my indebtedness to Lyle Gramley of the Federal Reserve Board's staff, whose contributions to this paper warrant recognition of at least coauthorship—if only he were in complete agreement with all of the strategy and conclusions.

tary economist, not in any way an official spokesman for the monetary authority.

While I'm slipping away from the constraint of the printed title of this session, let me go one small step further. Given the flood of research findings that happily have been emerging in recent years, I don't pretend to have absorbed all of the important contributions, particularly those in the unpublished doctoral dissertations academics hide in order to keep slugging me from behind. Moreover, many of the research reports presented to this group arrived too late—as usual—to be assimilated. So there will be major gaps in my presentation. The only consolation is that I came to learn, as well as to expound.

Turning to what is left of the assigned topic, it is apparent that the thrust of most recent research on policy criteria has been in elucidating the monetary process—on how policy actions are transmitted to the real world and with what intensity and timing. This is the area to which I will address the bulk of my remarks. But I cannot forbear expressing some dissatisfaction with this allocation of research efforts. In focusing on the policy transmission process, we have tended to leave untouched, or at least inadequately explored, fundamental issues relating to the objectives and appropriate scope of monetary policy. We have found it easy to agree on simple generalities, such as the proposition that social goals are multiple (or that there are multiple operating proxies for a single social welfare goal) and that there is an assortment of the economic policy tools available to government in achieving its goals. But where is the accepted specification of the social utility function policy makers must satisfy? Where are the tests of the compatibility among multiple goals? Where are the cost/benefit analyses to help policy makers evaluate alternative targets and alternative economic weapons systems?

To my knowledge, such studies are few and far between, and the conclusions reached rarely satisfy operating constraints. With apologies to my hosts, I must confess that I have found few useful answers advanced at this meeting. Professor Hildebrand, in his paper assessing the price stability/full employment dilemma,[2] offers little advice to the policymaker, other than prayer and moderation, and this in a context of despair suggesting that neither is likely to be effective. On the other hand, Professor Smith, in assessing whether the growth in private debt should be of concern to policy makers,[3] is determinedly optimistic, but it seems to me almost equally nonoperational. He jumps from a special case to a general conclusion that no one would probably want to dispute but which is likely

[2]George H. Hildebrand, "Structural Unemployment and Cost-Push Inflation in the United States", above, pp. 15–29.

[3]Warren L. Smith, "Is the Growth of Private Debt a Cause for Concern?" above, pp. 73–98.

to be irrelevant at most times when private debt is expanding rapidly. Aren't the policy problems different—and more difficult—when the total fiscal-monetary mix must deal with a fully employed economy? And can policy makers afford to dismiss the "credit quality" problem with the assertion that lenders "can presumably be depended upon to police lending practices in an appropriate way?" Such faith in the market economy is admirable, but it badly needs to be supported by more evidence before a policy maker can shrug off statutory responsibilities.

It is some progress, of course, to be able to divine what answers policy makers have in fact given to some of the questions of goals and tools in the absence of adequate professional guidance. I refer here to studies proposing to derive the implicit preference function of the monetary authority, such as that reported on at this meeting by my former colleague John Wood.[4] I believe it potentially a more useful approach than interviewing everyone in the central bank, from the charwoman to the chairman, as to his or her attachment to particular goals or tools. But I must warn John that interviewing the Federal Reserve *Bulletin* to determine the price variable in the Fed's utility function is just as futile. He would have been better advised, I believe, to have substituted the price variable —if any—he thinks compatible with other targets. And of course it's disappointing that he winds up unable to distinguish between the Fed's aspirations and the Fed's assessment of its powers.

However, my principal criticism of his investigation—and of the Johnson-Dewald predecessor[5]—is personal. I'm not sure that I really relish being the subject of public psychoanalysis, instructive as it may ultimately be to the patient. And I'm not sure that I welcome being considered *all* that stable and endogenous. I can see disquieting portents of technological unemployment as a result; it's just as uncomfortable to be automated out of existence by John Wood's computer as it is by Milton Friedman's slide rule.

On the assumption that the monetary authorities will likely stay around for a while, let's turn to the subject of its principal business and what it should be learning from current research. This research might be considered as directed toward answering three kinds of questions: (1) What are the effects of central bank actions on financial variables? (2) What is the impact of financial variables on decisions to spend for goods and services? (3) What financial variables should the central bank and its critics observe in guiding and evaluating the contribution of monetary policy to aggregate expenditures and income? Research directed toward

---

[4]John H. Wood, "A Model of Federal Reserve Behavior", above, pp. 135–66.

[5]William G. Dewald and Harry G. Johnson, "An Objective Analysis of the Objectives of American Monetary Policy, 1952–61," in Dean Carson (ed.), *Banking and Monetary Studies* (Homewood, Illinois: Richard D. Irwin, Inc., 1963).

the last question is, of course, the most directly concerned with the subject of this afternoon's meeting, but it is inevitable that answers to this last question will be contingent upon answers to the first two.

THEORIES OF THE MONETARY PROCESS

Monetary research has made progress recently in resolving the long-standing doctrinal dispute regarding the channels through which central bank actions communicate themselves to spending decisions. The core of the dispute revolves around the question of whether central bank actions affect spending decisions through their influence on prices and yields of financial assets—and on nonprice terms of credit—or whether the influence on spending is communicated through changes in the stock of money. The issue is fundamental, for it involves the very nature of how a central bank should be conceived—as a monetary or a credit agency—and how it could accomplish its objectives.

The interchange of views between neo-Keynesians, on the one hand, and quantity theorists, on the other, suggests that monetary economists appear to be approaching a reconciliation on this score—at least at a very high level of abstraction. As a minimum, some of the false issues which divided monetary economists into warring camps are being exposed, and the more important substantive issues are coming to the fore.

At the theoretical level, almost everyone now supports some version of a portfolio-balance approach to the demand for money and other assets—an approach in which stocks of assets play an important role, an approach in which all financial assets are potential substitutes for one another and for real assets.

Everyone also seems to agree, in principle, that analysis of central bank actions entails tracing out the implications of swaps of debt instruments between the public and the monetary system, and that these swaps affect spending decisions only if they initially alter prices and yields of financial assets, and thereby generate substitution between real and financial assets in the portfolios of investors.

The significance of agreement at this level of abstraction in terms of criteria for conducting and evaluating central bank policies depends importantly on the nature of the demand for money. Milton Friedman's views, in this regard, represent a polar position of professional opinion.

Friedman's restatement of the quantity theory of money gave it a more solid analytic substructure than had been characteristic of the classical quantity theory.[6] His theoretical reformulation was, by any standards, a

[6]Milton Friedman, "The Quantity Theory of Money—A Restatement," *Studies in the Quantity Theory of Money* (Chicago: University of Chicago Press, 1956), and "The Demand for Money: Some Theoretical and Empirical Results," *Journal of Political Economy*, August, 1959.

thing of beauty, but his empirical findings were potentially of considerably greater interest for central bank policy making.

Friedman argued that real per capita money demand was a stable function of real per capita *permanent* income. Recognition of the positive association between money demand and permanent income, he argued, makes it unnecessary to explain cyclical fluctuations in velocity by reference to the effect of interest rates on money demand, as miguided Keynesians are inclined to do. Variations in measured velocity over the cycle are mainly a reflection of the relative movements of permanent and measured income—empirically, the interest rate on market securities seems to play an essentially insignificant role in the demand for money.

The room for discretionary monetary policy decisions in Friedman's world is thus rather narrowly proscribed. All the central bank has to do is make projections of population growth and productivity trends to deduce the expansion in money balances consistent with full employment and stable prices. Since no one in his right mind would attempt to make precise annual estimates of productivity gains anyway, the prescription for central banking is to set the gears of the monetary machinery, using long-run trends in population and real output as guidelines, and then sit back and relax. It need not concern itself unduly with how monetary processes work. Nor should it worry about such grubby details as the interest elasticity of investment spending, or the stability of the investment demand function, or the size of the deficit in the federal budget, since (unless the money supply simultaneously is altered) they have no bearing on the level of income. In particular, the central bank should never, never worry about prevailing market rates of interest, which may give confusing signals about the direction and magnitude of policy actions. A careful control on the growth of money holdings suffices to insure the desired rate of expansion in money income.

The alleged close and stable relation between money demand and permanent income which Friedman discovered by studying time series extending back over most of our recorded economic history seems to have gotten out of kilter, however, in the postwar years. The real per capita money stock (defined to include time deposits at commercial banks, as Friedman defines it) *declined* almost continuously throughout the first decade and a half of the postwar period. Now I know Friedman thinks there are long lags between policy actions and their effects on spending, but I think he said the average lag was about 16 *months,* not 15 *years.* Accordingly, one encounters rather serious difficulties in explaining—in Friedman's terms of reference—why the U.S. economy was not in a state of almost complete economic collapse by 1960.

But generating a plausible explanation of why the first decade and a half of the postwar period does not fit a prewar model is not enough. For in the past four to five years the real money stock per capita has begun to increase again—somewhat more rapidly than real current income per head and, presumably, more rapidly than permanent income per head. Thus, an explanation must not only cover the peculiar relation between real income and the money stock in the first 15 years after World War II but must also account for the recent reversion to something close to the prewar pattern of growth that Friedman has focused upon. Friedman would surely find this task within his capabilities, but one might forgive policy makers for some skepticism about the value of a relationship that has served so poorly in the past two decades.

Friedman's model predicts poorly in the postwar period largely, I think, because it grossly underestimates the role of interest rates as a factor influencing the demand for money. An impressive number of empirical studies undertaken during recent years—including those of Brunner and Meltzer, de Leeuw, and Teigen, to name a few—have found that interest rates on money substitutes play a prominent role in the public's money demand function. Estimates of the interest elasticity of money demand are by no means firm at this point, but the evidence clearly indicates that central bankers cannot formulate policy on the assumption that money, however defined, is unique.

THE SIGNIFICANCE OF INTEREST-ELASTIC MONEY DEMAND

The significance for the conduct and evaluation of monetary policy of dropping the assumption that money demand is almost completely interest inelastic deserves more careful attention than it has been given in recent research. What I have to say on this score is certainly not new, but it bears repeating.

First, consider its implications for the use of the money stock as a policy guide. Interest elasticity of the public's demand for money breaks the tight linkage between the stock of money and money income. It permits fluctuations in propensities to spend, given the money stock, to influence equilibrium income as well as interest rates; it also allows fiscal policies to alter the level of aggregate expenditures for goods and services, quite apart from their influence on the stock of money.

The degree of financial restraint or stimulus imposed on the economic system, accordingly, is no longer reflected in any simple way by variations in the money stock. To illustrate, expansionary fiscal policies—as Brunner and Meltzer emphasize in their paper here[7]—tend to generate both increased income and rising interest rates on market securities, given a constant money stock. Interest-elastic money demand permits income to rise, although part of the fiscal stimulus is lost because rising interest rates impose additional financial restraints on spending.

In this example, the additional financial restraint is, by assumption,

---

[7]Karl Brunner and Allan H. Meltzer, "The Meaning of Monetary Indicators", above, pp. 187–217.

not the result of an overt central bank action to reduce the stock of money but the by-product of an expansionary fiscal measure. What Brunner and Meltzer are saying in their paper, I think, is that we ought not to give credit or blame to the central bank for the additional financial restraint in this instance—the gold star goes to the Treasury, not to the central bank. The central bank gets the gold star only when its overt actions—not its inaction—are the source of change in credit conditions.

But I am not particularly bothered by how the gold stars are distributed. What does concern me is that this reward is not what a central bank should be striving for in the conduct of its day-to-day policy operations. Central bankers should not be concerned merely with whether their overt actions, in isolation, are adding to or detracting from the degree of financial restraint or ease imposed on the private economy. Rather, they must decide, in the light of what they know about supply and demand conditions in the private economy, whether the degree of fiscal and financial restraint or ease imposed by overall governmental policies is appropriate. The ultimate test of monetary policy is not the state of financial variables; rather it is the reaction of real variables to the sum of fiscal, debt management, and monetary policies.

It is at this juncture that the central bank needs guidance in evaluating its own contribution by observing the behavior of financial variables. If a need for action has been determined, some way must be found to gauge how much action is enough. Monetary policy can, and does, move rapidly and usually in small amounts that are reversible if proven incorrect or if underlying conditions change. But even with the most sensitive of observing mechanisms, the feedback of information from markets for goods and services is often delayed too long. Does the response of the stock of money to policy actions tell us what we need to know?

The agreement mentioned earlier that we seem to be reaching at the theoretical level has something to say about this question. Once we recognize that central bank actions influence spending decisions through their impact on prices and yields of financial assets, it becomes evident that the money stock serves as a useful short-run guide to the effects of overt policy actions only to the extent that it serves as a proxy for the effects of policy in credit markets.

Certainly this has not been the case in recent years. Recent research, moreover, seems to point to the conclusion that changes in the stock of money are *not* related in any simple way to changes in either policy instruments or financial market conditions. Econometric studies increasingly have come to treat the money stock as an endogenous variable of the whole economic system. The Teigen and de Leeuw models of the financial markets perhaps come to mind immediately, but Brunner and Meltzer (in their paper at this meeting) also view the money stock as endogenously determined.

An important question at issue here is whether public decisions have much influence on the money stock, given specified values of the instrument variables over which the central bank has complete control—such as the quantity of securities in the Federal Reserve portfolio, the discount rate, required reserve ratios, and so on. Brunner and Meltzer argue that the public has little power to alter the nominal money stock, which they define to exclude time deposits.

Other research, however, does not seem to support this view. Hendershott of the Board's staff has tried to estimate the extent of variation in the stock of money ascribable to forces other than policy instruments—he finds that it is extremely high. Chase at Brookings and Gramley of the Board's staff, drawing on the de Leeuw model, contend that the behavior of banks in setting rates on time deposits within the limits imposed by Regulation Q has an important bearing on the public's money holdings, and that substitution between time deposits and market securities during the 1950s tended to generate procyclical variation in money balances, especially around turning points of economic activity.

One of the most difficult problems we face in trying to interpret rates of change in bank assets and liabilities, it seems to me, relates to a problem about which our present knowledge is extremely small—the significance of variations in rates on bank time deposits. Suppose, for example, that banks increase the rates they pay on time deposits. If money and time deposits are substitutes, the public's demand for money is reduced. A decline in the stock of money—or, in a dynamic context, a reduced growth rate of money balances—is essential if the posture of monetary policy is to remain unchanged. But if time deposits substitute for financial assets other than money, an unchanged posture of policy also requires an increase in the growth rate of total bank assets and liabilities—and hence in the Friedman definition of money. We have faced this kind of problem repeatedly in the past eight years, especially following periods of change in Regulation Q. And we must be prepared to face it in the future, since there is every reason to believe that bank rates on negotiable C.D.s will vary markedly over the course of the business cycle.

Thus, to formulate policy in the context of a banking system that competes aggressively for time deposits, we need to know much more than we presently do about substitutability between time deposits and other assets. Are we to believe Feige's conclusions that time deposits and demand balances are very weak substitutes for each other, possibly not substitutes at all? Or do we believe Friedman and Meiselman, who regard currency, demand deposits, and time deposits as almost perfect substitutes? Or do we accept de Leeuw's results, which suggest that time deposits and demand balances substitute for one another, but far from perfectly, in financial asset portfolios? Until we get better answers to these questions than we presently have, the significance of variations in the stock of money and in time deposits will remain highly ambiguous.

Earlier I noted that if the demand for money were extremely interest inelastic, as Friedman thinks it is, the task of predicting income, given the money stock, would be an easy one. The second question I want to explore concerning the meaning of an interest-elastic demand for money is this: Is there any simple way we can predict income, given the money stock, if we are *not* willing to accept Friedman's empirical judgments on the insensitivity of money demand to interest rates? In particular, is there any way to predict the effects of monetary policy actions on income without going through the maddeningly difficult job of determining how investment and consumption interact with policy variables, such as interest rates?

I would have thought not, at least before Brunner and Meltzer proposed a simple solution.[8] Their proposal involved estimating velocity, and then generating income estimates by multiplying the estimated velocity by known values or estimates of the money stock.

The Brunner-Meltzer method, as they propounded it, did not seem to entail the assumption of completely interest-inelastic money demand. In fact, their empirical estimates of the demand for money suggest a statistically significant elasticity. Nor was there any mention of the need to estimate investment and consumption functions. On the contrary, Brunner and Meltzer argued, macromodels based on flow relations are less useful for prediction than models based on stocks, because demand and supply functions for stocks are more stable.

The Brunner-Meltzer method for circumventing these difficulties entails concentration on stable demand and supply functions for assets that are of central importance to economic activity, such as the demand and supply functions for money. These two functions, it is alleged, have been shown to be stable under intensive empirical testing. Having established this to their own satisfaction, they then move to an estimation of a velocity function whose arguments are those entering the public's money demand function.

This velocity function is used to explain and indeed predict the level of income, without the need for an explanation of the determination of interest rates.

Thus, the Brunner-Meltzer procedure converts a theory of money demand directly into a theory of income determination. Under what circumstances is such a transformation valid?

If a Federal Reserve devil may be permitted to quote scripture, we can do no better than to turn to Friedman, who considered this question

[8]Karl Brunner and Allan H. Meltzer, "Predicting Velocity: Implications for Theory and Policy," *Journal of Finance,* May, 1963.

long ago. He stated that in order to convert an equation expressing income as the product of a velocity function and a known money stock into a theory of income determination (and here I quote):

> ". . . it is necessary to suppose either that the demand for money is highly inelastic with respect to the variables in [velocity] or that all these variables are taken as rigid and fixed."[9]

To state the matter bluntly, velocity must be assumed to be constant, for all practical purposes. But Brunner and Meltzer's theory and their own empirical results deny this. Constant velocity is not consistent with their theory, which postulates an interest-elastic demand for money. Velocity depends, as does money demand, on rates of interest.

Clearly then, what is needed for forecasting is a technique for predicting interest rates. The problem does not arise when measuring differences in past periods between actual velocity and velocity estimated by their equation. But what of the relation between money stocks and future income in which, as a policy adviser, I am understandably interested? Brunner and Meltzer get around this problem by plugging lagged values of the variables into their money demand equation. This strikes me as a sorry expedient, lacking any logic of its own and apparently violating their own logic, since I can find no provision for a lagged response of money demand to interest rates in the short-run model they advance.

But one could forgive logical lapses if accuracy of the results was sufficiently high to satisfy the "crude empiricists" of Washington. An examination of the results, described as fitting "reasonably well"—while missing the only recession in the period covered and achieving errors of up to $22 billion in *annual* forecasts—doesn't suggest that the approach has much operational value. I'm afraid that any policy maker would be justified in asking for tighter logic and better results before giving up "seat of the pants" judgment. Thus, another touted shortcut seems to lead to a blind alley.

There is a way out of this difficulty, but it involves getting down to the serious business of estimating expenditure responses—category by category—to changes in interest rates and other financial variables. Difficult though it is, this problem cannot be shrugged off.

PROGRESS

This is not to sound as though a new world remains to be discovered. It has been discovered, and is already being exploited. And the rate of progress is at least mildly encouraging.

One direction that recent empirical research has taken is the develop-

[9] Milton Friedman, *op. cit.*, p. 15.

ment of somewhat more disaggregated macromodels. The de Leeuw model probably represents as detailed a macrospecification of financial markets as is presently available. We have found the model very useful internally for estimating public demands for money and time deposits, given alternative assumptions about income and interest rate levels; we have also obtained from it preliminary estimates of short-run interest rate effects of specified changes in central bank instrument variables under given income and expenditure conditions.

Useful though it is, the de Leeuw model does not come close to the degree of disaggregation for which I yearn as a basis in formulating policy advice. I confess to being a "large model man"—a *very* large model —even though many of my colleagues keep warning me that the complexity of model building and running increases by the nth power of the number of equations. Perhaps I am hoping for too much—indeed, perhaps further empirical research will demonstrate that the kind of detailed model to which I aspire is inoperable or would add little, if anything, to our understanding of monetary processes. But I shall continue to hold and defend my prejudices in this regard until I am clearly shown to be wrong—or the computer breaks down.

Another and equally encouraging direction that recent research has taken is in emphasizing the development and testing of relationships at the micro level, using cross-section data for individual economic units. The large number of projects under way that are designed to crack the problem of asset selection at commercial banks through the application of more refined portfolio balance models is perhaps the best illustration. I don't know whether to be heartened or dismayed, though, by the number of dissertations on "commercial bank portfolio behavior."

But significant gaps still remain between what we need to know and what we do know about financial market behavior. For example, financial economists have been talking for a long time about credit availability—the nonprice rationing of loans—at banks and other institutional lenders, and its role in the transmission of monetary policy. As one looks back at what was done during the 1950s, he cannot help but be a little shocked to discover that there was hardly any empirical work done on the question, and—worse still—that a good many of the theories masquerading under the title of credit availability did not discuss the question at all. They treated the reasons for shifts in bank loan supply functions, not the question of price versus nonprice rationing of loanable funds.

More recently, there has been considerable progress in developing the theory of credit availability and some progress in orienting data collection programs to illuminate the problem. I take it that some agreement is beginning to develop that risk-avoiding behavior of lenders makes nonprice rationing consistent with profit maximization under conditions of uncertainty—a conclusion that was not obvious a few years ago. The empirical work in this area has, however, been minimal and what I've seen is not sufficiently convincing to shake my prejudices.

Also, there remains a number of questions to clear up on the money demand function. There are still several different theoretical approaches to the demand for money vying for contention, and the appropriate empirical representation of the function remains in doubt. This is not to deny the progress in recent years. There seems little doubt that interest rates are empirically important in the demand function, and we seem to agree that a wealth or permanent income variable helps to explain money holdings. But there remains some question about the appropriate interest rate or rates to include, and the role of current income, along with wealth or permanent income, as an argument in the function. The question of lags in the adjustment of money holdings, explored by de Leeuw in his paper here,[10] certainly is one deserving extensive further examination. Needless to say, in the face of these uncertainties, a statement that we already possess accurate estimates of the parameters of the money demand function would seem premature.

I am worried about still another kind of uncertainty. A few years ago, banks first began issuing C.D.s, which have become an extremely popular short-term investment among nonfinancial corporations and other large investors. One would expect that this innovation might have reduced the demand for money and resulted also in a decrease in the elasticity of money demand with respect to rates of interest on market securities. Some exploratory work in our own shop seems to confirm these expectations.

What bothers me is that this is but one of a series of developments that have occurred repeatedly throughout our economic history that must have affected money-holding attitudes enormously. Some examples would include: the introduction of deposit insurance, the advent of regulated interest rates on bank deposits, the extension of credit facilities to sectors of the economy which previously had minimal access to borrowed funds, variations in economic conditions which alternately give rise to extraordinary demands for liquidity on some occasions and to flights from fixed-value claims on others, and so on. How often we will have to patch up our empirical estimates to take account of such developments is a serious question.

RESEARCH ON THE IMPACT OF FINANCIAL VARIABLES ON SPENDING

While our knowledge of financial market responses to policy is weak, it exceeds by a considerable margin our knowledge of the relation between financial variables and expenditures for goods and services. This

[10] Frank de Leeuw, "The Demand for Money: Speed of Adjustment, Interest Rates, and Wealth", above, pp. 167–86.

is particularly chilling, because we have witnessed, in the past decade or so, a growing belief among financial economists (and also among their counterparts in the nonfinancial field) that financial variables play a significant role in spending decisions. Professional opinion has wobbled all over the map on this issue in the past, so it is never wise to jump on a current bandwagon of opinion too quickly. But I do think that the present trend results in large measure from empirical studies pointing to the conclusion that financial variables do matter. And I am not speaking here merely about the Friedman-Meiselman CMC paper, but also about the increasing number of studies suggesting that investment spending is responsive to interest rates. But the studies are suggestive rather than definitive, the results seem to vary too widely in response to methodological differences, and they comprehend as yet only a limited area of investment. The joint SSRC-Federal Reserve effort to study the impact of financial variables on expenditures—category by category—has only scratched the surface.

CONCLUSION

I'm afraid that these ill-tempered remarks about the state of our art reveal the frustrations I feel as one burdened with the task of persuading policy makers that economists can contribute some useful guidance in assessing the needs for and consequences of policy actions. There are times when I find it difficult to convince myself on this score.

But perhaps it is just as well that the logic of, or evidence underlying, apparently simple solutions is beginning to crumble. We may then be better prepared to come to grips with the hard task of formulating and quantifying the great many relationships involved in moving from the instrument variables to the target variables of policy. To quote from an expert in another discipline:

> Man likes to simplify things, to find single causes, to find an order in nature that corresponds with an orderly arrangement of ideas in his own mind. This surely is one of the great drives of thought leading to many of the great ideas of philosophy, religion and science. But nature is also frightfully complex, perhaps too complex ever to be 'understood' through the processes of our limited brains—and our fondness for single causes has probably got us in trouble more often than it has helped us.[11]

In assessing the state of the art to be rather primitive and the progress toward sophistication slow, I do not mean to pin the blame on academia or to exculpate policy makers and their staffs. *Mea culpa! Mea culpa!* And perhaps more deserving of censure, since we should be in the forefront of exploration and testing. If we haven't been in first place, then, like Avis Rent-a-Car, we'll be trying harder.

[11]Marston Bates, *The Forest and the Sea.*

CRITERIA FOR THE CONDUCT OF MONETARY POLICY—THE IMPLICATIONS OF RECENT RESEARCH; FOR ACADEMIA:*

G. L. Bach

When I accepted this assignment, I envisaged a succinct summary, complete with footnotes, of the major research advances in monetary economics during the past decade, with a running assessment of their implications for current policy. But more mature reflection told me that the end of three long summer days of learned discussion of the entire vista of monetary economics is no time to undertake still another summary, no matter how well intentioned. So instead I ask you to play a little game which may, happily, lead to the conclusions which the arrangers of the program had in mind. And it may be more fun.

Imagine that we have three composite economists, or groups of economists, charged with advising the Federal Reserve Board on current policy. One, whom we shall call 1960s man, reflects the wisdom that might be found in a group of a dozen or so of the leading monetary economists of our time. The second—1950s man—reflects the composite views of a comparable group of perhaps a decade ago. The third—1920s man—brings the accumulated wisdom of a comparable group in the late 1920s. The question is: What will be the advice of each? How much, if any, better will the advice of 1960s man be? And, if better, what has been the role of recent monetary research?

Let me specify just a few rules of the game. While the policy problem is simply the one confronting us today, each man must prescribe in terms

*I am indebted to my former colleagues at Carnegie Tech, Michael Lovell and Allan Meltzer, for helpful criticisms and suggestions. To understand the text, it is important to note that it was written in the summer of 1965.

of the analytical tools and the kinds of information that would have been available to him in his day. Thus, 1920s man can have only the kinds of factual information and the kinds of theory that he had at his disposal in the 1920s in offering his prescription. Second, what we are after is a kind of consensus that might emerge if we put a group of leading monetary economists together for each of the periods. For example, 1920s man might reflect the consensus of economists Irving Fisher, Edwin Kemmerer, Randolph Burgess, and Winfield Riefler from the U.S., and (since their works were so dominant in the 1920s) Hawtrey, Hayek, Keynes, and Robertson from abroad.[1] The group consensus behind 1950s man might include such economists as Arthur Burns, Milton Friedman, Alvin Hansen, Paul Samuelson, James Tobin, J. H. Williams, and, from abroad, J. R. Hicks and R. S. Sayers. For 1960s man, since the work has been largely done for me, I propose to take simply the groups of consultants to the Federal Reserve and the Treasury which have both met within the last six months and have, to a considerable degree, expressed themselves on precisely the question raised; some of you are here.

Each of you may wish to change the groups whose consensus our three mythical men are to reflect. My goal is not to pick the most influential monetary economists of the times, nor the ten best, but merely a highly influential, broadly representative group of the best in the profession at each of the periods. And, since of course there would be wide divergencies of views within each group, the game requires that we accept only those views which command a reasonable consensus within the group. Of course each of you may have your favorite economist (including yourself), who obviously knows the right thing to do much better than any of the others in the group, certainly better than the consensus of the group as a whole. But this is not a fair test of the state of knowledge as reflected by the leaders of the profession. What they cannot agree on for policy may be as interesting as what they can.

Lastly, to help organize the comparison, I propose that we imagine what each man might say under three broad headings: (1) the major goals, or basic objectives, of monetary policy; (2) the analysis of the situation to which policy is being applied; and (3) the mechanism which links Federal Reserve action to the real variables of the economy—all ending up with his recommendations on current policy.

I. 1920s MAN

It is difficult to know just how 1920s man would state the major goals of monetary policy. Much of his focus was on the money markets per se, and the details of their operation. W. R. Burgess wrote that "The most useful guides for policy have been shown by experience to be:

---

[1]It is interesting that my 1920s group includes two American economists employed full time as Federal Reserve Staff members, while neither of the later groups does.

(*a*) Changes in the volume of credit.
(*b*) Changes in the way credit is being used.
(*c*) Conditions of business.
(*d*) Prices.
(*e*) Gold movements and international conditions."

While this list is not unlike one we might find around the Federal Reserve today, the absence of full employment per se as a goal is striking (though one might say this was subsumed under "business conditions"). Other American economists might have placed more stress on "meeting the needs of trade." Fisher and the British economists stressed heavily a stable, or even gently falling, price level; and certainly close conformity of monetary conditions to international gold movements would have been given high priority. Lastly, concern with "business conditions" was essentially concern with avoiding crises and ensuing deflationary spirals; our leading economists were little inclined to challenge the notion that by and large, over the long pull, the system would tend to move back toward high employment under its own momentum.

How would 1920s man, with his range of economic information, size up the present economic situation as a basis for monetary policy advice? To make policy judgments, we must decide where we are now in relation to our goals, and, if indeed there is some lag in the effects of monetary policy, where we will be over the relevant months ahead in the absence of policy changes. Make your own guess. Mine is that he would say we are in a rousing boom, with substantial inflation, and with an alarming balance of payments deficit and loss of gold. Perhaps the main thing to remember is that he would have much less information to go on—no general unemployment statistics, no information on the national expenditure flows, no systematic information on inventories or capital investment, no current data on the money stock; indeed, mainly only rough indexes of prices and measures of industrial and farm production, data on interest rates and bank credit, and data on gold and central banks here and abroad. The most stylish forecasting device was the Harvard A-B-C indicators. Without unemployment statistics and with all the present signs of strong prosperity, including especially the recent rapid increase in total bank credit, it is hard to imagine that 1920s man would see anything other than the upper stages of a cyclical upswing, especially with the current upswing so long continued. And while it is hard to guess how he would assess the large gold stock we still have, it is not hard to imagine his reaction to the massive gold outflow over the past few years, untempered, one must remember, by presently-available indexes of unit labor costs in different countries and the like, and unilluminated by detailed data on current and capital account movements.

How about the monetary mechanism, connecting possible Federal Reserve actions with the variables to be ultimately affected? 1920s man probably would have first considered rediscount rate changes, then moral suasion, and then open market operations. His understanding of the basic mechanics connecting these moves with changes in bank reserves and the "money market" was good, even by our modern standards; concern with monetary and money market mechanics was the center of American monetary research. But his connection between "money market conditions" and the real economy now seems to us crude. Drastically oversimplifying, restrictive policy would have raised interest rates and decreased the availability of credit, pulling down prices and checking the boom, probably without inducing much unemployment, certainly not more than temporarily since wages would soon fall with other prices. Tighter money would also rectify the balance of payments deficit by reducing our prices relative to those abroad and reducing our imports relative to our exports. The disagreement among the experts would be considerable on precisely how these results would come about, and on the likely size and timing of them after any given policy action—a not unfamiliar situation today. While monetary policy could certainly influence business cycle fluctuations, its main effects in the long run would be on prices, since by and large Say's Law prevailed, and wages and other costs, with varying lags, would adjust with other prices.

So much for this attempt to piece together how today's world might look to 1920s man. What would his policy advice be? Put together your own conclusions. My guess is that, given primary focus on the money markets, on price stability, on checking the international gold drain, and on avoiding an "inflationary boom" which would almost inevitably bring about an ensuing collapse, he would prescribe tighter money—probably a rise in the discount rate and some open market sales, coupled with moral suasion to restrain speculation in the stock market and excessive loans to marginal borrowers elsewhere. Does it have a familiar ring? Remember that the modern sophisticated talk about the rise in the Consumer Price Index being due to its inadequate measurement of quality probably wouldn't have entered his head, though he might have been perplexed about the increasing spread between consumer and wholesale prices. Remember, too, his basic faith in the self-adjusting nature of the system to produce reasonably full employment over the long pull. And remember his acceptance of "the bigger the boom, the bigger the bust" as a crude approximation to reality. Above all, remember his lack of statistics on many of the wide range of variables we now use in analyzing the economic situation and its prospects.[2]

---

[2]A rough count shows about 38 pages of statistics per issue of the *Federal Reserve Bulletin* in 1928, compared to about 100 in 1965; the page comparison in the *Survey of Current Business* is much closer for the two years. But the striking difference to us is more in the big areas not covered at all in the 1920s, especially the flows of spending which make up aggregate demand.

II. 1950s MAN

By the 1950s, the goals recommended for monetary policy had undergone a substantial change. Maintenance of full employment had moved to the top of the list, with price stability important but much less so than to 1920s man. Our 1950s man would show little concern with gold and the international balance of payments; for a quarter century it had scarcely entered our thinking on monetary policy, except to generate a mild worry about our excess gold stock. Faster growth had come on the scene as a goal, but not as a clearly accepted one for monetary policy. For economists directly connected with the Fed, the state of the money markets continued a prime objective in its own right, but to a lesser extent for the academic economists in our panel.

Thirty years had seen an enormous improvement in the quantity and quality of information on the behavior of the economic system. 1950s man would have detailed national accounts; elaborate statistics on employment and unemployment, on production of major commodities and groups, on prices, and on the balance of payments; plus greatly enlarged monetary statistics of all sorts. While econometric forecasting techniques were just coming on the scene, the National Bureau's lead-lag analysis had replaced the old Harvard A-B-C indicators, and elaborate forecasting procedures built around the GNP accounts were widely used. At the risk of oversimplifying, it is probably safe to say that 1950s man's analysis of the current state of economic activity would not be far from 1960s man's, though his analysis of the possible stabilizing effect of governmental fiscal policies would have to do without the concept of the full-employment surplus and without much faith in public acceptance of stabilizing fiscal policies. Since 1950s man would be worried about the lags in monetary policy, he would feel a strong need to forecast economic activity, beyond the general concern with the state of the business cycle felt by 1920s man. Being an honest economist, he would admit sadly that his forecasting prowess was limited. However, built-in budget flexibility, plus monetary reforms like the FDIC and amortization arrangements on most debts, might reasonably lead him to have increased faith in a reasonably stable economy. What would he forecast for the year ahead? I don't see much reason to suppose it would be very different from 1960s man's.

What of the monetary mechanism? Here 1950s man has much theory and empirical research to draw on not available three decades earlier. On the linkage between Federal Reserve action and financial variables, this research had added little, and indeed there was little interest in the problem—although clear recognition of the powerful role of open market operations and reserve requirement changes had arrived. On the linkage between monetary-financial variables and the real economy, 1950s man has an elaborate theoretical mechanism, largely Keynesian, which leads him to minimize the probable effect of moderate changes in interest rates. He is little interested in the quantity of money per se; interest rates and possibly credit rationing are the critical monetary variables for influencing the real economy. But he has learned two vitally important lessons. First, wages and other costs are not as flexible downward as 1920s man was inclined to believe, so contraction of aggregate demand is likely to produce substantial unemployment along with, or as a substitute for, falling prices. Second, unemployment may persist from lack of aggregate demand. Thus monetary steps to help produce high employment must be concerned with long-run aggregate demand, real wage, and employment problems, as well as with merely leveling off the business cycle so as to avoid inflationary booms and ensuing collapses.

What would 1950s man prescribe as monetary policy for today? Again, the game is for you to guess. Mine is that, first, he would say it really doesn't matter much one way or the other; it's fiscal policy that counts. Second, with his overwhelming concern for high employment (reflecting strong memories of the 1930s), with little concern for a possible gold shortage, and with increased sophistication on the weaknesses of the rising price indexes as accurate measures of "actual" price changes, my guess is he would prescribe moderately easier money, with open market purchases. It is hard to say how much concern he might feel for the gently rising consumer price index; problems of postwar inflation would be still fresh in his mind, but his worry over our international competitive position would be much weaker than for 1960s man. He might think up fancy schemes like "the twist" to compromise domestic and international objectives; we can only speculate, but it seems not implausible, if indeed he thought such monetary manipulations worthwhile at all.

III. 1960s MAN

Now we come to today, when each of you can be his own 1960s man and feel appropriately superior to the crude consensus I try to describe. On goals, the picture has become more complex. While high employment clearly dominates stable prices, 1960s man suspects that the Phillips curve is real (though vague), and he is faced with a trade-off at somewhere around present levels of employment and prices; and he doesn't want to see prices rise much faster than they are now without an appreciable offset in improved employment. Perhaps more important, the international scene has come to bulk large again for monetary policy. While 1960s man says that the monetary authorities are badly overemphasizing the importance of gold drains today, he is by no means ready to advise them to forget about gold and the international scene in making monetary policy. He urges the authorities to play down their stress on "money market conditions," much more so than either of his predecessors, but again he's not ready to tell them to neglect this consideration entirely. Faster growth is a significant objective per se, and it leads him to worry about any policies which imply higher interest rates.

On where we are in relation to our goals, he has a sophisticated view, which you all know. We are in high-level, moderately satisfactory prosperity—but with employment not quite high enough. The prosperity looks surprisingly well balanced, though a shade shaky. Built-in flexibility looks promising and strong, and government fiscal policy over the year or so ahead looks promising. The banking and financial reforms that 1950s man had to count on are still here. Being an honest man, 1960s man also admits he cannot forecast very well, but he feels a little more comfortable about it for a year or so ahead than his predecessors had a right to do. He understands about the "fiscal drag" and the full employment surplus. All things considered, he is a shade worried on the domestic front about a mild shortage of aggregate demand for the year ahead.

What about the monetary mechanism? Messrs. Meigs, Dewald, Brunner, and Meltzer have undermined free reserves as a satisfactory guide to short-run open market operations, and our understanding of the links in the mechanism continues to grow. Interest in monetary mechanics has revived, and that in the linkage between monetary-financial variables and the real economy has snowballed.

But, alas, 1960s man has a badly split personality on just how the monetary-financial variables are connected with prices and real variables. The quantity of money looks more important in its own right than it did to 1950s man, but still interest rates and availability of credit appear to have a direct and understandable impact on investment and hence on prices, output, and employment. 1960s man talks in a sophisticated way about the twist and about a mix of monetary and fiscal policy to attain multiple goals. But that schizophrenia won't go away. He has a regression result to support almost every plausible hypothesis about the effects of monetary policy on prices and real variables, and it's very hard for him to make up his mind which regression to pay attention to when. For example, he has a wide range of respectable estimates on the responsiveness of private investment to interest rate changes, and on the importance of money (or liquid assets) in the consumption function; and he is thoroughly uncertain on the length of the lag in the effects of monetary policy.

Looking toward the international scene, he thinks that higher short-term rates relative to those abroad are critical for holding fluid short-term balances here; but he's much less convinced that long rates are important—and indeed it is possible that higher long rates might make the capital accounts worse through their indirect effect in lowering profit rates here relative to those abroad. He knows a lot more than his two predecessors, but sometimes he's not sure whether this makes him a better policy adviser, or just more knowledgeable about how uncertain he is about the channels of monetary policy and about the size and timing of the effects to be expected from different policy measures.

What does he prescribe? The answer is: monetary policy about the way it has been over the past year or two, but shading toward the easier side. If he didn't have to worry about the international scene, he would plump harder on the easy side, using primarily open market operations. But with the economy strong today and probably only a shade weak over the half-year ahead (which he suspects may be about the relevant lag period for monetary policy), and with his nagging worry about the possible effects of a gold scare and a run on the dollar, he's reluctant to advise the Fed to move much toward ease. He tells the authorities to work the twist as hard as they can, but he's skeptical that much more can be done than has already been accomplished. When he's asked what is the precise measure of how much easier money should be, he develops acute schizophrenia, vacillating between interest rates (long and/or short) and different measures of the money stock. While he knows of sophisticated research about the demand for money by households and business firms, he's far from clear just what this means for monetary policy, even if the desired level of aggregate demand is clear and especially when we confront the problem of multiple goals.

IV. WHAT HAS RECENT MONETARY RESEARCH CONTRIBUTED TO POLICY?

What are the lessons of this little game? In particular, what has been the contribution of recent monetary research to the (hopefully) superior performance of 1960s man?

If my answers in the preceding paragraphs are crudely right, the following general conclusions may be appropriate, but do the assessment on your own answers for the three mythical men. As I read the record, the biggest reasons for the improved performance of 1960s man are three:

1. From the Great Depression itself, and from research on it, we have learned that a major contraction of aggregate demand is perhaps the worst of all macroeconomic disasters. The prescription for monetary policy is clear, that priority is to be given to avoiding such cumulative contractions, through assuring adequate liquidity to the system if mass contraction begins and through positive measures to reverse it. We have learned that, given all the downward rigidities in the system, especially in wages, such contraction produces primarily lower incomes and employment.

2. Our goal system has changed substantially. High employment and rising output per se have become the dominant goals for 1960s man, though by no means exclusive goals. It would be a mistake to say that

we have simply had a shift in our value system, unrelated to economic research. On the contrary, one of the big reasons for this shift in goals is that research has illuminated the costs of unemployment and slack demand. It has showed that the effects of moderately rising price levels are much less drastic, in their impact on output and employment and in their inequities, than we had previously thought. Both theoretical and empirical research on the balance of payments and its interactions with domestic economic activity have illuminated the effects of monetary policies aimed at adjusting to balance of payments disequilibria; and they have generally led us to conclude that promptly correcting such payments disequilibria and drains on international reserves deserve a lower place in the goal structure than we had previously thought.[3]

3. Our third big advantage over 1920s man is that we know so much more about what is going on in the economy and where we are. To try to prescribe monetary (or fiscal) policy with the range of empirical information available to 1920s man would be a difficult, and ego-shredding, experience today. While such talk is not stylish among modern economists, our indebtedness to the fact-gatherers—the federal government, the National Bureau, and the others—appears great in explaining our superiority over the policy prescriptions of 1920s man.

These look to be the three big bases for our superiority as monetary policy advisers. Let me now add two others of lesser weight.

4. I suspect that most economists would add the discovery of fiscal policy, and its lessons against trying to accomplish too much with monetary policy alone in an uncoordinated way. Give this the weight you will. Clearly the discovery of fiscal policy is of major importance; whether it deserves major billing for improving our power to prescribe good monetary policy is another matter. And indeed, it is not clear that 1960s man is free from some schizophrenia as to what we really know about the relative powers of monetary and fiscal policy, and their interactions.

5. What of the role of monetary research itself, in the specific sense of investigations of the monetary mechanism, the linkages between monetary-financial and real variables, and the like, which have been the main subjects of this conference? Strikingly, none of the three big advances above rests heavily on monetary research in this narrower sense. Is it true that monetary research per se has added little to our policy-advising powers?

My initial instinct was that it has indeed greatly increased our understanding of the way the economy operates, and of the channels and effects

---

[3]One might argue that it is not the business of economists to prescribe value systems, and that it is not surprising that economists do not agree on value systems. But the above argument suggests that economists can have, and have had, great influence on policy makers' goal systems through clarifying and even quantifying the costs and benefits associated with various goals.

of monetary policy. The renaissance of money and monetary research has been an impressive one. We, plus the march of real world events, have reestablished that money matters a good deal. I well remember a meeting of distinguished fiscal-monetary consultants less than five years ago in which almost no one thought it mattered whether a proposed budget deficit was financed by new federal borrowing from the banks or from the nonbank public, even after the problem was specifically raised by a lonely monetary type. This doesn't happen today; monetary policy matters.

But recognizing this, if we put ourselves in the chair of the policy maker, it's not clear that recent monetary research has helped much. We are vastly more sophisticated than 1920s, or even 1950s man about the monetary mechanism and its interaction with the real economy. But to the policy maker who bears responsibility, our new theory and multiple regression results still look disputed and uncertain as foundations for establishing operating policy positions. Clearly monetary research per se has improved our ability—for example, in clarifying the role of free reserves as an immediate target of policy actions, in demonstrating some of the interacting forces determining the money stock, and in reestablishing the important role of money per se as a causal factor in at least many of the big swings. But on most of the day-to-day operating policy decisions, there are still too many conflicting arguments, too much conflicting evidence from recent monetary research, to make them look very reliable as guides to the responsible policy maker, except on the three big propositions suggested above. The lively, though fruitful, disputes of this conference are clear evidence of this lack of consensus. And above all, the real world policy maker ever confronts the problem of multiple goals—without being able to rely on the economist's neat theoretical one-control-for-each-policy-goal solution to the dilemma.

This situation is less discouraging than it may seem, however, if one thinks of the state of other "sciences." As knowledge accumulates, we often first develop consensus on big orders of magnitude, on major contours and relationships, long before we thoroughly understand all the variables and precise interrelationships involved. I think this has been true in many other areas. The biological scientists provide exciting theories and powerful basic research that has changed modern medicine; the use of antibiotics is a vivid example. But the doctor (the clinician who applies knowledge) still finds that medical research falls far short of giving him usable answers on many of his day-to-day decisions. So it is with the monetary policy maker and his economic scientist advisers. We know a lot more, and we can give some powerful advice on some big issues. But we're just not far enough along yet to have very clear answers on many of the day-to-day issues on which the Fed must act.

Conclusion? My personal assessment is that monetary research has made great progress in the past decade. We can give much better monetary policy advice than could 1920s man on the big issues where it matters most—on the need to avoid major deflationary pressure, on the dangers of overrating some of the traditional policy goals, on the needlessness of blindly checking prosperities to avoid depressions. Indeed, we can do more; we can help on many of the smaller issues. But we are still basically in the building stage which will take years, even decades, before we can be confident of our ability to give reliable policy advice on most operating questions, where quantitative, real-time answers are required and where merely looking at directions and at big magnitude changes isn't enough.

Most day-to-day monetary policy actions hinge not on sweeping discussions about big value judgments but on concrete issues like how much a small increase in the bill rate will pull funds from the Euro-dollar market; or how much and how fast would a hundred million dollars of new reserves affect bank lending for business investment in inventories and plant and equipment under today's conditions; or what would be the effect on bank deposits of a .5 percent change in the Regulation Q rate. If we as economists want to influence policy more, we will need to dig more deeply into such dirty "practical" quantitative operating details than has been stylish in recent years. If the Fed and its staff want to make the most of our resources, they could clarify more specifically what questions they consider vital for more effective policy decisions; they could push farther their own analyses of academic advances; and they could stimulate and conduct more active testing and evaluation of competing theories. If they need more or better economists to do these jobs, there is no better time than now. If the authorities need to make better use of the economists they have, continuing academic criticism may provide a useful stimulus.

CONTRIBUTED COMMENTS

Three Views on the Current Expansion

David I. Fand

Several times during the conference the discussion focused on the extent to which monetary and fiscal factors were responsible for the current economic expansion. Generally speaking, three views were developed: a fiscal view, a monetary view, and an eclectic view. The advocates of the fiscal view took the position that the duration and strength of the current expansion—the longest since the Civil War—is largely due to the tax cut of 1964. The monetary advocates, on the other hand, attempted to explain the current expansion in terms of favorable monetary policy. Finally, those upholding an eclectic position view the favorable mix of monetary and fiscal policy as the most telling factor in the expansion. Although this question came up several times and was actively discussed, it was not satisfactorily resolved. In this note we attempt to explore some of the issues.

THE SUBSTITUTABILITY OF MONETARY AND FISCAL POLICY

Everyone would agree that a given level of aggregate demand may be achieved with different combinations of budget and money policies and that at least to this extent there is some substitutability between monetary and fiscal policy.[1] Consequently, if we wish to stimulate the economy at a time when it is operating below capacity, we may do so at least in principle either by monetary means or by fiscal means (tax reduction or expenditure increases). Moreover, the persistence of unemployment and the fact that the economy is operating below capacity does not tell us whether we are being strangled by restrictive budgets or

[1]Quantitative estimates of the number of dollars of monetary action that may be substituted for a fiscal action of given magnitude is a difficult empirical question which has not been explored very much. The recent discussion concerning the relative stability of the money multiplier and autonomous expenditures multiplier may provide some indirect evidence. If either of the multipliers is very stable, it would seem to suggest that the rate of substitution is low, since the models used in deriving these multiplier estimates do not always contain both monetary and fiscal variables. See the discussion between A. Ando and F. Modigliani, M. DePrano and T. Mayer, and M. Friedman and D. Meiselman in *American Economic Review,* September, 1965.

starved by tight money and high interest rates. All we know is that the mix of policy is insufficient to maintain a high employment level of aggregate demand and that either fiscal stimulation (in the form of larger deficits or smaller surpluses) or monetary easing (in the form of increases in the money supply and lower interest rates) will move us toward a high employment level of aggregate demand. Consequently, when we are in a situation requiring a stimulus, the decision to choose monetary action or fiscal action, as well as the choice among fiscal actions, will often be based on additional considerations such as feasibility (a balance of payments deficit may be viewed as limiting the scope for monetary action), effectiveness (given the kind of magnitudes that will be acceptable to the Congress and to the business community, fiscal action may be more powerful), speed (the effectivenes lag—the lag between the taking of an action and the time it has its effect—may be much shorter for a tax cut than for expenditure increases), and value judgments (an expenditure increase may be preferred to tax reduction on the grounds that there is a greater need for public goods than for private goods).

The different views expressed (at the conference) as to the factors responsible for the current expansion cannot be traced to the immediate facts of the upturn that started in August, 1961, or derived from the events since then. For even if we demonstrate that fiscal drag (as measured by the full employment surplus) was an insurmountable barrier and that it alone was preventing us from achieving high employment in the late 1950s, this finding by itself does not mean that when we consider corrective policies we must offset fiscal drag by fiscal action or that we could not offset it by monetary easing; similarly, if an analysis of this period suggested that our difficulties in the late 1950s resulted from high interest or tight money. Stabilization considerations per se do not require that the punishment fit the crime. It may therefore appear that the different assessments of the current expansion rest, implicitly or explicitly, on the considerations (of feasibility, effectiveness, speed, and value judgments) mentioned above. This is undoubtedly true—but it does not appear to be the whole truth or the most interesting part of the truth. It seems to me rather that the different views rest largely on different theories of income determination.

1. The fiscal proponents do not have much confidence in the money multiplier—in the link between money (or its rate of growth) and money income. Instead they place much more emphasis on the relative stability of the consumption function and on the investment (or autonomous expenditure) multiplier. In addition, they can point to a substantial tax cut of approximately $10 billion for individuals and $3 billion for corporations for 1965 as a result of the Revenue Act of 1964.[2] Also, when assessing the

[2]The estimate of $10 billion attempts to measure the reduction in payments. If we restrict ourselves to federal income tax liabilities for individuals, the tax cut would be

impact of monetary policy on the economy, they tend to focus on interest rates rather than changes in the money supply. Since interest rates have been moderately stable since 1961, they conclude that monetary policy has been at most permissive. Accordingly, they see the current expansion primarily as a consequence of the tax cut, with monetary policy in the background as at most a permissive factor.[3]

For an example of the fiscal view we take Okun's recent estimates of the contribution of the tax cut to GNP presented at the 1965 meetings of the American Statistical Association.[4] In his analysis Okun argues that while in principle he would expect significant changes in the cost or availability of credit to have an important influence on business investment,

> in practice, dealing with the period of the last year and a half, I cannot believe that the omission of monetary variables can make a serious difference. By any measure of interest rates or credit conditions I know, there have been no significant monetary changes that would have either stimulated or restrained investment to a major degree.

He does, however, point out that "the maintenance of stable interest rates and stable credit conditions requires monetary action" and that at least to this extent, "monetary policies have made a major contribution to the advance." But in his view, "that contribution is appropriately viewed as permissive rather than causal."

2. The monetary proponents, on the other hand, do not have much confidence in the autonomous expenditure multiplier, but place considerable weight on the link between money and income. Moreover, focusing on money supply, its rate of change, and its variability, they can point to a considerable easing in Fed policy since 1961.[5] They do not, of course, deny that a tax cut may stimulate income, but argue rather that there was sufficient easing in monetary policy since 1961 to account for the expansion. And they also grant that a permanent tax cut may stimulate the economy, especially if it is associated with some easing on the mone-

---

$11.5 billion for 1965. See the excellent discussion of this problem in A. Okun: "Measuring the Impact of the 1964 Tax Reduction," a paper presented at the 1965 meetings of the American Statistical Association. An alternative measure of the tax cut is to estimate the reduction in the full employment surplus. See "Changing Attitudes Toward Fiscal Policy," a statement prepared by Gardner Ackley for the Joint Economic Committee in *Fiscal Policy Issues of the Coming Decade* (Washington, D.C., 1965), pp. 8–9.

[3]We may also list the views of an alternative group who basically subscribe to the fiscal view. These analysts agree that there was some monetary easing in the recent expansion but they go on to argue that the increase in money supply was largely *induced* by the growth in income which in turn reflects the tax cut.

[4]See Okun, *op. cit.*, pp. 14–15.

[5]For some evidence see the table prepared by George Morrison in "The Influence of Money on Economic Activity," a paper presented at the 1965 meetings of the American Statistical Association.

tary side. Finally, while they may on theoretical grounds argue that the tax cut was neither necessary nor sufficient for stimulating increases in employment and output, they may nevertheless concede that it may have been desirable on other grounds.

As representative of the monetary view we may cite the recent article by B. Sprinkel, who summarizes his views as follows:

> Although much emphasis is placed these days on the revolution in fiscal policy, perhaps the most fundamental and most important change has occurred in the monetary policy area. In my opinion monetary policy from 1961 through 1964, which was characterized by a relatively steady 3% growth rate in the money supply, has been largely responsible for the uninterrupted increase in total spending which will soon bring the longest as well as the largest peacetime expansion since the Civil War. This remarkable monetary record has been achieved despite conflicting views both within and outside the Federal Reserve System and despite the serious constraint imposed on monetary policy by the constant B.O.P. threat.[6]

According to this view monetary policy is gauged by the rate of growth in the money supply. This is justified on the ground that it is controllable by the Federal Reserve System and also because "the rate of growth of money supply is closely correlated with changes in total spending in the economy and is consistent with the argument that monetary change is causal." The evidence that total spending is determined essentially by changes in money is based on empirical tests of the quantity theory and the income expenditure theory along the lines of the Friedman-Meiselman study. Additional evidence is also brought in from the experience in other countries.[7] It is also argued that Federal Reserve performance in recent years has been superior because monetary growth has been less volatile and because it has been sufficient to increase spending at an accelerated pace without becoming so rapid as to bring inflation. While Sprinkel does not deny that the tax cut is expansionary, he nevertheless still concludes that recent monetary policy has been largely responsible for the longest (as well as the largest) peacetime economic expansion since the Civil War.

3. Those who take an eclectic position tend to view fiscal policy and

---

[6]See B. Sprinkel: "An Evaluation of Recent Federal Reserve Policy 1961–1964," *Financial Analysts Journal,* August, 1965, p. 6.

[7]Sprinkel in his study of "Relative Economic Growth Rates and Fiscal Monetary Policies," *Journal of Political Economy,* April, 1963, pp. 154–59, reports that for the seven major free market countries of the world, the rank correlation of monetary expansion and spending growth was very high, and that countries with the largest increase in the money supply from 1955–61 had the largest increase in dollar GNP. A similar finding is reported by Anderson who extended this analysis to include a larger number of countries (29) and a longer period of time (1949–61). See P. S. Anderson, "Relative Economic Growth Rates and Fiscal Monetary Policies: A Comment," *Journal of Political Economy,* February, 1965, pp. 74–80.

monetary policy as complementary mechanisms to promote growth and stability. On the basis of our post-Accord experience they also conclude that there may be a time lag of many months before these policies achieve their final effects and that both fiscal and monetary policy are on an equal footing in this regard. In assessing the current expansion, they note that it is fortunate that fiscal policy has a separate effect; for in an era of balance of payments deficits, militant use of credit expansion to restore full employment would not have been politically feasible. In their view, unemployment could not have been brought down from a 7 percent level to its recent 4½ percent level without expansionary fiscal policy.

Prominent among the eclectics is Professor Samuelson, who, after stressing the particular contribution of fiscal policy, also notes that the abandonment of the bills-only doctrine, the adoption of Operation Twist, and the raising of the ceilings on deposit interest set by Regulation Q did enable monetary policy to contribute to the economic expansion. Samuelson points to the "dramatic fact that the long-term interest rate remained low unprecedently long in the current expansion," and suggests that changes in Regulation Q may have resulted in "a willingness of commercial banks to reach out for riskier long-term investments in order to be able to offer high competitive interest rates on new certificates of deposit" —a factor which may have helped to keep down the long-term rate in the current expansion. Finally, in summarizing the impact of these Federal Reserve actions on bank portfolio policies, Samuelson makes the following observation:

> In a sense, one device we have used to stabilize domestic employment in the face of an international deficit has been a contrived deterioration of the quality of credit on a mild scale. It is a paradox that this may be sound social policy.[8]

This therefore leaves us with following questions:

1. In some ways the most appealing view is that the current expansion reflects both fiscal and monetary easing. But, if so, we face the difficult question of determining the relative contribution of each if we are to draw any lessons from our recent experiences.[9]

2. Those who take the fiscal view can account for the current expansion with multiplier values that are reasonable. But they can not completely avoid the question as to whether interest rate movements are the appro-

---

[8]See P. A. Samuelson, "Stabilization Policies in the Contemporary U.S. Economy," above, p. 8.

[9]Patric H. Hendershott in his "Monetary Policy, 1952–1962," a paper presented at the 1964 Econometric meetings, attempts to define more precisely the notion of tight or easy money. He defines a neutral monetary policy "as one that neither offsets nor reinforces the cycle but allows it to run its natural course" and calculates a neutralized money stock. This framework is intended to yield a better measure of Federal Reserve action and, in this way, may provide a basis for estimating the monetary contribution to the expansion.

priate measure of monetary ease—(especially in periods when interest rates do not move uniformly and when they may be responding to changes in the demand for credit).

3. Finally, those who take the monetary view can account for the expansion in terms of money. But this doesn't completely solve the problem, since monetary easing resulting from a fiscal deficit may have a somewhat different effect on aggregate demand from that of an equivalent monetary action brought about through an open market operation.

The Similarity of Quantity Theory and Keynesian Policy Prescriptions in Recent Years*

Paul Wonnacott

The controversy over the relative importance of monetary and fiscal policies has been a dominant theme in economic literature in recent years. The thesis of this note is that, regardless of the theoretical and broader policy significance of this issue, the prescriptions for recent U.S. policy which flow from both theoretical viewpoints are essentially the same. This similarity is a result of the balance of payments restraint within which policy has operated.[1] Specifically, the objective of stimulating aggregate demand has been subject to the limitation that interest rates must not be permitted to fall.[2]

If the quantity theory were strictly valid, the velocity of money would be constant; that is,

$$Y = cM \qquad (1)$$

Thus, money would be the critical policy variable. The implications of the strict quantity theory may be restated in such a way as to sharpen the contrast with Keynesian theory,[3] thus:

$$\frac{\partial Y}{\partial G} = 0 \qquad \text{when } M = \overline{M} \qquad (2)$$

In words, government spending has no influence on aggregate demand as long as the money supply remains constant.

---

*This note was stimulated by the address of Paul Samuelson on *Stabilization Policies in the Contemporary U.S. Economy*, above, pp. 5–8.

[1]Fixed exchange rates are taken as a given. Since both advocacy of and opposition to flexible rates cut across the Keynesian-quantity theory division, this important issue may be omitted.

[2]Or, more precisely, that they must be kept sufficiently high to prevent intolerable strains on the balance of payments.

[3]Whether this very strict formulation is adhered to by any quantity theorists need not be considered here; if the formulation is softened, the conclusions of this note will still follow.

If this represented the way the economy operated, then expansionary policy would depend on an increase in the quantity of money. The obvious way for this quantity to be increased is through open market purchases by the Fed. Such a policy may not, however, be directly undertaken because it would push down interest rates and thus violate the balance of payments restraint. The problem, therefore, is to find some device for creating upward pressures on the interest rate structure to offset the interest rate effects of open market operations.

This may be done through a decrease in taxation or an increase in government spending, which will augment the supply of government securities on the financial markets. All of the increase in government spending (or tax cut) need not be financed through security issues to the public; the restraint is only that interest rates must not be permitted to fall. As long as some fraction (x) of the increase in government spending is financed by issues to the public, the remainder ($1 - x$) may be financed by Federal Reserve purchases, permitting an expansion of the money supply, and therefore an increase in income.

Because the upward pressures on interest rates depend not only on the direct financial requirements of the government but also on the private demands for capital associated with the expanding level of income, the value of x may not easily be determined ahead of time. This, however, creates no insuperable problem: rather than undertaking to buy a given volume of securities, the Federal Reserve may simply buy that volume required to keep yields at the preexisting (or target) rate. The nice precision of monetary policy is, however, lost: even if the value of income velocity (c) is known, the desirable volume of official activity remains uncertain. Monetary policy has in a sense become passive, and the increase in the money supply results indirectly from government deficits; the relationship ($1 - x$) between reserve base expansion and such deficits is of uncertain size.

Keynesian theory rejects (2), above; that is, Keynesians hold that:

$$\frac{\partial Y}{\partial G} > 0 \qquad \text{when } M = \overline{M} \tag{3a}$$

and

$$\frac{\partial Y}{\partial T} < 0 \qquad \text{when } M = \overline{M} \tag{3b}$$

Changes in government spending and taxation become the major instruments for influencing aggregate demand. Monetary policy does not become irrelevant, but is relegated to a secondary role. Moreover, the key monetary variable is seen as the interest rate rather than the quantity of money. Thus, the effects of monetary policy may be shown by:

$$\frac{\partial Y}{\partial r} < 0 \tag{4}$$

In the recent situation, with the desirability of an expansionary policy indicated by the level of unemployment, the appropriate response is straightforward: taxes should be cut or government spending increased. This will directly increase income, and the effects will be augmented through the multiplier process. However, there will be one undesirable side effect if the total government deficit is financed through issues to the public: interest rates will be pushed up, thus tending to slow the growth of income. This effect is not required by the balance of payments restraint, and may be eliminated by Federal Reserve purchases sufficiently great to stabilize interest rates at the preexisting (or target) level. Thus, the policy prescriptions based on Keynesian analysis are in this case similar to those based on the quantity theory.

Although the above contains obvious oversimplifications, it may be taken as a reasonable summary of the policy that has, in fact, been followed. Taxes have been cut, the money supply has increased, and interest rates have been prevented from falling. In spite of the general recognition of this pattern, there has been considerable disagreement as to whether monetary policy or fiscal policy has been responsible for the vigorous expansion of the American economy. This disagreement is not particularly surprising in the light of the differences in the intellectual apparatus of the Keynesian and quantity theorists; in particular, it may be traced to the disagreement as to whether government deficits associated with monetization of government debt should be regarded as "fiscal" or "monetary" policy.

Comment on the de Leeuw Findings on Demand for Money

Harry G. Johnson

The most general, conclusive, and to some economists, surprising of de Leeuw's results is the revelation of the long lag in the adjustment of the quantity of money demanded to the interest rate and scale variables.[1] This finding appears to conflict with much of the established tradition of monetary theory, according to which money possesses in a unique degree the capacity of being readily convertible at small cost into goods or interest-yielding assets, so that one might expect that actual money holdings would be adjusted to desired cash balances with a very short lag. This expectation could, however, very easily be misleading and a result of superficial reasoning.

In the first place, it is necessary to distinguish sharply between the speed and cost with which something different can be done, if one knows what one wants to do, and the speed and cost with which one can acquire the information necessary to determine that one ought to do something different. None of the current theories of demand for money allows adequately for the costs and the time involved in gathering and assimilating the information necessary to take decisions of this kind. The Baumol-Tobin inventory-theoretic approach to the explanation of demand for money derives its appeal from the recognition of the transactions costs of converting money into interest-yielding assets and vice versa, whereas most previous theory ignored transactions costs; but transactions costs are only the most superficially recognizable of the costs involved in in-

[1] I personally was not surprised, since in an earlier study of the demand for money in Canada John Winder and I, using a version of the simple lag model of de Leeuw's equation (2) on which he has greatly improved, found a k of 0.66, implying a weighted average lag of half a year in the adjustment of the Canadian money-to-income ratio to its determinants (the Treasury bill rate, seasonally adjusted, and the average term to maturity of government debt held by the public); see Harry G. Johnson and John W. L. Winder, *Lags in the Effects of Monetary Policy in Canada* (Royal Commission on Banking and Finance Research Study) (Ottawa: The Queen's Printer, 1964). The findings are reported in Harry G. Johnson, *The Canadian Quandary* (Toronto: McGraw-Hill of Canada, 1963), pp. 180–82.

telligent portfolio management, those established by the market for already institutionalized procedures of utilization of market facilities. The costs involved in determining when to utilize the market for the exchange of different types of assets have scarcely been seriously considered.

One might hypothesize that, faced with the costs of acquiring and acting on information about changing conditions in an uncertain world, most asset holders would adopt some set of decision rules according to which their behavior would conform to the same "normal" pattern until its inappropriateness to changing circumstances—signaled by arrival at a portfolio composition that transgressed some threshold—required a reconsideration of the situation from which the "normal" pattern had been derived. At this point a new decision rule would be adopted, aiming either at a restoration of the original desired asset portfolio or at a new portfolio composition adjusted to the changed circumstances. In either case, the consequences would be an observed long lag in adjustment, discontinuities being removed by the dispersion of individual reaction times and changes in decision rules. This behavior pattern would, in its turn, lead to long lags in the adjustment of asset portfolios to changes in economic conditions, quite consistent with both ease of portfolio adjustment as between holdings of cash and holdings of yield-bearing assets and rationality of individual behavior in portfolio management. The long adjustment lag would apply to money holdings as well as to other assets.

Alternatively, and more in conformity with some existing approaches to econometric work on the demand for money and related problems, one might hypothesize that there is a long lag, not in the adjustment of actual money balances to the desired quantities, but in the adjustment of desired quantities to changes in the variables determining desired quantities. Or, one might hypothesize that actual money balances are adjusted instantaneously to desired quantities, but that desired quantities are determined by expected or "permanent" values of the determining variables, these being derived from past values by means of exponentially declining weights. Either hypothesis, as is well known, will generate de Leeuw's estimating equation,[2] as can be verified by expanding it in terms of past values of the variables on which the quantity of money demanded is assumed to depend, as he does in his equation (6). In short, the facility with which asset holders can convert into and out of money really carries no implications about the lag we should expect in the response of changes in money holdings to changes in their determinants, because the lag need not be located at this point in the decision processes of asset holders.

[2]Donald P. Tucker ("Dynamic Income Adjustment to Money Supply Changes," *American Economic Review* [forthcoming]) has derived the interesting conclusion that long lags in the adjustment of demand for money may offset long lags in the adjustment of interest rates and give monetary policy a more immediate control over economic activity than many writers have inferred to be the case from the magnitude of investment lags alone.

A different type of consideration which may help to rationalize the finding of a long lag—which I advance with some hesitancy since I have been unable to think it through fully—concerns the mechanism by which asset holders adjust actual to desired cash balances. Since the desired cash balances are defined in real terms, and the nominal stock of money is fixed by the monetary authority, the adjustment of actual to desired balances must come either through price level changes altering the real value of the money stock or through variations in the variables determining desired balances—broadly speaking, real output and interest rates. It is generally accepted that prices are sticky, and there is much evidence to the effect that the response of output to monetary changes, either on quantity theory lines or through the Keynesian mechanism of interest effects on investment and associated multiplier effects, is also slow; only interest rates are, presumably, very flexible in the short run. Thus the adjustment to changes in the quantity of money would fall initially on interest rates and only subsequently on output and prices, producing the kind of fluctuating adjustment of these variables that de Leeuw predicts from the lag in the adjustment of demand for money. This suggests that, by assuming a single common lag of the demand for money behind its determining variables, the technique used by de Leeuw (and others, including myself) may be picking up and attributing to the demand for money lags which properly belong to other parts of the economic system. The bearing of this point on de Leeuw's findings, however, is somewhat unclear, because he studies the demand for individual components of the money stock, the quantities of which may be altered by conversion into other components without calling into play the adjustment mechanism necessary for the adjustment of real balances as a whole.

Comment on Brunner and Meltzer's "The Meaning of Monetary Indicators"*

Patric H. Hendershott

Brunner and Meltzer argue that most of the indicators of monetary policy usually proposed by economists, for example, the money stock and free reserves, are endogenous variables. Hence, these indicators inaccurately measure current monetary policy:

> . . . their position or rate of change at any time is the result of the joint interaction of the whole system and reflects more than the effect of current monetary policy. Fiscal policies and non-controlled exogenous variables also influence the endogenous indicators. (p. 190).

They go on to say that the adjusted monetary base is exogenous and is the "true" indicator of policy if policy actions are restricted to open market operations (pp. 195–6).[1] They contend, therefore, that the adjusted base is not influenced by either the economic system (income and interest rates) or noncontrolled exogenous variables. In this comment I argue that the adjusted base is influenced by both the economic system and noncontrolled exogenous variables and thus is no better, in principle, than those indicators Brunner and Meltzer reject.

According to Brunner and Meltzer's hypothesis of how the economic system operates (described on pp. 192–4), the adjusted base is exogenous. That is, they *assume* that the adjusted base is not influenced by current income and interest rates. This assumption is not compatible with reality.

*Comments by Lyle Gramley on a draft of this note were helpful.

[1]Brunner and Meltzer have apparently switched from the monetary base to the adjusted monetary base—the base less member bank borrowings—as their indicator of Federal Reserve policy (both indicators are "extended" to include the reserves freed by changes in average reserve requirements and vault cash requirements). Their study for the Patman Subcommittee ("An Alternative Approach to the Monetary Mechanism") that David Meiselman referred to, when commenting on Robert Strotz's paper (p. 328 of Meiselman's comment), as indicating an infinite lag between the Federal Reserve's recognition of the need to act and the taking of effective action was based on an analysis of annual changes in the extended monetary base. (I might add that the long lag cited by Brunner and Meltzer was due almost entirely to the fact that they analyzed annual changes in the series rather than the series itself.)

The adjusted base is identically equal to the sum of the Federal Reserve's portfolio of government securities, the U.S. gold stock, Federal Reserve float, and Treasury currency outstanding, less Treasury cash holdings and deposits (other than those due to member banks) at Federal Reserve banks. Both the U.S. gold stock and Federal Reserve float are influenced by current income; U.S. imports are obviously related to income, and float is related to bank debits which are also positively associated with income. In addition, the U.S. gold stock is influenced by interest rates because the latter affect both U.S. and foreign short-term and long-term international capital flows.

The adjusted base is also influenced by noncontrolled variables whose relationship to current income and interest rates is sufficiently remote to warrant their classification as exogenous. Some factors that influence U.S. gold flows—such as foreign aid, U.S. military expenditures abroad, and foreign business cycles—fall into this category, as do many of the minor components of the adjusted base—Treasury currency outstanding, Treasury cash holdings, and deposits (other than those of member banks) at Federal Reserve banks.

According to Brunner and Meltzer, the "true" indicator of Federal Reserve policy cannot be influenced by either endogenous factors or noncontrolled exogenous variables. This, by definition, would seem to rule out everything (including movements in float, gold, and so forth) except explicit Federal Reserve actions.[2] Thus, in the case where Federal Reserve actions are limited to open market operations, the Federal Reserve's portfolio of government securities must be Brunner and Meltzer's "true" indicator.[3]

[2]One cannot argue that the Federal Reserve simply offsets these "technical factors" without facing the problem that Brunner and Meltzer wish to avoid. That is, if the Federal Reserve also offsets currency movements, then unborrowed reserves becomes the "true" indicator; if movements in borrowed reserves are added to the list, total reserves is the indicator. A few more additions and/or deletions could yield the money stock, free reserves, or even the bill rate as the "true" indicator because the Federal Reserve would then be treating the forces that influence one of these variables as "technical factors," and would be offsetting them.

[3]Of course, the observed values of the "true" indicator must be compared with the desired values, given the expected state of the economy, before the appropriateness of Federal Reserve actions can be assessed.

Rejoinder to Chase and Hendershott

Karl Brunner and Allan H. Meltzer

Chase makes a number of incorrect statements about our paper, and Hendershott argues that because some of the sources of the adjusted monetary base are not exogenous, the adjusted monetary base cannot be exogenous. Most of Chase's arguments do not bear, even remotely, on our paper, and Hendershott's argument involves a non sequitur, so it is important to reply to their criticisms. We will discuss Chase's comments first.

About the only points on which we agree with Chase are (1) that we regarded our paper "as more than an exercise" and (2) that "the idea of developing a quantitative gauge of monetary policy is appealing." To say that the paper is more than an exercise does not suggest that it is a definitive solution to the long-standing problem of measuring the size and direction of current or recent monetary policy operations. Chase chose to ignore our statements that we sought "to open discussion of an issue that is more frequently debated than analyzed," that "our tentative results are not presented as a resolution of the problem," and similar statements that we repeated throughout the text.[1] However, his misinterpretation of our intent is not confined to the issue of whether or not we regard our conclusions as applicable to current policy problems. The subject and purpose of our paper escaped him completely, so that his comments are either irrelevant or wrong. We will point out his main errors after summarizing the "indicator problem."

The problem discussed in our paper can be stated succinctly. (1) Economists have incomplete knowledge about the magnitude and timing of the response of output, the rate of change of prices, and other "goal variables" to monetary policy. (2) Analysis suggests that the response of the "goal variables" occurs after a delay (or lag), and that the lag is variable, not constant. (3) There is no agreement about the appropriate measure (or measures) of the *current* direction of monetary policy. Two

[1]One of us has since organized a conference on the subject of indicators and short-run targets to provide more opportunity for discussion and analysis than is available in our preliminary investigation. The papers prepared for the conference and a summary of the discussion will be published in a forthcoming volume.

commonly used measures—market interest rates and the money supply—frequently move in the same direction, rising in periods of economic expansion and falling in recessions. The two measures provide rather different interpretations about the direction of current or recent policy, since rising money supply is interpreted as an indication of an "easier," and rising interest rates of a "tighter," policy.

We know of only two ways to resolve the long-standing, largely futile and, at times, acrimonious debate about whether changes in interest rates, money supply, bank credit, or some other variable are a more reliable indicator of the current direction of monetary policy. One way eliminates most, if not all, of the problem but requires more information than is available. The other makes use of imperfect and incomplete information to compare the relative errors that are likely to result from the use of endogenous variables as indicators.

A validated, comprehensive, fully identified theory of monetary dynamics would permit economists and policy makers to state future goals and to compute the magnitude of current operations required to achieve those goals. Under these idealized conditions many (but not all) variables could be used to indicate whether the expected effects are being achieved at the expected rate. Preferences for particular indicators would be of no consequence, since the information provided by changes in one indicator is equivalent to the information provided by another, once the appropriate parameters and the observed rates of change are known. If the theory is identified, validated, and comprehensive, each endogenous indicator would give a consistent estimate of the size of future changes in output, employment, and prices.

The contrast between this desirable state of knowledge and current information is suggested by the fact that often we cannot agree about the direction of monetary policy. We lack the means of reconciling one indicator, which is widely interpreted as suggesting that policy will have a contractive influence on output or prices, with another that suggests the opposite. Our paper, therefore, attempted to answer the question: Given our imperfect knowledge, which of the endogenous variables is the least misleading indicator of changes in the direction and magnitude of monetary policy operations?

Chase's first criticism starts with the assumption that "all the elements of equation (A) [our equation (1)] are known." In this case, *all* of the responses of endogenous variables to changes in policy variables are known, and the gain or loss in utility resulting from each policy change is known also. There would be no reason to construct an indicator. The policy problem would be reduced to computing the values of the policy variables that maximize utility. The assumption of complete knowledge removes any connection between his criticism and our analysis.

However, Chase adds the additional assumption that the marginal utility of changes in each endogenous variable is constant. His utility function is linear; ours is not. Again there is no connection between the criticism and the paper. But, after a few additional assumptions, Chase reaches the absurd conclusions that:

> 'Good' policy presumably entails $I > 0$, 'bad' policy entails $I < 0$. Optimal policy requires maximizing u, which entails $I = 0$ . . . .
> (I is the indicator of monetary policy and u is social utility.)

It is either error or a strange ordering relation, indeed, that makes optimal the midpoint between good and bad. Had Chase considered the conclusion that we quote, he would have avoided this error and recognized that it resulted from his own assumptions. Chase's discussion of optimal policy appears to result from a confusion of our analysis with the analysis pioneered by Theil and others. The latter requires detailed knowledge of the trade-offs between social goals. In view of the lack of consensus about specific trade-offs in the social utility function, a main point of our paper is to provide a criteria for judging policy while avoiding a detailed statement of trade-offs.

Chase's second criticism also arises from his concern about the sign of the indicator function. He notes that the index can be rising or falling as a result of open market sales and concludes that "it seems strange to refer to monetary policy that reduces the rate of price increase during inflation as 'easing' merely because it is desirable in terms of social utility." This quotation (and several similar comments) suggest that there is a misunderstanding. The sign of the indicator has no bearing on the issues discussed in the paper. The reason is that the utility function is assumed to be unique only up to a monotone transformation. (See our footnote 4.) The indicator function provides an *ordering* of monetary policy, or a scale by means of which policy actions can be compared. If the utility function involves more than one argument, it must express a consensus about the effect on utility of a trade-off between various goals, as we stated. Moreover, it should be noted that the interpretation of a deflationary effect of policy as "easing" is entirely Chase's notion and is unrelated to our analysis.

The criticisms above are irrelevant because they apply to a paper that we would not consider writing; most of Chase's remaining criticisms are incorrect statements about a paper we might have written, but didn't. These comments are little more than a series of repeated assertions that our conclusions hold only for a model in which raising per capita real income is the only goal of policy and reflect some confusion about the results that would be obtained if the analysis were extended. Although we did not present the results of an analysis in which the price level is taken as the second argument of the utility function, the material in our appendix permits the extension to be made. The specific indicator, $\frac{dQ}{Q}$, that emerges in the case presented as an illustration is also obtained if the social utility function contains both per capita real income and the price level. Chase's conjecture that the values of the partial derivatives of the utility function would have to be known is incorrect. The derivatives of the utility function remain part of the scalar and are, therefore, not needed to construct the indicator.

Chase's final criticism is that none of our conclusions have been established because we compared the endogenous indicators (rates of change of the money supply, of interest rates, and so forth) to the optimal indicator implied by our model, $\frac{dQ}{Q}$. We would not be surprised to find on further extension of our analysis that the particular elasticities that form the weights in the index will change. But it would be surprising to learn that a solution of most systems of equations that connects monetary policy variables to output and the price level would not contain the variables that are manipulated by the policy maker, the principal components of $\frac{dQ}{Q}$.

Nevertheless, it is important to reiterate that the nonconstancy of the scalar $\epsilon(y,B^a)$ (the elasticity of real income with respect to the monetary base) in our indicator function restricts the use of the index. A similar restriction applies when the analysis is extended to the two-goal case. The problem is similar to the familiar "index number problem." The use of the index to compare policies at peaks and troughs or over relatively long time intervals requires more knowledge about the class of hypotheses than we have supplied thus far. We would need to know more about the structural parameters that are components of $\epsilon(y,B^a)$ or of the scalar that is part of the solution in the multiple-goal case.

However, we did not construct the indicator to compare policies over long periods. The index was constructed to illustrate that: (1) alternative policies can be compared at a given point in time; (2) rational statements can be made about short-term changes in the direction or size of policy operations; and (3) the relative merits of variables used to appraise the current direction of policy can be appraised. If our initial effort stimulates additional work on the indicator problem and provides "impetus to a needed discussion of an important issue," we must, reluctantly, disagree with Chase. The development of "an unambiguous indicator of monetary policy" is much closer than it has been in the past.

Hendershott emphasizes that the sources of the adjusted base include endogenous variables and argues that there is, therefore, no reason to select the adjusted base as an indicator of policy action rather than some other endogenous variable. We will grant more than Hendershott asks and *assume* for the moment that each of the source components is an endogenous variable. How does this affect our argument? Or, to phrase the question in another way, why would the adjusted base remain a measure summarizing the actions taken by the monetary authority when other monetary policy variables are unchanged?

One reason is that the stock of interest-bearing and noninterest-bearing debt issued by the government sector, and held by the private sector, is the cornerstone of modern monetary theory, as Patinkin has emphasized repeatedly.[2] This sum is obtained by consolidating the balance sheets of the Treasury and the central bank and is the total financial issue of the government sector to the private sector. The noninterest-bearing portion is the adjusted base—reserves and currency held by the banks and the public minus member bank borrowing from the central bank.

However, in our analysis, we separate the effect of changes in interest-bearing and noninterest-bearing debt. Again, this choice is not an arbitrary decision. It reflects the institutional arrangements that prevail in most countries—and certainly in the United States—which assign the primary responsibility for control of the two components to separate agencies. Congress and/or the Executive determine(s) the budget and the amount and type of interest-bearing debt that will be issued or retired. The Federal Reserve decides on the amount of base money that is issued.

Every dollar change in the adjusted base reveals a specific action of the monetary authorities, an action in principle avoidable. Needless to say, Federal Reserve officials may not view their actions in this way. They may choose to interpret their actions as changes in the volume of free reserves, total reserves, unborrowed reserves, and so on. From the standpoint of monetary theory (but not of monetary policy) their interpretations are not crucial, and their actions affect the economy only if they result in a change in the adjusted base.[3]

A second reason for rejecting Hendershott's argument is that it is insufficient for the case that he tries to make. The *levels* of the source components of the base, with the exception of float and foreign deposits, are predetermined relative to current monetary processes. *Changes* in some of the components are slightly more dependent on current processes. But even if every one of the sources responded to current monetary processes, the adjusted base would remain under the complete control of the Federal Reserve.

Again, the reason has nothing to do with the endogeneity or exogeneity of particular sources. It reflects the fact that the *uses* of the base—reserves plus currency minus member bank borrowing—are the total emission of the monetary authorities. As Hendershott correctly notes, the uses are

[2]See Don Patinkin, "Price Flexibility and Full Employment," as reprinted in F. Lutz and L. Mints (eds.), *Readings in Monetary Theory* (New York: The Blakiston Co., 1951), pp. 252–83. The definition is given on p. 264.

[3]We abstract, of course, from actions which change reserve requirement ratios, the rediscount rate, and so forth, which are discussed more fully in the text.

identically equal to the sum of the source components. It is the sum, and not the components, which is the critical policy variable in monetary theory.

This argument removes the alternatives that are mentioned by Hendershott. Treasury bill rate, free reserves, *et hoc genus omne* simply do not summarize in the same immediate and obvious manner the direct actions of the monetary authorities. Moreover, these measures require knowledge of structural detail that the policy maker does not possess. The use of the portfolio of government securities as a measure of monetary policy introduces an arbitrary dichotomy and an open invitation to irresponsible action. If the portfolio is increasing while the adjusted base is declining, monetary policy would be called expansive despite the withdrawal of base money. The tragic consequences of the early thirties, when open market operations were conducted in insufficient volume to offset the increased demand for currency, is adequate evidence on which to judge the consequences of using the Federal Reserve's portfolio of government securities as an indicator.

Comment on the Minsky Paper

Henry C. Wallich

Hyman Minsky is correct in his view that, other things equal, outside money makes for greater buoyancy and willingness to take risk than inside money. One would expect also on these grounds to find income velocity lower in economies where inside money predominates than in those where outside money predominates. Debtors must be expected to hold some idle money in anticipation of having to repay their obligations.

An impressionistic look at country data, based on IFS (International Financial Statistics) material throws a curious light on this hypothesis. It seems verified in countries with a high component of outside money where that outside money is due to government borrowing. Frequently, however, the higher velocity here seems to be the result of inflation rather than the effect that underlies Minsky's proposition. Where outside money largely reflects large foreign exchange holdings and where the inflow has not led to inflation, there seems to be no tendency toward higher velocity.

A high proportion of inside money thus seems to be associated with relatively low velocity. Typically, however, this condition is associated with price stability. It might well be the latter factor, therefore, that accounts for the behavior of velocity. I have not had an opportunity to make a formal analysis of the material that would permit me to say how far these observations are significant.

Comment on Daniel Brill's Interpretation of 'Predicting Velocity'

Karl Brunner and Allan H. Meltzer

Though we appreciate the interest that Dan Brill has shown in one of our earlier papers,[1] we cannot accept or even recognize the conclusion that he claims to have found there. We did not propose or even suggest that policy makers or economists could or should predict income solely from the demand and supply functions for money. Nor did we regard our description of a procedure for making such predictions as a central point of our paper.

On the contrary, we summarized our results by stating:
"The major purpose of this paper has been to compare a number of different demand for money hypotheses, using identical tests . . . .,"[2] and concluded that "monetary policy operates on interest rates or relative prices and through wealth and substitution processes on the level of income,"[3] a position quite different from the one attributed to us. Moreover, we carefully distinguished our use of the terms "prediction" and "forecast"[4] and wrote:

> These predictions are not forecasts, since in most cases the data would not have been available until after the year had passed. Our interest thoughout is the comparison of the explanatory or predictive power of the various models to increase our understanding of monetary theory.[5]

Lest there be any remaining doubt about our intention, we note that only a very small part of a lengthy paper considered the problem of predicting income and an even smaller part—described as a digression—was concerned with forecasting. We leave to the reader to decide whether the cautious way in which the results were presented, the qualifications intro-

[1] "Predicting Velocity: Implications for Theory and Policy," *Journal of Finance* (May, 1963), pp. 319–54.

[2] *Ibid.*, p. 349.

[3] *Ibid.*, p. 351.

[4] *Ibid.*, p. 323.

[5] *Ibid.*

duced, and the explicit reason for introducing lagged values (p. 341) warrant the scorn and the attention that Brill devoted to this section of our paper or the inference that he drew.

Finally, though we acknowledge the inadequacy of forecasts based on our one-equation method, we are disappointed to learn from Brill that policy makers have not yet given up " 'seat of the pants' judgment." We thought that they had been converted partially to econometric models of the Suits type. Since they have not been converted, one of the few justifications of our "forecasts" has vanished. Nevertheless, it may be instructive for economists and central bankers to learn that forecasts based solely on the demand and supply for money—poor as they may be—are often better than the annual forecasts reported by Suits,[6] which deny any influence of money on economic activity.

[6] D. B. Suits, "Forecasting with an Econometric Model," *American Economic Review*, March, 1962.

Rejoinder to Brunner-Meltzer Comments

Daniel H. Brill

. . . Once we know the factors affecting the demand for money, we know the determinants of income velocity. Knowledge of either one of these is tantamount to knowledge of the other. If we can forecast the velocity of money and control the supply of money, we can have substantial impact on the level of national income through monetary policy.

To obtain the predicted level of income from the prediction of velocity all that is required is that the predicted velocity be multiplied by the money supply . . . .

. . . In recent work, we have begun to explore the possibility that forecasts of national income made by this procedure would be an aid to policy makers and would add to our understanding of the economy . . . .

The results, though preliminary, are encouraging. They suggest that the average error in forecasting quarterly velocity is approximately 1½ per cent. These forecasts of velocity have been converted into forecasts of national income by multiplying the forecast by the actual supply of money . . . .[1]

. . . money matters. Measured income has been shown to respond closely to the demand and supply for money. We know of no other model of income determination that predicts income as accurately as the money supply and the wealth model of the demand for money . . . .[2]

[1]Brunner and Meltzer, "An Alternative Approach to the Monetary Mechanism" (Subcommittee on Domestic Finance, Committee on Banking and Currency, House of Representatives, 88th Cong., 2d sess.), pp. 72–73.

[2]Brunner and Meltzer, "Predicting Velocity: Implications for Theory and Policy," *Journal of Finance* (May, 1963), p. 343.

INDEX

INDEX

(Bold-face page numbers refer to a paper or other contribution by the participant indicated)

This book has been set in 10 and 9 point Caledonia, leaded 2 points. Part titles are in 18 point Futura Bold and display heads are in 18 and 12 point Futura Demi. The size of the type page is 27 by 45½ picas.